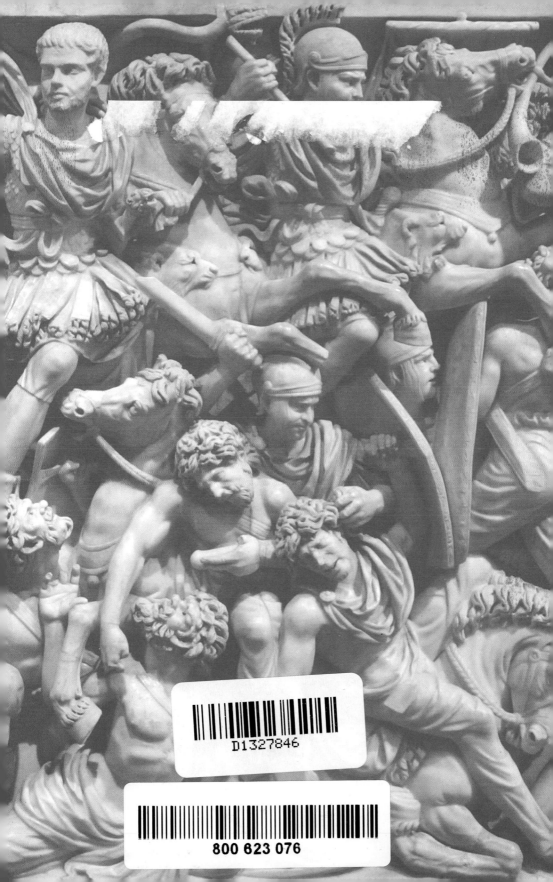

Imperial
Triumph

By the same author

Late Roman Spain and Its Cities
Hispania in Late Antiquity
Rome's Gothic Wars:
From the Third Century to Alaric

IMPERIAL TRIUMPH

THE ROMAN WORLD FROM HADRIAN TO CONSTANTINE

MICHAEL KULIKOWSKI

P

PROFILE BOOKS

First published in Great Britain in 2016 by
PROFILE BOOKS LTD
3 Holford Yard
Bevin Way
London
WC1X 9HD
www.profilebooks.com

1 3 5 7 9 10 8 6 4 2

Typeset in Garamond

Printed and bound in Great Britain by
Clays, St Ives plc

A CIP catalogue record for this book is available from the British Library.

ISBN 978 1 84668 370 1
eISBN 978 1 84765 437 3

FSC
www.fsc.org
MIX
Paper from
responsible sources
FSC® C018072

For Ellen and David

CONTENTS

CONTENTS

ACKNOWLEDGEMENTS

In a survey of this scale, one's debts are always numerous and often nebulous: practically everyone who's ever taught you something should have a place, and that kind of list has no limits. So I'll start by thanking John Davey, who commissioned the volume, Penny Daniel at Profile, and the exceptional teams both there and at Harvard University Press who brought it to fruition. Erin Eckley at Penn State has made it possible for me to do my job and still find moments to write. I am grateful for the research support I've received from my university, and for support from the Fund for Historical Studies in the Institute for Advanced Study, where I have spent a happy year as a Member of the School of Historical Studies and where the final draft of this book was completed.

In much broader terms, I'd like to thank those who taught me most of what I know, even though I often didn't realise I'd learned it until years later – and even though some of them would probably say I haven't learned a damn thing, least of all from them: Tim Barnes, Palmira Brummett, Jack Cargill, Angelos Chaniotis, Todd Diacon, Martin Dimnik, Jim Fitzgerald, Patrick Geary, Walter Goffart, Maurice Lee, Lester Little, John Magee, Ralph Mathisen, Sandy Murray, Walter Pohl, Roger Reynolds, Danuta Shanzer, Alan Stern, David Tandy and Susan Welch. Also my family, above all my grandmothers, as well as Oliver and Melvin.

Thanks go likewise to friends and colleagues who've inspired me, in ways too diverse to parse, and who have little in common save that fact: David Atwill, Bob Bast, Mia Bay, Joe Boone, Kim Bowes, Sebastian Brather, Tom Burman, Craig Davis, Deborah Deliyannis, Bonnie Effros, Hugh Elton, Catherine Higgs, Gavin Kelly, Maura Lafferty, Chris Lawrence, Hartmut Leppin, Mischa Meier, Eric Ramírez-Weaver, Josh Rosenblum, Kathy Salzer, Sebastian Schmidt-Hofner, Tina Shepardson,

Denise Solomon, Roland Steinacher, Paul Stephenson, Ellen Stroud, Carol Symes, Philipp von Rummel, Ed Watts, Clay Webster, David Wiljer and Christian Witschel. I owe Nicola Di Cosmo and Michael Maas special thanks for inviting to me to their symposium on 'Worlds in Motion' at the Institute for Advanced Study in Princeton in 2013 (now to be published as *Eurasian Empires in Late Antiquity*); it opened my eyes to a new and unimaginably rich historical world. To my colleagues in the Penn State history department, as whose head I served during the years I was writing this book, I owe an inexpiable debt, both for tolerating my periodic inattentions and for reminding me, continually and in big ways and small, that structural and social constraints operate on every system of governance. As much as all the foregoing, however, I would like to single out three fellow historians who have influenced my thinking – about history, about our profession, about what we as scholars owe society – so deeply that I'm rarely conscious of their having done so until I find myself unexpectedly reminded, and ever the more grateful, for it. To Richard Burgess, Guy Halsall and Noel Lenski: thanks.

Finally, the book's dedicatees, better friends than I ever expected to have.

LIST OF
ILLUSTRATIONS

23. Victory of Shapur, Naqsh-e Rustam. Photo: © Richard Slater/ Alamy Stock Photo
24. The Aurelian Wall of Rome. Photo: Luigi Strano on Flickr
25. Deeds of the Priest Kardir, Naqsh-e Rajab. Photo: The Circle of Ancient Iranian Studies (CAIS)
26. Maximian. Photo: Chris Hellier/Getty
27. Edict on Maximum Prices. Photo: Wikimedia Commons
28. Fausta. Photo: DEA/A. Dagli Orti/Getty
29. The Tetrarchs. Photos: www.cngcoins.com
30. Shapur II Hunting Boar. Photo: © The Smithsonian Museum of Asian Art
31. Sasanian Royal Bust. Photo: The Metropolitan Museum of Art
32. Constantius II. Photo: © Peter Horree/Alamy Stock Photo
33. Julian. Photo: DEA/A. Dagli Orti/Getty
34. Porphyry Sarcophagus of Helena. Photo: © Genevra Kornbluth
35. The Judgement of Paris (detail) from the Atrium House, Antioch. Photo: DEA/A. Dagli Orti/Getty

While every effort has been made to contact copyright-holders of illustrations, the author and publishers would be grateful for information about any illustrations where they have been unable to trace them, and would be glad to make amendments in further editions.

Maps

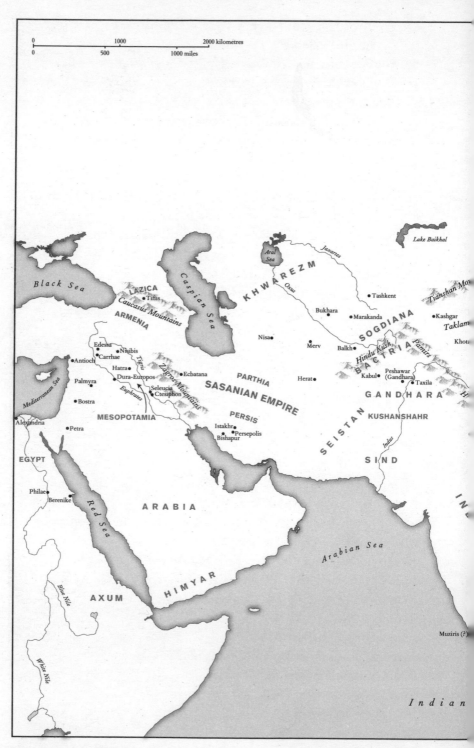

The Eurasian World

The Roman Empire under Hadrian

The Roman Empire under the Antonines

Aral
Sea

Caspian Sea

Black Sea

MOESIA
INFERIOR

ube

HRACIA

Byzantium

BITHYNIA

PONTUS

ARMENIA

PARTHIA

GALATIA

Tigris

ASIA

LYCIA

CAPPADOCIA

PAMPHYLIA

CILICIA

Euphrates

SYRIA

CYPRUS

CRETA

SYRIA
PALAESTINA

Alexandria

ARABIA

AEGYPTUS

Nile

Red Sea

Atlantic Ocean

North
Sea

Baltic Sea

BRITANNIA

GERMANIA
INFERIOR

BELGICA

Rhine

Danube

LUGDUNENSIS

GERMANIA
SUPERIOR

NORICUM

PANNONIA
SUPERIOR

DAC

GALLIA

RAETIA

PANNONIA
INFERIOR

AQUITANIA

ALPES

MOES
SUPERI

NARBONENSIS

DALMATIA

TARRACONENSIS

ITALIA

CORSICA

MACEDO

LUSITANIA

•Rome

EPIRUS

SARDINIA

ACHA

BAETICA

Mediterranean Sea

MAURITANIA
TINGITANA

MAURITANIA
CAESARIENSIS

SICILIA

CYRE

Carthage

NUMIDIA

AFRICA

N

TRIPOLITANIA

| 0 | | 1000 | | 2000 kilometres |
| 0 | 500 | | 1000 miles | |

The Severan Empire

The New Empire of Diocletian

The Parthian Empire

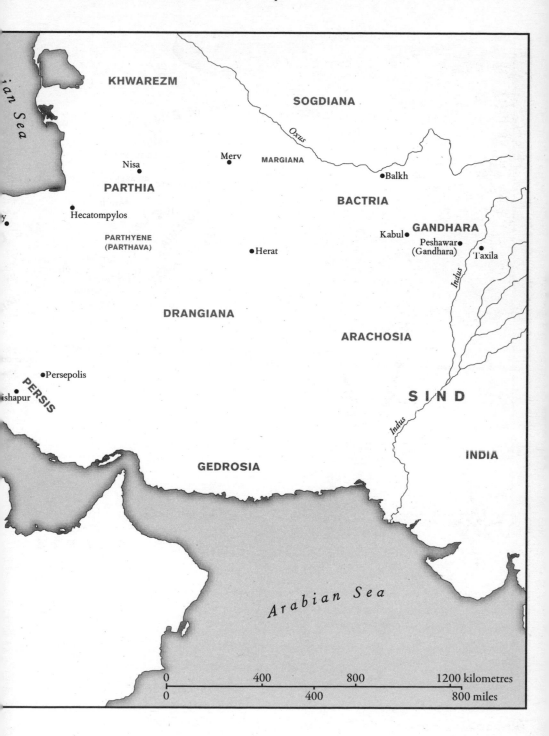

The Sasanian Empire

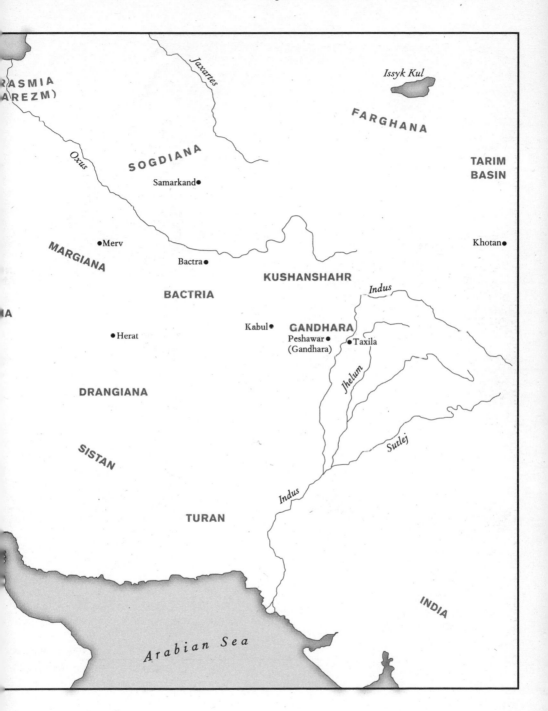

CHORASMIA
(KHAREZM)

Jaxartes

Issyk Kul

FARGHANA

Oxus

SOGDIANA

TARIM
BASIN

Samarkand●

●Merv

MARGIANA

Bactra●

Khotan●

KUSHANSHAHR

BACTRIA

Indus

Kabul● GANDHARA

●Herat

Peshawar● ●Taxila
(Gandhara)

DRANGIANA

Jhelum

SISTAN

Sutlej

TURAN

Indus

INDIA

Arabian Sea

INTRODUCTION

Rome started out as a very ordinary village on the Tiber river in central Italy perhaps a millennium before our story begins. For centuries, it was largely indistinguishable from its neighbours but, in the fourth century BC, it began aggressively to expand into the rest of the peninsula. Its leaders were magistrates elected each year by a citizen population whose votes were weighted to give the rich and powerful a decisive voice in their outcome. The system was in some respects genuinely representative of the citizenry's wishes and, virtually every year, the citizen army marched out, led by two elected consuls, to fight an enemy. Conquest accelerated in the third century BC, and a hundred years later Rome was unquestionably the superpower of the Mediterranean world. At the same time, however, the republican constitution began to break down, as rival generals tried to grab a monopoly of power for themselves and their cronies. The republic was destroyed by decades of civil war and, by the end of the last century BC, the sputtering machinery of republican government was replaced by the rule of one man, Augustus, the first Roman emperor.

Augustus, as he was known from 27 BC onwards, had started life as Octavianus, the great-nephew and adopted son of Julius Caesar, the first republican warlord to attempt to rule the Roman world alone. Caesar was assassinated for that presumption, but the republic was not restored, and the wars that followed his murder in 44 BC were even bloodier than those that preceded it. By the time they finished in 31 BC, the Roman world was exhausted, its far-flung provinces having been battlegrounds for three generations. Autocracy was welcomed as an alternative to more civil strife, and the fractious, ramshackle but representative constitution of the republic disappeared for good. Augustus outlived both his own generation and most of the younger one, too; by the time he died, very few people alive could remember the world before he ruled it. He styled himself the princeps, the 'first man' in the Roman state, rather than 'king' or 'emperor'. That polite fiction soothed the feelings of senators, the body of former magistrates who had long been accustomed to dominating the state. But the total hold he kept on actual power, and his preternatural longevity, allowed Augustus to transform Roman government.

We draw a line between Roman republic and Roman empire at the reign of Augustus to distinguish a Rome ruled by elective magistrates from one ruled by an individual autocrat, but the republic had already possessed a vast empire in Europe and the Mediterranean. This republican Roman empire was ruled by the Romans for the benefit of Italy, where a large majority of Roman citizens lived, and for that of the city of Rome, the largest conurbation the world had ever seen. The Augustan revolution gradually changed that. Republican provincial government, particularly in the immediate aftermath of Roman conquest, was frequently capricious and always rapacious, even when it brought new infrastructure and economic opportunities in its wake. Under the rule of the emperors, provincial life became rather more stable. The chieftains, burghers and nobles who ruled the empire's indigenous populations were free to retain their local authority, with two simple provisos. Peace must be kept and Roman citizens allowed to go about their business unmolested, and the state treasury must be kept full. This was a bargain that local elites eagerly seized, from the chieftains of western Europe to the Greek town councils and local dynasts of the eastern provinces. They and their subjects learned to make Roman governors happy, and many learned how to live like Romans. The enthusiasm of local elites for imperial rule, and for the peace that it brought, is the primary explanation of the Roman empire's success.

Augustus and his successors did more than reward collaboration. They also accepted many provincials into the ranks of Roman citizens. That was important. No other ancient state was as free with the privileges of its citizenship as was Rome under the emperors. Rather than guard citizenship for an imperial core, emperors granted it widely: sometimes to individual big men whom they knew personally; sometimes to favoured cities; sometimes to entire regions of the empire. This meant that from one end of the empire to another there were men who shared in legal rights that only Roman citizens possessed. They were equal before the law wherever they went in the empire, and their property and personal rights were valid regardless of the local jurisdiction in which they happened to live or find themselves. Readers may recall the story of the apostle Paul who, when threatened with a trial before hostile Jewish authorities, invoked his Roman citizenship and had his case transferred to Rome. This 'internationalism' of Roman citizenship was perhaps its greatest value.

In the course of the first century AD, the empire was transformed from a collection of subject territories exploited by Rome and Italy into a mosaic of culturally diverse provinces, all subject to the Roman emperor and now increasingly populated by provincial Roman citizens. Iberians and Gauls, Moors and Syrians, Thracians and Greeks – these and many other peoples could increasingly think of themselves as Romans, whatever else they might be as well. That self-identification, the sense of being Roman, became deeper and stronger in the centuries covered by this book: provincial Romans will gradually take centre stage in the political history of the empire. The Romans of the city of Rome will remain important, too, particularly the mass of the urban population known as the plebs. When Augustus imposed his autocracy, the plebs traded its right to participate formally in politics and choose its leaders in exchange for peace, prosperity and pomp: what the satirist Juvenal mocked as the 'bread and circuses' that kept the people quiet. It was a bargain the plebs could accept, but it did not come cheaply for the emperor. Cultivating the urban population meant not just money but also 'face time'. A princeps who cheated the plebs of either handouts or personal attention could expect rioting in the streets.

To make sense of our narrative, we need to pay attention not just to the imperial senate, or the urban plebs, or the Roman citizens in the provinces, but rather to the way all of them, together with the emperor and the army, fitted into the empire's system of governance, its unwritten constitution. This was deliberately ambiguous, because Augustus was extremely reluctant to expose the reality of his domination. The senate, whose members had once governed the republic and its provinces, accepted the autocracy of the new princeps not just because it brought peace, but because he put up a decent facade of deference to old republican principles. Senators could continue to hold offices with republican titles – quaestor, aedile, consul – even though they could no longer compete freely to win them, and they remained vital to the administration of the empire. As genuine memories of the republic faded, and those who had experienced its last decades died out, elite citizens could accept the political theatrics that cloaked the reality of one-man rule. They also accepted hereditary succession, which is slightly more surprising.

The republic's founding myth was the overthrow of the last king, Tarquin the Proud, supposedly in the sixth century BC, and the establishment of a senatorial government in which elected magistrates held office for just one year at a time. The word *rex*, 'king', remained a potent insult in republican politics till the end; the belief that Julius Caesar might in fact make himself king was one of the main justifications for his assassination. But though Augustus was squeamish about the language with which his power was described, neither he nor his subjects shrank from the reality of hereditary succession, as if the emperors were indeed monarchs. Augustus handed the state on to his adopted son Tiberius (r. AD 14–37), thus establishing the dynasty we call the Julio-Claudians, named after the two republican clans from which they descended. Three more members of that family succeeded Tiberius. When the male line of the Julio-Claudians was exhausted, in AD 68, there was a brief interval of civil war before its victor, Flavius Vespasianus (r. 69–79), established a new imperial dynasty that we call Flavian. By doing so, he proved that the empire could continue without its founding family, and that emperors could be created outside the city of Rome, by the army and in the provinces. This revelation was what the senatorial historian Tacitus called the *arcanum imperii*, 'the secret of empire'. It meant that other families could perpetuate the Julio-Claudian autocracy if they could win it on the battlefield.

The transition to a new dynasty made the real basis of imperial power more transparent. Vespasian had first been proclaimed emperor in a putsch by the provincial legions of the east, but was then acclaimed by the senate and people of Rome, which served to legitimise the accession. More significantly, the senate voted Vespasian a package of specific magisterial powers that had been exercised by the Julio-Claudians. These were powers that set the princeps apart from everyone else in the state, the foundation on which he claimed the right to act. Based on powers that the republic's elected magistrates had exercised during their time in office, their combination in one person gave the emperors their potency. Two powers were most important. The first was proconsular *imperium*. Under the republic, former consuls went out to govern the provinces as proconsuls, 'those acting for (*pro*) the consuls' in Rome. Proconsuls could conduct foreign policy, administer law and justice to citizens, and command obedience from citizens and non-citizens alike, but could do so outside the territory of the city of Rome in which the same powers were held by the annual consuls. What made the proconsular *imperium* of Augustus and his successors different was its extent: the princeps had proconsular *imperium* superior to that of any provincial governor, which made his every decision binding wherever in the empire he chose to act. The second of the two essential imperial powers was likewise rooted in republican history. The princeps possessed perpetual *tribunicia potestas*, which had been the right of a republican tribune to veto laws inside the city of Rome and command citizens within the sacred limits of the city. Like consular authority, *tribunicia potestas* under the republic was exercised for the single year in which a man held the office of tribune. But under the emperors, no one save the princeps possessed *tribunicia potestas*, and he possessed it in perpetuity.

When the senate voted to give Vespasian *tribunicia potestas* it confirmed that there were things the princeps possessed by virtue of his position not his person, and that the powers held by Augustus could be held by someone not of his family. But that was not the same thing as working out rules for how one actually became emperor; it only meant that whoever succeeded in being recognised as emperor, whether by heredity, by coup d'état or by military victory, would necessarily come to exercise those powers. But the ambiguity remained, because the fiction that Augustus had restored the republic made it impossible to specify precisely just what gave a Roman emperor his power to rule. For centuries, some combination of army, senate and people was needed to make a man emperor, but the balance between them was never clear and never subject to transparent or formal rules. Dynastic succession became the baseline norm, but it was never a principle: the empire was an autocracy with frequent hereditary succession, but it was never a hereditary monarchy.

The army, which we have mentioned only in passing thus far, was as crucial to making and unmaking emperors as were the senate or the Roman people. Imperial Rome's soldiers were long-serving professionals who enjoyed privileges that set them apart from the wider population of both citizens and provincial non-citizens. The goodwill of the soldiery needed constant tending because, in the final analysis, the success of the imperial autocrat depended on that goodwill: it was the loyalty of the armies, particularly the great provincial armies in Britain, Germany, the Balkans, Anatolia and Syria, that protected the princeps from challenges. Even more important was the loyalty of the praetorian guard, the emperor's personal troops quartered in Rome, who were invariably lethal when their ruler displeased them. Yet the soldiery's needs were generally predictable, as too were those of the Roman plebs.

The elites – the senators in particular – gave the emperor much more trouble, because they had to be handled as individuals, not propitiated as a group. To administer the empire, the emperor relied on an oligarchy of the rich and well born – the senators – and those who were merely very rich – the equestrians. The senatorial element in this oligarchy was self-reinforcing: holding certain magistracies conferred senatorial status, and that status accrued to a family for three generations, even if it was not sustained by office-holding in a particular generation. A senator needed to have a minimum fortune of a million sestertii to retain his senatorial status (an average townsman could live well on a thousand or so annually) and many senators actually had incomes that exceeded that figure every year. Given this exclusivity, there was a natural tendency for senatorial families to behave as a class apart from the rest of society, the *ordo senatorius*, but it was never a closed shop, precisely because of the connection to money.

Wealthy citizens who possessed a suitable net worth could choose to pursue the magistracies, starting with the office of quaestor, which conferred actual participatory membership in the senate. These wealthy men belonged to a second group within the larger Roman oligarchy, the equestrian order, or *ordo equester* (the name goes back to very early Roman history, when it referred to men with enough money to serve in the cavalry). Unlike senators, who needed to hold specific magistracies to confirm their status, equestrian status was an automatic consequence of a certain minimum fortune (400,000 sestertii). One was an eques by virtue of being, not of doing, and one remained equestrian whether one sought office or not. By the time our story begins in the next chapter, under the emperor Hadrian, the senatorial and equestrian *ordines* formed an international governing elite, into which new blood was incorporated whenever Roman citizenship was granted to a new provincial population: rich non-citizens would suddenly be transformed into Roman equestrians, eligible to seek a place in the senate if they so chose. Over time, it was the equestrian element in the oligarchy that came to predominate, occupying more and more of the offices through which the empire was administered. But the essential point is that the flexibility with which the ruling elite coopted new members into itself made for a basically stable oligarchic regime without which the emperors simply could not rule.

That is why, in the pages that follow, we cannot confine ourselves to discussing the emperor or the imperial family, and why we will not shy away from introducing a great many Romans, with their long, often unmemorable, names: these generals and bureaucrats, financiers and orators, made the empire what it was, even though they can be shadowy figures, known to us only by the long series of offices and commands that they held. Their motives, let alone their personalities, are often completely invisible. Yet to leave them out of the story, as popular histories sometimes do, is to simplify things in a way that cheats the reader and traduces the reality of the past: without reference to these oligarchs, with their complicated names and complicated careers, imperial history becomes a fantasy world in which only the emperor and the emperor's family count. They did count, of course, but the oligarchy counted just as much: autocracy could only work through, and with the consent of, its oligarchs.

It was a mutually re-enforcing relationship, but one we can get at only some of the time, because our sources for different periods of Roman imperial history are highly variable, both in quantity and quality. Readers will soon realise that we can narrate some eras in exponentially greater detail than others: the middle of the second and end of the third centuries, for instance, are almost a blank; the end of the second and beginning of the third are well documented. But there is another source problem besides the uneven distribution of evidence. Almost all the narrative sources we have are the work of senators or authors who identified with the senatorial order. For that reason, they tend to focus on the personalities of individual emperors, and the impact these had on the life of the senate and Rome itself. The emperors Caligula and Nero were horrible to senators and bad to the senate, so therefore they were tyrants, despite the fact that the latter was genuinely very popular in much of the wider empire. By contrast there is the stock type of the good emperor, the *civilis princeps*, who imitated Augustus as a well-mannered first among senatorial equals. Our elite historical traditions, then, tend to place every emperor into one stock type or the other. Good Vespasian's younger son Domitian followed the ugly pattern of Caligula and Nero. Vespasian and Trajan offered polite form its due deference and thus were fondly remembered. For all the concentration of our narrative sources on the character of the empire, we need to pay attention to the other evidence available, especially the vast number of inscriptions on stone that give us insight into how thousands of otherwise unknown individuals presented their lives and careers to the world. When we do that, we nearly always find that the emperor's personality, and the way the upper strata of the oligarchy experienced his rule, bore remarkably little relationship to the fortunes of the empire as a whole.

That was already true under the Julio-Claudians and it was even more true when our main narrative begins, in the year 117, with the death of the emperor Trajan and the accession of his distant relative Hadrian. To understand the reign of Hadrian, which in many ways determined the dynastic history of the whole second century, we need to sketch briefly the events of Trajan's time, and the sort of men who were now dominant in the ruling oligarchy. Vespasian and his sons were the first emperors not to have been Romans of Rome, hailing instead from an Italian municipality. They were descendants of Italians who had been granted Roman citizenship during the last century of the republic, and the family was senatorial on one side, equestrian on the other. This was novel. The Julio-Claudians were descended from two great senatorial clans of the late republic, and that contributed to the sense of their legitimacy and power. But under their dynastic rule, the old distinction between Roman citizens from Rome and Roman citizens from Italy came to matter much less, as the latter reached increasingly high positions in imperial government.

When Vespasian came to power, there was some sneering about country bumpkins that Vespasian seems to have revelled in, but no one thought his background made him unsuited to rule. And under his Flavian dynasty, a similar levelling of regional distinctions began to be felt outside the Italian peninsula. Colonial elites from southern and eastern Spain and from southern Gaul, descendants of republican veterans settled in the provinces they had conquered, began to enter the senate in growing numbers. A group of Spanish senators had already clustered around the court of Nero, while Roman senators from Gallia Narbonensis were so assimilated into the Italian aristocracy that it is notoriously hard to distinguish the two groups in the surviving evidence. As Italian elites had seen their prospects rise and broaden under the Julio-Claudians, so too did those of colonials under the Flavians. With the extinction of the Flavians, the new importance of the colonial elites became clear.

Vespasian's younger son Domitian was assassinated in September 96. There was no civil war like the one that followed the suicide of Nero, the last of the Julio-Claudians, in 68. Instead, the senate acted quickly and made Marcus Cocceius Nerva emperor. He was old, respected and childless, and his career went back deep into Nero's reign. His senatorial peers loved and trusted him. But he was unpopular with the plebs and the praetorian guard, and he was also weak and indecisive. The armies on the frontiers became restive. It seemed only a matter of time before one of the great commanders staged a coup like the one that brought down Nero and started a civil war. Rumours spread, but months passed and no coup came. We need to imagine the machinations taking place behind closed doors, because what really happened was carefully veiled from posterity. But seemingly out of the blue, in AD 97, Nerva announced the adoption of a powerful general, Marcus Ulpius Traianus, as his son and imperial partner. Known to us as Trajan, he was a Spaniard from Italica in Baetica, the rich southern province centred on the city of Corduba (modern Córdoba). The adoption had the desired effect, calming the soldiery with a man it was happy to call emperor. The senate, too, was pleased, and Trajan bent over backwards to be the very model of a *civilis princeps*, the antithesis of Domitian, an emperor whom he had in fact served quite faithfully.

Nerva soon died – naturally, by all accounts – and as sole emperor, Trajan (r. 98–117) deferred to the senate wherever possible, granting considerable discretion to senatorial commanders and provincial governors. We are fortunate to possess the letter collection of C. Plinius Caecilius Secundus, better known as Pliny the Younger, whose correspondence with Trajan gives us a window into the relationship between an emperor and a senatorial proconsul. Pliny is deferential, exaggeratedly worried not to take decisions that might displease the princeps. Trajan is exaggeratedly patient with his governor's indecisiveness, his repeated requests for guidance in small matters as well as large. The princeps knows that courteous tolerance behoves him when writing to a social peer. And the princeps also knows his instructions matter. Again and again, he reminds Pliny to share the genuine solicitude for the provincials that he himself feels as princeps, to let them live their lives in peace, to stop them hurting one another.

Trajan was forever remembered as *optimus princeps*, the best of emperors, and not just because he flattered the self-regard of senators. He manifestly protected the safety of his subjects and he brought new glory to the name of Rome, fighting a massive war on the Danube against the Dacian king Decebalus, and expanding imperial territory into the Carpathians by creating three new provinces in Dacia. These trans-Danubian provinces gave Rome control over the important mines of Transylvania and also made it possible to supervise barbarian client kings to the east and the west of the Carpathians. Dacia's subjugation made Trajan that rare thing among emperors, a *propagator imperii*, one who had extended the boundaries of the empire. Indeed, the epithet *optimus* was not simply posthumous – it appeared during his lifetime, an adjective sometimes treated as if it were part of his actual name.

The picture was complicated by the ambiguity of the imperial succession that we looked at above. Trajan had no children and he hesitated to designate a successor: the *optimus princeps* could hardly reveal his autocracy with an act of blatant dynasticism. At the same time, the absence of a clear succession plan could end in disaster, as the aftermath of Nero's reign had made clear. Moreover, if no heir apparent was designated, people would still speculate and factions would arise at court, with unpredictable consequences. Trajan compromised, unwilling to drop his persona as first among equals. He had one close male relative, Publius Aelius Hadrianus, the son of a maternal cousin and a product of the interlocking marriages among the Spanish colonial elites. Hadrian's father, Publius Aelius Afer, had died in AD 86, at which point the young Aelius Hadrianus and his elder sister Domitia Paulina became Trajan's wards. We are told that Hadrian was treated 'as a son' by Trajan throughout his life, that is to say, even from before he was clad in the *toga virilis*, the 'toga of manhood' that marked the passage from childhood to adulthood for a Roman male.

Trajan then brought the families of the Ulpii and Aelii even closer, by marrying Hadrian to his great-niece Sabina (she was the granddaughter of Trajan's sister Marciana). Marriage connections were the way Roman elites sustained themselves in a world of low life expectancy and high puerperal mortality: Hadrian's marriage to Sabina was consequential, but so too was that of his elder sister Domitia Paulina to the prominent general L. Julius Servianus, heirs to whose line would emerge into the political limelight throughout the second century. Trajan heaped honours on the women of his family, consciously echoing Augustus, who had done the same with his wife Livia. Thus Trajan's wife Plotina was given the title augusta, as was his sister Marciana, and thenceforth the senior women of the ruling family were generally designated as augustae. When Marciana Augusta died in 112, she was deified by the senate, after which Trajan conferred the title augusta on her daughter Matidia. Hadrian was thus married to the daughter of an augusta and the granddaughter of the deified empress, Diva Marciana.

While all this seemed to single Hadrian out as Trajan's heir apparent, there were counterindications as well. Trajan had not allowed his young relative special preferment on the *cursus honorum* (the phrase, literally 'the path of honours' or the 'series of offices' held by members of the Roman oligarchy, is untranslatable). This *cursus honorum* led through a number of minor qualifying offices and then into a series of magistracies that went back to the era of the republic: quaestor, aedile, praetor. Those who had served as praetors would go on to provincial governorships and then sometimes win the consulship after they reached the age of forty-four. As with the consulship, each of these traditional offices had a minimum age at which it could be held, and an interval between offices was enforced according to rules established by Augustus (these rules were called the *lex annalis*). For a man to hold an office in the first year he became eligible to do so was a great honour for which senators competed, but under the Julio-Claudians and Flavians, young members of the ruling dynasty were frequently exempted from the *lex annalis*, allowing them to leapfrog the normal sequence and hold offices well before those who were in theory their senatorial peers. Trajan did not allow Hadrian to do this. Presumably the emperor wanted to demonstrate his respect for the senate as a whole and the rules that bound all its members, but it also confused people. There were secret whispers that Trajan did not really think too highly of his ward.

It took until the year 113 for Hadrian's status as Trajan's likely heir to be secure, when he was designated to accompany Trajan on campaign as *legatus pro praetore*, which is to say an imperial *comes* ('companion') and special adviser. By 113, the ageing ruler had decided to launch another war of conquest. He was a restless man who disliked inactivity and preferred life in the field. His wars in Dacia had covered him in glory, and the lure of a war in the east was hard for him to resist. There were historical reasons for that allure, alongside the personal ones. Rome's eastern neighbour was the Parthian empire, the only other organised state in the Mediterranean or Near Eastern world in this period. The Romans had regarded the Parthians as their great ideological foe since at least 53 BC, when the great republican general Crassus was killed on the battlefield at Carrhae and several Roman legions were annihilated alongside him. Since then, any victory against Parthia had been regarded as moral as well as military, even though the Parthians tended not to reciprocate the Roman hostility. To follow in the footsteps of Alexander the Great, to finally avenge the death of Crassus, that was a worthy project for the *optimus princeps*.

Trajan's excuse was rivalry among claimants to the Parthian throne and Parthian interference in Armenia. In the early second century, Armenia was a client kingdom lying uneasily between the two great empires. Culturally, it was closer to Parthia, and its native dynasty shared the Iranian religion of the Parthian kings. Politically, however, it had long fallen within the Roman orbit and its kings were traditionally approved by Rome before being allowed to govern. Now, the Parthian king had deposed the Roman appointee in Armenia and installed a new ruler. That furnished Trajan with the only pretext he needed, and so, in 113, he launched an invasion of the Parthian empire with the explicit goal of conquering it and adding it to the Roman state. Hadrian's true position as heir apparent became clear on this campaign.

The emperor was sixty-one when the Parthian campaign began, old for a Roman, and he could not be expected to outlive it. The campaign itself was a great success, at least in military terms. Armenia was rapidly brought to heel, while petty kings flocked from deep in the northern Caucasus to swear their allegiance to Trajan. The Roman army then marched down the Euphrates river, capturing every city it passed. The Parthian capital at Ctesiphon fell, and with that, Trajan had excelled any previous Roman general. It was not enough him. He pressed on further south, to where the Euphrates meets the Tigris and they progress together into the Persian Gulf. There Trajan stood looking out, lamenting that he was too old to follow Alexander's ghost all the way to India. He would have to remain content with having placed a new king on the Parthian throne and mastered Rome's great rival.

The emperor's achievement was not quite all that it seemed. Before he had even left the Tigris island, near modern Basra in Iraq, eastern affairs were in disarray. Almost the whole of the conquered Parthian territory, and some of the allied kingdoms, was up in arms. More worryingly, the Jewish diaspora inside the Roman provinces had exploded into rebellion and proclaimed a Jewish king, a sign of dangerous messianic expectations. As was normal Roman policy, revolt on such a scale demanded overhelming reprisals. Trajan sent his best commanders to deal with the Jews, while he himself marched back through Mesopotamia into Roman territory, putting down the Parthian rebellions with great savagery. His health was failing and there was no obvious way to salvage the situation. Mesopotamia and Armenia would have to be written off. As he headed back into Roman Asia Minor, Trajan became too ill to travel and he died at Selinus in Cilicia on 8 August 117. Word of his death was covered up until Hadrian could be notified and presented to the soldiers, who duly acclaimed him. With the accession of Hadrian, our main story can begin.

THE EARLY YEARS
OF HADRIAN

Hadrian's reign did not begin well. People believed, or could affect to believe, that it was Trajan's widow Plotina to whom Hadrian owed the throne, rather than the wish of the dead emperor. It was true that he had been Plotina's favourite, and that many senators could imagine themselves a better successor to Trajan than this protégé of a dowager empress. Alternative names were bandied about, and Hadrian looked still worse when he immediately gave up Trajan's remarkable conquests. With hindsight, we can see that they were already a lost cause, and that even Trajan would have had to surrender them. But Trajan was dead and his memory revered. Hadrian was alive and not much liked, so he took the blame. Worst of all, though, were the murders. Either someone attempted a coup, or rumours of a coup were taken seriously. Regardless, four senior consulars, men who had held the consulship and now occupied the greatest commands in the empire, were put to death before Hadrian had returned to Rome from the east. He would always disclaim responsibility for the executions, but no one believed him. He seemed a poor contrast with a predecessor who, even when faced with genuine plots, had sent only two senators into exile during his reign and executed none of them.

Hadrian took his time getting back to Rome and his entry into the city was not greeted with enthusiasm. The plebs was restive – the murder of the four consulars was a scandal. Hadrian had to distribute large sums of money to calm them. He also forgave debts to private lenders and to cities that owed money to the emperor's own treasury, the *fiscus* (kept separate from the official treasury of the state, which was called the *aerarium publicum*, or sometimes the *aerarium Saturni* because it was housed near the temple of Saturn). He staged a very public burning of the tax registers in Trajan's Forum, hoping to win some popular goodwill. In the senate, too, he had to curry favour, but this was not easy. He swore on oath that he had not ordered the killing of the four consulars, and also took the now traditional vow not to punish any senator without a vote of the senate itself. But senatorial suspicions were irreversible and Hadrian was never well liked.

He had his adoptive father deified and Trajan's remains were entombed in the base of the column he had built to commemorate his victories on the Danube. This column, 100 feet high and decorated with a spiral frieze 600 feet long, depicting images from the emperor's Dacian wars, still stands in the forum that bears his name, and remains one of the iconic monuments of Roman imperialism. Hadrian's act of piety was in fact quite unusual and at one level sacrilegious. Trajan's Forum fell inside the traditional sacred boundary of the city of Rome, the so-called *pomerium*, within which burials were prohibited. Even emperors were buried outside the *pomerium*, in the mausoleum of Augustus on the Campus Martius. As with so many things he did, Hadrian's gesture would offend those who wanted to take offence, however well meaning he might have been.

Hadrian took other measures to secure his throne. He dismissed one of Trajan's two praetorian prefects, the chief administrators of imperial government and commanders of the praetorian guard, and accepted the resignation of the second prefect, a loyal old ex-centurion who seems not to have wanted to serve under Hadrian. (As the senior non-commissioned officers in the Roman legions, centurions generally gained equestrian rank upon discharge, which allowed them to hold the various offices of the imperial administration that were, like the praetorian prefecture, reserved for equestrians.) In place of Trajan's prefects, Hadrian appointed another ex-centurion, Marcius Turbo, who had long known Hadrian from the army, and who was at this time busy tidying up the Danube frontier in the provinces of Dacia and Moesia. The second new prefect was Septicius Clarus, an equestrian by birth, whom we know mainly as the dedicatee of Pliny the Younger's letter collection. Finally, Hadrian appointed a new *ab epistulis*, the equestrian official responsible for drafting imperial letters and replies: this was Suetonius Tranquillus, famous for his *Lives of the Caesars*, a series of gossipy biographies of the emperors from Julius Caesar (considered, incorrectly, to be the first emperor) to Domitian that has long been one of the most popular works of Latin literature.

Other appointments reveal the ways in which colonial elites who had prospered under the Flavians now became the dominant forces in government. Hadrian's urban prefect (a different post from that of praetorian prefect, in charge of the day-to-day running of the city of Rome itself) was the Spanish senator Marcus Annius Verus. His career went back to Vespasian's day and he would go on to become one of the very last private citizens in Roman history to hold three consulships, a privilege increasingly reserved for emperors and their heirs. The daughter of this Annius Verus, Annia Galeria Faustina, was married to a senator from Nemausus (Nîmes) in the province of Gallia Narbonensis: this senator, whose mouthful of a name was T. Aurelius Fulvius Boionius Arrius Antoninus, would later become the emperor we know as Antoninus Pius (r. 138–61). In the year 121, when old Annius Verus was consul for the second time, another M. Annius Verus, the consul's grandson, was born; this M. Annius Verus would in time become emperor as Marcus Aurelius (r. 161–80). These interlocking families would dominate the dynastic politics of the second century.

Annius Verus and Arrius Antoninus, like Hadrian, were different from the older generation to which a man like Trajan had belonged. Although they were of colonial stock, and continued to have relatives and clients in their familial homelands, they were themselves children of Italy, brought up in Rome and rare visitors to the ancestral provinces. For that reason, they were also closely interconnected with the Italian elites: another of Hadrian's appointees was Haterius Nepos, an equestrian of municipal stock from Umbria who had governed Armenia in the short period between 114 and 117 when it was a Roman province; he was now rapidly promoted through a series of posts to become prefect of Egypt, a hand-picked post reserved for equestrians and always given to the emperor's most reliable men. Hadrian's legionary commanders were a mixture of hold-overs from the Trajanic period and new faces: the new emperor's shaky hold on power made it essential to balance respect for continuity with the need for trustworthy supporters of his own.

Sometimes this quest for security led to innovations. A recently discovered inscription demonstrates that in the wake of the Jewish wars,

Hadrian created an extraordinary command, placing the Roman legions of Judaea and Arabia under the command of a single legionary commander. The gesture was meant to overawe the Jewish homeland and prevent its following the diaspora into rebellion, though it failed, as we shall soon see. The emperor himself spent the first three years of his reign in the city of Rome, despite his preference for the east and indeed for travel in general: a second-century emperor was expected to comport himself as a senator among senators, even if he was unpopular and wanted nothing so much as to be elsewhere. Hadrian endured the necessity of this 'face time' with the senate for as long as he could bear it, but thereafter, he moved out into the wider empire and stayed away from Rome whenever possible.

In 121, he went to Gaul and Germany, leaving Turbo and Annius Verus to look after the people and the senate. Trajan's widow, Plotina, stayed on, too, living in retirement. Matidia, Trajan's niece and Hadrian's mother-in-law, had died in 119 and was, like her mother Marciana before her, made a *diva*. Sabina, her daughter the empress, now became Augusta and travelled with the emperor: she and Hadrian disliked each other intensely but he feared that a woman of her authority would become the focus of plots if she were left to her own devices in Rome. Even travelling and under strict supervision, Sabina raised suspicions in her husband: late in 122, the praetorian prefect Septicius Clarus, the *ab epistulis* Suetonius and many others were dismissed abruptly from their offices after mysteriously unspecified interaction with the empress. Perhaps there had been a plot, or some indiscretion on Sabina's part (Hadrian reserved his affections for young men), but we actually have no idea what really happened. Sabina remained in the imperial party but Clarus was not replaced. That meant that Marcius Turbo, in office since Hadrian had first gone to Rome, would serve as sole praetorian prefect until the very last years of the reign.

Hadrian spent a decade and more in travel, touring the provinces of a vast empire. In 121 or 122 he visited the provinces of the Upper Danube, Raetia and Noricum, now parts of Switzerland, southern Germany and Austria, and in Noricum he inspected the imperial mines, as coins struck to commemorate his visit make clear. He honoured both provinces, raising several Norican communities to the status of *municipia* – a technical status with special rights under Roman law – bestowing a new theatre on the governor's residence at Virunum (near modern Klagenfurt), and in Raetia raising Augusta Vindelicum (Augsburg) to municipal status as well. From there he aimed for Britain, probably sailing down the Rhine

Asia Minor

as far as Colonia Agrippensis, modern Cologne, the capital of Germania Inferior ('Lower Germany', so called because it was further downriver than Germania Superior). It seems likely that the underdeveloped areas of Germania Inferior, which included parts of modern Flanders, were deliberately improved by Hadrian and that the *civitas Tungrorum*, modern Tongres, was raised to the rank of *municipium* at this time. The governor of Germania Inferior, Platorius Nepos, went with Hadrian to Britain in 122, eventually becoming his legate there, in a province that would long remain one of the empire's great military commands.

Britain had been struck by either rebellion or frontier trouble the year after Trajan's death, and had required the presence of a senior general. In 122, Platorius Nepos brought with him an entire legion, the VI Victrix, from Castra Vetera in Germania Inferior (now Xanten, at the confluence of the Rhine and the Lippe), and thousands of additional legionaries from Spain came to Britain along with the imperial party. Britain would long remain one of the most difficult and least remunerative provinces in the empire, while the main result of the imperial visit of 122 was the plan for Hadrian's Wall, perhaps the most famous Roman monument outside Rome itself. The emperor spent much of the year in the island province, returning to the continent by the winter of 122–3.

Once in Gaul, Hadrian made for Spain, his familial homeland, which now enjoyed the glories of a full imperial visit. Hadrian journeyed there via the south coast of Gallia Narbonensis, erecting a memorial to Trajan's widow and his own adoptive mother Plotina in her home city of Nemausus. In Apta (Apt) he put up a monument to Borysthenes, his beloved hunting horse, who had died there and whose tomb was adorned with some not very good verse composed by the emperor himself. From Narbonensis, Hadrian took the coast road to Tarraco (Tarragona), the capital of the huge province of Hispania Citerior, where he overwintered well into 123. In spring of that year, he held a major *conventus*, or assembly of provincial Roman citizens, in the forum and temple complex constructed in Tarraco by the Flavians. After that, he visited the northern part of the province, including the legionary fort of the Legio VII Gemina (León) and the north-western administrative centres like Asturica Augusta (Astorga). We do not know whether he visited the other two Spanish provinces, Baetica and Lusitania, but he deliberately refused to visit his *patria*, his ancestral home, at Italica. He did, however, lavish funds on the town: Italica constructed virtually a whole new public centre during the course of his reign. Also while in Spain, Hadrian introduced a levy on provincial citizens to provide recruits for the legions. He wanted to supplement the army of the Parthian frontier, for in 124 he intended to move eastwards.

We have no real notion of the route by which Hadrian travelled to the east, but we know for certain that he personally negotiated peace with Parthia, conceding token support to one side in a dynastic dispute there and forestalling any actual fighting between the two empires. Instead, he spent the rest of 124 touring the eastern provinces. We know that he travelled through mountainous Cappadocia up to the great Black Sea port of Trapezus (Trabzon) and that a major renovation of its harbour was undertaken on his orders. He also toured the more easterly, Pontic sections of the dual province of Bithynia et Pontus before moving into Bithynia proper and staying at Nicomedia (modern Izmit). It is possible, though impossible to verify, that Hadrian here met the country boy Antinous, a Greek from outside the Bithynian town of Claudiopolis, who would become his great love and the subject of romantic fancy down to modern times.

From Bithynia, the imperial party crossed over to the European side of the Propontis, probably visiting Perinthus, the capital of the province of Thrace, before returning to the province of Asia. Cyzicus was Hadrian's first and perhaps most important stop, for he honoured it extravagantly, restarting work on a great temple begun by king Attalus of Pergamum hundreds of years earlier, and granting the city the status of *neokoros*, which is to say one of the provincial centres of imperial cult. To be *neokoros*, and have a temple to the deified emperors and the ruling imperial house, was a coveted status in the province of Asia and peninsular Asia Minor more generally. The old cities of Pergamum, Ephesus, Smyrna and Sardis already enjoyed it, as Roman imperial rule fuelled a renaissance of local Greek urbanism, sentiment and pride. Only the provincial capital, Pergamum, and Smyrna, home of the sophist and philosopher Polemon who was Hadrian's travelling companion, were more greatly honoured than Cyzicus, for Hadrian designated both cities as twice *neokoros*, a towering privilege. No wonder that he began to gain a reputation as a Hellenophile, something regarded as not altogether seemly by the more censorious Latin senators at Rome. That said, Hadrian's visit to Asia encouraged many high-born Greeks who were already Roman citizens and possessed an equestrian fortune to pursue senatorial careers.

Hadrian lingered at Ephesus for some time in August 124, before making for mainland Greece by way of the island of Rhodes. He had been in Athens before as a young man, but that had been a decade earlier, when he first showed signs of his unabashed love for all things Greek. Now he came as ruler of the Roman world and his primary aim was to be initiated into the Eleusinian mysteries, the great religious rites of ancient Attica which were celebrated in late summer or early autumn and had long fascinated Roman admirers of Greek culture. Hadrian also renewed old acquaintances, like the young Herodes Atticus. Herodes was the son of one of Athens' wealthiest men, Claudius Atticus, who had looked after Hadrian during his time there a decade before, and Herodes himself would go on to be the great patron of mid-second-century Attica. Now, Hadrian adlected him into the Roman senate as quaestor *inter amicos*. Adlection (*adlectio*, 'reading into the rolls') was a way emperors could honour their favourites by making them senators of a particular official rank without their having to serve in the minor qualifying offices. Herodes now enjoyed the same rank that he would have had if he had actually served as quaestor, and he was also made one of the emperor's *amici*, 'friends', a rare and coveted, if only quasi-official, status.

While the court was based in Attica, Hadrian toured the Peloponnese and much of central Greece, restoring buildings and dedicating new ones. He imagined himself to be restoring the ancient glories of Greece, but was more often putting a new and imperial stamp on its landscape. Hadrian's Hellenophile enthusiasm was just one symptom of a much larger revival of interest in the cultural glories of Classical Greece that characterised the second century: it was in just this period that the learned antiquarian Pausanias, who came from Lydia in Asia Minor, was embarking on his massive *Description of Greece*, which is to this day a vital source for the geography and history of the region. Hadrian, for his part, returned to Athens in time for the Dionysiac Games of 125, where he played the role of *agonothetes*, or master of the games. He then visited both Delphi and Corinth, known respectively for its oracular shrine of Apollo and as the great Roman colony founded by Julius Caesar for veterans of his victorious civil wars. Hadrian then sailed up the Gulf of Corinth to Nicopolis, the settlement that commemorated the final triumph of Augustus over his rival Mark Antony, and then to Dyrrachium in Epirus (now Dürres in Albania), whence he set sail back to Italy for Brundisium (modern Brindisi). He had been away from Rome for four years.

Hadrian's sojourn in Greece and Asia Minor tells us a great deal about the public role that Roman emperors had to play. For instance, while there he accepted election as archon, chief magistrate of Athens, a very specific type of philhellenism that gave symbolic endorsement to ancient Greek traditions that had been hollow memories for many centuries. The Greek elites loved it when Hadrian meandered through their cities as if on historical tour. In the provinces of Achaea and Asia, in Syria and Egypt, Hadrian re-enacted and re-commissioned versions of Greek history. Among countless other examples, he rebuilt the supposed tomb of Ajax at Ilium, site of the Trojan war in Asia Minor, just as in Arcadian Scillus he visited the tomb of the great Athenian general Xenophon. On another eastern visit, he restored the tomb of Alcibiades in Melissa, deep in northern Phrygia. At Mantineia in Arcadia, he put up a memorial to the Theban Epaminondas, remembered as a liberator of the Greeks 400 years after his death. At Athens, he initiated a building programme that would continue through the century under both local and imperial patronage. Hadrian's major personal contribution to the city was to order the final completion of the great temple of Olympian Zeus: the Athenian tyrant Peisistratus had begun it in the sixth century BC but the work was unfinished till Hadrian's day. At Delphi, he was more aggressively philhellenc: he undid the oligarchic dominance of the Amphictyonic Council that managed Delphi's prophetic shrine, which had been imposed on it by the emperors Augustus and Nero, widening the membership to what he imagined was its pristine, original state when the Greek world was still a mosaic of tiny, independent *poleis*. It was a fantasy version of Greek antiquity, but one that appealed to his audience. When he arrived in Egypt for the first time, in the year 130, there followed another orgy of historically symbolic acts, beginning with the restoration of the tomb of Pompey at Pelusium and continuing from there with a procession down the Nile.

Hadrian's type of philhellenism marks an interesting stage in Roman imperial history. During his reign, it was still possible for disappointed rivals and others who disliked him to deride Hadrian as effete and un-Roman, a *Graeculus*, 'little Greek'. In doing so, they recalled a very old strain of fear and jealousy that went back to the republic. Greek culture was self-evidently so much older and more sophisticated than Rome's home-grown traditions, that affected disdain for all things Greek served a defensive function. A fondness for the hunt, for instance, was a stereotypically Greek pastime that Roman aristocrats had once thought of as beneath their dignity. Likewise romantic or affective homosexuality: no one minded if Roman men preferred sex with other men, but romance was not meant to come into it and was an embarrassment if it did. The two cultures had long since come together in a great many ways, and Hellenistic tastes in art and literature tended to dominate in both Greek and Latin contexts, but at the start of the second century, to ride to hounds or to erotise the love of young men might still make one a *Graeculus*: old stereotypes still carried a sting. Hadrian's long reign drew much of that poison, not because Latin senators ever warmed to the man himself or his philhellenic enthusiasms, but because his embrace of the Greek aristocracies propelled many more of them into the upper reaches of the Roman senate and the increasingly transnational elite it symbolised.

2

THE LATE REIGN AND THE SUCCESSION

Though in antiquity Hadrian was best remembered for his relationship with Greek culture and the Greek cities of the eastern Roman empire, he is nowadays most associated with the great wall stretching across the north of modern England – about as far as one could get from the Greek world and still be inside the imperial frontiers. The wall that bears Hadrian's name was a monumental construction, a series of earthworks and fortifications that used the local topography to its best advantage and symbolically closed off the line of the Tyne–Solway isthmus from South Shields in the east to Bowness in the west.

The emperor marked out frontiers wherever he went, his trip to Germany coinciding with the construction of a frontier infrastructure anchored by massive palisades. While in Spain, Hadrian seems to have suppressed a revolt of the Mauri (presumably Moorish tribesmen from across the straits of Gibraltar in the province of Mauretania Tingitana). He may not actually have crossed the straits himself, but he initiated the development of Tingitania as an urbanised frontier bulwark for the rich and peaceful Spanish provinces. In the same way, deep on the desert frontier of Numidia, Hadrian's reign marks the earliest phases of another fortified *limes*, on much the same scale as that of Germany: the camp of Numidia's garrison, the Legio III Augusta, was transferred fully 150 miles southwards, to Lambaesis, while still another 150 miles south of there a

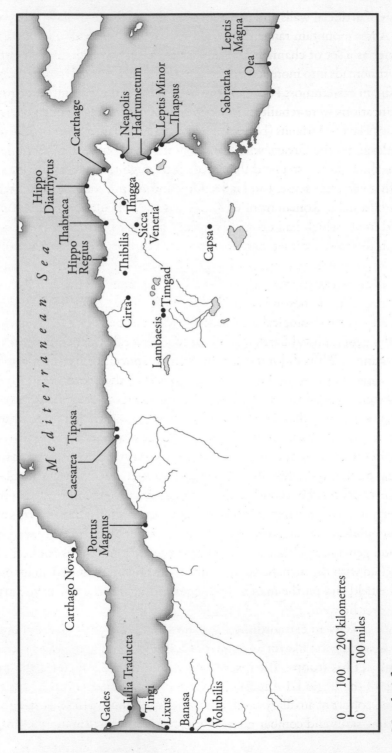

North Africa

series of artificial walls and trenches were dug in the semi-desert, beyond the Aurès mountain range. These did not so much provide a continuous barrier as a set of channels through which to control the movement of desert nomads into more settled regions during their annual transhumance. Again, in easternmost Pontus at the edge of the Caucasus, various timber fortifications were rebuilt in brick and stone by the Hadrianic governor Lucius Flavius Arrianus (better known to us as Arrian, author of a history of Alexander the Great), who learned at first hand how to repel nomads from the Eurasian steppe if they made it through the Caucasus passes.

In a very real sense, the Hadrianic building programmes were what created a stable Roman frontier, and it is not a coincidence that the Latin word *limes*, which had originally meant 'military or frontier road', now began to mean 'frontier, barrier or border'. The fortifications made clear that the infinitely expansible empire of the first century AD no longer existed; henceforth there would be a Roman empire on the one side and a barbarian world beyond it on the other. The two worlds had always been separate in an ideological and conceptual sense, but Hadrian's activities fixed a geographical barrier, more or less permeable depending on circumstances. Walls did not alter the Roman conceit of having mastered the whole world – the Latin *orbis terrarum*, or the *oikumene* as Greek philosophers liked to call it – but they foreclosed the prospect of further conquest in a way that the Augustan age would have found inconceivable.

Just as he took care of the frontiers, Hadrian worked hard to provide a model for the troops: in a world where continuous conquest was no longer on the cards, different sorts of activity would have to take its place. In the course of the second century, legionaries turned into construction experts, not just for siege machinery and fortifications, but as road- and town-builders, the engineering corps of the Roman world. Moreover, like a good general, Hadrian set an example of discipline to his soldiers. He marched with the men, he ate the same food, and he eschewed all luxuries in the field and on the march, walking or riding like the rest of the army wherever he went.

We possess an extraordinary inscription revealing, in Hadrian's own words, what it was like for an emperor (or indeed any commanding officer) to inspect his troops. The inscription comes from Lambaesis, the new camp of the Legio III Augusta in Numidia. In it, Hadrian addresses the second cohort of auxiliary cavalry in spring 128. Along with praise for their building skills and combat manoeuvres, he offers criticism of open-order cavalry tactics, deploring them as inherently dangerous and contrary to good military science. Manoeuvres and constant drill were the centrepiece of Hadrianic military discipline.

The orator Fronto, tutor of Hadrian's adoptive grandson and eventual successor Marcus Aurelius, would – decades later – mock Hadrian for insisting on constantly training his troops while being unwilling to let them off their lead and fight. The irony is real, but so too was Hadrian's belief in the value of his disciplinary regimen, as is attested by the *Tactica* of Hadrian's Greek friend Arrian, whom he had appointed to the vital governorship of Cappadocia near the Armenian frontiers. In Arrian's little work on military tactics, which he dedicated to the emperor at the very end of his reign, he specifically praises the revival of supposedly long-defunct practices that were good for the troops. Hadrian's training-heavy example, as it was described by Arrian, was seen as the model of good, old-fashioned discipline right into the fifth century. When emperors appealed to some vague ideal of ancient military conduct, or late antique authors lamented the fallen standards of their own day, they were thinking of Hadrian's army. A longer-lasting military reform was meant to ensure that recruits for the legions, now permanently garrisoned on the frontiers, could be raised locally. Local recruiting would remain a problem in the frontier zones, where there were few communities of Roman citizens, so long as the historic restriction of legionary service to citizens remained in place. Going right back to republican times, only enfranchised Romans could serve in the legions; non-citizens were recruited into auxiliary units, served longer terms at lower pay, but gained the coveted Roman citizenship upon their honourable discharge. Because of that distinction, frontier regions had tended to supply the *auxilia* while Italy and the old overseas provinces in Spain, Africa Proconsularis and the islands, had furnished the legions with recruits. Now, by raising one or two cities near the frontier forts to the status of *coloniae*, Hadrian turned their residents into Roman citizens and ensured a permanent supply of young men eligible for legionary service to the garrisons near where they were born.

If we turn back from these structural reflections to our narrative of Hadrian's reign, we find the emperor returning to Italy in 125, after four years away and a stop-over in Sicily, which had never before been visited by a Roman emperor. His precise route back to Rome is unknown, but he may well have personally dedicated the victory arch of Trajan at Beneventum (modern Benevento) along the way. By late summer of 125 he was in Rome, and shortly thereafter had retired to his country estates at Tibur (modern Tivoli), where an enormous palace was constructed for him where a rather modest villa had once stood.

The year 126 opened with Annius Verus, urban prefect for the past seven years, as consul for the third time. As we saw, this was a great – indeed now unique – honour for a private citizen. It foretold Hadrian's eventual predilection for Verus's grandson, another Marcus Annius Verus, whose father had died and who had then been adopted as a son by his thrice-consular grandfather. This young Annius Verus spent a great deal of time in the company of the emperor, was enrolled as an equestrian at the age of five and became a Salian priest at the age of seven (the Salii were an archaic priesthood revived – or perhaps invented – by Augustus, and concerned with the ritual protection of the Roman army). Because this younger Annius Verus would eventually succeed to the throne as the emperor Marcus Aurelius, some have suspected that Hadrian already considered him a potential successor in the 120s, but there is no clear evidence to that effect. On the other hand, Verus's family was highly favoured: not just the elder Annius Verus, but both of his sons-in-law, Aurelius Antoninus and Ummidius Quadratus, were consulars and among the empire's most senior statesmen.

Hadrian found life in Rome very dull after so many years of travelling and, although he stayed in or near the city throughout 126, he spent much of 127 touring the Italian countryside, including the regions north of the Po that were now becoming heavily urbanised centres of imperial administration – a role they would enjoy even more during the coming centuries. In early August 127, Hadrian celebrated his *decennalia*, the tenth anniversary of his accession, in Rome, and he now also accepted acclamation by the senate as *pater patriae*, father of his country, an honour he had previously declined. In 128, he travelled for some months to Africa to tour Rome's provinces there. We know little of his itinerary, but since all the governors of the African provinces were recent appointees, it is possible that he had planned to undertake a thorough peregrination. He definitely visited both Numidia and Mauretania Caesariensis, the long coastal strip of modern Algeria. The emperor strew privileges in his wake, granting colonial status to Utica and providing a major new aqueduct for Carthage. Other cities, too, became *coloniae*, and many peregrine (non-citizen) communities were raised to municipal status, a half-step towards enfranchisement that gave local municipal officials an automatic right to

Roman citizenship. Nevertheless, Africa would remain a patchwork quilt of legal statuses for generations to come, with *coloniae*, *municipia* and unenfranchised *peregrini* all sharing overlapping provincial space; this was in strong contrast to Spain and Gallia Narbonensis, which were by now entirely colonial or municipal, and also to northern Gaul, Britain and the Balkans, which were overwhelmingly populated by non-citizen *peregrini*.

Before mid-summer 128, Hadrian returned to Italy, but he had no intention of staying there long. Instead, he would once again go to the east. By autumn he was in Athens, where he stayed with Claudius Atticus, who was soon to be honoured with the consulship; his son Herodes Atticus had just returned from his first senatorial posting as quaestor. The emperor again took part in the Eleusinian rites and was now initiated into a higher ritual grade, that of *epoptes*, which meant that he had not merely taken part in the procession and prayers, but had actually witnessed the mystery itself – whatever that was, for we moderns have no idea. More ambitiously, Hadrian began planning the creation of the Panhellenion, a league or association of all the 'Hellenes', centred on Athens and meeting in the Olympeion, the temple of Olympian Zeus begun by Peisistratos back in the sixth century BC and now nearly complete. Unlike any previous Greek league, this one was meant to include every Greek city founded before the age of Alexander, another sign of the imaginary Classical world Hadrian was trying to recreate for Greece. It is impossible to doubt the emperor's enthusiasm for this project, which was reciprocated by his Greek subjects who henceforth referred to him as *Sebastos Olympios*, the Olympian Emperor.

When he left Athens for the east in 129, Hadrian was accompanied by many of the Hellenic intellectuals and grandees whose company he enjoyed, among them Julia Balbilla, widow of the prominent Athenian Philoppapus and a friend of the empress Sabina. Hadrian's sister Paulina may have travelled with the imperial party as well, though his brother-in-law, Paulina's husband Julius Servianus, remained in Rome. The imperial party travelled from Athens to Ephesus and then through the southern provinces of Asia Minor. We can find evidence of Hadrian in Caria, as well as further inland in Phrygia and Galatia, then moving via Cappadocia to Lycia and ultimately to Syria on the other side of the Taurus mountains. He spent some time in Antioch, showering the city with privileges, but he also honoured other Syrian cities, among them Tyre, Damascus and Samosata. All three were now, like Antioch, permitted to call themselves by the Greek title *metropolis*, as jealously guarded a status as that of *neokoros*.

While in Syria, the emperor's Hellenism took a new and dangerous turn, as he intervened in a quarrel between local Jews and Greeks. Both communities had special privileges under Roman rule, but they also had a long-standing mutual dislike, which surfaced whenever they were forced to live together. Hadrian came down precipitately on the Greek side. In a harshly worded edict that reeked of Hellenic anti-Judaism, Hadrian forbade circumcision, thereby outlawing a central part of Jewish ritual practice. He also decided to rebuild Jerusalem – destroyed by Vespasian and Titus after the Jewish revolt of the 60s AD – as a Roman *colonia*, placing a temple of Jupiter Capitolinus on the site where the Jewish temple had once stood. Offensive as that was, it was really the ban on circumcision that sparked the last and most brutal Jewish rebellion against Roman rule.

Hadrian spent the winter of 129–30 in Syria, venturing as far east as the caravan oasis of Palmyra in the Syrian desert, before travelling via Arabia and Judaea to Egypt in the summer of 130. He went overland from Gaza to Pelusium and, as noted above, he entertained his historical predilections at the latter site by reconstructing Pompey's tomb and inscribing his own verse on it. He was in Alexandria in August, where he restored to the city the privileges it had lost after the Jewish revolt of 116–17, and he conversed there with the scholars of the Ptolemaic Museion (whence comes our own word 'museum'). He also probably visited the double-legionary camp at Nicopolis. This housed the Legiones XXII Deiotariana and the II Traina, which together made up the whole Roman garrison of Egypt. His plan was to sail upriver into Upper Egypt after the Nile's annual flood subsided.

Hadrian's visit to Egypt was a long one, and rather different from his earlier tours. In Egypt, there were very few Greeks and very few Greek communities on whom he could lavish the privileges he had showered across the rest of the eastern provinces. He had therefore to exercise his philhellenism in a different way, by founding a brand new Greek *polis*. It would possess all the urban institutions of a proper *polis* and it would stand as one of just four Greek cities in Egypt, alongside Alexandria, Naucratis and Ptolemais. The rest of Egypt was a sea of native villages that had changed relatively little since Alexander's successor Ptolemy took over from the last pharaohs and retained most of the pharaonic dispensation rather than remake it in the Greek image. Hadrian's plan for a new Greek city was an important early step in the Romanisation of Egypt, or rather its Hellenisation within a Roman imperial mainstream, that we will return to in our discussion of the third century.

Hadrian's Egyptian tour went on to Naucratis and Ptolemais, the other Greek cities of the north, and then started up the Nile late in 130, beginning at Heliopolis, the birthplace of the mythical Phoenix, near where the river starts to spread out into its gigantic delta. Further upriver, the pyramids and sphinxes of Memphis had been a tourist destination for Greeks, and later Romans, for half a millennium and we have evidence that the imperial touring party of 130 followed in the footsteps of earlier visitors by carving its graffiti – names and doggerel verse – on the Great Pyramid. From Memphis, they continued on to Oxyrhynchus, an important administrative centre for Middle Egypt and a site in whose sands are preserved many of the papyri on which our understanding of Ptolemaic and Roman Egypt is based. In October, they reached Hermopolis, the site of the temple of Thoth, identified with the Greek god Hermes, which was another frequent tourist destination for curious Greeks and Romans. Here, Hadrian was able to witness the great festival of the Nile, which commemorated the self-sacrifice of the Egyptian god Osiris who was responsible for ensuring the Nile flood and thus the fertility of Egypt itself.

It was at Hermopolis that disaster struck. Hadrian travelled with a large party, not least his wife Sabina and her entourage of learned women. The emperor's own personal companion was the Bithynian boy Antinous. We learn very little of Antinous in contemporary literary sources and, for that reason, he has been the source of much modern conjecture, not least the homerotic romance made famous in Marguerite Yourcenar's 1951 novel, *Memoirs of Hadrian*. That Antinous was the love of Hadrian's life can hardly be doubted, but the historical record leaves him a blank slate on to which modern scholars can project their own visions. He may have been travelling with Hadrian since the visit to Bithynia in the early 120s, but there is no proof of that. If he did, we have no idea how public their companionship was or whether Antinous was given some minor Roman office to keep him busy. Scholars also differ over whether Hadrian was publicly endorsing the kind of romantic love between males that was central to the Classical Athenian culture to which he was so devoted. If he was, then Hadrian was playing *erastes* to Antinous' *eromenos*, in a paternal and nurturing, but also actively homosexual, love affair between adult man and adolescent boy. The one thing of which we can be absolutely sure is that Antinous was Hadrian's favoured hunting companion and that his death by drowning in the Nile at Hermopolis occasioned an outpouring of public grief quite alien to Roman emperors. There were hostile rumours that the boy's death was voluntary, a magical recreation of the death of Osiris perhaps designed to restore Hadrian's health or ensure his long life, and Hadrian had to insist on the accidental nature of the drowning. What we do know is that Hadrian finally decided to found his new Greek city here, opposite Hermopolis on the right bank of the Nile, and to call the province's fourth autonomous city Antinoopolis after his dead favourite.

Grief did not prevent the imperial party from continuing its journey, which progressed in November south to Ptolemais, Thebes and Philae, and visiting the famous singing statue of Memnon (the Pharaoh Amenophis III) at Thebes; here, as at Memphis, they commemorated their passage with verse scribbled on the singing statue itself. Before the year was out, Hadrian was back in Alexandria, where the official deification of Antinous was promulgated and spread almost instantly throughout the Greek east. For the Egyptian audience the dead boy was assimilated to Osiris, and we have a hieroglyphic monument to a new hybrid deity Osirantinous. Elsewhere, though, Greeks had long been happy to accept the divinisation of mortals and the cult of Antinous joined many others, his statues reproduced from one end of the empire to another, the whole Roman world thereby sharing in the emperor's private grief.

Hadrian began the new year of 131 in Alexandria, before returning to Syria and taking a journey by land up to Cilicia and Pamphylia in south-eastern Asia Minor. From the south coast, Hadrian went by ship to Ephesus, which was now made twice *neokoros*, and then ventured into the far north of the province of Asia on the border of Bithynia. There, it can be conjectured, he paid his respects at Bithynium, the home of Antinous, but soon there was more bad news – Hadrian's sister Paulina had died and was now honoured as Diva Paulina. Hadrian was again making for Athens, where he overwintered in 131–2, participating in the Eleusinian mysteries for the third time. In the spring of 132 he celebrated the dedication of the temple of Olympian Zeus, so many centuries delayed, and inaugurated the first Panhellenion, his great festival of all the Greeks.

All the while, however, trouble had been brewing in Judaea. Hadrian's prohibition of circumcision, his rebuilding of the Jewish temple as a Greek cult site and the foundation of a Roman *colonia* where the ancient Jewish capital had once stood together proved too great a provocation. For several years Jewish militants had been stockpiling weaponry, fortifying remote strongholds and planning rebellion. In 132 the storm broke and the Roman legate Tineius Rufus found it impossible to fight an enemy who refused to meet his legions in open battle and relied instead on guerrilla warfare from hidden bases. The governor of Syria brought in reinforcements, but the Romans were soon suffering massive casualties. The initial success of the revolt seems clearly to have been the result of its coherence and unity, under the authority of a single 'prince of Israel', Shimon bar Kokhba, known as Bar Cochebas in much later Christian sources written in Greek. Contemporary Greek and Roman writers do not so much as mention his existence, but the Romans clearly understood the messianic cast of the rebellion and struck directly at the Jews' religious leaders. Bar Kokhba was supported by the rabbi Akiba, one of the most influential of the post-Flavian rabbis, and he and many others lost their lives as the legions suppressed the rebels.

Their unity and military prowess is what separates this revolt from that of 116–17 under Trajan: despite its disruptiveness, that earlier revolt was put down relatively easily and ended in the annihilation of the Jewish population in provinces such as Cyrenaica. During the Bar Kokhba revolt, by contrast, the rebels actually took control of provincial territory and held it for several years, until 135. We do not know that they ever took Jerusalem, but they certainly did force Hadrian to return briefly to Judaea in person and to summon his best general, Sextus Julius Severus, from faraway Britain. A man skilled at handling difficult natives, he was now meant to bring his expertise to the Jewish revolt. Tineius Rufus had already been wreaking reprisals on the Jewish civilian population, but Severus continued this policy and extended it, adopting small unit tactics, cutting off rebel outposts, starving or smoking them out, and then massacring them indiscriminately. Hundreds of Jewish villages were wiped off the map, hundreds of thousands of Jews were killed, and many more enslaved. It was a return to the methods of subjugation that had characterised early phases of Roman expansion and it was one that would have a long future along the northern frontiers, where the periodical sowing of terror among native populations was thought to be the best means of controlling them.

In Judaea, it took until 135 and the death of Shimon bar Kokhba for the last Jewish fortress to fall. After that, Jews were forbidden to enter the territory of Aelia Capitolina, the Roman *colonia* on the site of Jerusalem.

Within a few years of the end of the war, even the provincial name Judaea was erased – the province was henceforth called Syria Palaestina.

While Julius Severus continued to deal with the revolt, Hadrian returned to Italy via the Balkans. He was back in Rome by May of 134, in which year his widowed brother-in-law Julius Servianus achieved his third consulate. This honour, though long delayed, may have been a sign of Hadrian's plans for the succession, since he was ageing fast and generally in ill health. The year 137 would mark his *vicennalia*, the twentieth anniversary of his accession. He was the first emperor since Tiberius to have reigned so long, although no one at the time would have made so unflattering a comparison explicit. Hadrian was now actively planning for his death, building a gigantic mausoleum in the Ager Vaticanus, across the Tiber from the Campus Martius: it is the monument now known as the Castel Sant'Angelo after its conversion to a papal fortress during the Middle Ages. Planning for the succession, unlike planning for the mausoleum, was a disaster, thanks to Hadrian's failing health and his alienation from many old friends at this time. Hadrian was childless and had done even less than Trajan to signal his choice of heir. In the later 120s, his great-nephew, Pedanius Fuscus – the grandson of Paulina and Julius Servianus, whose father, another Pedanius Fuscus, had probably died soon after his consulship in 118 – imagined himself to be heir presumptive. As the emperor's nearest male relative, the younger Fuscus had travelled with Hadrian to Greece. But back in Rome, compelled by health to choose a successor, Hadrian passed Fuscus over.

Instead, in his *vicennalia* year, Hadrian adopted as his son one of the year's consuls, a young senator of Gallic origin named Lucius Ceionius Commodus. Hadrian renamed him Lucius Aelius Caesar at his adoption. The choice was unpopular, perhaps because it was inexplicable. Commodus was a virtual unknown. His sole recommendation was that he was married to a daughter of Avidius Nigrinus, one of the four Trajanic consulars executed back in 118. Some argue that the adoption was Hadrian's way of expiating that crime, but that is far-fetched: the imperial rationale must remain a mystery. The frustrated Pedanius Fuscus took poorly to the adoption of Lucius, and Hadrian had him put to death in 137. His 90-year-old grandfather, Hadrian's brother-in-law Julius Servianus, was forced to commit suicide; at least two other forced suicides are named, and we are told that there were 'many other deaths' as well. Hadrian's unloved wife, the Augusta Sabina, also now died – a natural death, despite inevitable rumours of poisoning – and she was duly deified by the senate.

Hadrian's reign was poised to end in the same high-profile bloodshed with which it had begun, when the sudden death of Aelius Caesar revealed the pointlessness of it all. He had been sent to the armies on the Danube both to get some military experience and to impress a sense of dynastic continuity on the soldiers. Tubercular even before he left, the Balkan weather did him no good. When he returned to Rome late in 137, on the night before he was meant to address the senate, he fell sick and died before the morning, coughing blood. He left behind a 6-year-old son, also named Lucius Ceionius Commodus, and a daughter, Ceionia Fabia, who was already betrothed to the younger Marcus Annius Verus (that is, the future emperor Marcus Aurelius).

Hadrian moved quickly to name an alternative successor. He turned sixty-two on 24 January 138, and was by then himself dying of tuberculosis, disturbed by wild dreams, and sometimes too ill to come to the senate house. The new heir was Aurelius Antoninus, like the late Aelius Caesar a man of southern Gallic descent, but anything but an unknown. On the contrary, he had a long and unexceptionable history of service in the senate. Born in 86, he was the maternal grandson of the great marshal Arrius Antoninus, who had been consul for the second time in the year 97, when Trajan was adopted by Nerva. By the year 110 he had married Annia Faustina, daughter of the thrice-consular Annius Verus, and was thus launched on a career among the luminaries of the Hadrianic age. Antoninus was allowed to keep his name upon his adoption, but he was also made to adopt two heirs. One, Lucius Aelius Ceionius Commodus, was the son of the dead Aelius Caesar, and now renamed L. Aurelius Commodus; he was betrothed to the younger Faustina, daughter of Antoninus and Annia Faustina. The other was the 16-year-old Marcus Annius Verus, already Antoninus's nephew by marriage, who had been favoured since his birth in 121 and was betrothed to Ceionia Fabia, daughter of the dead Aelius Caesar. Now, with his adoption by Aurelius Antoninus, he was to change his name to Marcus Aurelius Verus, uniting in his person and family the great clans of Trajanic Rome: his mother, Domitia Lucilla, was an heiress of enormous personal wealth, and his sister, Annia Cornificia, was married to Ummidius Quadratus, one of Hadrian's favoured generals.

With these multi-generational adoptions, Hadrian would in effect fix the imperial succession for at least two, perhaps three future reigns.

Antoninus, we are told in the desperately scant literary evidence for this period, hesitated a long time before accepting what Hadrian was offering him. This was more than the gesture known as *recusatio imperii*, a show of reluctance and feigned refusal that even the most avid aspirant to the purple was meant to display. Antoninus was a modest man. He may genuinely have preferred the privileged life of a blameless senator to the responsibilities of imperial rule. But a blameless senator was also a dutiful one and, on 24 February 138, a month after Hadrian's birthday, the adoption ceremony went ahead and Aurelius Antoninus became T. Aelius Caesar Antoninus. He received the title *imperator* as a type of praenomen or first name, implying that he had already received a military acclamation as emperor, and was given the tribunician power, an essential part of the package of powers that made up imperial authority. He never did stop using his own nomen Aurelius, and was designated for the consulship of 139, his second.

Important men who opposed this succession, or were thought to do so, now went into retirement, and the old praetorian prefect Marcius Turbo, who had been there since the very start of Hadrian's reign, was finally relieved of his post. Turbo's anomalous role as sole prefect was allowed to set no precedent, and the office now reverted to two prefects, Gavius Maximus and Petronius Mamertinus, both of whom could be trusted to support the succession plans. They would ensure a smooth transition in government, for Hadrian's death was fast approaching. Dropsy had set in, and he is said to have begged for someone to kill him, by poison or the sword: his personal physician committed suicide rather than administer a killing draught. Unable to die and in great misery, Hadrian set about writing an autobiography in imitation of Augustus: the work itself has not survived, but it was used as a source by authors whose work we possess. Death finally came on 10 July 138 at Baiae, a holiday resort on the coast of the bay of Naples. Antoninus was at the emperor's side. Hadrian died, as a later author put it, 'hated by all'.

The executions at the end of his reign, recalling as they did the executions at its start, had left only bitter memories. The emperor was buried temporarily at one of his villas in Campania, to await the completion of his mausoleum in Rome. In the city itself, Hadrian's adoptive grandson Marcus sponsored the gladiatorial games that traditionally accompanied the mourning for a Roman of status, but he did so in his capacity as a private citizen, using his family's own inheritance, the pious duty owed to a revered ancestor. With the death of Hadrian, our main story can begin. These preliminaries have been necessary because the networks of marriage, patronage and inheritance that stretch from the Flavians, through the reigns of Nerva and Trajan, and into that of Hadrian definitively shaped the next fifty years of Roman history.

3

PEACE AND WAR AT
MID-CENTURY

＊＊＊＊＊＊＊

As we saw in the last chapter, Hadrian adopted two sons in succession. The second, Aurelius Antoninus, had been an alternative to the short-lived Aelius Caesar. Antoninus had little governing experience, just the standard *cursus honorum* of a not very ambitious senator: first quaestor, then praetor, and then the by no means assured dignity of a consulship. His brief administrative stints had been as a consular governor in Italy, part of a short-lived and unpopular Hadrianic experiment in administering the peninsula as if it were a province, and as proconsul of Asia, a very prestigious but entirely untaxing appointment. He had never laid eyes on an army. Still, his father and grandfather had each been consul twice. That kind of ancestry counted for something. Better still, he was rich, had a reputation for good management and was popular in the senate – all told, the perfect qualities of a *civilis princeps*, a reputation Hadrian had never achieved.

Each of the qualities Antoninus was already thought to possess at his accession became patent in the course of his long and quiet reign, not least its opening act, when he won the sobriquet Pius, by which he is generally known. He earned the name because of the insistence with which he honoured both the ancestral gods and, more specifically, his adoptive father Hadrian, whom he had deified despite resistance in the senate. Indeed, that venerable body acquiesced in Hadrian's deification only to ensure that Pius would accept his imperial inheritance: he publicly declared that if Hadrian's memory were to be condemned, then all his acts would be invalidated, not least Pius's own succession, and he would be forced to retire forthwith. It was an inspired argument. The senate could not deny the insistent wish of an autocratic princeps, but Pius handed them a face-saving argument that spared him any need to insist and them any public show of subordination. Construction of Hadrian's mausoleum was finished, his remains brought from Puteoli to Rome and, after the ceremony of *consecratio* by which he was deified, Hadrian was interred in the giant tomb he had planned for himself.

That act of necessary piety accomplished, Antoninus was free to tamper with any number of Hadrianic arrangements, in particular the betrothals of the heirs Antoninus had adopted on Hadrian's insistence: instead of the young Ceionia Fabia, daughter of Aelius Caesar and sister of L. Aurelius Commodus, Marcus Aurelius Verus (the future emperor and former Marcus Annius Verus the Younger) was to be betrothed to Faustina the Younger, Antoninus's own daughter, whose betrothal to Commodus was now dissolved. Marcus was also designated consul for the year 140 and had the name Caesar added to his own, thus making him the more serious of the two heirs apparent and raising him distinctly above his adoptive brother in public esteem. As cover for this change to Hadrian's plans, and perhaps also to make up for the unpopularity of Hadrian's *consecratio*, some of the now deified emperor's least popular measures were reversed: death sentences issued at the end of Hadrian's life were commuted and his experiment in imposing consular governors on Italy in imitation of provincial governance was abolished.

In other respects the opening years of Antoninus's reign advertised continuity with the past. Pius entered on his second consulship, his first as augustus, on 1 January 139; his colleague was C. Bruttius Praesens, also consul for the second time. Praesens was that rare old friend of Hadrian who had escaped displeasure in his notorious final years. When he and Pius stepped down to make way for suffect consuls, Praesens replaced the last urban prefect of Hadrian's reign, Scipio Orfitus. Though he died in that office in the following year, his descendants and those of Pius formed an association that would last across three generations, each of which included marriage connections to the ruling dynasty. Both of Pius's praetorian prefects were held over from the final days of Hadrian, which suggests that their initial appointment may have been the work of Antoninus, as he prepared to succeed. One prefect was M. Petronius Mamertinus, a relative of the African orator Fronto; the latter had become tutor to the senior heir apparent, Marcus, and his descendants would eventually marry into the imperial family. The other prefect was M. Gavius Maximus, a trusted equestrian official under Hadrian whose career as guard prefect would last nearly to the end of Antoninus's reign: when he died of natural causes in 156 or 157, he became the only praetorian prefect in imperial history to survive that long in office without acquiring dangerous personal ambitions or falling from grace under suspicion of having done so.

All told, the empire under Antoninus Pius almost appears to have no internal, and very little external, history. Narrative sources tend to go silent during times of peace, in every age and in every culture. In the second century AD, however, we are particularly disadvantaged. We know of very few histories written in this period, and even those that were written are either completely lost or survive in fragments that leave entire decades blank. Late imperial *breviaria*, what we might call 'very short histories', offer literally a sentence or two per reign. The major surviving source is a fourth-century compilation known as the *Historia Augusta*. Its author was a crackpot, plain and simple. He took a now lost collection of sober imperial biographies from Nerva to Caracalla (that is, from AD 96 to 217, and thus a continuation of Suetonius Tranquillus's lives of the first twelve emperors), mixed in juicy titbits from the rather more gossipy collection put together in the early third century by a senator named Marius Maximus, and then started to fantasise: he fabricated lives of imperial heirs apparent and when that got boring he carried on his sequence into the third century AD, with biographies of the period's little-known and short-lived emperors that could run through forty or fifty pages of pure invention. Then, to top it off, he pretended to be six different biographers writing more than half a century before the late 390s. The reader can imagine the inordinate effort made by modern scholars panning for gold among these maddening tanks full of dross, and we will have cause to lament the *Historia Augusta* and regret the existence of its author more than once in chapters to come. Yet for the reign of Antoninus Pius, it seems certain that our unlovable fabulist had next to nothing to work with. Even a near-contemporary, like the author of the biography from which our fourth-century author borrowed his framework, found nothing exciting, still less scandalous, to say about political events of the time. It is as if history were happening elsewhere.

As a result of all this, the modern scholar's main way into the political life of the reign is to carefully trace its senatorial and equestrian career paths and how these issued in success or failure, under Pius himself or during later reigns. There is a great deal of information to be found in these careers, though little of it makes for exciting reading. Contemporaries were fully aware of the peaceful felicity of their era. The Greek orator Aelius Aristides left us a beatific picture of Antonine prosperity deliberately conjured up by Edward Gibbon, the great Enlightenment historian of Rome's rise and fall: Rome's empire, under the pious Antoninus, 'comprehended the fairest part of the earth and the most civilised portion of mankind'. More importantly, it was at peace.

Aristides could paint a picture of free and happy Greek cities, prospering like never before under the loving gaze of their benevolent emperor, in large part because the eastern front stayed quiet while Pius reigned. There had, it is true, been some trouble there not long before Hadrian's death: the Roman client king of Caucasian Iberia, one Pharasmanes, had induced a confederation of semi-nomadic warriors from the trans-Caucasian steppes known as the Alani to invade the territory of his neighbours in Armenia and Albania. In the aftermath, these Alans raided both Parthian and Roman territory. The legate of Cappadocia, the famous historian Arrian, acted swiftly and there was no full-scale invasion of the Roman provinces. Pharasmanes was playing at the intrigues common to eastern client monarchs, but on the frontiers small triggers could spark major wars. It was thus a pleasant relief when the Iberian king travelled to Rome in person to pay homage to the new emperor and exculpate himself for his mistake.

In general, Antoninus's frontier diplomacy seems to have been similarly successful, as when the Quadi, a coalition of barbarian tribes dwelling along the middle Danube frontier, asked the emperor to choose their king for them; the event is commemorated on coins showing Pius appointing a submissive barbarian king under the legend REX QUADIS DATUS ('a king given to the Quadi'). In the north-western provinces, Quintus Lollius Urbicus went from governing Germania Inferior to Britannia, where he left behind the line of Hadrian's Wall and drove Roman control north to the narrower Clyde–Forth line. There he built a new wall out of turf piled up behind a deep ditch, the so-called Antonine Wall. As a result of this renewed activity, the northern British tribes rose up in one of the disturbances to which they remained prone; the military map of south-western

Scotland suggests that it was never properly pacified. The rising or risings late in Antoninus's reign were suppressed by the general Gnaeus Julius Verus, who decided to solve the longer-term threat by reverting to the line of Hadrian's Wall, which had been refortified at just the same time that the frontier line was driven north. Roman occupation of the Borders had lasted a mere twenty years, proving once again that Britannia was a disproportionately challenging province to control.

Western Mauretania was less difficult, but not by much. Most of the Roman Maghreb consisted of a tiny strip of fertile coastal land dotted with cities and backing on to forbidding mountains populated by the perpetually unsettled tribes of Mauri. In between the provinces of Caesariensis and Tingitania, the mountains ran all the way to the coast, making consistent control that much more difficult. Neither province ever had a proper legionary garrison – constant low-grade raiding did not merit the permanent expense – but this meant that expeditionary forces had to be gathered from as far away as Britannia when a major revolt blew up among the Mauri, as it did in 145. The subsequent campaign, which lasted for several years, flared up periodically into the next reign. Also in 145, in September, one Cornelius Priscianus 'disturbed the peace of Spain' and was condemned to death by the senate for doing so, as we are informed by a lone inscription. This may have been an attempt at usurpation, although Hispania Tarraconensis had only a single legion, the Legio VII Gemina, stationed in the future city of León, far from the seat of provincial government at Tarraco. And so this Priscianus affair, whatever it was, exhausts the list of disturbances during an astonishingly tranquil reign.

In Rome, the peace was kept and government ticked smoothly along. The empress Faustina died late in 140 and Pius had her deified, never remarrying, but taking Faustina's freedwoman, Galeria Lysistrate, as his concubine until his own death two decades later. He divided his time among his many villas in the countryside near Rome, at Baiae on the bay of Naples, and in the city itself when he was needed, but mainly he played the role of the frugal senator and careful estate manager to the full. For that, senatorial opinion would pay him the highest tribute possible, claiming that he remained the same man as emperor as he had been as a private citizen. The young heirs to the throne, Lucius Aurelius Commodus and Marcus Aurelius Verus, accompanied their adoptive father on his peaceful country rounds. In March 145, Lucius assumed the *toga virilis*, and in April of that year Marcus married the younger Faustina, to whom he had been betrothed since the death of Hadrian. The teachers of Marcus had won strong preferment from early in the reign. Herodes Atticus, the Athenian millionaire and philosopher whose friendship with Hadrian we noted in the last chapter, was ordinary consul in 143, a suitable (and expected) honour for a man of his rank whose father had attained the consulship in the previous reign. But Marcus's tutor, Fronto, an African and a *novus homo*, also won a suffect consulship in that year, thanks to his connections to both Marcus and the guard prefect Petronius Mamertinus. (Suffect consuls were appointed a couple of months into each year, the 'ordinary' consuls who gave their names to the year having stepped down – the practice not only spread consular dignity more widely, but also ensured a sufficient supply of men to hold provincial commands for which only ex-consuls were qualified.)

As is often true during this period of imperial history, but especially so in the reign of Pius, it is easier to describe the shape of government and its personnel than it is to reconstruct the course of big events. The families at the centre of Antonine government were a varied lot, many of whose senatorial roots went back two or at most three generations, to the Flavian revolution. Many had roots in the colonial aristocracies of Baetica, Hispania Tarraconensis and Gallia Narbonensis, though their Antonine descendants were by now thoroughly Italian. At the same time, a leavening of Africans, Greeks from Asia and Achaea, and even the occasional Syrian family, now began to register in the *fasti*, 'lists of magistrates'. These families were closely interconnected by marriages that pulled in new blood but constantly reinforced existing ties. Thus a man like Sextus Erucius Clarus, who replaced Bruttius Praesens as urban prefect and kept the post until his death in 145, had a senatorial career that went back to the time of Trajan and had family roots that were older than that.

Others, by contrast, had come to prominence in the later reign of Hadrian. Claudius Maximus, consul in 144, governed one of the three great military provinces, Pannonia Superior, in 150–54, and was proconsul of Africa in 158; Gnaeus Julius Verus, who suppressed the British rising of the late 150s, was probably the son of the Sextus Julius Severus who had been Hadrian's most trusted general and the victor of his Jewish war. Quintus Lollius Urbicus, an African like Fronto and Mamertinus, was governor of Britannia early in the reign and became urban prefect near its end. The family of the Ummidii Quadrati, already prospering under Hadrian, continued to do so under his successor. The elder Ummidius

Quadratus was married to Cornificia, sister of the senior heir apparent Marcus Aurelius Verus; the children of Ummidius and Cornificia, Marcus Ummidius Quadratus and Ummidia Cornificia Faustina, would be important in the dynastic politics of the coming reigns, even though the elder Cornificia (Marcus's sister) had died by 152 – when, upon the death of Pius, Marcus acceded to the throne as Marcus Aurelius Antoninus, he transferred a substantial part of his family's private fortune to the younger Quadratus so as not to mingle it with the imperial *fiscus* or the public *aerarium*. Other relatives of the imperial house also did very well. The Ceionii Commodi, the family of the junior heir Lucius, prospered. Lucius's cousin M. Ceionius Silvanus was consul in 156. In 157, it was the turn of M. Vettulenus Civica Barbarus, Lucius's uncle, while his sister Ceionia Fabia's husband, Plautius Quintillus, was consul in 159. This barrage of multi-barrelled names cannot help but daunt the reader, who may well have skimmed the last paragraph taking very little in. That reaction is entirely natural, but nothing can illustrate the self-sustaining coherence of the Antonine aristocracy as well as these tangled webs of similarly-named Roman grandees.

From the start of Antoninus Pius's reign, the elder of his adoptive sons, Marcus, was steadily advanced through the stages of a public career that made clear his coming succession to the throne. Lucius was clearly signalled as the junior partner, for despite receiving such honours as a consulship at the age of eighteen in 154, he was never granted the same constitutional powers as Marcus. More symbolically, while Lucius accompanied the praetorian prefect Gavius Maximus in official processions, Marcus travelled alongside Pius. And Marcus looked likely to provide for the future succession as well. In 147, Faustina gave birth to their first child, Domitia Faustina – only a daughter, but still an important signal that the marriage would be fertile. In that same year, Pius conferred upon Marcus the *tribunicia potestas* and consular *imperium* superior to any proconsul's. That is to say, Marcus now possessed the proconsular *imperium* first enjoyed by Augustus in the 20s BC, and the equivalent *tribunicia potestas* at Rome itself; long the basis of imperial power, they were formalised as such by the senatorial law that had granted imperial powers to Vespasian the better part of a century earlier. A decade into the reign, Marcus's official nomenclature changed yet again. In 147, Marcus Antoninus Verus (formerly Marcus Annius Verus) became Marcus Aurelius Caesar. This renaming finally cemented a precedent that had grown up slowly over the previous century, according to which the cognomen of the dictator Julius Caesar, who was by now remembered as the first emperor, became part of the imperial titulature, and was specifically used to designate the heir to the throne: a caesar was now an augustus in waiting.

At the same time that Marcus became caesar, his wife Faustina was given the title augusta, with which emperors since Trajan had honoured their most senior female relatives. Marcus Caesar and Faustina Augusta would go on to have many children after their first, Domitia Faustina, who died some time in the 150s. Twin sons were born in 149 and duly commemorated on coinage, but both were dead before the end of the year and buried in the mausoleum of Hadrian, where their funerary inscriptions still survive; in March 150, there arrived another girl, Annia Aurelia Galeria Lucilla, known to history by the last of those names and for her prodigious influence after Marcus's death; another son was born in 152, but he too died young; either the year before or the year after that, another daughter, Annia Galeria Aurelia Faustina, was born; one more son was born but died before 158; two daughters, Fadilla and Cornificia, were born in 159 and 160 respectively; then, in 161, when Marcus had already succeeded his adoptive father as emperor, Faustina gave birth to two more children, twin boys named T. Aurelius Fulvus Antoninus and Lucius Aurelius Commodus – the latter would be the only male child to survive Marcus and would in fact accede to the throne at his death; finally, in 162, there arrived yet another boy, Marcus Annius Verus, who failed to survive despite being given Marcus's birth names.

In studied contrast with Marcus, Lucius was neither married nor, so far as we know, betrothed, presumably lest he produce an heir who might challenge Marcus's dynastic primacy. Pius, a frugal and careful man, would live to the age of seventy-five, but he was beginning to tire by the mid 150s. With the death of the trusted praetorian prefect Gavius Maximus, more and more power began to devolve upon Marcus Caesar, who already shared nearly all the constitutional authority that his father possessed. Marcus and Lucius were made joint ordinary consuls in 161, the year in which Antoninus Pius finally died, on 7 March, as peacefully and uneventfully as he had reigned.

There was no transition in government with Pius's death, for Marcus had shared all of his adoptive father's authority save for the title of augustus and the religious office of *pontifex maximus*. Marcus refused to accept these powers and titles unless his brother was given an equal share in the imperial power. That was something that Antoninus had never wanted, as every one of his decisions had long made clear and despite the fact that, decades earlier, his patron and benefactor Hadrian had envisaged just such a joint succession. Observing Lucius's mediocre intellect and complete lack of interest in governance, Antoninus had continually promoted Marcus over his younger adoptive son. Marcus, however, possessed an almost overwhelming sense of duty, based on a deeply held Stoic philosophical outlook that pervades his own writings – throughout his life, while on campaign or struggling through the daily duties of an emperor, he jotted down his philosophical thoughts in pithy, occasionally moving, Greek prose, leaving to posterity the still widely read collection of his *Meditations* (or *Eis heauton*, 'To himself').

In 161, whatever Pius might have wanted, Marcus felt a powerful obligation to honour the plans made by his adoptive grandfather Hadrian. The senate could only oblige, and the praetorian guard accepted the arrangement on the promise of a suitably large donative. Lucius therefore became co-emperor, an augustus like Marcus, with tribunician power, the highest *imperium*, and a priesthood. Both Marcus and Lucius now changed their names yet again, Marcus taking on his late adoptive father's main cognomen, Antoninus, while Lucius took on Marcus's original cognomen, Verus. The two emperors, whose shifting nomenclature has dizzied the reader through the past dozen pages, thereby became Marcus Aurelius Antoninus Augustus and Lucius Aurelius Verus Augustus, the names by which they are generally known to posterity. The 30-year-old Lucius, prevented from marrying by Pius, was now betrothed to Marcus's eldest surviving daughter, Lucilla, eleven years old at the time. Marcus, having shared in Pius's rule for so long, and being ten years older than Lucius, had clearly decided to remain the senior partner, but the parity of constitutional power between the two men was a novel experiment rarely repeated in Roman history.

Pius was deified and laid to rest in the mausoleum of Hadrian. The peace of his reign was fraying. Britannia had begun to give trouble yet again and the general Statius Priscus was en route to the island from his posting in Moesia Superior when the old emperor died. The Chatti had invaded Germania Superior, although this may have been no more than a testing probe to see what the new rulers were made of. At the same time, the client kings on the borders of Cappadocia grew restive. The Parthian king Vologaeses III invaded Armenia, deposed its Roman client king and

Samosata

Antinonopolis

Tigris

Bezabde

Edessa
Apamea
Nisibis
Zeugma
Batnae
Carrhae
Resaina

Singara

Cyrrhus
Europus

MESOPOTAMIA

Antiochia
Hierapolis

Seleucia Pieria
Beroea

Barbalissus
Nicephorium

Orontes

Laodicea
Apamea
SYRIA
Resafa
Zenobia

Epiphaneia
Circesium

Raphanaea
Dura-Europos
Euphrates

Mediterranean Sea
Tripolis
Emesa
Palmyra

Byblus
Heliopolis
Berytus

Sidon
Damascus

Tyre

Ptolemais
*Lake
Tiberias*

Tiberias
Scythopolis
Gadara

Caesarea
Maritima
Pella

JUDAEA (PALAESTINA)
Gerasa

Bostra

Jordan
Aelia Capitolina
Philadelphia

Gaza
Madaba

Raphia
*Dead
Sea*

Elusa

ARABIA

N

Petra

0   100   200 kilometres
0   100 miles

Aila

Mesopotamia, Syria and Palestine

set up his own relative Pacorus as ruler. The governor of Cappadocia, Sedatius Severianus, distinguished enough to have been honoured with a suffect consulship in 153, launched a hasty reprisal across the Euphrates that ended in the annihilation of his legion and his own remorseful suicide. At the same time, Lucius Attidius Cornelianus, governor of Syria, was routed by a Parthian army.

This meant war on all fronts for the new emperors. Aufidius Victorinus, the son-in-law of Marcus's old tutor Fronto, was sent to govern Germania Superior and punish the Chatti for their border raids. Pannonia Superior was entrusted to a distant relative of Hadrian, L. Dasumius Tullius Tuscus. Faraway Britannia would have to wait, for the experienced Statius Priscus was needed to fight the Parthians. That campaign, like all eastern campaigns, had considerable symbolic importance and required the imperial presence, even if its conduct could not be entrusted to the inexperienced Lucius. His presence in the east would help inspire troops, and he took titular command of the whole eastern expedition, although in the field the great military marshals would take charge. One of the guard prefects, Furius Victorinus, accompanied Lucius along with a portion of the praetorian guard and several senior senators with long experience of military command to advise him. Marcus's cousin M. Annius Libo was sent along to replace the defeated Attidius as governor of Syria. Three full legions were sent east from the European frontiers, the V Macedonica from Moesia Inferior, the II Adiutrix from Pannonia Superior and the I Minervia from Germania Inferior.

The Parthian War was long and hard fought, along both the Cappadocian front under Statius Priscus and the Syrian front under Annius Libo and, nominally, Lucius. But Lucius had fallen ill en route to the east and travelled slowly, overwintering in Athens, where he imitated his adoptive grandfather Hadrian in becoming an initiate of the Eleusinian mysteries. We do not know when he actually arrived in Antioch, the main staging post for eastern campaigns, but he had taken in many of the Asian holiday resorts along the way. Once in Antioch, he divided his time between the city and the nearby resort of Daphne, and took no personal role in the fighting. That soured his relations with Annius Libo, whose death soon after Lucius's arrival was inevitably attributed to poisoning.

In 163 Statius Priscus secured the Cappadocian frontiers, advanced into Armenia and captured the kingdom's capital at Artaxata. This major success restored the traditional balance of power on the eastern frontier and allowed the emperors to add the victory title Armeniacus to their names. It did not, however, make the Parthians more willing to come to terms, and the fighting went on. Priscus remained in Armenia, which was brought firmly under Roman control. A pro-Roman Arsacid, and thus a relative of the ruling Parthian dynasty, who had received Roman citizenship and become a senator, was placed on the Armenian throne, not in the traditional capital at Artaxata but in a new capital built to Roman specifications. Statius Priscus died or retired soon after this victory, but other generals carried the fight to Parthia, invading the client state of Osrhoene and confronting Parthian forces there. While Julius Verus, another legacy of the previous reign, took over from the late Annius Libo as governor of Syria, C. Avidius Cassius, a Syrian from Cyrrhus who had been Hadrian's *ab epistulis*, was made legate of the III Gallica, an appointment with serious and lasting consequences.

In the meantime, Marcus's eldest surviving daughter Lucilla went to the east in 164, accompanied by Lucius's uncle, Marcus Vettulenus Civica Barbarus. There she married Lucius, to whom she had been betrothed since the start of the reign. She was made augusta, and gave birth to a daughter in the following year. In 165 the eastern high command launched a major invasion of Parthia. Edessa was taken and the kingdom of Osrhoene occupied, while Avidius Cassius pressed southwards along the Euphrates with the III Gallica to Dura-Europos, a city on the right bank of the river which now became a Roman garrison site for the first time. (Once famously among the best-preserved frontier posts of the east, it has now re-entered history tragically, having been looted wholesale in 2014 under cover of the civil wars in Syria and Iraq.) In the winter of 165–6, Cassius pressed on further into Parthian territory to the point where the Tigris and Euphrates flow beside each other at the twin cities of Seleucia and Ctesiphon. These lay forty miles north of ancient Babylon, the one a Greek foundation of the first Seleucid king from around 300 BC, the other the Arsacid administrative centre for their Mesopotamian province.

Cassius's success echoed Trajan's, the first time a Roman army had penetrated so far east in half a century. Ctesiphon was sacked, its palace razed, and, to reward his troops, Cassius let them sack the much older and richer Greek city of Seleucia as well. It became a ghost town, still lying in ruins when another Roman army passed through it 200 years later. With Cassius's victory, Lucius became Parthicus Maximus, and he and Marcus were again acclaimed as *imperatores* – victory titles of this sort were always taken by the emperors, whether or not they had been present at the fighting, and they are a precious resource for the modern historian, sometimes letting us date events, or even learn about campaigns that are not otherwise attested. Cassius, one of only two Syrian senators known from the reign and himself a descendant of Seleucid kings, was designated for a consulship in 166. In his consular year, he led his army out beyond the upper Tigris into the ancient territory of Media so that Lucius was now Medicus as well as Parthicus Maximus. An emperor other than Marcus might have been jealous of such heroics – the last Roman general to win so many conspicuous victories on the eastern front was Domitius Corbulo, executed by the suspicious Nero as a reward for his successes. Marcus was a different sort of emperor: Cassius inspired such confidence that he was promoted to the governorship of Syria and remained in overall command of the eastern front for the better part of a decade. In Cappadocia, on the other side of the Taurus mountains and guarding the Armenian and Caucasian frontiers, Martius Verus had an equally long and trusted tenure.

Towards the end of the campaigning season of 166, after two years of continuous fighting, the combined Roman expeditionary forces marched back to Antioch in good order. Late in the year, the three legions seconded from Europe returned to their home bases on the Rhine and the Danube. On 12 October 166, a triumph was celebrated in Rome to commemorate the eastern conquests and two of Marcus's sons, Lucius Commodus and Annius Verus, were raised to the rank of caesar. But Marcus, and indeed the whole empire, was soon to learn the true cost of the eastern triumph, for the victorious legions had brought a lethal plague home with them. The true epidemiology of this plague has never been established, and there is no agreement as to what pathogen was responsible. Ancient sources for epidemics tended to pattern their accounts consciously on Thucydides's account of the Athenian plague during the Peloponnesian War, but whatever struck the empire in the 160s, morbidity and mortality were both very high among a population that had suffered consecutive bad harvest years in 164 and 165. Much of the legislation that survives from the latter part of the decade concerns death and burial, while the legions needed disproportionately large numbers of new recruits in this period as well: in 169, for instance, the Legio VII Claudia required twice the normal complement. The epidemic raged for more than a decade, brutally culling the Roman population and sparing neither age nor rank: Marcus himself would eventually fall victim to it, if modern inferences about the cause of his death are correct.

Plague or no plague, however, Marcus and Lucius could not rest on their eastern successes. Marcus believed that the barbarian groups beyond the Rhine and the Danube had been allowed too much freedom of action while three of the regional legions had been fighting in the east. Indeed, both archaeological evidence and the scant literary sources suggest that the balance of tribal power beyond the middle Danube and in Bohemia had changed dramatically around this time, though for reasons that remain obscure. Relative imperial neglect probably played a part, allowing unexpected and undesirable violence to break out. Authorised warfare between tribal clients was a healthy part of Roman policy as it created a managed instability that prevented any one group from becoming too powerful and channelled the excess energy of martial societies away from Rome and towards one another. But unauthorised warfare beyond the northern frontier was something different: without sufficient Roman oversight or surveillance, it might rapidly flare up into something more threatening. Defeated war bands, occasionally whole tribes, might try to seek refuge in the empire, and while that was often a desirable way of bringing new farmers and soldiers into the empire, it only worked when such population movements could be controlled.

Nowadays Rome's European frontiers, with their 'Germanic' barbarians, loom disproportionately large in the historical imagination, both popular and scholarly: the frontier is often imagined as a breakwater against which barbarian tides lapped endlessly across centuries until the dam burst and the empire fell. In fact, the political dynamics on the Rhine and Danube frontiers were similar to those in Africa, Arabia, Britain and wherever the socially more complex and technologically more sophisticated empire confronted tribal groups whose power structures rarely stayed stable for long. For those neighbours, the empire was a juggernaut towering on the horizon. Roman actions, and fear of Roman actions, shaped the decisions of barbarian elites everywhere, even those at three or four removes from the frontier itself. The churning landscape just beyond the European and African frontiers was as much a product of Rome as the barbarians: even the smallest Roman expedition could wipe out whole sections of a population, lay waste to years' worth of seed grain and stockpiled wealth and render a group's homeland uninhabitable. When the empire was distracted, it presented an opportunity. Not to correct the immeasurable disparity in power, that could never happen; rather to seize momentarily a small piece of Roman prosperity, accessible along well-built roads leading deep into the imperial provinces. To do so was worth the inevitable and often devastating response. We have no idea what was happening beyond the Danube frontier when some of its garrison legions were detached to the Parthian War. But the return of the legions either directly provoked a violent response or triggered an outbreak of intertribal violence that drove a medium-sized barbarian army into Pannonia.

Marcus's response was determinedly punitive. Iallius Bassus, who had been with Lucius on the eastern campaigns, was made governor of Pannonia Superior, traditionally the most senior command on the Rhine–Danube frontier. At the same time, a man named Tiberius Claudius Pompeianus first enters the historical record as the governor of Pannonia Inferior. Pompeianus is a remarkable example of the way in which the oligarchic elite that dominated imperial government could open itself to conspicuous talent. Pompeianus was the son of a minor equestrian official from Antioch in Syria, a part of the Hellenistic east that had as yet launched very few of its native sons into the international elite of equestrian, let alone senatorial, government. On his personal merits alone, however, Pompeianus would go on to enter the senate, becoming a special friend of Marcus, marrying into the imperial family and remaining a central figure in Roman politics for the rest of the century.

Pannonia Inferior was Pompeianus's first significant command, and both he and Bassus would experience very heavy fighting. Late in 166 or early in 167, several thousand Langobardi and Obii invaded Pannonia Superior. They had come from a region well beyond the immediate frontier zone, which was settled with Marcomanni opposite Pannonia in the modern Czech Republic, Quadi opposite the Danube bend, and the Sarmatian Iazyges in the land between the Danube and the Carpathians. These distant invaders were rapidly annihilated by Bassus, but the prospect of reprisals frightened the client kings closer by. Eleven of the middle Danubian tribes chose as their spokesman the Marcomannic king Ballomarius and he sued for peace before Bassus. Ballomarius protested his own and his fellow clients' loyalty to the emperor and dismissed the actions of the Langobardi and Obii as a freak aberration. The plague had detained Marcus at Rome, so Bassus concluded a provisional peace and waited until his emperor was ready.

In spring 168, Marcus began a personal inspection of the Danube frontier. No one doubted that this was a preamble to war. Lucius would accompany the expedition as well, in part because the troops knew him from the Parthian War, and the project's scale can be judged by the number of important men involved. Furius Victorinus, the experienced guard prefect who had accompanied Lucius to the east, now went north with both emperors, but he and many of his guardsmen would die, probably of plague, en route to the frontier. He was replaced by M. Bassaeus Rufus, previously prefect of the *vigiles* (the urban security force of Rome) and briefly prefect of Egypt. The other guard prefect, M. Macrinius Vindex, came, too, which suggests that Rome was left ungarrisoned in the emperors' absence. Marcus's other trusted generals – Aufidius Victorinus, Dasumius Tullius Tuscus, Pontius Laelianus, the last two of whom had both served stints on the Danube frontier – were with him, not with specific portfolios but as *comites Augusti*, companions of the emperor.

Our sources are confused and two centuries of modern scholarship have yet to produce a fully satisfactory chronology of what we call the Marcomannic Wars and what Marcus referred to as his *expeditio Germanica*. The frontier of Pannonia Superior had not been settled by the treaty of Ballomarius and Bassus, and by 168 a Marcomannic king (perhaps, but not necessarily, Ballomarius) had been killed in battle there. The tribal leaders asked Roman permission to choose his successor and Lucius argued that this was success enough: why not call off the whole campaign and spare themselves the expense and the danger? Marcus demurred, planning to spend winter outside Rome for the first time since becoming emperor, choosing instead the Adriatic hub of Aquileia which was equidistant from the capital and the frontier. In the end, sickness in the ranks proved so bad that Marcus acceded to Lucius's wishes and agreed to return to Rome. But having got his way, Lucius proved unlucky: just days after leaving Aquileia, he had a stroke and died at Altinum. Marcus returned to Rome with his adoptive brother's body. He was now sole emperor, as Antoninus Pius had always intended.

There was little time for grief, but Marcus had his brother deified as duty required. Lucius's death left Marcus's 19-year-old daughter Lucilla the widow of a *divus*. She may already have begun to show the ambition and ruthlessness that would define her later career, or Marcus may have felt that a marriageable princess was too tempting a target for court intrigue. Regardless, he scandalised senatorial opinion by marrying Lucilla off again before the mourning period for Lucius was over. Worse still, she was given not to a senatorial grandee, but to the equestrian marshal Ti. Claudius Pompeianus. Marcus had good reasons for this decision. Only one of his daughters was ever given an aristocratic husband, lest it lead to a dynastic challenge to the heir apparent, Lucius Commodus (he became the emperor's only surviving son after the youngest, Annius Verus, died in summer 169). Pompeianus proved a loyal supporter of the dynasty, as well as an important patron for other equestrians. Most significant of these was Helvius Pertinax, the equestrian son of a freedman, who was adlected into the senate without ever having set foot in the senate house, or serving in the qualifying posts of quaestor, aedile or praetor. That he would eventually become emperor, even if only briefly, illustrates some of the social change that was overtaking Roman society, not least under the combined pressure of plague and war and the indiscriminate death toll they took on the traditional elites.

The marriage of Lucilla to Pompeianus – which both she and her mother Faustina had vigorously opposed – was not the only scandal of 169. New legions had to be raised for the Marcommanic campaigns and, in order to finance them, Marcus auctioned off property from the imperial household. The event was proverbial in antiquity, and has become a handy shorthand for imperial crisis in the modern scholarship, but it was a gesture of neither ostentatious self-sacrifice nor personal frugality. It was, rather, the only way to generate fresh revenue without raising taxes at a time when a badly depleted population might not be able to pay them. Fresh soldiers were in such short supply that Marcus authorised the recruitment of gladiators into the legions, an unprecedented action which drove up the price of public games across the empire and fell so heavily on local magistrates that Marcus soon enacted price-capping measures.

These varied financial expedients were ultimately successful and by late 169 Marcus was ready to return to Pannonia. Faustina stayed in Rome with the young and sickly heir to the throne, Lucius Commodus. Pompeianus came with Marcus as his chief counsellor, which meant that Lucilla did, too, as did many veteran commanders of the eastern wars: Pontius Laelianus, Dasumius Tullius Tuscus, Claudius Fronto. Where they overwintered is unclear, perhaps at either Singidunum or Sirmium (respectively Belgrade and Sremska Mitrovica in modern Serbia), both now coming to prominence as major imperial cities. Indeed, Marcus's Danubian wars mark a transition in the history of the Balkan provinces, previously cultural backwaters but thereafter increasingly urbanised and studded with wealthy farms and villas that would make the region central to imperial history in the coming centuries: as our story continues, a much longer list of Balkan towns – Mursa, Naissus, Poetovio, Serdica, Viminacium, Nicopolis ad Istrum – will join Sirmium and Singidunum in these pages.

Marcus himself led the major offensive of 170, pushing deep into Marcomannic territory. It was a fiasco: imperial propaganda was capable of turning a trivial skirmish into a towering victory, but now there is not so much as a whiff of success in the sources. Instead, the campaign triggered a massive barbarian invasion of Italy. Aquileia was besieged and the North Italian plain penetrated. This was an early harbinger of later history – Italy had to be defended at the Alps or, better still, just beyond them. If Alpine defences failed, the peninsula was effectively ungarrisoned and helpless. In 170, the Balkans also experienced heavy damage. The Costoboci, a tribe whose name is otherwise barely known, made it all the way to the province of Achaea, indeed as far as Attica, where they violated the shrine of the Eleusinian mysteries. The invaders' numbers, their divisions, their routes, all are unrecoverable, but they did more than ravage crops and kidnap farmers, which the government usually tolerated as an acceptable loss. Instead, there was a lot of hard fighting against Roman forces, with conspicuous and high-level deaths: in 170, the governor of Moesia Superior, whose name is not preserved, was either killed or cashiered for incompetence. His command was given to the governor of Dacia, the experienced Claudius Fronto, who himself fell in battle before the year was out. The emperor's own army got cut off beyond the Danube, and a special fleet command, under Valerius Maximianus, was needed to carry supplies to Marcus and his troops.

Meanwhile, Claudius Pompeianus, with Helvius Pertinax as his chief lieutenant, began to clear northern Italy of its unwanted guests. Fighting at the frontier continued in 171, when Marcus was headquartered at Carnuntum near modern Vienna. A barbarian army that Pompeianus had chased out of Italy was now trapped at the Danube crossing and destroyed. Marcus divided the plunder he retrieved among the provincials, and these victories, though small, contained the damage well enough to allow a return to the traditional policy of setting one group of barbarians against another. That seemed to work. As the end of the campaigning season approached in autumn 171, Marcus received various embassies at Carnuntum. The Quadi made peace, offering to supply the Roman army and agreeing to prevent the passage of either the Marcomanni or the

Iazyges (their western and eastern neighbours, respectively) through their territory. Other defeated barbarians were allowed into imperial territory and settled deep in the interior provinces. It was all starting to look like a return to frontier business as usual, welcome because there was now trouble elsewhere: the Mauri who had caused trouble under Antoninus Pius were again raiding across the straits of Gibraltar into Spain, which required an emergency arrangement combining the imperial province of Hispania Tarraconensis with the ungarrisoned senatorial province of Bactica under a single military commander.

In the next year, 172, the value of Marcus's Quadic treaty became clear. With the middle Danube bend and the Dacian fronts calm, Marcus was able to launch a second invasion beyond the river, focused solely on the Marcomanni in what is now Bohemia. It was another arduous campaign, during which one of the praetorian prefects, Macrinius Vindex, was killed in battle. But Marcus had gained the confidence of his troops and they began to attribute to him a supernatural ability to call down aid from the gods. In one case, he was said to have summoned a thunderbolt to destroy a barbarian war engine, an event duly commemorated on coins; in another, he (or rather his favourite, the Egyptian magician Arnouphis) had apparently summoned a rainstorm to revive his parched and exhausted troops: they proceeded to win a victory against all odds. Both miracles are depicted on Marcus's column in the Piazza Colonna at Rome, and coins seem to credit Mercury for the miraculous victory. The scale of actual military achievement may not have been equal to the propaganda triumphs, though both Marcus and the caesar Commodus had taken the victory title Germanicus before the start of 173. Commodus may have been at the front with his father, which would mean that most of the imperial family, including Faustina, Lucilla and her husband Pompeianus, were at Carnuntum late in 172. In the following year, Faustina was hailed as *mater castrorum*, mother of the camps, a sign that the soldiers regarded her as a protecting patron. Not long afterwards, the rest of the family also joined Marcus and Faustina on the Danube: Fadilla, now married to Lucius Verus's nephew Plautius Quintillus; and Cornificia, married to Petronius Sura Mamertinus, grandson of Pius's praetorian prefect Mamertinus. And then bad news came from the east.

4

THE LAST OF THE ANTONINES

In 172, while Marcus was proclaiming success on the Danube front, there was either a fully fledged uprising or an outbreak of intensive banditry in the Egyptian delta. At the same time, the Parthians attempted to bring Armenia back under the tutelage of Ctesiphon, no doubt emboldened by the detachment of some imperial troops from Cappadocia to the Danube. But the scale of the Danubian war meant Marcus could not give the east the attention it needed, and there was no longer a Lucius Verus available to serve as the face of the imperial dynasty. Avidius Cassius, the long-serving governor of Syria and a native Syrian himself, was granted extraordinary *imperium* in the east, of the kind that no one outside the imperial family had possessed since the days of Augustus's trusted lieutenant Agrippa a century and a half before. In practical terms, Cassius had become Marcus's plenipotentiary east of the Bosporus and the suppression of Lower Egypt was his first task.

Meanwhile, Marcus passed most of the campaigning season of 173 beyond the Danube, possibly reaching as far as the headwaters of the Vistula. The Quadi were certainly one target, perhaps because they had broken their oath not to help the Marcomanni. In the following year, he turned against the Iazyges beyond the Danube bend, in the Great Hungarian plain between the river and the Carpathians, or, in Roman terms, between Pannonia and Dacia. He did well enough to refuse the

Iazyges the peace terms they sought, preferring to continue the fighting in 175. That year brought something far worse than another round of frontier warfare: Avidius Cassius, perhaps the most reliable man Marcus had, revolted and claimed the imperial title.

The proximate cause of rebellion was a rumour that Marcus had died on the Danube. Our sources, retrospective and unreliable, suggest that Faustina became worried that Marcus would die of an illness he had contracted and sent word to Cassius to prepare to seize power if Marcus died. While not intrinsically implausible, the story cannot be proved. But whether he believed the rumour to be true, or whether it served as a useful pretext for his ambitions, Cassius was acclaimed emperor by his troops early in 175. The governor of Cappadocia, Martius Verus, stayed loyal to the emperor and sent word to the Danube as soon as he learned of the uprising beyond the Taurus mountains. When Cassius learned the truth – Marcus was not dead and thus he was now de facto a usurper – he decided to press ahead with his rebellion and fight for the throne. He was popular in the east – his royal Seleucid background lent him real status there – and backing him he had the powerful Syrian army, which had won the throne for generals in the past. The whole of the Roman Near East south of the Taurus sided with him, including Egypt and its vital grain supply. But he got no encouragement from his fellow senators in the west, and he would need to deal with the loyalist Martius Verus, at the head of the Cappadocian legions, sooner rather than later.

For Marcus the situation was very alarming. In bad health himself, he was fully aware of Cassius's strengths. He moved quickly, sending Vettius Sabinianus, governor of Pannonia Inferior, to hold Rome. The senate had obligingly condemned Cassius as a *hostis publicis*, but Marcus knew it would duly reverse itself if the 'public enemy' looked likely to pull off his coup. The teenage caesar Commodus, back in Rome when news of the coup arrived, oversaw the distribution of *liberalitas* (the emperor's free gift of coined money) to the people to calm them in their emperor's absence. He rejoined his father on the Danube, where he immediately assumed the *toga virilis*, well before the March festival of the Liberalia when Roman boys traditionally marked the transition to adulthood. He received the title *princeps iuventutis* and was presented to the army, which was meant to signify that Marcus had an heir who would succeed him when he died, and to play on the long-standing military habit of dynastic sentiment.

Marcus declared publicly, to the army and the senate, that he hoped Cassius would not be killed or take his own life, still less force war upon the empire, and that he should instead allow Marcus to make him an example of his mercy. This was implausible, even from as forbearing and philosophical an emperor as Marcus: it was an iron law of Roman history that, once committed to his usurpation, an imperial challenger should not be permitted to live. Before Marcus was forced to take action, however, one of Cassius's own centurions assassinated him, to the emperor's great relief. Martius Verus advanced into Syria to settle affairs. On the emperor's orders, he burned Cassius's correspondence unread. With this act of leniency, Marcus not only exculpated those genuinely implicated in Cassius's rebellion, but also any innocents who might have been suspected by dint of having written to the usurper in times long past.

Given how much support Cassius had enjoyed, Marcus could not afford to delay a trip to the east. He concluded a peace with the Iazyges, took the victory title Sarmaticus and enlisted a large number of their cavalry into the auxiliaries, sending them to faraway Britain. Pompeianus was left on the Danube frontier as Marcus's proxy, while the imperial family began a tour of the eastern provinces that had supported Cassius. Along with Marcus, Faustina and Commodus went one of the year's consuls, none other than Helvius Pertinax, son of a freedman, and thus even more than his patron Pompeianus an indicator of the changes overtaking the ruling class of the empire. The imperial party overwintered in the east, where Faustina died, at the village of Halala near Tyana in Cappadocia. Marcus renamed the village Faustinopolis and the senate, as was customary, deified her as *diva Faustina*.

On the whole, Marcus was extremely lenient, granting Cassius's younger children freedom of movement, and only banishing his elder son Heliodorus. He did, however, ostentatiously spurn the city of Cyrrhus, where Cassius had been born, and forbade public spectacles at Antioch, the capital of the revolt, also stripping it of its rights as a *metropolis*. He treated Alexandria in Egypt more lightly, and Antioch would have its privileges restored by Commodus after his father's death. More significantly, Marcus decreed that henceforth no man should be allowed to govern the province of his birth, lest that kindle dangerous ambition. On the overland journey back to Rome, the imperial party stopped in Athens, where Marcus and Commodus were together initiated in the Eleusinian mysteries. The emperor also endowed professorships of the arts and sciences in the city in, among other topics, Stoic, Epicurean, Platonist and Aristotelian philosophy.

In the autumn of 176, the family returned to Rome, and later that year, on 27 November, Commodus was granted *imperium maius*, thus standing beside Marcus as Lucius Verus had once done. The two of them celebrated a joint triumph for the Danubian victories. The next year opened with Commodus and his brother-in-law, Fadilla's husband M. Peducaeus Plautius Quintillus, as consuls. At fifteen, Commodus was the youngest consul in Roman history, an explicit exception to the Augustan *lex annalis* that still cloaked imperial government in republican dress – at the time, it was seen as an affront to ancient tradition, but child emperors would become an increasing feature of imperial government as the centuries wore on. A month after inaugurating the year as consul, Commodus received the tribunician power. This meant that, like Marcus in the last years of Pius, he now had all the constitutional trappings necessary to be emperor, and he was officially made an augustus in the middle of 177. In final celebration of his son's accession, Marcus cancelled all outstanding debts to the *aerarium* and the *fiscus* going back to the year 133; Marcus's adoptive grandfather Hadrian had done the same thing in 118, so the gesture emphasised dynastic memory as much as it bought good will.

Marcus still expected to die soon, and he was unsettled by what he saw on the frontiers. The Mauri in Tingitania remained uncontrollable: a group had again crossed into Baetica to raid and had even laid siege to the town of Singilia Barba (modern Antequera in Málaga province). Meanwhile, the Danube was again calling and, though Marcus would take personal charge of the campaign, he wanted Commodus to gain the experience of real war. To shore up the dynasty before they set out, he married Commodus to Bruttia Crispina, the descendant of a leading Hadrianic aristocrat; her father, Bruttius Praesens, already a prominent man when he was made consul in 153, was designated as consul for the second time for 180. In August 178, the emperors left for the Danube front. Old Pompeianus went with them as always, and now Commodus's father-in-law Bruttius did, too. Both guard prefects, Tarruttienus Paternus and Tigidius Perennis, accompanied the expedition and both would keep their posts into the next reign. Helvius Pertinax was made governor of Dacia, to support the flank of the main army, and Paternus was put in charge of the field army; the campaign proper was launched in 179 into Quadic territory at the Danube bend. Modern scholars are divided over

whether Marcus intended to conquer and hold a new province of Marco-
mannia beyond the Danube, but the sources, written and archaeological,
reveal dozens of Roman forts throughout what is now Slovakia and the
Czech Republic, and it is certainly possible to discern in them a prelude
to occupation and provincialisation.

At the start of the next year's campaigning season, however, Marcus
fell gravely ill yet again. It may be that he had finally succumbed to the
plague, but he had never been particularly robust, so we cannot be sure.
Nor are we sure quite where he was when this final sickness overtook him
– perhaps near Sirmium. He summoned Commodus, commended him to
the counsel of his own senior advisers and begged him to continue the war
effort whether or not he was personally inclined to do so. The old emperor
then proceeded to starve himself, perhaps hoping that this would cure
his illness, perhaps trying to hasten death. After seven days, on 17 March
180, he knew he was dying. When the duty tribune asked him for the
day's watchword, which it was the emperor's task to set, Marcus sent the
man to Commodus: 'Go to the rising sun,' he said, 'for I am now setting.'

Commodus's first decision as sole emperor, so far as we can tell, was
to conclude a treaty with the Marcomanni and the Quadi. This left intact
the old line of the Danube frontier, scotching any plans Marcus might
have had for imperial expansion, and it brought to the region a peace that
endured for half a century. The terms were very much in Rome's favour.
The defeated tribes were required to supply the empire with an annual
tribute of grain and to collectively contribute more than 20,000 soldiers
to the Roman army. They would be posted to distant auxiliary units and
kept away from their homeland to break down any lingering sense of
tribal identity they might have. Back home, both the Marcomanni and the
Quadi were partially disarmed and forbidden to attack their neighbours –
the Iazyges, the Buri and the Vandals – without Roman permission. They
were also forbidden to make use of the Danube islands and even of a strip
of land on their own, left bank of the river. Large-scale political meetings
could take place only when a Roman centurion was present to supervise.

In many ways, Commodus's decision to end his father's war was wise.
It restored the old imperial preference for client kingships in regions
not worth the effort of conquest and it made sure those clients would
be dependent upon Rome for their hold on internal power. An unin-
tended, but ultimately more lasting, consequence was the efflorescence
of civilian life and Roman civil society in the Danubian provinces, which

had developed very quickly thanks to two decades of wartime investment in the region's infrastructure. Thus it is not true, as many have argued, that Marcus's worthless son threw away the chance to create a great trans-Danubian province as his father had planned. There is no definitive evidence that Marcus was planning to extend the frontiers into central Europe, and the return to the pre-war status quo was both strategically sound and tactically sensible. What is more, however much Marcus's trusted old adviser Claudius Pompeianus, brother-in-law to the new emperor, might argue against the return to Rome, Commodus would have to present himself to the people to be acclaimed by them and the senate. Delay would breed their resentment, while the military's dynasticism would keep the frontiers quiet for a time. As soon as the treaty was concluded, Commodus presented himself at Rome as the son of the deified Marcus and the bringer of peace through conquest. He celebrated a formal triumph on 22 October 180.

Spectacular as that triumph may have been, Commodus's reign did not begin well – Saoterus, his *a cubiculo* (private chamberlain) and a Bithynian freedman, rode with the emperor in his triumphal chariot. Whether known or merely rumoured to be Commodus's lover, Saoterus was deeply resented by all who thought they had a stronger claim on the emperor's attention, and the presence of the low-born imperial favourite antagonised senatorial sentiment. On the other hand, the first consuls of the new reign were both sons of consulars, a traditionalist move that may have appeased some portion of senatorial opinion, and Pompeianus stayed loyal to Commodus despite his brother-in-law's unwillingness to take advice. The new emperor got no such loyalty from his own sister, Pompeianus's wife Lucilla, who attempted to organise a coup, perhaps in 182. The motives behind imperial court intrigue are never easy to uncover, because contemporary writers were often as much in the dark as we are. The mere jealousy imputed to Lucilla by our sources is surely not enough and it may be that she found her younger brother insufficiently pliable and resented playing second fiddle to Commodus's wife Crispina.

Lucilla manifestly loathed old Pompeianus, her father's creature and a husband to whom she had never reconciled herself. She therefore conspired against Commodus with her lover, Ummidius Quadratus, the adoptive son of Marcus's nephew. Their fellow conspirator, Claudius Pompeianus Quintianus, was a nephew of Pompeianus himself, a reminder that 'dynastic crime and secret politics' were central to the palace intrigues of the principate. Lucilla relied upon Quadratus and Quintianus to have her brother killed, but their farcical effort ended in shambles. As Commodus entered the amphitheatre, Quadratus confronted him and stagily proclaimed the enmity of the senate, rather than simply doing the job. The coup ended before it began, Quadratus and Quintianus were seized and executed, and Lucilla was exiled and later killed at a discreet moment.

Claudius Pompeianus withdrew from public life, knowing how lucky he was to have survived. The guard prefects, both of whom had been appointed by Marcus before the last Danubian campaign, used the disruption to do away with the hated *a cubiculo* Saoterus; he was murdered by the *frumentarii* ('inspectors of the grain supply'), who were often used as secret police and special agents by the early Roman emperors. With Saoterus dead, the guard prefect Tigidius Perennis assumed the position of trust that the *a cubiculo* had once held. He got Commodus to make his fellow prefect Tarruttienus Paternus a senator, thus rendering him ineligible for the equestrian post of guard prefect, and then put it about that Paternus had been party to Lucilla's conspiracy, for which crime the newly minted senator was executed. The prominent jurist Salvius Julianus (whose son was betrothed to Paternus's daughter), several ex-consuls and the emperor's own *ab epistulis*, Vitruvius Secundus, were executed at the same time. Two of Marcus's trusted advisers, the brothers Quintilii, were also executed. In the provinces, other senators and commanders who might have been involved in treasonable conspiracy were hunted down and killed. Many others who had been appointed in the last years of Marcus's reign or at the very start of Commodus's sole reign were thrown out of office, among them three future emperors: Didius Julianus, then governor of Germania Inferior, forced into retirement at his native Mediolanum (Milan); Helvius Pertinax, the governor of Syria; and Septimius Severus, legionary legate of IV Scythica. C. Aufidius Victorinus, who had been appointed *praefectus urbi* at the end of Marcus's reign, remained in favour and in office until 186, but in that year he was forced to commit suicide, the last of the old guard to have survived so long.

Commodus himself, so we are told, proceeded to retire from the business of government altogether, leaving state affairs first to his prefect Perennis and later to another favourite, M. Aurelius Cleander (actually a freedman of Marcus's who had taken the praenomen and nomen of his former master when he was manumitted). The period of Perennis's domination was a bad one – he was deeply hostile to the senate, having started off his career as *praefectus annonae* (the equestrian official in charge of the grain supply of the city of Rome). Government, where we can see it in action, was dominated by equestrian officials; the emperor's advisory council, the *consilium principis*, is documented by the occasional inscription and at times it met with no senators present, something hitherto unprecedented. Equally unheard of was the explicit inclusion of a freedman in the *consilium*, even one like Cleander who had had free birth bestowed upon him retrospectively by a legal fiction known as a *restitutio natalium*. Throughout Roman history, freedmen and eunuchs could gain tremendous influence with their masters, but that was always a source for scandal and meant to be handled with discretion. A freedman taking part in an imperial council that excluded senators offended every sense of propriety.

Worse, although Commodus's generals continued to win frontier victories and he continued to be acclaimed *imperator* for them, relations between the court and the senatorial legates were poor. In Britannia the general Ulpius Marcellus, who had won a major victory against a rebellion there, was overthrown in a mutiny. Thereupon the legates of all the British legions were cashiered and replaced by senior equestrians, risen from the ranks. Indeed, we can see a consistent trend towards the appointment of equestrians to positions of power in this reign, with only the most prestigious, chiefly the consulship, remaining the preserve of the old consular families. The downgrading of the most important legateships was one among many insults felt deeply by the senate. It was Perennis who shouldered the blame, because the emperor was known to have no interest in governing. The prefect's fall came soon enough. Precise circumstances are murky, for our sources all contradict each other, but it seems that a military delegation, possibly of British troops, negotiated the guard prefect's dismissal and execution in 185. In this, they were abetted by the *a cubiculo* Cleander, who now took control of government.

He was determined that no praetorian prefect should disrupt his hold on Commodus and so the prefecture passed through numerous hands between 186 and 190, while Cleander took to styling himself *a pugione*, 'dagger man', and the emperor's personal guardian, dominating each of the successive prefects. Thanks to Cleander, the enemies of Perennis were all now brought back to their lost commands, among them the future emperors Septimius Severus and Helvius Pertinax. By contrast, some of Marcus's remaining trusties, like the *praefectus urbi* Aufidius Victorinus, committed suicide rather than put up with Cleander's habit of openly selling public offices. In 185, while Pertinax was sent to govern Britannia and mollify its restive troops, Severus received his first provincial governorship, in Gallia Lugdunensis. Pertinax was faced with yet another violent mutiny of the British troops, but, unlike Ulpius Marcellus a year earlier, he was not recalled to court in disgrace. Instead, he played upon the emperor's paranoia, claiming that Commodus's brother-in-law Antistius Burrus was plotting to seize the throne in concert with another Numidian general named Arrius Antoninus, a relative of the imperial house who had recently been honoured with the proconsulate of Asia.

We cannot be quite sure what lay behind these intrigues, but they may be the first hints of tentative jockeying for the succession as it began to dawn on people that Commodus would at some point be overthrown. We know that several of the main intriguers, among them Pertinax, Burrus and Arrius Antoninus, had all first risen to prominence in the last years of Marcus Aurelius during the Marcomannic wars. They would have got to know each other well in the intervening period and shared strong views on the manifold failings of the Commodan regime. Burrus and Antoninus, with their connections to the imperial house, were genuinely plausible candidates for the throne, while Pertinax returned a hero from Britain and took up the *cura* of the *alimenta*, an honourable post in which he could keep his head well down. Cleander, meanwhile, grew bolder, having both Burrus and Antoninus executed in 189 and also eliminating Atilius Aebutianus, a praetorian prefect who showed too many signs of independence.

As Cleander thrived, so too did Pertinax, who went to Africa as proconsul in summer 188. We should note how extraordinary this appointment was for a man like Pertinax: the proconsulates of Asia, Africa and Achaea were strongly associated with the old senatorial governorships of the republic and, as such, were the jealous preserve of the highest born senators. Pertinax was the son of a freedman and, though he was himself equestrian at birth, his successes had come thanks to the patronage of the similarly *arriviste* Pompeianus and later the hated Cleander. That he was a brilliant commander whose talents more than justified his promotion could not stifle the whiff of improper novelty in his ongoing successes, something that was not helped when he returned from Africa to take up the post of urban prefect.

The British disturbances, with all their subsequent consequences for palace intrigue, were not the only rumblings in the empire at large. In

185 a certain Maternus revolted in Germania Superior, in what is known as the Deserters' War, the *bellum desertorum*. This was an unfortunate consequence of Marcus's unremitting warfare on the Danube, which had required the forced impressment of many soldiers with little professional loyalty. Left idle, they rebelled, joined by discontents of various stripes, from runaway slaves to indentured labourers to impoverished peasants. Thus reinforced, Maternus's rebels dared to challenge a Roman legion in the field: the VIII Augusta was given a new honorific title, *pia fidelis constans Commoda*, for resisting the rebel army. The rebels were suppressed by summer 186, probably by M. Helvius Clemens Dextrianus, but the episode demonstrates the social problems endemic to the military provinces of the empire, where it took only the right combination of events to release surprising reserves of latent violence.

The escalation of paramilitary violence in the provinces, and the continuing intrigue at court, meant that the orderly conduct of government began to suffer. Thanks to Cleander's sale of offices, there were fully twenty-five consuls in the year 190, among them the future emperor Septimius Severus. Cleander had been hated, even by those who profited by him, ever since he had done away with Paternus and established his hegemony over the paranoid but inattentive Commodus. He had hung on remarkably well for a dominant favourite without family connections in the imperial elite. But the rise of a more suitable equestrian rival, the *praefectus annonae* Papirius Dionysius, would end his hold on the court.

In the spring of 190, Papirius manipulated the grain supply of the capital to cause a bread shortage. The plebs predictably rioted, perhaps during the *ludi Caeriales*, held in the Circus Maximus on 19 April. The angry crowd was met by a group of children who were let into the circus and began to chant, calling down blessings on Commodus and curses on Cleander. This carefully orchestrated spur to public expression was taken up by the assembled masses, who marched several miles out of Rome to the villa where Commodus was ensconced. When the imperial mistress Marcia learned what was going on, she urged the emperor to execute Cleander, knowing that a mob of this sort would turn still uglier if not propitiated. The terrified emperor had his *a pugione* executed at once, and not one of Cleander's protégés, least of all the urban prefect Pertinax, lifted a finger to protect him. They had got what they needed from the former slave who had smoothed their path to power; his death rid them of a nasty reminder of an embarrassing debt.

Cleander's execution sparked more killing. His protégé, the guard prefect Julius Julianus, had his colleague Regillus murdered, before being executed in turn on the emperor's orders. Despite the many conspiracies, real and imagined, no one had yet actually managed to eliminate Commodus. In the early 190s, however, it seems clear that the emperor stopped behaving with the mere caprice of an absolute ruler and began his descent into actual madness. He proclaimed a new Golden Age of Commodus on his coinage, and he implicitly rejected the memory of Marcus by ceasing to style himself Marcus Antoninus and instead minting coins in his original name, Lucius Aelius Aurelius Commodus, thus recalling the emperor Hadrian. He also amplified his appeal to a Hadrianic precedent by becoming an Athenian citizen and having himself inscribed in the same deme (the traditional Athenian voting group) as Hadrian had done, inaugurating a tradition that would last at least as late as the reign of Gallienus (r. 253–68) – the people of Athens reciprocated by making the emperor their archon, or chief magistrate, in the year 188/9. (All the various Greek calendars used a year that overlapped two different Roman years.)

Meanwhile, Commodus's identification with the god Hercules became more intense. It had played a small part in dynastic propaganda ever since Marcus had made the boy a caesar in 166, but in the 190s coins began to show Commodus as an actual personification of the god. Statues of him dressed as Hercules, with the traditional attributes of lionskin and club, were put up everywhere. While this heroic disguise may have been calculated to appeal to the soldiers and particularly the urban plebs, it offended the senators intensely. They would happily deify emperors once they were safely dead, but had no desire to serve a self-proclaimed divinity. Modern scholars disagree about how seriously Commodus took his new Herculean identity. Some argue that we are looking at an aspect of formal propaganda in which the emperor had a distinct role to play before different audiences, but which he did not necessarily have to believe in. Although it is possible that he was merely trying to convey his special relationship to the divine, the whole historical tradition, though hostile, uniformly claims that he did believe he was a god. Other traces of madness exist as well.

The emperor had always been fond of the arena and enjoyed the company of gladiators. Now, his power unchecked, he began to appear in the arena himself. The gladiator, though often a popular hero, was by definition a slave, a barbarian or a criminal. That the ruler of the Roman world should choose to play such a debased role was yet another gross offence to traditional values. Worse still, it conjured the awful historical exemplum of another tyrant who had revelled in inappropriate behaviour – Nero, the actor and cytharode. Whether as god or gladiator, Commodus could be nothing but a hate figure for the senatorial elite, and the emperor began to reciprocate. The *ordo senatorius* was violently purged. No fewer than twelve ex-consuls were put to death during the last two years of Commodus's reign. These killings, unlike the earlier purges of the reign, destroyed not just individuals but whole families.

No story was too implausible to believe of a megalomaniac tyrant whose father, in striking contrast, had been able to swear on oath that he had never caused the death of a senator: Commodus, it was rumoured, went so far as to order the execution of anyone, senator or not, whose hunting skills equalled or excelled his own. Criminals, it was said, stalked the streets of Rome with poisoned needles, infecting victims with plague – a rumour that had previously surfaced in the reign of Domitian, another archetypal tyrant. But, as in the past, all the hatred he inspired among the senate could not in itself bring Commodus down. It took his own household to do that.

Along with the new imagery, the emperor surrounded himself with new protectors: there was a new praetorian prefect, Q. Aemilius Laetus, a Numidian, who held the office alone, and there was also a new *a cubiculo* named Eclectus, who had served Lucius Verus and Ummidius Quadratus before. Eclectus, while in the service of Quadratus, had known the latter's freedwoman concubine Marcia, who after Quadratus's execution was used by Commodus for the same purposes. While Commodus disported himself in the arena, Eclectus and Marcia ruled the palace, and Laetus more or less ruled the empire. The provincial appointments made by Laetus are essential to our understanding of the aftermath of Commodus's fall, even though it is a struggle for scholars to explain them convincingly. Septimius Severus, for instance, who had never served on the northern frontier, was given command of Pannonia Superior and its three legions, while his brother Septimius Geta held Moesia Inferior, with two. Another African senator, Clodius Albinus, was given Britannia – still a very difficult military command – while his relative Asellius Aemilianus was made proconsul of Asia. Cornelius Anullinus, later a key prop of the Severan regime, also got his first appointment in this period. These were not the only Africans holding provincial commands at this time and we can perhaps link them together through joint service under Helvius Pertinax; a new prefect of Egypt, Mantennius Sabinus, was also probably related to Pertinax in some way. Pertinax had proved himself a survivor, actually managing to prosper through all the upheavals of Commodus's reign. His term as urban prefect had been successful enough that he and the emperor were designated to inaugurate the year 192 as ordinary consuls. By the time they did so, old Pertinax had joined a plot to overthrow the emperor.

Laetus, for reasons that are genuinely obscure, had decided to make Pertinax Commodus's successor. As sole guard prefect, and on cordial relations with the palace staff, he was in a position to ensure that a plot against the emperor did not go awry. Allies were in place across the northern provinces, while the large and potentially hostile Syrian army was under the command of Pescennius Niger, something of a nonentity who owed his appointment, it was said, to one of Commodus's favoured athletes.

The conspirators were encouraged by the fact that Commodus's behaviour was becoming ever more bizarre. In 192, he officially renamed Rome the *colonia Commodiana*, in effect subordinating the eternal city to himself, while he renamed each month of the year after his grandiose, indeed imaginary, imperial nomenclature. (He had by now added unprecedented names like Amazonius and Exsuperatorius to his title, which are attested in inscriptions, not just in hostile literary texts.) In the guise of Hercules, he revelled in new orgies of bloodshed. At the plebeian games of November 192, the emperor slaughtered thousands of red and roe deer, lions and leopards, and shot the heads off ostriches with special arrows so that they continued to run headless for a time. In a scene famously described by the senatorial historian Cassius Dio, who was present at the time, Commodus brandished the head of a decapitated ostrich at the assembled senators, forced to watch the display from their special gallery, proclaiming his wish to decapitate the whole senate in the same way.

He went further, replacing the solar portrait head of the colossal statue that gave the Colosseum its name with his own portrait, an unfortunate echo of its builder, the tyrant Nero, and providing it with the attributes of Hercules – a club and a crouching bronze lion. These excesses made wild rumours seem plausible – that the emperor would shoot spectators at his games, forcing them to play Stymphalian birds to his Hercules, or that he planned to personally murder the ordinary consuls of 193 (Sosius Falco and Gaius Erucius Clarus) dressed as a gladiator and then assume the role of

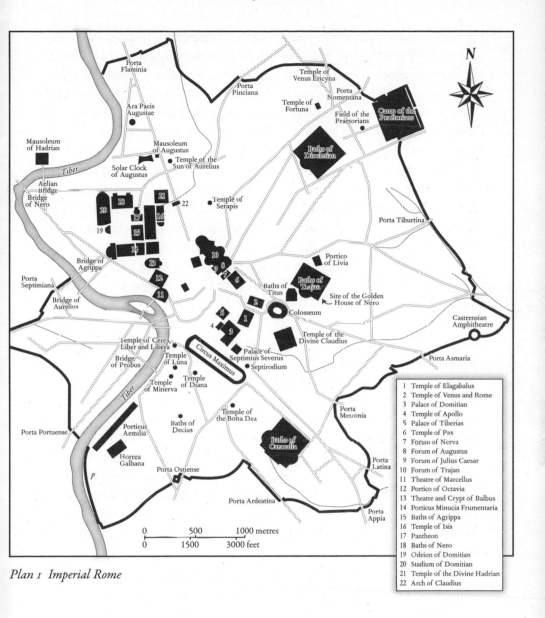

N

Porta
Flaminia

Temple of
Venus Ericyna

Porta
Pinciana

Porta
Nomentana

Temple of
Fortuna

Field of the
Praetorians

Camp of the
Praetorians

Ara Pacis
Augustae

Mausoleum
of Hadrian

Mausoleum
of Augustus

Temple of the
Sun of Aurelius

Baths of
Diocletian

Tiber

Solar Clock
of Augustus

Aelian
Bridge
Bridge
of Nero

21   22

Temple of
Serapis

Porta Tiburtina

20   18

17   16

19

15

14

Bridge of
Agrippa

13

Portico
of Livia

Porta
Septimiana

12

Bridge
of Aurelius

11

10

8
9 7 6

Baths of
Titus

Baths of
Trajan

Site of the Golden
House of Nero

Colosseum

Castrensian
Amphitheatre

5

4   3

1

2

Temple of the
Divine Claudius

Porta Asmaria

Temple of Ceres,
Liber and Libera

Circus Maximus

Palace of
Septimius Severus
Septirodium

Bridge
of Probus

Temple
of Luna

Temple
of Minerva

Temple
of Diana

Porta
Metronia

Temple of
the Bona Dea

Porta
Latina

Porta Portuense

Porticus
Aemilia

Baths of
Decius

Baths of
Caracalla

Horrea
Galbana

Porta Ostiense

Porta
Appia

P

Porta Ardeatina

0 500 1000 metres	1 Temple of Elagabalus
0 1500 3000 feet	2 Temple of Venus and Rome

1 Temple of Elagabalus
2 Temple of Venus and Rome
3 Palace of Domitian
4 Temple of Apollo
5 Palace of Tiberias
6 Temple of Pax
7 Forum of Nerva
8 Forum of Augustus
9 Forum of Julius Caesar
10 Forum of Trajan
11 Theatre of Marcellus
12 Portico of Octavia
13 Theatre and Crypt of Balbus
14 Porticus Minucia Frumentaria
15 Baths of Agrippa
16 Temple of Isis
17 Pantheon
18 Baths of Nero
19 Odeion of Domitian
20 Stadium of Domitian
21 Temple of the Divine Hadrian
22 Arch of Claudius

Plan 1 Imperial Rome

sole consul. Even the gods seemed angry, as a portentous earthquake made clear: the fire it caused destroyed many of Rome's libraries and archives and the enormous temple of Peace was consumed by the flames. So, too, was the temple of Vesta; in order to save the sacred Palladium, the Vestal Virgins were forced, in an unprecedented act, to expose it to public view and carry it openly through the city down the via Sacra to safety in the imperial palace on the Palatine. Commodus, who had given up residing on the Palatine for a more private villa on the Caelian hill, would not be permitted to anger the heavens any further.

Laetus and Eclectus brought the emperor's concubine Marcia into their plot. On New Year's Eve 192, she administered poison to the emperor. It put him to sleep but, burly and strong, he soon awoke in a fit of vomiting and began to recover. Eclectus and Marcia had to bring in Narcissus, a wrestler with whom Commodus regularly trained, to strangle him in his bath.

By the next morning Pertinax had been proclaimed emperor. Our sources agree that the final decision to kill Commodus was taken quite suddenly, but also make clear how long the plot had been in train. Even Claudius Pompeianus, the original sponsor of Pertinax, who was now over a decade into his retirement, was in Rome when Commodus died. Having been married to Lucilla, a daughter of Marcus and the widow of Lucius Verus, Pompeianus could lend moral support and a tangible sense of dynastic legitimacy to the sudden change of regime. With his advanced age and uncanny instinct for avoiding trouble, he did not put himself up as contender for a throne that had been secretly designated for another. Pertinax got the news of Commodus's murder when he was already at the praetorian camp, proof of his deep complicity in events. With an escort of praetorians, he made his way before dawn to Commodus's residence on the Caelian. There, he was presented to the troops guarding the court as their new *imperator*, successor to the dead Commodus. These soldiers responded slowly and suspiciously, refusing to believe that Commodus had died naturally. But by morning of New Year's Day 193, the soldiery had acclaimed Pertinax their emperor.

When the senate house was opened, Pertinax made the now traditional gesture of *recusatio imperii* – he did not want the burden of the imperial purple, so he said. But he was widely acclaimed by his senatorial peers, who heaped abuse upon the memory of Commodus and loudly demanded that his body be abused – 'dragged on a hook' was the phrase. But Pertinax had more sense than that, knowing that Commodus's memory was revered rather than execrated by much of the army. He allowed his predecessor's statues to be pulled down, but he had already arranged for the body to be safely buried in the mausoleum of Hadrian. He dared not provoke those who still honoured Commodus's memory.

The praetorians remained grudging and suspicious, and the extravagance of the dead Hercules had so denuded the treasury that Pertinax auctioned off items from the imperial household to pay the guard his accession donative. Meanwhile, news of the coup went out to the provincial governors. By March, all had announced the succession of Pertinax, though none, it seems, were quite satisfied. The latter half of 193 would witness a flurry of imperial proclamations and inaugurate a confused half-decade of civil war. One of the imperial aspirants was Septimius Severus, the governor of Pannonia Superior. We need to give some attention to his origins before returning to our narrative, for he and his future rival Clodius Albinus illustrate how far the provincial Roman world had come in displacing the old dominance of the imperial centre.

5

SEPTIMIUS SEVERUS
AND HIS RIVALS

***

Septimius Severus came from Leptis Magna in Tripolitania, near modern al-Khums in Libya. Leptis was an ancient Punic foundation which remained a different sort of place from the urban centres of Numidia and Africa Proconsularis, with their orientation towards Italy and closer integration into its economy. The Jebel desert lay a mere handful of miles away from Leptis's coastal greenery, and in the countryside Neo-Punic remained the language of many people right through the imperial period. Leptis itself had enjoyed a relationship with Rome since the days of the middle republic, becoming a federated city when Rome was fighting against the Numidian kingdom of Jugurtha. It continued to enjoy the status that came with this very early Roman connection even after it was laid to waste for supporting the Pompeians against Julius Caesar during the African phase of their civil war in the 40s BC.

But then the rich families of Leptis threw themselves wholeheartedly into the new Augustan world. They embraced the imperial cult and, from the time of Claudius, many received Roman citizenship, so that important families like the Marcii and the Annaei traced their enfranchisement back to proconsuls of the Claudian era. By the end of the Julio-Claudian period, the urban elites had stopped using Punic names. Finally, in the late 70s, the town was honoured with the status of a *municipium ius Latii*, with the special privilege that its pair of chief local magistrates could retain their old Punic title, *sufetes*, rather than Latinising it to *duoviri*, as most *municipia* would have been expected to do. The granting of municipal status and the Latin right meant that local magistrates automatically became citizens of Rome by virtue of holding local office. That in turn meant that the richer among them would enter the equestrian order at the same time as they gained their citizenship. The first Lepcitanians in the *ordo equester* appear under Trajan, who promoted the municipality to the rank of *colonia*, known as *Ulpia Traiana fidelis*; that meant that its whole population was now enfranchised and the Punic *sufetes* were finally replaced with Roman *duoviri*. Told in isolation, the success of Leptis seems very impressive, but the city was in fact an outlying latecomer to the Romanisation of the western provinces, long after places like Africa Proconsularis, let alone the Spanish provinces and Gallia Narbonensis, had begun to produce not just Roman equestrians but even senators. The mark of their provincial origin remained clearly visible on generations of Tripolitanians who joined Roman government, among them the future emperor Septimius Severus.

By the end of the second century, most of the important families of Leptis owned property in Italy as well, the Septimii Severi among them. The precise ancestry of the future emperor has some hypothetical stages, but we know that the family had Italian estates in the region of Veii and elsewhere north of Rome. Severus's grandfather, after whom he was named, came to Italy in the reign of Titus or Domitian, and there studied with the famous rhetorician Quintilian. In Italy, this first of the Lepcitanian Septimii Severi entered the *ordo equester*. The next generation of the family, which included the emperor's father Geta, came of age under Hadrian and Antoninus Pius and also witnessed the first senators to come from Leptis – two uncles or fraternal cousins of the emperor advanced as far as a consulship. The future emperor himself was born on 11 April 146. By the time Pius died in 161, Severus had followed his brother to Italy for further education and perhaps an entrée into the imperial service. He, and indeed the family as a whole, were models of a kind of provincial notable on the make that could be found in any corner of the empire where citizenship was confined to a relatively small and wealthy minority. He had connections, he came from a good provincial family, and there was plenty of money to go around, so the only question was whether he would pursue a senatorial or an equestrian career in imperial service.

We have already seen that the empire, for all its hierarchy and breathtaking dependence upon patronage, was also remarkably merito-cratic. Even as its bureaucracy grew more complex, the distance between the lowest level of the imperial hierarchy and the highest was far narrower than the gap between a junior civil servant and a modern head of state, however tiny that state might be. The demonstrably able could always expect to be noticed alongside the well born and politically savvy, and if ability was sometimes hazardous, the right admixture of good luck could produce dramatic results. Links of patronage brought the young Septimius to the attention of the new emperor Marcus Aurelius – the African was granted the *latus clavus*, the symbolically broad stripe on the toga that would allow him to enter a senatorial career, starting with the minor qualifying offices of the vigintivirate and progressing thence to the quaestorship and beyond. In 162 or 163, at the request of his uncle (or perhaps cousin) C. Septimius Severus, who had recently been consul under Antoninus Pius, Septimius Severus entered the vigintivirate in 164. He showed no early promise, and he got no military tribunate, even though his brother Septimius Geta was serving as a tribune of the II Augusta in Britain. Presumably he worked on his oratory as a barrister in the courts hoping to draw favourable attention, but during the plague years of 167 and 168 he returned to Africa and survived a prosecution for adultery that might have ruined him.

In 169, he had returned to Rome to enter the senate as quaestor on 5 December. It was a time when the dual pressures of plague and the Mar-comannic War stretched the resources of the governing classes very thin, and Severus had to serve a second consecutive term as quaestor. While his brother Septimius Geta was a curator of Ancona, Severus was slated to go to Baetica as quaestor to the proconsul Cornelius Anullinus, later one of his staunch supporters as emperor. But when the invasion of the Mauri discussed in chapter 4 led to the brief subordination of Baetica to the governor of Hispania Tarraconensis, Anullinus was sent to Sardinia instead. Severus spent his second quaestorship there, in one of the least taxing positions in the empire. Then, five undistinguished years after entering the *ordo senatorius*, luck intervened.

In 173, his uncle (or cousin) C. Septimius Severus was chosen as proconsul of Africa, one of the three most prestigious provincial commands for a senator, and he brought his nephew along as *legatus pro praetore*. This was progress. In that same year, Severus married a Lepcitanian wife, Paccia Marciana, who probably accompanied him back to Rome in 174, where he became tribune of the plebs as one of the emperor's own *candidati*. Who pulled the strings for him is unclear, but his fortunes were very much on the rise and in 176 he was designated praetor, serving as *iuridicus* in Hispania Tarraconensis while the governor was engaged in military duties. His next command was as legate of the Legio IV Scythica in Syria, to which he was appointed either in the very last weeks of Marcus's reign or at the start of the sole reign of Commodus.

There were three legions in Syria: the IV Scythica, near Antioch; the XVI Flavia at Samosata; and the III Gallica at Raphaneae, near Apamea. The IV Scythica was the senior command, a sign of how far Severus had come, and, while serving in Syria, he formed a connection that had immense consequences for the future. At some point during his legateship, he journeyed deep inland, to the Arab town of Emesa (modern Homs), the easternmost Syrian city still inside the empire, before one came to the true desert, in which lay the oasis and caravan city of Palmyra (to use its Greek name, although it was called Tadmor in the local Aramaic dialect). Emesa was a foundation of the first century BC, a relic of a city state left over from Pompey's destruction of the Seleucid kingdom. The city was an important Roman ally, courted by various late republican dynasts. After the turn of the millennium, the Emescnes were imperial clients who remained generally loyal against both the Parthians and rebellious Jews. When the native royal dynasty died out, however, at some point in the Flavian period, the city was absorbed into the Roman province of Syria. Collateral descendants of the royal house continued to prosper and Emesa remained a cultural hinge, sitting socially somewhere between the Arab interior and the Syrian coastal cities, with their Phoenician and Hellenistic, rather than Arab, roots.

Emesa was famously the home of the god Elagabal (meaning 'El of the Mountain': the 'gab' is the same Semitic root-form *jeb* that gives us the originally Arabic Gibraltar). This ancient deity was worshipped in the immanent form of a black stone, but was also frequently equated to a sun god because, with an easy if false etymology, educated Greek-speakers could transform his Semitic name into the Hellenised Heliogabalus. The hereditary priests of the cult of Elagabal were descended from the old royal dynasty and by the later second century they had gained Roman citizenship. At the time Septimius Severus stayed at Emesa, the high priest was a citizen named Julius Bassianus, his cognomen perhaps a coinage from the Semitic *basus*, a priestly title. Their acquaintance was important, for Severus would later marry Bassianus's elder daughter, Julia Domna; long thereafter, Bassianus's younger daughter, Julia Maesa, would oversee the resurgence of the Severan dynasty in the second decade of the third century.

Severus was dismissed from his Syrian command on the orders of Commodus's praetorian prefect Tigidius Perennis, as discussed in chapter 4, after which he spent time in Athens and travelled through the east, staying away from Italy until the fall of Perennis in 185. He was then sent off to govern Gallia Lugdunensis, a large province but not a significant military command, as it had no legions. Paccia Marciana died in Gaul and, no later than 187, Severus sent to Emesa to request the hand of Julia Domna in marriage from his old acquaintance Julius Bassianus. The wedding took place in 187, and on 4 April 188 a son named Bassianus was born to the new couple. By 188, Severus and Julia returned to Rome, where he was designated for the command of Sicily. By the time he took up this new, though again not very significant, governorship, a second son, P. Septimius Geta, had been born. In 190, whether through the favour of Pertinax or Cleander, Severus became one of the notorious twenty-five consuls of that scandalous year, though Cleander had fallen by the time Severus returned to Rome from Sicily. There he was accused of treason and tried before the praetorian prefect Julius Julianus, probably because his preoccupation with oracles and prophecy, well attested in his later career, seemed like a threat in the paranoid last years of Commodus. Severus was acquitted, and his accuser was crucified, but some of the dirt stuck, and he spent a full year out of office in the aftermath.

Luck was once again on his side. The next upheaval at court brought Severus back to power, when the regime of the new guard prefect Laetus appointed him to govern Pannonia Superior in the summer of 191, an astonishing promotion for a man whose *cursus* had been relatively indifferent hitherto. Pannonia was one of the great armed provinces of the empire, with fully three legions and easy access to Italy. Only trusted men could be given that sort of power, which makes it extremely probable that he was a party to the conspiracy against Commodus. Given that all the senior commanders on the northern frontier stayed loyal to the regime of Laetus and his new emperor Pertinax, it seems likely that they had gone out to their commands knowing a coup d'état was in the offing. But no one could have predicted how unstable a ruler Pertinax would prove.

The praetorians, as we have seen, were hostile to the new emperor from the beginning, for reasons that are not entirely clear, and they eventually brought down his regime. One attempted mutiny followed almost immediately on the accession, and a second took place as soon as Pertinax left the city to consult with the procurator of the grain supply at Ostia, who happened to be a Syrian from Emesa named C. Julius Avitus Alexianus, the brother-in-law of Julia Domna. The rioting praetorians attempted to place the consul Sosius Falco on the throne, but when the mutiny failed and the senate condemned Falco to death, Pertinax pardoned him, with the assurance that no senator would be put to death under his regime – a significant variation on the standard oath of emperors not to put senators to death unless they were condemned by the senate itself. It was pious gestures of that sort that most contributed to the posthumous esteem in which Pertinax was held, but they did nothing to keep him alive. A few soldiers were put to death after the mutiny and the desultory attempt at usurpation, but Pertinax was heard to abuse the faith of the soldiery in the senate, and promptly faced a third armed uprising. The new emperor may also have been rather less generous than he had claimed, disbursing a smaller accession donative than he had promised and then dissimulating about it. In the end, Laetus turned on his imperial ally and refused to intervene to stop his praetorians from taking action on 28 March 193.

The emperor returned to the palace that morning to find himself set upon by hundreds of mutinous praetorian guardsmen who were joined by many of the palace staff; these latter had preferred life under the spendthrift Commodus to the proverbially stingy Pertinax. Rather than call out the *vigiles*, who were commanded by his father-in-law Sulpicianus, or the still loyal horseguards, Pertinax stood on his personal authority and confronted the mutineers. His calm shamed and cowed them for a time, but then a Tungrian guardsman named Tausius (it is rare that we learn the name of a common soldier) drew his sword and attacked the emperor. The chamberlain Eclectus, who had been personally responsible for the murder of Commodus, defended Pertinax alone, wounding two guardsmen before he was himself killed. Pertinax offered up a prayer to Jupiter, covered his head with his toga in imitation of Julius Caesar's dying moments, and was cut to ribbons. His head was struck off and fixed on a spear, and with that his eighty-seven day reign ended. It had been a plain and pure mutiny, unconcerted and unforeseen. No successor stood ready to take the throne, and the city was briefly paralysed.

Sulpicianus, the urban prefect, thought of seizing the purple for himself as the father of Pertinax's widow, but the praetorians would accept no relative of the man they had just butchered. Instead, a detachment of guardsmen assembled in front of the senate house until they spotted a likely candidate in Didius Julianus, the most senior living senator of consular rank, and began urging him to take the throne. Upon escorting him to the praetorian camp, however, they found themselves in a stand-off with rival guardsmen who supported Sulpicianus. What followed remains notorious in Roman history: the praetorians auctioned the empire to the highest bidder. The throne hung in the balance, as Julianus and Sulpicianus threw out ever higher figures for accession donatives, until, with an offer of 25,000 sestertii per man and a promise to restore the memory of Commodus and grant amnesty to the murderers of Pertinax, Julianus finally outbid his rival. With the praetorians in full battle array under two new prefects, Julianus was escorted to the senate house that evening, where the senators had been awaiting the results with bated breath. Faced with this *fait accompli*, they acquiesced.

The urban plebs was less forgiving. By the next day, 29 March, Julianus was already being pelted with stones as he returned to the senate house, and the streets were ringing with rhythmically chanted insults, claiming that he was a robber and a parricide. This sort of rhythmic chanting, which we have already seen in the fall of Cleander, became an increasingly important form of political communication between emperors and their subjects as time went on. Though it could also be orchestrated to signal approval, when sentiments were hostile, it was an extremely menacing form of behaviour. The same chanting crowd then began to call out the name of Pescennius Niger, governor of Syria and master of three legions, to come and rescue the city from its captivity. It was clear that Julianus should expect a challenge to his rule.

Severus's Danubian armies were ready to act faster than Niger's were in Syria, Severus having been kept apprised of events by relatives and allies at Ostia and in Rome itself. Less than two weeks after Pertinax was murdered, Severus went into action. The neighbouring governors and legionary legates backed him – his brother Septimius Geta in Moesia, his friend C. Valerius Pudens in Pannonia Inferior, and the German and Alpine commanders as well. On 9 April, twelve days after Pertinax's murder, Severus was acclaimed augustus by the Legio XIV Gemina, normally stationed at Carnuntum. He would, he told the troops, avenge the murder of Pertinax, whose memory was still honoured by the Pannonian, Moesian and Dacian legions that he had commanded at various times under Marcus. And Severus publicised his loyalty to the murdered emperor in his new titulature: Imperator Caesar L. Septimius Severus Pertinax Augustus. Having accepted the imperatorial proclamation of his soldiers, however, he ostentatiously refused to claim tribunician authority until he had been properly acclaimed by the senate. His next move was to neutralise his only potential rival in the west, Clodius Albinus in Britannia.

Albinus was, like Severus, an African, though he may also have been a maternal relative of Didius Julianus. He also commanded a truly vast army, composed of three battle-hardened legions and even more *auxilia*. Severus could not risk a challenge on his north-western flank if he was about to march on Italy. He therefore offered Albinus the title of caesar, which would designate him Severus's imperial successor. Albinus accepted, taking the name D. Clodius Septimius Albinus Caesar. From Albinus's point of view, and given the extreme youth of Severus's own children (Bassianus was five, Geta three), it was clearly wiser to await events in Italy than to waste energy on a civil war along the northern frontiers. That there would be war was quite certain: Pescennius Niger, already mooted as emperor by the Roman mob, had proclaimed himself just as soon as news of Pertinax's death reached Antioch in Syria, shortly after Severus's proclamation at Carnuntum. The whole of the eastern empire, wealthy Egypt included, supported Niger and so it became ever more important for Severus to reach Rome and gain the legitimacy that acclamation in the senate and the conferral of tribunician power would ensure. He would be in a strong position once that was done, with sixteen western legions to Niger's ten from the east. The legate of the III Augusta in Numidia had chosen to side with Severus, closing off Africa to Niger, and the emperor's brother Septimius Geta advanced out of Moesia, seized Thrace, and with it the crossing points to Asia Minor.

Didius Julianus lacked similar strategic good sense. He failed to garrison the Alpine passes, allowing Severus's army to descend on the North Italian plain via Emona (modern Ljubljana) and Aquileia and seize Ravenna, the seat of the Adriatic fleet. Severus moved by forced marches, often sleeping in his armour and sharing the rigours of the camp with his bodyguards, pausing to sacrifice at each city he passed, but neither stopping nor delaying. Julianus tried ineffectually to fortify Rome (our main source, Cassius Dio, is scathing) and he had both Laetus and Marcia killed. The two had once been kingmakers, but Julianus feared such agile politicians:

they were likely to pick and then assist the winning side, and much better dead than hostile. None of this did him any good, however. The senatorial embassy he sent to meet Severus deserted to the advancing marshal, as did many of the few troops Julianus could command. The senate began to disregard him. When Julianus tried to acknowledge Severus as his co-emperor, it was an empty and pointless gesture: Severus could not even be troubled to respond. Julianus had lost all support and Claudius Pompeianus, that greatest of survivors among the Antonine elite, pointed the way. Having managed, so improbably, to outlive his vicious brother-in-law Commodus, Pompeianus publicly refused to advise Julianus, still less to accept the floundering ruler's desperate offer to share in his imperial power.

By the end of May, Severus was poised at Interamna, the main staging post between Ancona on the Adriatic sea and Rome beyond the Apennine mountains, from where he issued a direct order to the praetorians, commanded by Veturius Macrinus. Septimius ordered the murderers of Pertinax to be arrested and held for trial. Wishing to be seen to do its part for the new cause, the senate condemned Julianus to death, deified Pertinax and acclaimed Septimius as augustus. A common soldier (unnamed in our sources, unlike the killer of Pertinax) cut Julianus down in the palace, alone save for one relative and the second guard prefect Flavius Genialis, who had stayed loyal. Meanwhile, Severus's agents went searching for Pescennius Niger's children for use as hostages. They also seized the offspring of Asellius Aemilianus, proconsul of Asia and a relative of Clodius Albinus who had reluctantly sided with Niger, as well as the children of the other eastern governors. Fabius Cilo, one of Severus's long-trusted allies, was sent to take the Greek city of Perinthus and prevent access to Thrace from Asia Minor, while Marius Maximus, later to write scandalous biographies of the second-century emperors, besieged the Greek city of Byzantium, the only European city to have declared for Niger.

Back in Italy, Severus remained in full campaign mode, camped at Interamna and playing his hand for all it was worth. He greeted a delegation of 100 senators while still wearing a military breastplate and the *paludamentum* of a general in the field, and had them searched for weapons before they were allowed into his presence. Theatre this may have been, but it was expertly threatening theatre. He distributed gifts to those in attendance, welcomed the palace staff who had travelled en masse to greet him at Interamna, and allowed those senators who wished to do so to accompany him on the final stages of his march on Rome. Before setting out, he publicly retained Veturius Macrinus as one of the guard prefects and appointed Flavius Juvenalis as the second. Juvenalis was an African and, like Macrinus, a very senior equestrian officer whose career had been blighted in the later years of Commodus. Knowing that both his prefects could be trusted, Severus decided to take radical action against the unruly and mutinous guards. He ordered them to assemble outside the city, unarmed but in parade uniform, to take the oath of allegiance to him. Seeing this as the price of their continued employment and a suitable accession donative, they obeyed. But rather than welcoming them with the speech of thanks they had expected, Severus had them surrounded by his Pannonian troops, berated them for their disloyalty and the murder of Pertinax, and discharged them from the ranks. They were stripped of their uniforms and the ceremonial daggers which only praetorians were permitted to wear, and ordered to remain beyond the hundredth milestone from Rome on pain of death. With this act, Severus ended a 200-year-long history and reconstituted a new praetorian guard, manned by the cream of his Danubian legions.

After this, Severus finally entered the city of Rome. In a characteristic *coup de théâtre* he dismounted before the gates, stripped off his officer's uniform and donned the civilian toga, while his army accompanied him in full battle array. He mounted the Capitol to sacrifice and then took up residence in the palace, while his armies camped in all the public places throughout the city, eating the Romans out of house and home. The victory had been bloodless, but Rome was not to doubt that it was under military occupation. Addressing the senate, while his soldiers clamoured for a colossal donative outside the *curia*, he made a show of bargaining down his troops' demands – but still struck an extraordinary issue of coins to pay the donative, with the names of the Rhine, Danubian and Dacian legions on the reverses. The mint also struck in the name of Albinus Caesar, a sign of how seriously Severus was taking the alliance at this point. The senate officially bestowed the name Pertinax on Severus, endorsing the fiction that his proclamation at Carnuntum had all been in aid of avenging a murdered predecessor. As the pious son of a deified emperor, he ordered a state funeral for his 'father'. He also adlected to the senate a variety of loyal equestrians. Among them were Julia Domna's brother-in-law, Julius Avitus Alexianus, who had managed the Ostian grain supply under Pertinax, and Aquilius Felix, an ex-centurion who was given an extraordinary triple command, over the public works and the two financial offices of the *patrimonium* and the *res privata* (as the *fiscus* was coming to be known). Together with Albinus Caesar, Severus was designated for the ordinary consulship of 194.

None of this was enough to keep him in Rome, however. He stayed less than thirty days. Like Hadrian before him, he always preferred travel in the provinces to life in the capital city. His immediate concern was Niger. While still in Rome, Severus had begun to assemble three brand new legions, the I, II and III Parthicae. Although their names proclaimed their purpose to be a new Parthian campaign, few can have been deceived: they were destined for the now inescapable civil war against Niger. Severus strengthened the garrison of Africa, and perhaps of Tripolitania as well, and he kept tight hold on the hostages he had available to him – most of the children of Niger's governors were in Severus's hands, even if Niger's own children were still in hiding. Neither imperial claimant had yet openly declared war on the other when Niger handed Severus a propaganda triumph: he sent a detachment to resist Fabius Cilo's peaceful occupation of Perinthus, thus publicly opening hostilities. It was all that Severus needed to have him and Asellius Aemilianus declared *hostes publici* by the senate before setting out for the Balkans and the inevitable campaign.

Facing down an attempted mutiny on the via Flaminia just outside Rome, Severus resigned himself to paying his soldiers handsomely until the civil war was won, and after that, things went more smoothly. He marched north to Aquileia and then down via Singidunum and Viminacium to Naissus. He altered the Balkan legionary commands as he marched, securing his line of retreat, and then settled in with Fabius Cilo at Perinthus while Marius Maximus kept Niger besieged in Byzantium. The latter began to doubt his prospects and, like Didius Julianus in similar straits, offered Severus an equal share of the empire. Severus responded by offering Niger his life if that of Asellius Aemilianus was forfeited. Niger refused, but his position remained grim. In autumn 193, Claudius Candidus took one of the Pannonian legions across the Propontis into Asia Minor and put Aemilianus to flight before capturing and executing him. His soldiers continued to resist, however, retreating to Bithynia under their junior officers. Niger, having managed to slip out of Byzantium, joined his troops at Nicaea, which supported him simply because its local rival, Nicomedia, supported Severus. At Nicaea, Candidus tempted Niger into open battle, rallied his men from the beginnings of a rout, and proceeded to decimate Niger's army.

With the few troops that remained to him, Niger retreated to Antioch, reckoning that if he ceded Asia Minor to Severus he could make a credible stand beyond the Taurus mountains. These mountains channelled all the military traffic between Cilicia and Syria down into the plains of Issus, where a set-piece battle should give both sides an equal chance of winning. By 31 January 194, when news of Candidus's Bithynian victory reached Rome, Egypt had defected to Severus, as had several Syrian and Phoenician cities, among them Laodicea and Tyre, which Niger punished severely. Marching towards the Taurus passes, Candidus and the other Severan commanders levied massive fines on the Asian cities that had thrown in their lot with Niger and Aemilianus: their emperor had a large number of very expensive troops to pay and the various imperial treasuries were all nearly empty.

Severus himself remained at Perinthus, where he was joined by the proconsul of Africa, Cornelius Anullinus, a contemporary and a loyal ally throughout his life, to whom he now gave charge of the whole campaign against Niger. Anullinus marched out through Galatia and Cappadocia and forced the Taurus passes in a battle which is barely noticed by our sources. Instead, it was at Issus in Syria that, as Niger had intended, the climactic battle was fought. A massive thunderstorm coming down off the Taurus sowed confusion, giving Anullinus the cover he needed for a classic outflanking manoeuvre – the Severan cavalry under Valerius Valerianus got round the back of the Syrian legions and began to roll up their ranks from the rear. It is claimed that 20,000 of Niger's troops died on the battlefield, a number that is by no means impossible. Niger fled into the city of Antioch, still hoping to escape as he had from Byzantium, but he was captured and executed. His head was sent to Severus, and thence to the city of Byzantium, in the hope that Marius Maximus could lift his siege after the city surrendered. The Byzantines declined to do so, even with their emperor dead. That stubbornness would eventually cost them dear.

Probably by the end of May, Severus arrived at Antioch. He was now master of the Roman world, and he lost no time in making the east realise it was spear-won territory. Cities like Antioch that had supported Niger to the end were punished by loss of status. Those that had switched sides in a timely fashion were rewarded – Tyre, for instance, was granted the *ius Italicum*, the highest honour a provincial city could receive, making it legally a part of Italy and therefore exempt from tax. Severus revisited the various places he had first seen as a legionary legate more than a decade before, but now in the company of his Emesene empress, who began to be formally addressed as the *mater castrorum*, mother of the camps. Thus deemed patroness and guardian of Severus's armies, she would accompany Severus on the other campaigns he was now planning. He had decided to make good on the pretence that the three new legions raised in 193 were meant for a Parthian war. The minor kingdoms of Osrhoene and Adiabene, as well as certain Arabs known as Scenitae, had all given aid to Niger, while some of Niger's routed troops had fled to Parthia. It was a good excuse for a punitive campaign beyond the Euphrates that would both add to Severus's glory and allow the soldiers, who had so recently been fighting one another in a civil war, to come together against a common, foreign foe.

The first kingdom to fall was Osrhoene, incorporated into the empire as a province in 195, although its capital Edessa was allowed to remain under the autonomous control of its king Abgar, the last ruling member of a dynasty that had vacillated so frequently between Rome and Parthia that neither side ever trusted it. The new Severan province extended as far as Nisibis nearly on the Tigris river. When Adiabene surrendered without resistance, Severus took appropriate victory titles and, with these annexations, the provincial outline of the late imperial eastern empire begins to come into view. Further eastern conquests would need to wait, however, as Severus had determined to rid himself of his ally Albinus, whose support he no longer needed.

6

THE REIGN OF
SEVERUS

The emperor was still in the east late in 195, from where he rejected the senate's offer of a triumph. He did not want to be seen to triumph over fellow Romans. But he made a more interesting propaganda decision at the same time, declaring himself the son of Marcus Aurelius. Inscriptions at Rome record him as *frater divi Commodi*, 'brother of the deified Commodus', and a flurry of coins was issued in both east and west, with the legend *Hercules Defens(or)*, 'Hercules the Defender', and a depiction of the god, in a clear reference back to Commodus's favourite deity. Severus's elder son Bassianus was now renamed Marcus Aurelius Antoninus, though we shall herein call him Caracalla, the nickname by which he is referred to in all our sources. In the context of this genealogical charade, Julia Domna's title of *mater castrorum* makes perfect sense, since it was Marcus Aurelius's wife Faustina with whom the honorific is most associated.

When the recently renamed Bassianus was swiftly promoted to the rank of caesar, Clodius Albinus must have understood himself to be the target. With the Parthian frontier secure, Niger's legions safely absorbed into his own army and rebellious Byzantium finally subdued, there was nothing to prevent Severus from turning on his erstwhile ally in Britannia. It was put about that Albinus was behaving as if he were already an augustus and that powerful, though unnamed, senators had invited him to come to Rome to supplant Severus. That may have been no more than Severan propaganda, as the rumour that Albinus had plotted the murder of Pertinax certainly was. Regardless, as Severus began his march back to the west, the senate declared Albinus a public enemy on 15 December. There was rioting in the circus among a populace who wanted an end to warfare.

Albinus now did proclaim himself augustus, as he had to, but Severus was lethally efficient: Fabius Cilo went on to secure the loyalty of Moesia and its legions; the emperor's brother-in-law, Julius Avitus Alexianus, was made legate of the IV Flavia at the strategic river crossing of Singidunum. At Viminacium, in the presence of the Dacian governor Claudius Claudianus and Severus's brother Septimius Geta, Caracalla was displayed to the troops who would provide the strike force of the expeditionary army under the command of Claudianus. Supporters of Albinus were hunted down in Noricum, and Julius Pacatianus took control of the main passes into Italy with detachments from the new Parthian legions. Fulvius Plautianus became prefect of the *vigiles* at Rome at the same time, able to enforce discipline on senate and plebs alike. By early 196, Cornelius Anullinus, who had overseen the campaigns against Niger, was installed as urban prefect, thus tightening still further Severus's iron grip on the city of Rome.

Albinus, too, had acquired some supporters. The large and wealthy province of Hispania Tarraconensis went over to him with its governor Novius Rufus, while Albinus expelled the Severan governor of Lugdunensis and took up residence at Lugdunum (Lyons). Belgica was largely in his camp, but there was resistance in the two Germanias, where the important garrison at Moguntiacum (Mainz) under Claudius Gallus stuck with Severus. Rather than invade Gaul immediately, Severus crossed the Alps and entered Rome, where a series of coins greeted his *adventus* and others advertised Caracalla's ostensibly Antonine heritage with the customary title of *princeps iuventutis*. Severus spent several months in Rome, exercising the traditional imperial roles of lawgiver and judge, hearing petitions, and perhaps sounding out the mood of the senate, too many of whose members may have remained favourable to Albinus.

The plan of campaign was now set. As 197 dawned, the emperor returned to Pannonia and then moved west along the northern edge of the Alps, descending from the north on to Albinus's capital at Lugdunum. Although Albinus had the large army of Britannia with him, Severus led much the larger force, with the combined legions of Dacia and the

Danube. Battle was joined on 19 February outside Lugdunum. As with many of the decisive battles in Roman history, it was a close run thing. Albinus's legions feigned retreat, but only to ensnare the Severan forces in trenches and embankments. Trying to rally his faltering troops, Severus was thrown from his horse and caught up in the general retreat. It took Julius Laetus to rescue the day with a charge of the auxiliary cavalry.

Lugdunum was put to the sack by the victorious Severans and Albinus took his own life. His decapitated head was sent to Rome, while his body and those of his wife and sons were cast into the Rhône. The mopping-up operations in the west lasted a long time, and became proverbial for their brutality. Britannia needed re-enforcement rather than chastisement, because the tribes beyond Hadrian's Wall used the absence of Albinus's legions to lay waste the north, and Severus not only returned most of the British legions but re-enforced them with his Danubian troops. Elsewhere, though, the punishments were severe. Novius Rufus, the governor of Tarraconensis who had sided with Albinus, was put to death, while Claudius Candidus, a loyal Severan butcher, made sure that the proscriptions of Albinus's supporters in Hispania bit deep. Throughout Lugdunensis, vast tracts of private land were brought under state control from the properties of those proscribed and Lollianus Gentianus undertook a new census in the province to extract additional revenue. The proscriptions in Africa required the creation of an entirely new equestrian office to register and manage the lands confiscated to the imperial *fiscus*. The Rhineland was generally spared, having stayed loyal; indeed, Severus was touring the German provinces when he learned that the Parthians had invaded the east. Julius Laetus, the victor of Lugdunum, went east at once to take command, while Claudius Gallus, whose legion had held Moguntiacum for Severus, followed after Laetus with a newly raised campaign army.

Severus himself made for Rome, in the company of his horse guards and the praetorian prefect Fulvius Plautianus. No matter how dangerous the Parthian situation might become, the loyalty of the senate needed to be tested and re-enforced. Though senators made a variety of pacific gestures to him, the emperor went out of his way to appear menacing. He quartered one of his new legions, the II Parthica, at Alba a few miles south of Rome, and he did so without reducing the complement of the praetorian guard in the city. That was a larger garrison than Rome had seen in a very long time. He publicly derided the clemency with which Julius Caesar had once treated his enemies, and praised instead the republican exempla of Sulla and Marius, famous for their ruthless destruction of those they defeated in civil war. His demands that Commodus be deified as his brother and that he himself be known as Marcus's son were also meant to inspire terror, for no emperor since Domitian had been as hated and feared by the senate as Commodus. None of these were empty gestures, for Severus also purged the senate, executing twenty-nine senators and keeping many others under arrest. To drive home to the *ordo* its reduced status, he gave his three new legions equestrian rather than senatorial legates. By contrast, he treated his armies handsomely, allowing them to gorge on the influx of confiscated wealth. Pay rose substantially for every type of soldier, and the conditions of military service were formally altered so that, for the first time in Roman history, soldiers could contract valid marriages. This not only recognised the long-standing fact that many soldiers took concubines who were wives in all but law, but it also helped bind the army closer to Severus and his dynasty: the emperor needed his men to follow him willingly on the many campaigns that he planned.

The emperor's Second Parthian War began in 197. He left Rome for Brundisium (Brindisi), and sailed from there to Aegeae in Cilicia, the shortest sea route between Italy and the east. From Asia Minor he went via Epiphaneia and Nicopolis to Antioch in Syria. Julia Domna, the *mater castrorum*, went with him, as did the royal children, Caracalla and Geta. The emperor left all three at Antioch and marched quickly inland, receiving embassies from the region's few remaining client kings before joining Julius Laetus at Nisibis. Laetus had already repelled the Parthian invasion, so Severus returned to Syria to prepare a full-scale war against Parthia. Late in September a supply fleet had been assembled on the Euphrates and Severus had discovered a plausible claimant for the Parthian throne to lend a tincture of respectability to the expedition. The army met little resistance as it marched downriver, taking a string of famous cities: Seleucia, Babylon and Ctesiphon itself, the Parthian capital from which the king had fled. The city was put to the sack, probably in December of 197, and the royal treasury fell to Severus as part of the spoils.

By the end of January 198, Severus took the title of Parthicus Maximus and accepted his eleventh acclamation as *imperator* by the troops. He did so on the hundredth anniversary of Trajan's accession to the throne. The symbolism was patent: Trajan had been the first true conqueror of Parthia and he, Severus, the second. To emphasise the point, Severus raised Caracalla to the rank of augustus. His younger son, Geta, was made caesar. Severus was re-enacting, on a larger scale and in a single person, the successes of his great predecessors Trajan and Marcus Aurelius. As he aggrandised his own family, many of those who had helped him in his rise to power found themselves either pushed to the sidelines or dead. The only real winner was the guard prefect Plautianus, who like other prefects before him envisaged himself as the emperor's companion in the ruling of the empire. Claudius Candidus, who had won the campaign against Niger and been the hammer of Albinus's partisans in Spain, was executed and his name subjected to *damnatio memoriae*. Where this took place, and on what pretext, we do not know, but the destruction of Julius Laetus, by contrast, happened almost within sight of the emperor. As soon as Ctesiphon fell, Severus marched back up the Tigris, intending to punish the independent principality of Hatra for having sided with Niger five years previously. Today Hatra is, with Palmyra and Dura Europus, one of the most conspicuous victims of the Islamicist iconoclasm (and remunerative looting for the antiquities market) that has characterised Middle Eastern conflicts since the American invasions of Iraq and Afghanistan. When Severus set out, though, it had long been an important buffer between the Romans and the Arsacids. It controlled the caravan trade across the Mesopotamian steppes from Babylon in the south up to Singara and Nisibis, and then across to Zeugma, a popular crossing point on the Euphrates. Its hereditary rulers, in theory subject to the Arsacids, were powerful enough to use the Syriac royal title *malka* and their kingdom was more populous and wealthy under the Parthians than ever before, or indeed since. The suppression of Hatra required two separate sieges, which proved unpopular with the troops, who began to grumble about their preference for Laetus over their emperor. That was enough to doom the general, who was arrested and executed for treason. Though it is unlikely that Laetus had ever contemplated usurpation, the rumour was now spread that he had held back at the battle of Lugdunum, hoping that both Albinus and Severus would be killed so he could become emperor.

Hatra never did fall to siege but its king submitted to Severus as a client and, with that, the emperor could with some justification claim to have succeeded Trajan as a conqueror of the east. Unlike Trajan's successor Hadrian, Severus made an effort to hold large parts of the conquered lands. Osrhoene was to remain a province centred on the city of Carrhae, and Severus created the new province of Mesopotamia, based on the territories of the old kingdom of Edessa but with a new capital at Nisibis;

a hundred years later, Nisibis would be the creative engine of a Syriac cultural world that we will discuss in the sequel to this book. This Mesopotamian province was defended by two of Severus's new legions, the I Parthica at Singara and the III Parthica at Resaina. With these annexations, Severus fundamentally remade the map of the Near East, shifting the front line of confrontation between Rome and its Mesopotamian and Iranian neighbours away from the border of Syria and deep into the land between the northern Tigris and the Euphrates. Right until the Muslim conquest of the Middle East in the seventh century, control of the Severan provinces would be contentious, but Roman Syria, with the great city of Antioch-on-the-Orontes at its core, flourished more than ever now that it was further from the actual zone of confrontation.

Severus returned to Palaestina after the siege of Hatra, at the end of 198. More provincial reorganisations followed in 199. The emperor split Syria into two: Syria Coele ('Hollow Syria') to the north, garrisoned by legions at Samosata and Zeugma and still anchored by the metropolis at Antioch; to the south, Syria Phoenice had its capital at Tyre, which was now made a Roman *colonia* as a belated reward for supporting Severus against Niger. More significantly for future events, the caravan city of Palmyra, which had possessed colonial status since Hadrianic times but had long remained an independent player between Syria and the Euphrates frontier, was now incorporated into the newly formed Syria Phoenice and allowed to continue its main function of policing the Syrian desert against Arab tribesmen further south.

In 199, while these changes were being promulgated, Severus, his family and the court went to Egypt, travelling overland via Pelusium. Like Hadrian's visit half a century earlier, the whole expedition was a sort of historical re-enactment. Severus sacrificed at the tomb of Pompey. At Alexandria he gazed upon the tomb of Alexander the Great and then had it permanently sealed up, so that no one should ever look upon it again and acquire the ambitions of Alexander. He took care likewise to correct his predecessors' injustices. Alexandria, long and with good reason the object of imperial suspicion, was finally given the right to have a *boulé*, or city council, like any normal city in the Greek world. The city thus finally achieved the legal status that its size, commercial importance and historical significance had always merited. From Alexandria, the emperor moved on to a grand tour of the province, pressing on up the Nile to Memphis and Thebes, where he visited the singing statue of Memnon. He likewise visited the great sphinx, which the Egyptian prefect had recently had repaired – not the last time that a conquering power has attempted to restore Egypt's monuments to their former grandeur. Severus lingered on his tour into the new year of 200 and made it as far as Philae (modern Aswan), where he celebrated its secret cult acts in May. We do not know whether he went any further south, to the provincial frontier, but by August 200 he was back in Alexandria, ready to return to the eastern provinces. This time he went by ship to Antioch, although we do not know where he spent the year 201. He inaugurated the new year of 202 at Antioch, holding the ordinary consulship together with his son Caracalla, who having now turned thirteen could wear the *toga virilis* that signalled he had reached adulthood

The early 200s were the quiet years of the reign. The guard prefect Fulvius Plautianus remained Septimius's partner in government – he was consul for the second time in 203 – and plans were made to marry his daughter Plautilla to Caracalla. The dominance of Africans in the high commands remained unchallenged, not least thanks to the patronage of Plautianus; the several new legionary commanders of the Danubian provinces known from 202 were all Africans. Those old-time supporters who had survived the purges in Syria continued to do well. Ti. Claudius Candidianus, who had been with Severus since 193, was now made consular legate of Pannonia Superior, the same post that Severus had held when he claimed the throne, and Fabius Cilo, likewise present from the beginning, was promoted to the urban prefecture. Nevertheless, the influx of easterners into the Severan government, which had begun by 198, continued under the influence of Julia Domna and her family's many connections. A relative of Julia, Aemilius Papinianus, became the *a libellis* of the emperor, in charge of answering petitions, and Domitius Ulpianus, a distinguished Roman lawyer from Tyre, served under Papinian. Both would be significant figures in later reigns and were central to the development of a late antique governmental culture that transformed the empire in the third century. Other sections of Julia's family also witnessed important promotions – her nieces (daughters of her sister Julia Maesa) both married well and their offspring would continue the Severan dynasty into the 230s, after Septimius Severus's direct heirs had disappeared. Those heirs, Caracalla and Geta, travelled with their parents during this period. Their tutor was a famous sophist from Egyptian Hierapolis named Aelius Antipater. Although an Egyptian sophist was no novelty, the larger role of Egyptians in government was changing thanks to Severus's decision to allow Egyptians to become senators for the very first time. The first Egyptian to become a senator, one Aelius Coeranus, was – predictably – a client of Plautianus's. What strikes the modern historian in all this, and what is so important for the transition between high empire and late antiquity, is the dominance of provincial senators and provincial equestrians at the heart of Severan government. Rome would continue to play an important role in imperial politics for another century, and would remain the ideological heart of empire for longer than that, but Roman and Italian elites would never again provide the indispensable foundation for government.

Soon after the New Year's celebrations at Antioch, the court began its overland journey to Rome, where Severus's *decennalia* were to be celebrated. The journey provided an occasion to restore many cities that had fallen into disfavour because of their support for Niger – Byzantium was raised up again, and Nicaea was given equality with Nicomedia, perhaps partly as a favour to the senatorial historian Cassius Dio, who composed laudatory histories of the civil war that met with the emperor's strong personal approval. The official story made Caracalla responsible for these acts of beneficence and restoration and the Severans give us a better sense of a dynastic image being carefully curated over time than do most other dynasties in Roman history.

Back in Rome, the marriage of Caracalla and Fulvia Plautilla was celebrated with great largesse to the urban plebs and the praetorian guard – a gold aureus for every person for each year of Septimius's reign, and hence a vast expense, the *liberalitas tertia*, or third great distribution of largesse to the people, which he proclaimed on coins issued for the occasion. The celebration of the emperor's *decennalia* followed the wedding with games which lasted for seven days, during which, along with the usual gladiatorial and hunting shows, 700 of the rarest animals in the Roman world – including the Indian hyena – were displayed to the audience, and then slaughtered.

For all the splendour of these shows and the lavish gifts bestowed on the people of Rome, Septimius disliked the city. Not long after the *decennalia* celebrations ended, he left for Africa, his first visit since becoming emperor more than a decade before and, in another Severan echo of Hadrian, only the second time any emperor had visited that province. Arriving at Carthage with the entire court in tow, he honoured this greatest of African cities with the ancient *ius Italicum*, thereby exempting it from taxation, just as he had Tyre in Phoenicia for its support in the civil wars. He visited Numidia and the legionary fortress of Lambaesis, and presumably many other cities as well, before going overland eastwards past the cities of Tripolitania to Leptis itself – a *patria* which he had not seen in thirty years. Here, too, the *ius Italicum* was received as a great honour. The winter of 202/203 was spent in Leptis, and the New Year opened with Plautianus and Severus's younger son Geta sharing the consular fasces. But the long visit also opened an ugly rift between the emperor and Plautianus. The prefect's statues were put up alongside those of the royal family all around Leptis, not unnaturally given that these two sons of Leptis had conquered the world together. Yet the parity implied by the statues could not help but cause offence and Severus had some of his prefect's images melted down. After that, a permanent breach was almost inevitable, although for the moment the two men renewed their alliance.

Early in 203, Severus took part in a campaign south into the desert against the tribe of the Garamantes, who lived in the Sahara oases and had long been the primary threat to the Tripolitanian frontier. New frontier posts were constructed, deep into the Sahara, and in the same period the Mauretanian provinces to the west were also expanded into the southern steppe and desert. Numidia, which had long functioned as an independent province under the command of its legionary legate, rather than as a part of Africa Proconsularis, was now formally constituted as its own separate province.

By June, when the Garamantes had been suitably chastised, the imperial party set sail for Rome, to which they had returned by June 203. There the emperor celebrated an *ovatio*, a sort of mini-triumph, for his African victories, and his imposing triumphal arch, which still towers over the north-eastern corner of the Roman Forum between the *rostra* and the *curia*, was built in this year. Its placement, directly in front of the temple of Concordia, may reflect the pious wishes of a senate that in reality mistrusted an emperor who had so little time for the city of Rome and its ancient ways. But Severus was never to have a smooth relationship with the Italian aristocracy, no matter how much either side might have wished it otherwise. Even the consuls for 204 were chosen for dynastic reasons, rather than to conciliate senatorial feelings: Fabius Cilo, from the beginning one of the great Severan marshals, was consul for the second time, while Annius Libo, a distant and undistinguished descendant of

Marcus Aurelius, was chosen for his connection to the dynasty from which Severus claimed his fictional descent. The year 204 was another celebration of Severan monumentalism, for the secular games, meant to be celebrated only once a century (Latin *saeculum*, hence the name) were held for the seventh time in Roman history.

The Romans of the empire celebrated not one but two types of 'secular' games. On the one hand there was an archaic and originally Etruscan ceremony, based on an eccentric cycle of 110 years, that had been revived in 17 BC by Augustus, with his notorious penchant for reviving (or inventing) long-lost traditions. These Augustan games were repeated by Domitian, and then again, as we have seen, by Septimius Severus. On the other hand, there were other games also described as 'secular' in all our ancient sources. These were determined by a simpler counting from the supposed foundation of the city of Rome, according to a basic cycle of 100 years – and were held by Antoninus Pius, and then again in the 240s by Philip. Severus claimed to be celebrating the games for the seventh time – they were the *ludi septimi*, following on from Domitian's *ludi sexti*. Preparations for the Severan secular games were complex and lasted throughout the first half of 204. They also involved the senate to a very large extent, since the *quindecimviri sacris faciundis*, the fifteen men in charge of sacred affairs, were all senators, usually from the very pinnacle of the *ordo*.

The *quindecimviri* of 204 are a study in how much the empire had changed since the last time the secular games had been held, under Domitian: almost none of the Severan *quindecimviri* were descended from families of Rome itself, but instead were from municipal Italian families grown grand or from provincial dynasties, Africans among them. After months of solemn preparation, the three days of the games themselves began on the night of 1 June, the Kalends. While Julia Domna led 110 of the great matrons of the city in rites sacred to Juno and Diana, Septimius presided over the sacrifice. Caracalla, now honoured as *pater patriae*, opened the prayers, and Geta concluded them. These two heirs apparent were the designated consuls for 205 – which meant that the new *saeculum* would open not with the dynastic founder, but rather with the dynastic future.

That dynastic future was cemented by two deaths in the year of the secular games. First, Lucius Septimius Geta, Severus's brother, died naturally in 204 without male issue. Then, Fulvius Plautianus, the most powerful and longest serving of Severus's supporters, was put to death. Plautianus's son-in-law was, of course, Caracalla, whose hatred of his wife

Fulvia Plautilla is well documented, and it was Caracalla who engineered the prefect's downfall. In January 205, he recruited three centurions to claim before Septimius that Plautianus had ordered them to kill both augusti so that he could seize the throne for himself. Septimius, suspicious of his prefect ever since the affair of the statues in Leptis, summoned him to the palace. Plautianus protested his innocence, but Caracalla set murderously upon him so that Septimius had to personally restrain his son. It is the first glimpse we catch of the furious rages to which Caracalla was later prone. But though Severus had held back Caracalla from murder, it was not with the intention of sparing Plautianus. He had the prefect killed by a waiting guardsman and his body cast into the road outside the palace.

Caracalla divorced Plautilla and she and her brother were exiled to the tiny Aeolian island of Lipara to live out their lives. The imperial *fiscus*, drained by so many wars, was now revived with a massive influx of funds from Plautianus's private property, a large enough windfall that a special official was needed to administer it. A further purge of senators, chiefly those who had been on good terms with Plautianus, now followed. The middle years of the decade thus witnessed a new low point in the relationship between Severus and the senate, but politics quieted down after the fall of the great prefect. It was in these years that Severus composed his autobiography, now lost.

In choosing Plautianus's successor, Severus reverted to the more usual scheme of having two guard prefects – Q. Maecius Laetus and Aemilius Papinianus – rather than one, though only Papinian matters for our story. He was neither a military man nor a member of the great aristocracy, but rather a Syrian from Tyre, a distant connection of Julia Domna who had been serving as Severus's *a libellis* since the end of the Parthian War. The guard prefecture had always been an equestrian office, but placing it in the hands of a very learned jurist would have historical consequences to which we will return in a later chapter.

Severus was ageing by now and he had not led an easy life. It was only natural that Caracalla should begin to exert more authority alongside his father. But whatever else the late Plautianus might have been, he had been a check on the passions of his son-in-law, the younger Augustus. After his execution, the full force of Caracalla's long-festering hatred turned on his younger brother Geta, the last potential rival to his dominance. It is reported that both youths behaved very badly during these Italian years, corrupted by power and the almost infinite pleasures of the world's largest city. A string of coin issues proclaiming fraternal harmony can have done nothing to disguise their mounting enmity. The constant discord wore on Severus, for whom getting his sons away from Rome seemed like a possible solution.

Our sources attribute two other causes of displeasure to the emperor: not only was a younger generation of military commanders leading successful campaigns outside Italy, but in the peninsula itself, even with the emperor present, a brigand by the name of Bulla was running out of control, terrorising Italy for two years before he was captured in 207. Banditry was a fact of life in the empire, a menace to travellers and country folk, but no more than an irritant to government – it cannot have been enough to stir the emperor to action, but the fact that he was no longer the greatest and most active general in the empire may well have rankled the old man. He was also deeply superstitious, putting great store by his birth horoscope. He fully expected death to come for him soon. Perhaps he thought it better to die on one last victorious campaign than remain trapped between his squabbling children in a city that he could hardly bear. He began to prepare for a major campaign in northern Britannia.

There had been disturbances there, as there usually were, and we do not know the scale of the disruption that prompted Severus's last adventure. There is a great deal of speculation, which ranges from a maximalist hypothesis positing a major revolt by the native Brigantes of the Pennines alongside invasions by tribes from the Scottish Lowlands or even Caledonian highlanders, to the minimalist proposition of slightly increased raiding activity of the sort to which all Roman frontiers were prone. The imperial procurator Oclatinius Adventus and the senatorial governor L. Alfenus Senecio, operated simultaneously along Hadrian's Wall in the early 200s, a type of collaboration in military affairs that was quite unusual, but that is partly explained by the archaeological evidence for a comprehensive rebuilding of the local infrastructure to support an army led by the emperor in person.

Back at court, the kinsmen and favourites of Julia Domna were increasingly in the ascendant. Julia's brother-in-law Julius Avitus Alexianus was one of Severus's *comites* on the expedition, as was his son in-law, Sex. Varius Marcellus, who succeeded Oclatinius Adventus as procurator of Britain. Of the two guard prefects, the Syrian Papinian was chosen to go north with the emperor. The year 208 was seen in by another joint consulship of Caracalla and Geta, and the expedition set off for Britannia. Both consuls travelled north with their 63-year-old father, but only Caracalla and Severus would see any actual fighting. Geta was left behind, perhaps at Eboracum (York), ostensibly to manage civilian administration. Caracalla accompanied his father beyond the Wall and into Scotland, where the war was to take place. The 209 campaigns penetrated deep into the Highlands, where the Caledonians formally submitted to the emperor. We have evidence of massive marching camps right up the eastern edge of Scotland, and the beginnings of a major legionary base, clearly designed for a permanent occupation that never came, have been found at Carpow in Perthshire. This was more than a punitive raid, then. It was a concerted decision to take and hold Britain north of Hadrian's Wall – Severus would then be able to claim to have extended the frontiers of the empire in Britannia as well as in Mesopotamia. When the campaign was over, the imperial party returned to Eboracum, and Severus and Caracalla took the victory title Britannicus. The lowland Maeatae, in whose territory the new fortress at Carpow was being built, revolted and another large campaign was needed in 210.

Indisputably successful though it was, the British campaign foreshadowed its brutal dynastic aftermath. There is some evidence that Caracalla contemplated assassinating his father, and he did not trouble to conceal a public desire to kill Geta. His plans were checked by the revolt of the Maeatae, against whom he had to campaign on his own; Severus had become too ill for the rigours of the field, whether from arthritis or gout is unclear. The emperor now knew for sure that he was dying – the stars had foretold the span of his life and his sickness proved that they were right. In these last days, although he must have suspected it would be too late, Severus moved to secure his younger son's future. Towards the end of the year 210, he promoted Geta to the rank of augustus and for two or three months the empire had three augusti. Then, on 4 February 211, Severus died at Eboracum, still on his last campaign – the *expeditio felicissima britannica*, that most happy British campaign – at the age of sixty-five. His advice to his sons, supposedly quoted verbatim by Cassius Dio, is famous: 'Don't argue between yourselves, enrich the soldiers, and scorn all the rest.'

7

THE LATER SEVERANS

Julia Domna was with her two sons at Eboracum when Severus died in 211. His body was cremated at once and his ashes placed in an urn made of porphyry, the purple stone of emperors and kings. Twenty-five-year-old Caracalla, so it was rumoured, had badgered the doctors to kill Severus off sooner; he executed quite a few of them as soon as his father died. The household freedmen who had been closest to his father, and who might have tried to protect his plans for the succession, were likewise killed. But the chief ministers of government, many of whom had long served under Severus, remained in place for the time being, notably the guard prefects Papinian and Q. Maecius Laetus.

While the court began to prepare to return to Italy, Caracalla remained with the campaign army in the north, urging it to make him sole emperor, without immediate success. He quickly made peace with the Maeatae and the Caledonians, agreeing to withdraw from their territory and return to the line of Hadrian's Wall. He and Geta lived apart while they travelled and Julia had a difficult time even pretending that they could be reconciled.

Back in Rome, the brothers found it impossible to be together, supposedly bricking up passageways in the imperial palace to prevent contact with one another. By the end of the year, Caracalla decided to act. He had already dismissed Papinian and the urban prefect, replacing them both with one man, a relative by marriage. Sextus Varius Marcellus was the husband of Julia Soaemias, the niece of Caracalla and Geta's mother Julia Domna. During the Saturnalia of December 211, on the twenty-fifth day of the month, Geta was stabbed to death in the palace in his mother's arms, while Caracalla took himself to the praetorian camp and announced that he had escaped Geta's attempt on his life. Anyone who might have supported Geta was now put to death, among them the former guard prefect Aemilius Papinianus, and all the male relations of previous emperors, including some quite distant ones: Caracalla's harmless cousin, another Septimius Severus, died, as did Helvius Pertinax, the son of the emperor, and Marcus Aurelius's venerable daughter Cornificia and her son; even old Severan trusties like Fabius Cilo were marked for death. Varius Marcellus was tasked with erasing the memory of Geta from the public record, while Caracalla secured the allegiance of the Legio II Parthica at Alba. He addressed the senate as well, dressed in full military regalia, but this was a perfunctory move. It was the army that counted, and he had won its support by promising a major pay rise. Confiscations, and the recall and reminting of the coinage of Geta, would underwrite these costs.

Caracalla proved to be a monumentally bad emperor, a menace to the senate, a builder on a grandiose scale, a lavisher of money on anything and everything that might make him seem larger than life, and, in the end, the accidental architect of the late imperial world. In the five years of his sole reign, the emperor's cruelty and incompetence was inflicted mainly on those within easy reach. Like Commodus before him, he tried to win favour with the populace by competing in the arena and the circus, but, unlike Commodus, it seems not to have won him much support from the plebs. He was energetic enough, but his temper and bad sportsmanship had put the Roman crowd off him before the first year of his reign was over. Thereafter, he saved his energy for the life of the camps and for playing at soldiers with the troops. Provincial government remained in the hands of those Severus had chosen before his final campaign, which ensured a stability that Caracalla could not quickly wreck.

Syria Coele was governed by Marius Maximus, a long-time supporter of Severus going back to 193 and later a consul – and a prolific and scurrilous biographer. His brother Marius Perpetuus governed Moesia Superior; the *praefectus* of Egypt was Ti. Claudius Subatianus Aquila, a Numidian, and his relation Subatianus Proculus governed Numidia itself. Other Africans held both Pannonias (Septimius Castinus, a relation of Severus, and Egnatius Victor), while Aiacius Modestus Crescentianus governed Germania Superior. They kept the great military provinces safe, though Caracalla feared the concentration of power in any one general's hands. For that reason, he split the single British province into a Britannia Inferior, governed by the legate of VI Victrix at Eboracum, and a Britannia Superior, with a governor at Londinium and command of the II Augusta at Caerleon and the XX Valeria Victrix at Chester.

While he could control the provincial governors relatively easily, Caracalla remained a shadowy figure to much of the populace. With his chronic insecurity and megalomania, he determined on a suitably grandiose way of introducing himself to the subjects of whom he was now sole ruler. He did so with a legal measure that we call the *Constitutio Antoniniana*, but which was actually an imperial edict. With it, he extended to every free inhabitant of the Roman empire the privileges of Roman citizenship, excluding only the small category of *dediticii* (former enemies who had surrendered, keeping their personal freedoms but losing all communal rights). At a stroke, millions of people who had not had access to Roman law, but only that of their local communities, were turned into Romans. Although the line between Roman citizen and non-citizen *peregrinus* had been blurring in the provinces for over a century – and despite the extension of Roman citizenship to the provincial elites in almost every civilised province, particularly in the towns – the consequences of this action were enormous. Suddenly, local practices that were considered normal under local law (like sibling marriage in Egypt) became illegal; equally, testamentary privileges and exemption from certain forms of punishment were now universal. It would take decades to sort out the legal consequences, and it is no coincidence that the great age of Classical Roman law should be the earlier third century: the jurists of Caracalla's successors, prompted by the sudden accession of so many new Romans, had to clarify and spell out what Roman law actually meant and required in a systematic way.

Though over time the Antonine constitution would completely transform the culture of many provinces, contemporary authors took little notice of the measure. Indeed, if we had only the works of the historian and senator Cassius Dio to go by we would believe the emperor's sole motive for the granting of citizenship was to raise more of the inheritance taxes that Roman citizens were required to pay. Apart from Dio, no literary references to Caracalla's far-reaching edict survive, which means we are most fortunate that a fragmentary papyrus (known as the Giessen Papyrus) preserves the preamble of the imperial edict itself and gives us insight into the mind of Caracalla.

This emperor, having just murdered his brother and let loose a bloodbath at the imperial centre, sticks to the official story: he had been saved from Geta's wicked plot and, because the gods had spared him, he would thank them by leading more of his subjects to them. By granting them the privilege of Roman law, he not only brought the gods new worshippers, he allowed his people to share in his good fortune. We should not dismiss this rhetoric out of hand. The ideology of Roman government encouraged a close identification of the populace with the emperor as an embodiment of a universal order. One can argue that this was a form of hegemony that made imperial subjects complicit in their own subordination, but it was no less powerful for that. The new citizens took Aurelius for their nomen, after Caracalla's official name of Marcus Aurelius Antoninus, which announced their direct connection to the emperor who enfranchised them. It was this symbolism that mattered most; if, as the cynical Dio had it, the citizenship edict happened to raise more money for the treasury, then that was simply a bonus. For Caracalla certainly needed money.

Like any other emperor out to prove himself, Caracalla had to be seen to defend his empire. By the start of 213 at the latest, he marched north to the upper Danube frontier, personally leading the campaign in the same year that he was *consul ordinarius*. Late in the campaigning season, he passed beyond the Danube from Raetia into the region that would later be called Alamannia, after the barbarian people who dwelt there and who are first mentioned by our sources in the context of Caracalla's campaign. Within the month he had declared victory and may even have won it: the capacity of Roman armies to rain destruction on the disorganised agricultural populations beyond the northern frontiers is a constant of the period. His movements are only sketchily recorded, but he shared his father's compulsion to travel. In 214, he marched across the Balkans to the east, crossing into Asia Minor at Troy and sacrificing to the spirit of Achilles in imitation of Alexander the Great. From the Troad, he continued on into Bithynia, where he wintered at Nicomedia, and then moved to Antioch in Syria in the spring of the following year. He forgave the Antiochenes for siding against his father in the civil wars of the 190s. Having been stripped of its privileges in the aftermath of Severus's victory, Antioch was now exalted with the title of *colonia* and given the right of *ius Italicum*, a privilege that had ceased to have much legal importance since the citizenship edict, but which still meant sharing in the Italian peninsula's exemption from taxes, and was thus a real mark of status. Caracalla also returned to the city its right to celebrate Olympic games as it had always done in the past. He may have visited his mother's city of Emesa, and he certainly bestowed colonial rank upon it, although the gesture did nothing to reconcile him with Julia Domna, who never forgave her surviving son for murdering his brother. Late in 215, Caracalla left Syria for Egypt, arriving in Alexandria in November or December. He would spend the winter in the city, leaving only in April 216, with destruction in his wake.

Just as his antics had angered the Roman plebs in the first year of his reign, so too did he alienate the even more unruly populace of Alexandria, notoriously among the most fractious citizenries of the empire. Precisely how he gave offence we do not know, but crowds began to gather and chant that he was a fratricide and a fraud, certainly not another Alexander. To an emperor with Caracalla's temper, this was tantamount to treason – had he not sacrificed to Achilles at Troy as the great conqueror had done, and had he not left his soldier's cloak and many other gifts at the conqueror's tomb? What was more, he had not murdered Geta – the whole world knew that the gods had preserved him from his brother's malevolence. After ordering those who were not Alexandrian citizens to depart from the city, he unleashed a massacre. Precise numbers are impossible to come by, but whenever soldiers were sent into the streets with orders to discipline the citizenry, it meant thousands of deaths, not hundreds. His vengeance partly satisfied, Caracalla departed the city intending to prove the Alexandrians wrong – he would be a new Alexander and subdue the Parthians as the great conqueror had the Persians.

Caracalla arrived at Antioch in late spring 216 and marched out on campaign shortly after 27 May. The timing was auspicious. He had already made an example of Abgar of Edessa, king of Osrhoene, deposing him on the specious pretext that he had mistreated the Mesopotamian tribes. Travelling from Arbela to Edessa, he was consciously tracing the footsteps of Alexander, who had defeated Darius there. He overwintered in the former royal capital of Osrhoene, celebrating his *vicennalia* there on 28 January 217 and raising the city to the status of *colonia*. That spring, he was prepared to march out into the Parthian kingdom itself. He never made it. Caracalla was murdered at Carrhae in Mesopotamia on 8 April.

His courtiers feared disaster going into a Parthian war with an emperor who relied more upon astrologers and an Egyptian charlatan called

Serapio than on expert military advisers. The praetorian prefect Opellius Macrinus and the high command of the expeditionary force were behind the putsch. They suborned a ranker called Martialis who had reason to hate the emperor. Martialis stabbed Caracalla to death during a toilet break as he was travelling to the temple of the local moon god. Caracalla's loyal bodyguard then killed Martialis, burying the true story of the coup but saving the army from a dangerous war that the generals did not want. The prefect Macrinus spent several days canvassing support, securing the assent of the Mesopotamian garrison and winning the acquiescence of his fellow guard prefect Oclatinius Adventus, who now became urban prefect. Four days after the murder, M. Opellius Macrinus was proclaimed emperor.

His position looked strong. His family was from Caesarea Maritima in Mauretania, thus at the other end of civilised, urban Africa from Septimi-us's Tripolitania. They were of Moorish origin in the same manner that the Severans had been Punic, but their origins were lower than the Severans. Now in his early fifties, Macrinus had a son named Diadumenianus, only nine years old but still a potential dynastic heir. Macrinus also stood at the head of an army which had known him for some time and his long career had earned him a large clientele in the imperial bureaucracy. Two such clients were among his first appointments: the procurator Ulpius Julianus and the prefect of the *cursus publicus* now replaced Macrinus and Adventus as praetorian prefects. But the new emperor was less secure than he imagined. The people of Rome were furious that he did not immedi-ately rush home to curry their favour and were already rioting before the year was out.

The senate, meanwhile, was appalled at the elevation of this low-born equestrian to the purple. The historian Dio, than whom few writers are more snobbish, probably speaks for his order in condemning the presumption of Macrinus and his promotion of uppity men just like himself to positions of power. They could also charge him with cowardice. The Parthian king Artabanus V had been mustering his forces to meet Caracalla when the emperor was killed and, though Macrinus tried to reach a negotiated peace, Artabanus invaded Roman Mesopotamia. At Nisibis, late in 217, Macrinus suffered a bloody defeat. The humiliating cost of peace was reportedly the staggeringly high figure of 200 million sesterces, money that could not have been found in the treasury without additional taxes or confiscations.

Overwintering in the east, while trying to raise the funds for the peace tribute, nothing Macrinus did went right. He proclaimed Diadumenianus as caesar and began to mint coins in each of their names, but the idea of his founding a dynasty appealed to no one. He had promised the soldiers that Caracalla would be deified, but he could not deliver that in the face of senatorial hostility. Searching for economies, he reduced the pay of new recruits, a recipe for unrest. He appointed some of Caracalla's favourites to positions of power in Rome, while the senate griped and the citizenry rioted. Had he gone to Rome he might perhaps have defused the situation, but he was not given the chance to find out.

Caracalla left no heirs, but he did not lack for living relations. That Macrinus chose not to follow his predecessor's example and massacre them proved a mistake. Julia Domna, sick with cancer, committed suicide at Antioch shortly after learning of her son's assassination. Her family lived on, however, in their home city of Emesa. Julia Domna's younger sister, Julia Maesa, had two daughters named Julia Soaemias and Julia Mamaea, born of her marriage to Julius Avitus, consul during the reign of Septimius Severus. Both daughters had been married to strong supporters of the Severan dynasty, Julia Soaemias to Caracalla's prefect Sextus Varius Marcellus, Julia Mamaea to the senior procurator Gessius Marcianus. Both men had died of natural causes before 217, but both marriages had produced male heirs. These second cousins of Caracalla would perpetuate the Severan dynasty and ensure that the reign of Rome's first equestrian emperor was painfully short.

Julia Soaemias and Varius Marcellus's son, Varius Avitus, was a boy of thirteen or fourteen at the time of Caracalla's death. It is unlikely that he had ever left Emesa, where he served in a role that had long belonged to his ancestors as hereditary priest of Elagabal (or *'lh'gbl* in the Syriac), the local manifestation of the ubiquitous Semitic deity Baal, here worshipped in the form of a black meteorite. The young Avitus, as the god's earthly priest, took his deity's name and is known to the Classical sources as Elagabalus (or, traditionally but less correctly, Heliogabalus). Julia Mamaea's son Bassianus Alexianus, who was younger than Elagabalus, accompanied his mother back to Emesa after Julia Domna's suicide. Soaemias and Mamaea together plotted the coup that would bring down Macrinus. The sisters had spent their lives near the centre of power in the Severan empire and they had supporters everywhere. They knew about the discord in Macrinus's camp, and did everything in their power to make it worse. The Legio III Parthica, under the command of one P. Valerius Comazon, had taken up its winter quarters near Emesa and was therefore the natural audience for a potential Severan comeback. The legionaries witnessed Elagabalus celebrate the festivals of the sun god, and whispers began to go round the camps that the handsome young man looked an awful lot like Caracalla; perhaps he was actually the emperor's son by his cousin Mamaea? Meanwhile, the oracle of Bel at Apamea, home town of Varius Marcellus, began to utter ominous prophecies about Macrinus's longevity. Having led a successful coup himself, these whispers must have worried Macrinus, but he did nothing, and that paralysis was fatal.

On the night of 16 May 218, a freedman of Mamaea's brought Elagabalus to the camp of the III Parthica, where Valerius Comazon let them in. By morning, a new emperor had been proclaimed, taking the name Marcus Aurelius Antoninus – a bold assertion of his descent from the legitimate dynasty. Supporters of Macrinus tried to act. Ulpius Julianus, legate of the Legio II Parthica, marched his men to Emesa, but there the Legio III declined to fight them, instead displaying images of Caracalla alongside their new emperor Elagabalus. After a few officers loyal to Macrinus were killed, both legions returned to quarters, the III Parthica near Emesa, the II Parthica at Apamea. Macrinus then tried to intervene personally, asking the II Parthica to acclaim his son, the caesar Diadumenianus, as his fellow augustus. They consented, in return for a large donative, but during the celebratory banquet presented the augusti with the head of their loyal legate Ulpius Julianus. The conditional loyalty of the II Parthica, which had so blithely murdered its own commanding officers, could clearly not be relied upon, so Macrinus and his son retreated to Antioch with only the praetorians to defend them. The supporters of Elagabalus marched on the Syrian capital, the III Parthica under Valerius Comazon leading the way.

The decisive battle, fought on 8 June, was hotly contested until Macrinus left the field and his troops began to desert. The emperor made for Rome, while trying to send Diadumenianus into hiding, but that simply revealed his fundamental incompetence. Had he made for Rome sooner, before the end of 217, he would probably still have faced an eastern rebellion of the Severan cadet line. But that would have been a civil war, in which he might have rallied the support of the western and Balkan legions to his side. As it was, his reign was a rout from start to finish. Macrinus was caught at Chalcedon, about to cross to Europe from Asia; Diadumenianus had already been arrested at Zeugma. Both were soon executed by their captors – Macrinus at Archelais in Cappadocia, en route back to Antioch. The equestrian officials on whom Macrinus had relied and promoted to higher office were killed, too. Back in Rome, a long-time servant of the Severans, the consular Marius Maximus, conducted a purge of the Syrians' potential enemies.

The centurion who had executed Macrinus, Claudius Aelius Pollio, was made a senator and given command of Bithynia, later on being sent to hold Germania Superior. Elagabalus and his mother remained in Antioch for some months, until it became clear that they should not repeat the mistake of Macrinus and neglect the city of Rome. Before the end of 218 they began their journey west, wintering in Nicomedia. The boy did not finally arrive in Rome until late summer 219, making a formal *adventus* into the city, but his new imperial subjects were ill prepared for the spectacle their emperor presented. He might have gone by the name Marcus Aurelius Antoninus – and there is no question that he looked physically like a member of the family – but there the resemblance to his Severan forebears stopped. He dressed as a high priest of the cult of Elagabal at all times, travelling with the earthly manifestation of his god and conducting his rites wherever he went. Upon arriving in the eternal city, he ascended the Capitol and placed the image of his Baal in the temple of Capitoline Jupiter, the chief god of the Roman state religion. Romans lacked a sense of blasphemy in its later Christian valence, but they did have an acute awareness of what was and what was not acceptable religious conduct. The advent of a Syrian god, with no pedigree as an object of Roman worship, into the most solemn cult site in the empire could only be felt as a pollution, even if the emperor himself claimed to be the god's high priest and even if his cult could be rationalised as a form of solar devotion.

Things got worse when, in 220, Elagabalus made himself appear still less traditionally Roman by adopting a new and bizarre title. Emperors had long been chief priests of the state cult, ever since Augustus had permanently taken over the role of *pontifex maximus* from his dead rival Lepidus. But now Elagabalus began to call himself the *sacerdos amplissimus dei invicti Solis Elagabali, pontifex maximus* – 'the highest priest of the invincible Sun God Elagabalus and pontifex maximus'. If the title had been calculated to outrage conservative sensibilities it could not have done so any more effectively. Marriage to the impeccably high born Roman heiress Julia Cornelia Paula could do nothing to alter the offence, which the emperor exacerbated by declaring Elagabalus to be the chief god of the Roman state, above the Capitoline triad of Jupiter, Juno and Minerva that had long since protected the empire. The headstrong young emperor must himself have insisted upon this course of action, for no sane adviser could have endorsed it. But perhaps Elagabalus had surrounded himself with equally bizarre advisers. We cannot know, since the available sources become painfully deficient and grow more so as the century progresses: the excerpts in which Cassius Dio is preserved become patchier, while the biographies of the fourth-century *Historia Augusta* are pure fiction where they do not merely draw on Herodian, whose deeply unreliable narrative is still extant.

Despite our ignorance of precise facts, what seems clear is that Elagabalus conducted himself in a fashion that seemed, from the Roman perspective, mad at best, and dangerous at worst. This view was painfully reinforced by the events of 220, when Elagabalus divorced the blameless Cornelia and instead married a vestal virgin, Julia Aquila Severa, in order to celebrate the marriage of the deity Elagabalus to the goddess Minerva. Minerva was the Roman version of the Greek Athena, whose statue, the Palladium, was moved to the temple of Jupiter to accompany her new husband. That the emperor did this with great ceremony, in public processions in which the Roman populace was meant to take part, only made matters worse. In the following year, this charade – for so it must have seemed to many observers – was repeated, with the divine Elagabalus divorcing Athena and marrying the Punic Astarte, and the emperor Elagabalus divorcing Julia Aquila Severa and marrying Annia Faustina, a distant descendant of Marcus Aurelius. The marriage to Faustina did not last very long either, but by the time the emperor had discarded her and chosen other brides unnamed in the sources, his court had had enough of him.

The sisters Julia Soaemias and Julia Mamaea had come to Rome along with their sons, the former the emperor Elagabalus, the latter the somewhat younger Bassianus Alexianus. Mamaea now decided that her nephew's conduct as emperor was simply too bizarrely damaging to tolerate any further. In this judgement she seems to have enjoyed the support of Valerius Comazon, the former commander of Legio III Parthica whose defection from Macrinus had sealed the latter's fate, and who now held the urban prefecture. In June 221, Bassianus – who had been born in 208 – reached adulthood, taking the *toga virilis* to symbolise that transition. He was also made caesar to Elagabalus's augustus and given the name Marcus

Aurelius Alexander. As the second adult male in the imperial family he also gave anyone who wanted it a focus for resistance at court.

Two factions now vied for control in Rome, some siding with the emperor, some with the new caesar. Elagabalus tried to dismiss Valerius Comazon for disloyalty, but was forced to reinstate him after some murky negotiations. At the start of the New Year, when Elagabalus became consul for the fourth time and Alexander for the first, the situation worsened and Mamaea moved to force a coup. Alexander disappeared into hiding in March, whether in genuine fear or, perhaps more likely, to bring the cold war between him and his cousin to a boil. On 11 March 222, Elagabalus went with Julia Soaemias to the camp of the praetorian guard, hoping to reassure them of Alexander's well-being, but the guardsmen had turned mutinous. Elagabalus tried to hide himself in a trunk, but was discovered and beheaded, along with his mother and their main supporters, including both guard prefects and the urban prefect who had briefly replaced Comazon.

With her sister dead, Julia Mamaea came into her own. The 14-year-old Alexander was proclaimed emperor by the army on 13 March, and a day later was made augustus, *pater patriae* and *pontifex maximus* by a senate only too glad to be rid of his cousin. At the same time, he added Severus to his nomenclature to reassert his dynastic connections, while the rumour was spread about that he, too, was actually the son of Caracalla, rather than of Mamaea's husband Gessius Marcianus. The memory of his predecessor was condemned in a formal *damnatio* and a new era of peace was to ensue. Or so it was hoped.

For the better part of a decade, peace may indeed have done its bit, although in truth we know next to nothing about Alexander's reign. The *Historia Augusta*'s account is almost pure fiction, offering an idealised portrait of the 'good emperor' to balance the stereotyped orientalism of its Elagabalus and the barbarous caricature of its Maximinus, Alexander's eventual successor. Herodian, for his part, is limited by his ignorance and his distance from events, as well as an eternal preference for rhetoric over content. Dio remains our best account, not least because he himself played an important role in the politics of the moment.

We last met Dio as a junior senator in the reign of Commodus, of whose mad self-indulgence the historian gives a frightening and at times quite amusing account. He became and remained a good servant of the Severan dynasty, however, even though Elagabalus must have seemed at times like Commodus reincarnate. Dio spent most of the Syrian boy's reign in his own home city of Nicaea, as a senatorial curator in charge of its administration. (*Curatores* were a special type of short-term senatorial appointment, generally charged with supervising the finances of provincial cities that had got themselves into fiscal trouble.) Thereafter, he became proconsul of Africa, a senatorial province still ostensibly chosen by lot from among the consulars in the senate, though frequently assigned by imperial fiat from among those eligible. His conduct in the proconsulate must have been impressive, for he was then appointed governor of two imperial provinces, first Dalmatia and then Pannonia Superior, the latter a key military province. In 229 he was honoured with a second consulate, sharing it with the emperor himself. The conspicuous favours showered on Dio reflect, on one level, a deliberate policy of Alexander's regime – whereas Caracalla and Elagabalus had tended to honour those who emerged from their personal service, be that household or equestrian bureaus, the reign of Alexander was dominated by men of senatorial background. Indeed, much of what we know about the reign must be inferred from its official appointments, since its narrative history is all but a blank. One thing is clear – the equestrian and court favourites of Elagabalus and Soaemias were going to be excluded from the government of Alexander as much as possible. Instead, senators whose careers had begun under Septimius Severus – and sometimes even held their first consulships during his reign – would hold the main offices of government.

That fact alone explains why Alexander's reign was remembered as a golden age in later centuries, irrespective of any conspicuous success, thanks to a tradition dominated by senatorial writers like Dio and Marius Maximus. The provincials, insofar as we can grasp their views, and even for the most part the legions, remained passive throughout. Rome itself was much less quiescent. The praetorian guard was unhappy from the start of the reign and never really settled down. Alexander's new praetorian prefect, Domitius Ulpianus (known to us more frequently as the jurist Ulpian), whose career had begun under Severus's praetorian prefect Papinian, was a harsh disciplinarian. His ideas about the law, and about fairness and justice, sat ill with a group of soldiers who were used to demanding and getting what they wanted. Ulpian has plausibly been identified as the first proper theorist of human rights, the first to articulate that broad category as a concept, and his careful clarification of and systematic approach to Roman civil law – an approach he shared with other Severan jurists of the time – not only shaped the following three centuries, but revolutionised European legal thought when his ideas were rediscovered and disseminated in the twelfth century AD and after. But in his own day, the praetorians objected to his sternness and disliked many of his appointees, to the point that the guard's discipline broke down completely in summer 223.

Ulpian's enemy Marcus Aurelius Epagathus, an equestrian freedman who had succeded him as the *praefectus annonae* in charge of Rome's grain supply, fanned the flames of resentment. Ulpian escaped an attempt to kidnap him at home by fleeing to the palace, but a detachment of guardsmen caught him there and, in the presence of the emperor and his mother, murdered the prefect who had so enraged them. The hostility between the guard and the officials favoured by the emperor's household continued: Cassius Dio, for one, was unable to remain in Rome during his own second consulate in 229 because of the praetorians' threats. There were other problems, too – at some point in 225, Alexander was married to Gnaea Seia Herennia Sallustia Orbiana, the daughter of L. Seius Herennius Sallustius. She was given the title of augusta, while it is possible, if by no means certain, that her father was named caesar. But then, in 227, something went wrong – perhaps a conspiracy or an attempt at usurpation. At any rate, Herennius was executed and Orbiana banished to Africa, never to be heard of again.

The discontent that had simmered in Rome from the start of Alexander's reign seems to have grown throughout the empire over time, perhaps in reaction to a young and cloistered emperor with little capacity to lead on his own behalf: mutinies and unrest afflicted many frontier regions and, sometime before 229, the Mesopotamian garrison went so far as to murder its legate. They were undoubtedly facing a novel threat to their east, from the new Persian king Ardashir, who had only a few years earlier overthrown the last Parthian king. Events in Central Asia and the Parthian empire will occupy much of the next chapter, but we can briefly trace their role in the downfall of the Severan regime here. Around the year 230, perhaps slightly later, the new Persian ruler Ardashir attacked Rome's province of Mesopotamia, at the same time that a man named Uranius may have claimed the imperial purple (it is very unclear whether this is a misplaced, or even a correct, reference to the later usurper Uranius Antoninus known from his coins). Ardashir besieged Nisibis and his troops threatened the borders of Syria itself. The regime of Severus Alexander did not begin to mount a proper defence until 231, when the young emperor left Rome for the eastern front, collecting troops en route and summoning the Legio II Traiana from Egypt, the whole army converging at Antioch before the winter of 231–2, during which further mutinies are attested. The campaign of the next year was on a huge scale, with armies assaulting Armenia in the north, Osrhoene in the centre and Mesopotamia in the south. But the armies failed on their northern and southern fronts and our vague accounts suggest massive losses with little to show for them.

Then, at the end of the campaign season, news came of trouble on the upper Rhine and Danube. The Alamanni, or some group among that emerging confederation of barbarians along the upper Rhine and upper Danube frontiers, had launched a large raid or a full-scale invasion: details are as impossible to reconstruct as Alamannic motives. In response, the emperor and his mother made for the west, returning to Rome in 233 celebrating a Persian triumph, before moving on to Moguntiacum on the German frontier. Severus planned to chastise the barbarians in the approved manner, personally invading their territory and sowing havoc. He appears to have done so successfully, since it was a rare day on which a Roman army met serious opposition beyond the northern frontiers. Unfortunately for Alexander, while the campaign army had been laying waste Alamannia, some parties of Alamannic raiders had done the same to civilian settlements near the Rhineland garrisons. The emperor's soldiers, or at least some of them, found their homes destroyed upon returning to winter quarters after their successes across the river. Distraught and enraged, they proclaimed the equestrian commander C. Julius Verus Maximinus as their new emperor, deposing and killing Alexander and his mother Mamaea. The coup brought Severan dynasty to a painful and sorry end, on 19 March 235.

One historical commonplace understands the death of Severus Alexander as the breaking point between the early empire and the hiatus or caesura of a third-century crisis. We will consider the concept of imperial crisis at greater length in the following chapters, but for now it is enough to insist that the four years after the murder of Alexander continued to play out the political tensions of his reign without any real substantive break. The usurper Maximinus belonged to the growing class of equestrian officials whose influence had increasingly supplanted that of traditional senatorial families since the late Antonine period. He was a senior officer, with a long but to us obscure career of reliable service behind him. The senatorial historical tradition, on which we are mainly reliant, deliberately casts Maximinus as a barbarian outsider, a rhetorical stance deployed throughout later antiquity by the civilian elites who wrote our extant histories; in the fourth-century *Historia Augusta*, after the pornographic luxuriousness of Elagabalus and the inspirational perfection of Alexander, we are given a physically monstrous and monstrously cruel Maximinus, the embodiment of pure id, although each of these portraits is equally lacking in basic fact. But we should not doubt how bitterly the senatorial elite of the late Antonine and early Severan periods resented the capacity of men with no birthright to achieve more and more genuine power as the third century wore on.

We do not know when Maximinus was born, but he came from Thrace in the Balkans, hence the inauthentic cognomen Maximinus Thrax by which he is still sometimes known, and the spurious imputation of barbarism it still connotes. He had risen to high equestrian rank through service in the army and civil service, and he was not young when the German troops mutinied and made him emperor. His portrait, on coins and the rare portrait busts, shows him as distinctly middle-aged, probably born in the last years of Marcus and entering imperial service during the civil wars of the 190s. He had, presumably, been on the winning side and had reached at least the rarely attested, and not very senior, rank of *praefectus tironibus*, 'prefect of the recruits', perhaps a sort of very senior sergeant-major. At the time of his accession he was married to a Caecilia Paulina of whom nothing is known and the two had a by-then adolescent son, C. Julius Verus Maximus.

Given his career, Maximinus fully understood the Severan policy of enriching the soldiers in order to keep the army under control. Alexander and Mamaea had never been hugely popular with the army, but it was their stinginess with donatives that got them killed. Maximinus promised his supporters both a large donative and a doubling of military pay. But promises like that called for desperate measures. Although posthumous slander clouds almost every aspect of Maximinus's reign, and we will never know quite who were the main targets of his confiscations, he seems authentically to have lowered subsidies to the Roman grain supply and to the city's imperial cult. Relying on its subsidies, and unable to feed itself entirely from its own market gardens or its wages, the Roman plebs was necessarily affronted; just as bad, the imperial cult regulated large parts of the urban calendar, and interfering with the schedule of religious observance could alienate the senatorial elite as much as the plebs. That

Maximinus seems not to have cared very much about the offence he was causing at Rome only magnified its impact, and while he reigned he never did go to Rome, instead sending back images of his military exploits on the Rhine and the Danube. These campaigns are poorly documented, but in 235 and 236 he was fighting on the Rhine, probably against the Alamanni, and in later 236 and thereafter he was on the Danube frontier fighting the Sarmatians; he appears as Germanicus Maximus, Dacicus Maximus and Sarmaticus Maximus on the coinage by the time of his death in 238.

For all that he was a hate figure for Roman plebs and Roman senate alike, what mattered more was that he could neither afford the donative he promised his soldiers nor double their wages as they believed he had agreed to do. Conspiracies led by two otherwise unknown officers named Magnus and Quartinus are reported in our only source of value; they were probably acting on discontent in the ranks. Worse, the consecration of Maximinus's wife Paulina, who died in 235 or 236, and the raising of the young Maximus to the rank of caesar did nothing to create the sense of a successful ruling dynasty. Indeed, the main structural point we can glean about the reign, beyond the narratives of its beginning and end, is that many men whose careers blossomed later in the century (including at least two future emperors, Valerian and Decius) either continued unchecked or actively prospered under Maximinus. That said, Maximinus seems nowhere to have generated any great enthusiasm, which is why an initially trivial revolt in Africa Proconsularis could spiral out of control in 238 and bring down his regime while achieving next to nothing on its own account.

The revolt of the senatorial regime in Africa Proconsularis forms the climax to the histories of Herodian which, though moralising and rhetorically mannered, preserve a detailed and broadly comprehensible account of events: an unnamed imperial procurator, while raising the funds his emperor Maximinus required, annoyed the well-born population of Proconsularis – some of them from the senatorial class, many of them clients of senatorial families now in Italy. The 'young men' of the province then rose up, murdering the offensive procurator and proclaiming as emperor the proconsul himself; this was the senator M. Antonius Gordianus Sempronianus Romanus Africanus, known to us as Gordian I. An old man of no special distinction, he had had a long career – governing Britannia under Caracalla, and Achaea under Elagabalus – which meant plenty of his fellow senators knew and might support him. He made the necessary show of refusing the purple, but swiftly got word back to the capital, where the senate acclaimed him and had Maximinus's praetorian prefect Vitalianus killed. It then declared Maximinus himself a *hostis publicus* and took the unprecedented and ultimately quixotic step of appointing a board of twenty men (the *vigintiviri*) to lead the senatorial opposition to the emperor they had publicly condemned. Gordian's son, who had held a suffect consulate under Alexander and was in 238 serving as his father's consular legate in Africa, was now made his co-emperor. Coins of both Gordians were struck at Rome, word went out to all the provincial governors and legionary legates and, in the east at least, Maximinus seems to have had no support whatsoever. He proved luckiest in Africa, of all places: Capelianus, the legate of Legio III Augusta and thus also the governor of Numidia, marched on Proconsularis, a province that had been ungarrisoned since the time of Augustus. Capelianus put down Gordian's revolt without difficulty, killing the younger emperor in battle and inducing the tired old man to commit suicide after a reign of just twenty days.

In Rome, events continued on their unprecedentedly peculiar course: not content with having supported the shambolic revolt in Africa, the senate now made two of the *vigintiviri* augusti, equal colleagues to replace the dead Gordiani. These men, Marcus Clodius Pupienus and Decimus Caelius Balbinus, were to have a reign as unhappy as it was short, and that despite their fine pedigrees: Balbinus was a patrician from an old family, probably from the Spanish province of Baetica where families of republican origin had lived for centuries – he had governed Asia as proconsul (which was, with Africa, one of the two most prestigious posts in the empire), and he had already enjoyed a second consulate in 213, with Caracalla as consul prior; Pupienus was a career soldier, perhaps the first in his family to enter a senatorial *cursus*, but extremely successful, starting out under Septimius Severus and continuing with governorships of Bithynia, Illyricum and Germania, as well as the proconsulate of Asia and then a second consulate under Severus Alexander.

The news of their proclamation was met with outrage in Rome, not by supporters of Maximinus – of whom there were few in the capital – but by loyalists of the Gordiani, who succeeded in stirring up a mob. Riotous crowds proclaimed as emperor the dead Gordian's grandson, and the two new senatorial augusti conceded to him the rank of caesar in an effort to unite the opposition to Maximinus. Each of the successive rivals to the sitting emperor struck coins in profusion, though those of the first two

Gordiani are now quite scarce and aurei of Balbinus and Pupienus virtually unknown: all conveyed the message that Maximinus was an illegitimate tyrant against whom the steady hand of honourable senators would restore the dignity of their republican forebears. Contrasts in the coin portaiture tell their own story: the first Gordian clean-shaven, firm of chin, civilian and classical; his doomed son young, vigorous and military; Balbinus fat, jowly and be-togaed; Pupienus grim, determined, wearing the beard of a philosopher-soldier like Marcus, but not the stubble of a contemporary warrior like Maximinus. And then, following them all, the boy Gordian, only thirteen when the crowds acclaimed him, a promise of the future on whom the viewer could project whatever they liked. The contrast with the professional, military and equestrian ethos of Maximinus could not be stronger; in 238, with the vigintivirate and the abortive support of the Gordiani, the senate was asserting its own sense of aristocratic privilege, which it now began to couch as a civilian contrast to the soldierly virtue that was all Maximinus had to offer.

The rioting had upset not just the senate, but also the praetorians, some of whom had lost their lives. For some days there was open warfare in the streets of Rome, but the plebs – or enough of them to make a difference – seems to have sided with the senate and besieged the praetorians in their camp, cowing them into submission. While this was going on – and possibly before he had even heard of Capelianus's lightning victory in Proconsularis – Maximinus invaded northern Italy in March 238. Here he made a critical mistake. Rather than moving south with all speed, he stopped to besiege Aquileia, a key strongpoint on the route between Pannonia and northern Italy. Perhaps he was worried about leaving that nearly impregnable base of opposition in his rear, but the siege did not go well. After a couple of months, in late spring 238, the disgruntled soldiers mutinied, killing Maximinus and his son Maximus, and then holding fast in the north of the peninsula without advancing any further. When news of this reached Rome, instead of the expected rejoicing, the bloodbath continued. The praetorian guard, so recently in violent conflict with plebs and senate, now rallied behind the young caesar Gordian III, proclaiming him augustus on the people's behalf and murdering Balbinus and Pupienus.

Survivors coalesced around the court of Gordian III, the sixth emperor to have held the imperial title, however briefly, in 238. The butchery stopped and the equestrian and military men who had prospered under Maximinus now came to dominate the new government: in Balbinus and

Pupienus, a core of old-fashioned privilege had tried to reassert itself and failed miserably. With a boy barely in his teens on the throne, a palace junta ran the empire. That pattern of rule by committee, and the slaughters at Carthage, Rome and Aquileia, foreshadow what we have long called the third-century crisis, to which the next chapter will turn.

8

EURASIAN HISTORY AND THE ROMAN EMPIRE

⬥⬥⬥⬥⬥⬥

The crisis of the third century. The age of the soldier emperors. The military anarchy. *Die Weltkrise.* Call it what you may, the years between 235 and 285 have long been treated as a dark time in Roman history, a caesura between the high and later empires, a world that had to be saved from ruining itself by the smack of firm government – which was duly administered by the authoritarian Diocletian during a reign of twenty years (r. 284–305). On the surface, this dire reputation might seem deserved. After all, dozens of different men claimed the imperial purple in the course of five decades. Some of them were indisputably legitimate, whether on account of hereditary succession or timely senatorial recognition; others were usurpers by any definition, ancient or modern. But rather more were of some dubious status in between, as if the whole notion of imperial legitimacy had become open to a question that was usually answered in bloody civil wars among rival claimants. What is more, the eastern provinces of the empire faced persistent and sometimes devastating invasions by the new Sasanian dynasty in Persia and Mesopotamia, while less damaging but still alarming raids were a regular part of life along the Rhine and Danube frontiers, as well as the Atlantic and Black Sea coasts. Further evidence for decline can be found in the breakdown of the early

117

imperial currency, and the total debasement of its silver coinage. On the religious front, we find new cults and enthusiasms, prophets like Mani with strange dualistic beliefs, as well as the steady spread of Christianity and the outbreaks of violent persecution which that engendered. Topping it off, a major plague – perhaps a haemorrhagic fever – struck at mid-century, with a mortality that is only just now coming to be recognised. Set out starkly, it is difficult to read the era in any terms other than crisis.

And yet the picture is in fact far less clear. For one thing, as we began to see in chapter 7, the chronology of the supposed age of crisis does not really fit – the kinds of instability generally cited as defining the middle years of the century began with the death of Caracalla in 217. Equally, the geographical range of the crisis was far more restricted than a general model of collapse implies. A few parts of the empire did indeed suffer repeatedly from invasion and civil wars, with the consequence that some regions that had not seen a Roman army for many centuries now had to deal with soldiers living in their midst and the inevitable depredations they brought. On the other hand, many regions that suffered badly for a couple of years went on to experience decades of uninterrupted peace. Still others – much of Britain, Africa and Spain, for instance – prospered throughout the century. Likewise, while the economy of some provinces clearly stuttered, the trans-provincial export agriculture that fed the empire on an industrial scale continued as before and there is little evidence for supra-regional, still less empire-wide, economic crisis, despite the travails of the imperial currency.

On those and many other grounds, the traditional model of crisis and decline has been widely challenged over the past three decades. We need to treat the third century as a period with a historical dynamic of its own, not merely as a way station on the road between early and late empires. Such an analysis would recognise the way changes to Roman government and society under Hadrian and the Antonines continued to shape the course of third-century history: the disappearance of the state that Augustus had created as the patrimony of a single family; the rise of a new equestrian elite that penetrated much deeper into provincial lives than earlier types of Roman government had done; the changing composition of the senatorial aristocracy, and with it the bridging of divisions between the Greek and Roman cultural worlds.

One key aspect of this analysis is the recognition that a much larger world of historical events, some very far away indeed, began to have an impact on the Roman empire in the third century AD. During the last two centuries BC, when Rome conquered the Mediterranean from its Punic, Celtic and Greek rulers, Romans knew almost nothing about the interiors of the continents that ringed their inner sea, and had even less to fear from them. But then, as the last republican dynasts and the first emperors consolidated Roman rule in the Near East, the Balkans and parts of central Europe, their military machine, unprecedented in its sheer expansionary violence, played havoc with the traditional societies of the European interior. Still, Rome did not yet notice the waves of social upheavals rippling out beyond its immediate conquests, through mountains, forests and steppes as far as Scandinavia, Russia and the Caucasus, and nor did Rome feel the impact of those upheavals. In that same period, from the last century BC right through the last of the Antonines, the sprawling Parthian empire was both a meaningful barrier to further eastern expansion, and also a safe and stable antagonist, which itself benefited from stable societies on its own Central Asian frontiers. The destruction of the Parthian dynasty of the Arsacids, and the triumph of the Persian Sasanians, altered that cosy status quo for ever.

Now, events in the Roman empire, and the priorities that Roman emperors and their officials needed to set, could be determined at second or third hand by events in the Hindu Kush, in the Taklamakan desert, in the Hexi corridor (in China's modern Gansu province), or even in the Ordos desert south of the Yellow river bend. Put another way, in the third century AD the Roman empire entered Eurasian history for the first time: its connections to India via the Red Sea and Indian ocean, to Central Asia via Iran and the steppe, to China through both of those, and most of all to the Eurasian steppe itself, were all now historically meaningful, if still tenuous and indirect. To understand why this should be so, and to set the scene for episodes of fourth- and fifth-century history that cannot be understood without reference to this much wider world, we need to take a brief excursion into the history of the Parthian Arsacids.

The Parthians have been a somewhat faceless presence in this book until now, but the empire that they ruled in Mesopotamia, Iran and Central Asia had survived in one shape or another for more than 500 years. But just like the Roman empire, they felt the impact of the changing third-century world. It was not just Rome and Parthia. Every corner of Eurasia changed during the third century AD in ways that could have an impact on every other.

But before turning to politics, we need to understand geography and climate. Northern Asia is divided into four broad climatic zones, particularly east of the Ural mountains, which arrest the prevailing western winds and their water-bearing clouds: the tundra north of the Arctic circle; south of that, the taiga or northern forest; then, where the forest thins, it shades into wooded steppe, then grassland steppe too arid for sustained agriculture, and then into actual desert; and south of that runs a whole series of mountain ranges from Anatolia and Armenia, through the Caucasus and the Alborz mountains of northern Iran to the Kopet Dag between Iran and Turkmenistan, and then into the larger complex of the Hindu Kush, Pamirs, Tian Shan, Kun Lun and the Himalayas. The further east one goes, the narrower the band of steppe and the broader the bands of desert, which is only sometimes punctuated with oases fed by streams from surrounding mountain ranges. The third of these bands, the Eurasian steppe both wooded and grassy, was the connective tissue of the continent, a continuous stretch of traversable lands running uninterrupted, apart from the Altai and Sayan mountains of southernmost Siberia, from the Pacific ocean to the basin of the Danube river nearly 5,000 miles away. From the Hexi corridor at the Chinese frontier, then around what is now the autonomous region of Xinjiang and its enormous Taklamakan desert, then around the Tian Shan, Pamirs and the Hindu Kush, the steppe runs almost up against highlands of one sort or another. Then, west of the Hindu Kush, it is separated by the deserts of modern Kazakhstan from the intermittently arable zones of ancient Margiana, Sogdiana and Bactria (parts of modern Turkmenistan, Uzbekistan and Afghanistan along the Murghab, Syr Darya and Amu Darya rivers). Then, south of the Ural mountains and north of the Caspian sea and the Caucasus, the grass and forest steppe narrows, becoming a still thinner strip of grassland to the north of the Black Sea, in present-day Ukraine and Moldova, where the temperate central European forest zone spreads much further south than elsewhere. The steppe then tapers into a small gap between the eastern edge of the Carpathians and the Black Sea coast that funnels travel south towards the Danube basin and the Rumanian Dobrogea; a similar strip of steppeland funnels travel south along the Caspian into the steppes of modern Azerbaijan and Iran. In geological terms, the Hungarian Puszta, the open plains between the Danube bend and the southern Carpathians, constitutes a small extension of the Eurasian steppe, although it is too small to sustain the true nomadism found further east.

Events in this enormous steppe world are hard to follow, sometimes even impossible: it is only when the literate cultures of China, India and the Mediterranean world were affected by steppe polities that we glimpse something of what went on there, with occasional help from the coinage and inscriptions of the Parthian and Iranian empires. But even 6,000 years ago, steppe cultures were mobile enough for aristocratic symbols to be shared by people as far apart as western Mongolia and the Carpathians. The fluid exchange of technologies, portable art forms and symbolic markers of prestige and power among the steppe world's warrior classes crossed linguistic groups, ethnicities and political structures. It is that fluidity which helps explain our difficulty – and that of the ancient sources, Greek, Roman, Iranian and Chinese – in drawing sharp distinctions among the different steppe peoples.

The Romans and Chinese knew next to nothing about one another, despite the role that Persia and Bactria played in the exchange of ideas and luxury items between them, but both were connected in significant ways by the steppe polities of Central Asia. The semi-nomadic and nomadic pastoralists of the steppe depended politically and economically upon their interactions with the settled agricultural and urban worlds of China, Iran and eventually Rome; reciprocally, manpower from the steppe was a resource for the armies of the settled states, even when the steppe warriors also preyed upon them. That symbiosis is found at every connective point between the two worlds. What is more, because the steppe was surprisingly populous and also had virtually no barriers to travel, political disruption in one of its corners could set off ripples of distress a very long distance away. This was not a matter of direct knock-on effects, of huge migrations pushing each other onwards into the frontiers of Roman, Chinese and Iranian civilisations. Very substantial migrations did sometimes take place, but the old-fashioned picture of nomadic waves lapping over one another across the steppe not only understates the diversity of ancient steppe empires, but ignores the fact that devastating invasions do not require the movement of very many individual people at any one time. That is the flaw in the old belief that the Huns who appeared with such sudden violence in the Graeco-Roman world of the 360s were identical with the Xiongnu (sometimes written Hsiung-nu), whose empire was destroyed by China's Han dynasty in the first century BC, launching them on a trek to the west that took centuries.

Linguistically, there is no doubt that Xiongnu, Hun or Hunnoi (Latin and Greek, and their modern derivatives), Chionitae (the Latin and Greek word for Central Asian nomads subject to the Persian empire), Huna (Sanskrit) and Xwn (Sogdian) are different ways of writing the same indigenous word, or that this indigenous word is almost certainly what these people called themselves. But neither that nor the cultural parallels visible in both written and archaeological records mean that a single ethnic or political community travelled together over four centuries and thousands of miles, with its identity – still less its genes – intact. Cultural behaviours, names with a prestigious history, attitudes towards rulership, all these were transferable, and very few biological descendants of the Han's Xiongnu enemies need to have found themselves among the Chionitae and Huns for the name to have stayed the same, and for a half-real and half-imaginary sense of continuity to have existed in the minds of the fourth-century people who bore that name.

We will return to the history and identity of the Huns in the sequel to this volume, but raise their example here because they are paradigmatic and illustrate the degree to which disturbances in the steppe, difficult as it is for us to diagnose their causes, could have an impact from one end of Eurasia to the other – and without our needing to posit mass migration to account for them. That becomes clearest in the third century. The Han dynasty had united northern and southern China from its capitals in Chang'an (modern Xian) and Luoyang for four centuries. When the last Han emperor fell in the 220s, the empire's northern territories broke up into a series of rival dynasties, which in turn created opportunities and incentives for neighbouring steppe polities, who were further encouraged because the warring princes of post-Han China found them useful. The power of these new steppe confederacies disturbed nomadic neighbours further west, which in turn disturbed Sogdia, Bactria and north-eastern India – the eastern edge of the Parthian and then the Sasanian empires. And because Parthian and then Persian rulers rubbed shoulders with the Roman empire in eastern Anatolia, Armenia and Mesopotamia, trouble in the steppe zones north and east of Iran could have a surprisingly direct impact on Rome's own eastern frontier.

It is for that reason that a brief glance at the Parthian empire's history in relation to the Mediterranean world on the one hand, and to Central Asia on the other, will illustrate themes we should keep in mind when thinking about Rome's relations along its eastern and north-eastern frontiers. We need to begin in the 320s BC, when Alexander the Great conquered Achaemenid Persia, pushing deep into Central Asia, reaching the Indus river in Gandhara, modern-day Pakistan, Bactria in modern Afghanistan and Sogdiana and Margiana in modern Turkmenistan and Uzbekistan. Alexander's astonishing empire was entirely the product of his own personality, and it fell to pieces at once when he died in 323. The wars to succeed him lasted decades, during which the vast area from Syria, across Mesopotamia and Persia and into Margiana to the borders of Sogdiana, Bactria and north-eastern India fell under the control of the Seleucid dynasty. The first Seleucus, a very minor figure and a most unlikely winner in the early succession wars, lacked the means to change things in the huge territory on which he had gained a parlous hold: he and his descendants essentially perpetuated the Achaemenid Persian dynasty's administration of their eastern provinces, imposing the occasional Greek or Macedonian overseer. Their gaze was perpetually levelled on the politics of the Hellenistic Mediterranean, the centre of the world from which the dynasty had sprung. As a result, their hold on their eastern provinces was always fragile. Bactria and Gandhara were swiftly lost to Seleucid control, becoming independent kingdoms under local Graeco-Macedonian dynasties that lasted for a couple of hundred years, while the old Achaemenid satrapies (provinces) along the eastern shores of the Caspian gradually devolved to native rulers.

One such satrap, as these provincial governors were known, was a nobleman named Arsaces, who came from either Parthava (in Greek, Parthyene) or Bactria. His family, which we know as the Arsacids, had been Achaemenid courtiers and were also closely tied to the nomadic communities of the intermittently arable lands between the Caspian and Aral seas. Arsaces revolted against the Seleucid kings in the middle of the third century BC and established himself as king in the city of Nisa, in modern Turkmenistan to the north-east of the Alborz mountains. Arsaces's successors brought under their control Hyrcania, Parthyene, Margiana and Sogdiana – the ancient regions in which the Central Asian steppe is penetrated by oases watered by the Atrak, Tejen, Murghab and lower Amu Darya rivers. Under the Arsacids, this stretch of territory due east of the Caspian was more intensively settled and cultivated than at any time before or since. Beyond it, to the north and east, the Amu Darya (Oxus) and Syr Darya (Jaxartes) rivers flowed too swiftly and too violently to be used for irrigation, except right beside the Aral sea itself. This preserved a desert buffer between the steppe and those eastern provinces first brought under

Arsacid control. They became frontier provinces for the dynasty once it set out to displace the Seleucids from central Iran as well.

The Seleucids had maintained the old Achaemenid satrapies which, as they fell to the Arsacids, were simply reconstituted as subordinate kingdoms under cadet branches of the ruling house. With the Iranian heartlands secured, and the formidable ruling families of the Persian nobility conciliated and willing to lend their feudal levies of mounted troops to the Arsacid cause, the dynasty increasingly concentrated on Mesopotamia and the Hellenistic world, from which their Seleucid adversaries had sprung. But at the same time, the Arsacids maintained their interest in, and symbolic association with, Central Asia, especially in the style of military dress cultivated by the royal family and its immediate followers – trousers worn with short, fitted jackets rather than the long tunics and cloaks worn by the majority of their Iranian and Mesopotamian subjects.

This symbolic insistence on a Central Asian or steppe nomadic fashion is particularly striking because the Arsacid kings hung on to it even as they gradually shifted their power base westwards, consciously refashioning themselves as Achaemenid successors. Nisa was left behind to serve as a cult centre and funerary precinct for dead kings, although the discovery there of late second-century Aramaic documents on ostraka (ceramic sherds used for keeping ephemeral records) demonstrates the importance of Mesopotamian-style administration to the emerging Parthian empire. After Nisa, first Saddarvazeh – better known by its Greek name Hekatompylos (today Sahr-e Qumis, near Damghan) – and then Ecbatana (modern Hamadan) were the main Arsacid residences.

In the long reign of Mithridates II (124/3–88/7 BC), Mesopotamia and Armenia fell under Arsacid control and the city of Ctesiphon, beside the Greek *polis* of Seleucia-on-Tigris, became the main seat of Parthian government, with Ecbatana continuing to be used as a winter residence. Mithridates, as his coins show, also began to use the old Achaemenid title 'king of kings', explicitly claiming the legacy of his Iranian predecessors, but using the Hellenistic medium of silver coins. Probably during the same reign, a new Pahlavi script was designed to write the Parthian language of Middle Persian: in the first century AD, this script would go on to replace Greek on Arsacid coinage. For all the symbolic assertion and actual consolidation of royal power, the local aristocracies retained enormous power throughout the Parthian empire. Indeed, some satrapies were effectively autonomous, whether as independent kingdoms in what is now Iraq and eastern Turkey or as tribal chiefdoms in the valleys of present-day western Afghanistan.

The importance of the Arsacid connection to Central Asia grew when, at the end of the second century BC, the last of the Greek kingdoms of Bactria and India were conquered from the north by a people called the Yuëzhi. The Yuëzhi had been long been known to Han China: in the first millennium BC, they had controlled the oases and grasslands of the Hexi corridor, and with it the main trade route for white jade (pure nephrite) mined only in Khotan, in the south-western Taklamakan, and prized in China above all other precious materials. Han Chinese sources, in particular the *Shiji* of Sima Qian, suggest that whereas once the Yuëzhi were the most important militarised pastoralists on the frontiers, around 175 BC they were driven west, beyond the Tarim basin, by more northerly tribes – most probably as a consequence of the growing power of the Xiongnu confederacy in the Altai mountains, Mongolia and the north Asian steppe.

There remains some controversy over the ethnic and linguistic identity of the Yuëzhi – they almost certainly spoke an Indo-Iranian language called Tocharian and are sometimes referred to by that name (the mountainous region in eastern Bactria where some of them settled was later called Tokharistan) – but how they were related to other groups in the steppe is unclear. Regardless, groups of these Yuëzhi established control first at Balkh in Bactria along the upper reaches of the Amu Darya river in the 140s BC, and later at Begram, near Kabul in modern Afghanistan, though there seems never to have been a single unified Yuëzhi state, but rather several at a time. Then, some while after the turn of the millennium, a Yuëzhi chieftain called Qiujiuque in the Chinese sources, and Kujula Kadphises in Indo-Greek, conquered his various rivals. This Qiujiuque had ruled a group of Yuëzhi called the Kushans, and the empire he established is known to us as the Kushan empire – *Koshshanon* on the coins he issued in imitation of the Indo-Greeks – and Kuei-shuang in the Chinese. During the first century AD, the Kushans took over the Arsacids' easternmost satrapies, dominating southern Bactria, the Hindu Kush and the plains of Sind, from a capital at Gandhara (Peshawar) in what is now Pakistan. The Kushans were Buddhists, and much of the most spectacular art – a unique combination of Iranian, south Asian and late Hellenistic styles – that is nowadays being looted from Afghanistan and the tribal territories of Pakistan dates to the Kushan era.

A ruler known as Kanishka, whose dates remain a topic of controversy but who may have been a great-grandson of Kujula Kadphises, pushed Kushan hegemony to its greatest extent, towards the end of the first or the beginning of the second century AD. Despite frequent contestation with various Parthian rulers in the area where Iran, Pakistan and Afghanistan now meet, the existence of the Kushan empire brought a fundamental stability to the Arsacids' eastern frontier. Stretching at its height in the second century AD from the Tarim basin in Xinjiang down through the Pamirs and the Hindu Kush into northern India and the Ganges plain, Kushan hegemony linked the Parthians to China. The eastern parts of the Parthian realm and the Kushan empire were thus a crossroads of the world, where Chinese lacquers circulated alongside Mediterranean artworks and Roman glassware (whose manufacture was as yet unknown in China and India) and where new ideas percolated and fermented among the diversity of different cultures. It is no wonder that it was in the Kushan period that Buddhism came to be known to the Roman and Chinese worlds, that a Parthian nobleman was among the first Buddhist missionaries recorded in China, or that the Persian revelations of the prophet Mani spread into both the Roman empire and China via the oasis of Dunhuang where the desert comes closest to the grasslands of the Hexi corridor.

To give some sense of the cultural diversity these overlapping worlds engendered, one need only look at the spoken and written languages in Central Asia: all were linguistically forms of Middle Iranian, but in Khorezm on the lower Amu Darya, and in Sogdiana between the Amu Darya and the Syr Darya, two very different languages were both written in local scripts derived from ancient Aramaic; in what is now northern Afghanistan along the upper Amu Darya near Balkh and beyond to Begram, Bactrian was written in the Greek alphabet – a legacy of Alexander; across the Pamirs, in the oasis of Khotan on the edge of the Taklamakan desert, the local Iranian language ('Khotanese') was written in the Indian script known as Brahmi, whose life in the region would extend far into the Middle Ages when it was used to write entirely different, Turkic languages. Further east, north of the Kunlun Shan and the Himalayas, Chinese was written in the oases of Turfan, Hami and Dunhuang, while along the edge of the Tian Shan mountains, in the north of the Tarim depression, Indo-European languages were written in the same Brahmi script that served Iranian speakers at the southern edge of the Tarim.

Arsacid rule in Iran and Kushan in Central Asia opened up a hitherto unprecedented amount of trade from one end of the Eurasian continent to the other, both on the silk road routes across Central Asia and by ship across the Indian ocean. On the land route, Roman traders seem to have played no part, but ocean trade was another matter. All along the Malabar coast, for a hundred miles around modern Kerala, Roman coins and their imitations are found in large quantities, from the first to the fifth centuries AD, and Roman traders were prominent enough in the Indian port of Muziris (the exact location of which is unknown) to erect a temple to the imperial cult there. Similarly, between the time of Vespasian right through to the late Roman period, the desert route from Berenike on the Red Sea coast into the Nile valley was carefully guarded by a series of fortlets, wells and wagon routes, all of which were needed to bring imported Indian goods – pepper and pearls in particular – into the Mediterranean. Under Hadrian and Antoninus Pius, there were even small Roman garrisons in the Farasan islands, off the coast of the Arabian peninsula almost at the mouth of the Red Sea – more than 500 miles south of Roman Egypt's borders. Also on the Arabian side of the Red Sea, a Roman temple, its dedications in both Nabatean and Latin, was built under Marcus Aurelius and Lucius Verus at al-Ruwafa, deep in the Hisma sand desert of north-western Arabia, to serve the Thamud Arab allies who helped Rome protect trade through its desert frontiers. Other Eurasian connections were less direct but longer lasting: on a gustatory note, for example, the pomegranate was introduced to China from Iran in the Kushan era, while peaches and apricots came west, eventually reaching the Mediterranean as the oriental delicacies they would remain for many centuries thereafter.

Despite the role of Greeks and Romans in direct contacts with India, for most of the period up to the second century AD, the kaleidoscopic world beyond Arsacid Mesopotamia was barely known to the Romans, appearing chiefly in novels inspired by the romance of Alexander. Indeed, Romans liked to think of Parthia – as they named the conglomeration of Mesopotamian, Iranian and Central Asian territories ruled by the Arsacids – as a weak and divided state. Modern scholars once tended to follow suit, seeing the Parthian period as a sort of hiatus between the glorious peaks of Achaemenid and Sasanian Persia. But the Arsacids ruled for nearly five centuries and what Romans ascribed to weakness is better understood as a lack of Rome's entrenched culture of militarism.

The Arsacids, for their part, had experienced Roman aggression as early as the last century BC. The great republican general Sulla had negotiated with representatives of Mithridates in 96 BC; thirty years later, when the conquering dynast Pompey the Great put an end to the rump Seleucid kingdom in Syria, he defied the warnings of Phraates III to respect the river Euphrates as the boundary between them. Then, in 54 BC, Pompey's rival Crassus, seeking military glory to match that of Pompey and Julius Caesar, launched an attack on Parthia that saw the annihilation of his army at Carrhae in Mesopotamia, his legionary standards falling into Parthian hands. Though the emperor Augustus secured the return of the standards many decades later in negotiations with Phraates IV (r. 38–3/2 BC), his arrangement created the complicated imperial fixation on its Parthian neighbour that we considered in chapter 1. At one level, Romans were willing to see in Parthia a state of greater ideological importance and scale than any other that they knew, while on another they thought of their Parthian foes as weak and degenerate, the perfect representation of the decadent easterner (an idea that had roots reaching all the way back to the fifth century BC and Greek stereotyping of the Achaemenids and their subjects).

That said, throughout the first century AD, Roman emperors behaved with a certain diffidence in their eastern policy and, by the latter part of Nero's reign, there was even a de facto understanding about the difficult case that was Armenia: a favoured Arsacid would accede to the Armenian throne, but he would do so only with the consent of, and 'designation' by, the Roman emperor. Trajan's glorious but ultimately pointless conquest of Mesopotamia down to the Arabian Gulf was no more than a temporary shift in the balance of power. The second-century wars were different. The gradual Roman fortification of a habitable zone between the upper Euphrates and the Tigris meant that a route straight downriver to Ctesiphon and Seleucia-on-Tigris was always available to Roman armies, and it was this strategic disadvantage that generations of Persian rulers would, from the middle of the third century, attempt to nullify.

A far more visible way in which those Persian rulers continued the Parthian – and indeed Achaemenid – legacy was in religion. The Arsacids had long previously adopted the Zoroastrianism practised at the Achaemenid royal court. The teachings of Zarathustra, known as Zoroaster to the Greeks and Romans, date back to before the first millennium BC, and are transmitted in an epic work known as the *Avesta*, which consists of a small number of hymns (*Gathas*) written by Zarathustra himself, and the much larger Younger Avesta, composed by his followers but accepted as having been inspired by his teachings. Zarathustra brought new ideas to very ancient Iranian traditions that also have parallels in the Indian Rigveda. For Zarathustra, there was one supreme divinity, Ahura Mazda (or Ohrmazd, in the later Persian), who had created the universe and all that was good in it, including many subordinate divinities representing various aspects of earthly good. But in contrast to all that was ordered and good in the world, there existed also 'nothingness' or anti-creation, which all living beings must fight against: this had been created by Anra Mainiyu (later, Ahriman), who dwelled in darkness, and the struggle between Ohrmazd and Ahriman was fought out in the human world. The dualism of this Mazdean worldview coloured the actions of Iranian rulers from the Achaemenid era down to the Islamic conquest of Persia at the end of late antiquity. These Avestan teachings were transmitted orally or in written fragments for a very long time, before finally being committed to textual form in the fifth century AD. The original *Gathas*, as they are called, are in such an archaic language that they were probably only partly comprehensible by the Achaemenid period, and it is the Younger Avesta and another text, the *Phalavi Zand*, that lay out clear doctrines only implied in the *Gathas*. Temple worship was introduced into Iran from Mesopotamia under the Achaemenids, and it was the temple priesthood, tending eternal flames in honour of Ohrmazd, who seem to have transmitted a relatively stable corpus of Avestan texts and commentaries through the Seleucid and Arsacid periods. As the Arsacids expanded their control, they too made use of the temple priesthood in administration and to organise the fiscal life of the countryside. While adopting many elements of Greek religion, they also increasingly sponsored the religious culture of the Mazdean priesthood.

Then, in the first century AD, we start to notice changes. Arsacid coinage ceases to use Greek, the occasional Mazdean symbolism appears on it, as it had long continued to do in the sub-kingdom of Persis, and the new Parthian script starts to provide the coin legends. Literary sources (of later date, but seemingly valid for this period) suggest that at this point, too, native Iranian names began to reappear in place of their Greek equivalents: the city that is now Mary in Turkmenistan starts to again be known as Merv rather than by its Greek name of Antiochia Margiane. The Sasanian dynasty that succeeded the Arsacids was deeply committed to portraying its predecessors as negligent guardians of Zoroastrian purity, failures in their duty to fight against the evil in the world. But, despite that, it seems clear that the later Arsacids both sponsored and responded to an increasing Iranisation of culture throughout their empire. That said, however, the Arsacids ruled a far more culturally and religiously diverse empire than the one their heirs strove to create.

Because of the looseness of Parthian rule, dynasties tended to form at regional courts and satrapies often became hereditary as well, not only on the frontiers, and sometimes with surprising regional autonomy. Thus in the province known in Greek as Persis or in Persian as Fars (now the modern Iranian provinces of Fars and Bushehr), which had been the old centre of Achaemenid dominance half a millennium earlier, the provincial dynasty had been issuing coins for local use since the second century BC – for a time using Zoroastrian iconography not yet taken up by the Arsacids. Not long thereafter, they began calling themselves 'shah', or king, writing that Middle Persian word in the Aramaic script of Mesopotamia. How these early kings of Fars were related to the other Iranian dynasties of the region is unclear but, by the start of the third century, the most important regional family was that of the Sasanians, which was closely associated with the Zoroastrian temple of Anahita in Istakhr. Istakhr was very near to ancient Persepolis, once the Achaemenid capital, and thus close to many of the Zoroastrian holy sites constructed there almost a millennium before. Anahita, whose temple the dynasty tended, was a goddess in the Zoroastrian pantheon: though created like all the other (good) deities by Ohrmazd, she was one of the three foremost subordinate deities. Devotion to – and codification of – Zoroastrian belief would become a central part of Sasanian ruling ideology in a way that even the most zealous of the Arsacid rulers could not have imagined.

The origins of the Sasanian family itself are deeply obscure, though the stone-carved imagery from their victory monuments clearly shows them linking their dynastic victories to a Mazdean mythology of good triumphing over evil, their royal investiture in the trust of Ahura Mazda himself. The literary evidence, on the other hand, is disappointingly hard to decode. There are colourful, contradictory and highly fictionalised accounts in the scanty Greek sources, most of them very late: Agathias in the sixth century and George Syncellus in the ninth give us our most complete accounts, but there is no scholarly consensus about where they found their stories. The Arabic evidence is even later, though it may have borrowed from authentic Sasanian sources, but the Syriac evidence, which seems highly and plausibly detailed, has been revealed as a genealogical farrago. None of that should surprise us: successful rulers of obscure parentage must necessarily mystify their origins.

What seems beyond dispute is that a man of Fars province named Papak demanded from the Arsacid king some sort of rulership for his son, Shapur. This Shapur died before anything could come of the dispute, and another of Papak's sons, Ardashir, ended up spearheading a rebellion against Arsacid rule that had, by the later 220s, penetrated beyond Fars into Elam on the eastern coast of the Persian Gulf, and thence to Mesopotamia, the province known as Assuristan in Parthian and Persian. The 'Sasan' who to this day gives his name to the dynasty may well be a fictional ancestor, or perhaps a minor spirit in the Zoroastrian pantheon claimed as a divine progenitor of the family. The sources are too obscure to let us decide. But Ardashir son of Papak, and then his son Shapur (Shapur I, in our dynastic reckoning), were the kings who set the family on the path that led to the overthrow of the Arsacids.

Despite the legends canvassed above, it is not really clear what sparked the outright rebellion of the Sasanian family against Arsacid rule, but there had been serious unrest in the empire ever since civil conflict broke out in the year 208 or so. The division of the Arsacid dominion between Artabanus V and his brother Vologaeses III, one based in Ctesiphon, the other based in the eastern part of the empire, weakened their capacity to work in concert. Thereafter, the distraction of Artabanus in his fight against Caracalla and Macrinus, considered in chapter 7, only exacerbated the willingness of the Persians to defy their putative overlords in Ctesiphon. Early Sasanian campaigns were devastatingly effective, their shah leading a highly mobile army based not on the combination of phalanx and horse archers favoured by the Arsacids, but instead on a hard core of heavily armoured lancers drawn from the Iranian and Parthian nobilities. It was probably in the course of the campaigns that destroyed Arsacid power that Ardashir attacked the caravan city of Hatra, a crucial buffer between east and west in central Mesopotamia, and so powerful that it had twice held out against the full force of the Roman imperial armies without falling. Sometime around 226/227 the Hatrans defeated Ardashir's army, firmly resisting his attempts to do away with the Arsacid tradition of giving them their autonomy under the local client king. This experience drove the Hatrans into a Roman alliance, despite a long enmity, and, for twenty years in the middle of the third century, the city became a key part of Rome's eastern defences. The fortifications of Hatra, until their recent destruction by the Islamist militants of Daesh (or ISIS, ISIL), long bore witness to the engineering expertise of Roman legionaries. Yet that Roman connection would ultimately prove fatal to the caravan city.

In the north, Armenia seems to have fought off Ardashir's attacks, even if the sources on this period of Armenian history are too confused for us to be sure quite what happened. But on his other western fronts, Ardashir was as successful as he had been in the eastern satrapies. In the Arab city of Hira, on the western edge of the Syrian desert, he made tributaries of the ruling family of the Lakhmids and of their chieftain Hamr ibn Hadi. As dependants of the Sasanians, these Lakhmids would extend their hegemony deep into the Arabian peninsula. Driving his forces into the peninsula Hamr took Spasinou Charax, the main ancient port on the Satt al-Arab, the western tongue of the Persian Gulf. The control of Spasinou Charax brought control of a major trade route in Arabian spices and incense and Far Eastern luxury goods into the hands of an imperial power rather than the caravan cities of the Syrian desert, and later Sasanian rulers placed much greater emphasis on controlling trade to and from the Far East. That was to the particular detriment of Palmyra, the oasis city that had long acted as an intermediary between the Roman and Parthian empires. Now, like Hatra, Palmyra bound itself firmly to Rome.

Much of the middle of Ardashir's reign was spent on eastern campaigns, about which we know little or nothing, though evidence from the reign of his son and successor suggests that the great Parthian feudal clans – the Varaz, Suren, Mihren and Karen – went over to him, and that he coopted or subjugated Khorasan, Merv, Kerman and Seistan. He almost certainly campaigned still further away, in the Kushanshahr and in Bactria, because his campaigns made enough of an impression to create a new calendrical era: documents in Bactrian were dated according to an era of Ardashir until the arrival of the Muslim Abbasids in the ninth century. In whatever sequence these campaigns took place – and it is likely that the flood of new Sasanian coin types currently entering the market from clandestine digs in modern Pakistan and Afghanistan will eventually clarify the chronology – it seems certain that by the later 230s, most of the eastern territories that had been actually or nominally subject to the later Arsacids were now under Sasanian control. The Sasanian determination to expand the Arsacid realm north and eastwards, as far as the Indus and into the Central Asian desert and steppe, would mean that the Persian shahs were continually torn between fighting nomads and pastoralists on their north-eastern frontiers and the Roman enemy to the west. Even though Rome would increasingly face its own threats from the steppe, Roman imperial psychology remained fixated primarily on the threat of Persia itself.

In some ways, that fixation made more sense after the Sasanian overthrow of the Arsacids. More than the Parthian dynasty ever had, the Sasanians would contest the Roman right to rule the lands between Mesopotamia and the Mediterranean. There is some ambiguous evidence that when Severus Alexander wrote to Ardashir to congratulate him on his accession, and to signal the desire to maintain the peace he had enjoyed with the Arsacids, the new shah instead demanded Roman withdrawal from Syria and Asia Minor. The story may well be Roman propaganda, which always tended to overstate eastern interest in Rome's affairs. Even if true, there remains a question of Ardashir's motives. Our two contemporary Greek sources attribute to him the desire to take back from the Romans all the lands that had been held by the Achaemenid Darius the Great, while the ninth-century Arab historian al-Tabari, whose work preserves authentically old traditions, states that Ardashir's revolt against Artabanus stemmed from a desire to avenge the blood of Darius III, whose empire Alexander the Great had destroyed. The evidence, in other words, is all of a piece, but there is no way of knowing if it is based on actual Sasanian traditions, let alone contemporary ambition.

On balance, a programmatic restoration of Achaemenid glory is probably a Roman invention, based on the centrality of Alexander the Great to Graeco-Roman cultural memory. It is true that Ardashir's son Shapur appropriated to the Sasanian royal dynasty the Achaemenid necropolis at Naqsh-e Rustam near Persepolis, but that was a monument for local consumption by the Iranian nobility of Fars, and not a statement of ambition against the Roman east. Indeed, it is only in the fourth century that we find a Persian shah explicitly making the claim of kinship with the Achaemenids, and that might well have been the result of the Sasanian court having absorbed and adapted a hundred years' worth of projected Graeco-Roman ideologies. That said, the absence of ideological motive did not make the Persian military onslaught any less of a threat to the Roman east. Ardashir's initial advances into Roman territory had, it is true, suffered setbacks and Severus Alexander had claimed a Persian victory just before he was killed by his mutinous army in Germania.

But Rome's eastern frontier remained unstable during the last years of Ardashir, and the would-be successors of Severus Alexander had their own rivalries to deal with. By the time Ardashir was entering old age, most of the Iranian nobility had concluded that his overthrow of the Arsacids would be permanent. The only question was which of his several sons would succeed him. The outcome was decided by the successful campaigning of one of them, Shapur I, who consolidated his own authority against his fraternal rivals after victories on the Mesopotamian frontier with Rome: some time between April and September 240, a Persian army succeeded in taking Hatra in northern Mesopotamia, which had earlier survived the initial invasions of Ardashir. This Sasanian victory seriously compromised the line of fortified cities in Roman Mesopotamia, and both Nisibis and Carrhae had fallen to Shapur and Ardashir before the latter's death in 242. For Hatra, the consequences were worse: the caravan city's two-decade-long alliance with the Roman emperors doomed it to decay under Persian hegemony, and it was deserted a hundred years later. The fall of Hatra prompted the equestrian junta that ran the government of young Gordian III to organise a massive invasion of Persia, which they began planning as early as 238.

We will return to that campaign in chapter 9, but it will first be useful to consider another big change in Eurasian societies that would have a profound effect on later Roman history. Europe is a relatively small corner of the Eurasian landmass, and changes there took place over a much smaller area than in the deserts and steppes of Central Asia. But in the third century, the barbarians of central Europe began to develop more complex political structures in response to the example and the violence of Roman imperialism. The mutiny that ended in the death of Severus Alexander and his mother took place in Germania Superior, the Roman province centred on Moguntiacum (Mainz), opposite a tract of territory that was in the process of becoming Alamannia. Between the 90s and the 160s, the Roman frontier had been extended further eastwards, to provide a shortened route between Moguntiacum and Augusta Vindelicum (Augsburg) in Raetia.

This Roman territory within the Rhine–Danube salient became known as the Agri Decumates, and was intensively settled in a relatively short amount of time. Imperial expansion, and the economic opportunities it opened up, caused major changes among the tribal populations who lived beyond the new frontier. The first reference to a barbarian group known as the Alamanni comes in Greek accounts of the campaigns of Caracalla in 213. Thereafter, sometimes in concert with a people called the Iuthungi, the Alamanni come to dominate the evidence for Roman military activity on the upper Rhine and upper Danube, and by the 280s the lands opposite Germania Superior and Raetia had been known as Alamannia for quite some time. It used to be thought that the sudden appearance of Alamanni in the early third-century sources represented a clear-cut case of invasion: a new barbarian tribe arriving on the edge of the empire and threatening the frontiers. A more nuanced understanding of the evidence – derived particularly from the archaeological record – now suggests that the 'arrival' of the Alamanni was nothing of the sort. The Alamanni had always been there, they simply had not been called Alamanni or thought of themselves as such. There had instead been a scatter of disunited tribal groupings along the lines sketched by Tacitus in his early second-century treatise, *Germania*. But then, the Roman provinces of Germania Superior and Raetia, increasingly urbanised, populous and wealthy on both sides of the Rhine and Danube, provided a focus and a contrast against which the diverse tribes could define themselves.

At the same time, Romans – administrators and authors both – borrowed names of people on their frontiers and gave them a geographical focus that they did not necessarily have before. This is what happened in Alamannia and, at nearly the same time, in Francia to its north and west: the barbarians opposite Germania Inferior got classified as Franci and those opposite Superior as Alamanni, and over a generation or two people beyond the frontier came to see themselves as being more alike than they once had. That was partly a response to the Romans with whom they traded and fought, and whose armies periodically devastated their lands when an emperor needed a quick victory, and partly because they were becoming more alike in their material culture and probably in their political and linguistic cultures too.

Archaeology suggests a greater militarisation all across central Europe in this period as well, and perhaps an uptick in warfare. The readier availability of Roman technologies even at very great distances from the frontier, particularly high-quality swords, may have something to do with that. Chieftains leading bands of 400–600 warriors were increasingly able to raid over considerable distances, many hundreds of miles, without necessarily intending to conquer or settle territory. Some scholars have suggested that the arrival and settlement of small war bands from the Elbe region provided the leadership that created a unified sense of being Alamanni among the different frontier barbarians. That is certainly possible, though widely disputed. However, what is absolutely certain is the growing social stratification of the region in the third century, with increasing numbers of high-status burials and lavish grave goods: the traces left by a new ruling elite whose human and monetary capital came in part from their relationship with the empire. In the course of the third century, especially as the imperial government faced one political crisis after another, these chieftains or frontier kings gained increasing power over their agricultural populations, and in turn became more valuable as clients of the empire – and more dangerous as potential enemies. We shall see a great deal more of the Alamanni and the Franci in the coming chapters, but the point here is the interconnectedness of the Roman empire to a much larger world, from one end of Eurasia to another, on every one of its many frontiers. That interconnectedness will emerge all the more clearly as the third century progresses.

9

FROM GORDIAN III TO VALERIAN

✦

The bloodletting of summer 238 ended, in Italy at least, in a relatively stable peace. The 12-year-old emperor Gordian III, acclaimed caesar in February, and then augustus in May or June, was watched over by a cabal of mainly equestrian officials who determined imperial policy. These men were led by C. Furius Sabinius Timesitheus, the praetorian prefect, whose power was such that he married his daughter Tranquillina to the emperor himself in May 241, as soon as she was old enough. But whatever stability had accompanied the end of the civil war proved illusory. The proconsul of Africa, M. Asinius Sabinianus, who had replaced old Gordian, revolted soon after the new regime had settled. He was an old Severan, having been consul in 225, and it may be that he objected to the sidelining of the consular elites after the failure of Pupienus and Balbinus's regime. Sabinianus's putsch failed, put down by the procurator of Mauretania, Faltonius Restitutianus. He was replaced as proconsul by L. Caesonius Lucillus Macer Rufinianus, who had been one of the *vigintiviri* alongside Balbinus and Pupienus, which suggests that we must not read events in terms of senatorial and equestrian factions at court, but instead as rival factions within equestrian and senatorial *ordines*.

Nevertheless, with Timesitheus at the centre of things, the government continued to have the professional, systematising outlook of the bureaucratic classes – among the equestrians known to have prospered greatly during the reign we find M. Gnaius Licinius Rufinus, as *a libellis*; C. Attius Alcimus Felicianus, whose career had begun under Elagabalus and whose financial posts clearly made him something of an expert in the field; Gnaeus Domitius Philippus, who was prefect of the *vigiles* at the start of the reign; Faltonius Restitutianus, who put down the revolt of Sabinianus in Africa; and two brothers from Arabia, Julius Priscus and Julius Philippus, the latter becoming emperor within a few years: by the early 240s, the world in which the accession of Macrinus had been resisted because he was not a senator no longer existed.

In 238, the regime's first order of business was Persia. As we saw in chapter 8, the Sasanian kings who replaced the Arsacids in Persia and Mesopotamia were much more expansionary than their predecessors had been, bringing to heel the semi-independent satraps of Mesopotamia and the Caucasus, in part provoked by the survival of the Arsacids in Armenia, where kings like Tiridates II (r. 217–52) attempted to rally other frontier dynasts as far away as India against Ardashir. By the time the regime of the young Gordian had settled, much of Roman Mesopotamia was exposed to Persian invasion, Nisibis, Carrhae and Hatra had all fallen, and other fortress cities like Singara could not be re-enforced. The prestige of the new regime at Rome would be much enhanced if it could secure the eastern frontiers in a way that Maximinus had failed entirely to do.

Leaving behind Alcimus Felicianus to run Rome, and having appointed Julius Priscus as his fellow praetorian prefect, Timesitheus and the young emperor marched east in 242, evidently having found it difficult to muster a campaign army. They signalled the gravity of their intentions by opening the doors of the temple of Janus in Rome itself, probably the last time in history that this archaic ritual declaration of war was performed. They then progressed overland through Moesia and Thrace, their crossing from Europe to Asia, probably early in the summer of 242, being commemorated with an issue of gold medallions with the legend *traiectus*, 'crossed over', to important courtiers. Antioch in Syria served, as it usually did, as the staging point for the campaign against Persia, but delays were endemic. The year 243 was spent in Syria, but not until the winter of 243–4 do we find the army fighting along the Euphrates. It may be that the death of Timesitheus sometime in 243 had contributed to the delay. His successor as prefect was Julius Philippus, brother of the other prefect Julius Priscus. The joint prefecture of two brothers was unheard of, but in the circumstances, the two men had become indispensable: they came from Shaba

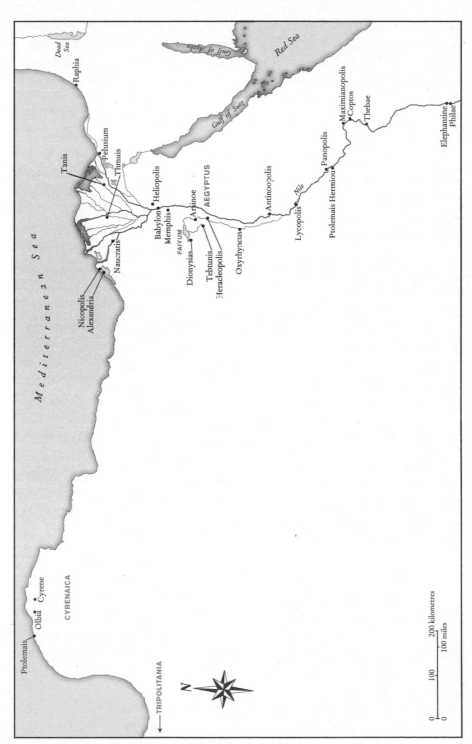

Egypt and Cyrene

in Arabia, had risen through the equestrian grades (Priscus, at least, had once been a fiscal procurator), and their local connections made them a good conduit to the region's elites whose cooperation was necessary if the campaign was to go smoothly and the army was to be properly supplied.

At first, the fighting went the Romans' way and a victory over Persian forces is recorded in the sources, perhaps at Resaina in Osrhoene, and possibly in battle against the Persian shah himself. This was now Shapur I, ruling alone after the death of Ardashir in 242, though he had been effectively in charge since 240, when he was crowned co-ruler with his father. Shapur, even more than Ardashir, was the true architect of Sasanian power. Though he had not yet articulated an ambition to recreate the Persian empire of the Achaemenids, there is no question that he embraced an Achaemenid more than a Parthian model of display. What is more, he took to new levels his father's militance, campaigning on every frontier of his empire and imposing Sasanian governors, often members of his own house.

Much of what we know about Shapur's early reign comes from the monumental inscription he put up to commemorate his victories at Naqsh-e Rustam. The site is significant, for it lies a few miles outside the ancient Achaemenid city of Persepolis and houses the rock-cut tombs of several Achaemenid kings, including Darius the Great and probably Xerxes I. By appropriating for his own display the necropolis of the last conquering dynasty to come from Fars, Shapur was perhaps implying a continuity with them, and certainly displaying himself firmly in a Persian rather than a Mesopotamian or Parthian light.

Of the two earliest Sasanian reliefs at Naqsh-e Rustam, one shows Shapur on horseback, with a Roman emperor kneeling in supplication before him. The other shows Shapur's father Ardashir being invested with his crown by the supreme Zoroastrian divinity Ohrmazd. A more elaborate version of the Shapur monument appears at Bishapur, a town that served as a staging post between the Sasanian dynastic centre at Istakhr and the old Parthian capital at Ctesiphon in Mesopotamia. Back at Naqsh-e Rustam, a square tower known as the Ka'ba-i Zardusht (or the Kaaba of Zoroaster) stood opposite the rock-cut tombs of the Achaemenids, and had served as a Zoroastrian fire sanctuary since the reign of the Achaemenid Darius. On it, Shapur's son Ohrmazd I had inscribed a text in three languages – Parthian, Middle Persian and Greek – that his father had composed in the last years of his long reign, outlining an official version of his glorious deeds and his piety. The inscription gives Shapur's title as His Mazdayasnian Majesty Shapur, King of Kings of Iran and not-Iran (or of the Aryans and the non-Aryans) Whose Seed is from the Gods. Shapur's father Ardashir had already revived the Achaemenid title of shahanshah ('king of kings') and asserted a personal connection to Ohrmazd, but Shapur now added an explicit claim to universal rulership that matched that of the Roman emperors. The rest of the text gives us the Persian account of Shapur's struggles with his neighbours and is often strikingly different from what we find in the Greek and Latin sources, sometimes completely contradicting them. It also, to some extent, confirms the strong focus of Shapur on his conflicts with the Romans, rather than with other parts of his realm, for the battles that he commemorates on his inscription are all those that he fought against the Romans, rather than on his eastern and north-eastern frontiers.

And yet we also know that Shapur inherited the same problems his Arsacid predecessors had faced on the eastern frontier. Early in his reign, he may have subjugated Khwarezm, the northernmost of the Central Asian oases, at the delta of the Amu Darya beside what was then still the Aral sea, though it never became a province of the empire. It was also Shapur, though when in his reign we do not know, who reduced the Kushanshahr to a client state of his dynasty, marked by a series of coinages that we know as Kushano-Sasanian. Here, as elsewhere, we continue to learn a great deal that is new in Sasanian history from the numismatic evidence – much of it, sadly, coming to light from the clandestine excavation and looting made possible by conflict in present-day Afghanistan and Pakistan. Most significantly, the heavy concentration of Sasanian minting in places like Merv and elsewhere in the east, some of it by die-workers clearly trained in the metropolitan mint at Ctesiphon, demonstrates how much military force was needed to control the east under Shapur and how many campaigns he must have fought there.

In his inscription, he lays claim to Sind and 'the Kushanshahr up to Peshawar and up to Kashgar, Sogdiana and the mountains of Tashkent', but he does not tell us about the fighting that was clearly necessary to control that region. Instead, he focuses on his Roman victories – reciprocating the kind of focus that Roman emperors had for their eastern neighbours. This Sasanian focus on Rome marks a change from the Arsacids' more balanced division of attention between their eastern and western frontiers, although Shapur did continue the Arsacid policy of farming out control of the Syrian and northern Arabian deserts to clients, most particularly the Lakhmid king of Hira, Imru'ulqais, who had succeeded his father some years before and went on to serve not just Shapur but also his successors Ohrmazd I and Varahran I as satrap of Iraq and the Hijaz.

For historians of the Roman empire, this Sasanian interest in Rome offers a valuable counterpoint to the sparse imperial evidence. On the Naqsh-e Rustam monument, Shapur claims to have defeated and killed the emperor Gordian at Misiche (or, in Persian, Mishik) on the middle Euphrates. Of the three Roman emperors depicted on the victory monument, one lies dead on the ground, one is supplicant and the third has been taken captive – Gordian, Philip and Valerian, respectively. Shapur also renamed Misiche Peroz-Shapur, or 'victorious is Shapur'. By contrast with Shapur's explicit claims, the Roman sources are ambiguous. None straightforwardly attests Gordian's death in battle. Indeed, the best Roman evidence suggests that Gordian died further north than Misiche, at Zaitha, sometime between mid January and mid March 244. He was certainly buried there, at least temporarily, in a massive tumulus that could still be seen more than a hundred years later, when another Roman army was invading the region.

What actually happened will never be known, but Gordian was a teenager and had little military experience. Few can have expected great things of him on the battlefield. It may be that a mid-winter defeat by Shapur on the edge of Persian territory, one in which the emperor himself was perhaps badly wounded, prompted a disgruntled soldiery to assassinate him at Zaitha. An opaque passage in the life of the philosopher Plotinus, who had been accompanying the imperial expedition on a sort of research trip for esoteric knowledge, suggests that there was rioting in the Roman camp when Gordian was killed. As one would expect, many sources – from the near-contemporary apocalyptic text known as the *Thirteenth Sybilline Oracle* to the fourth-century Latin tradition of abbreviated histories – blame the man who profited from Gordian's death for causing it, Julius Philippus, the praetorian prefect who had succeeded Timesitheus. But Philippus (or Philip the Arab, as he is conventionally known) was not with the army at the time of Gordian's death, though his brother Priscus may have been. That fact could explain why the older and presumably predominant brother did not himself take the throne – throughout late Roman history, councils of army officers sometimes chose an imperial candidate who could achieve consensus precisely because he was not present on the spot to take part in debate about the succession.

Regardless of how Gordian died, it took a lot of negotiation for the army to extricate itself from disputed territory, and the new emperor had to act personally as a supplicant in the peace talks. The settlement, which was all Philip could have hoped for in the circumstances, was the root of endless further conflict between Persian and Roman monarchs. According to the Roman sources, Philip 'betrayed' Armenia to the Persians, which must mean that he acknowledged Shapur's right to determine that kingdom's succession, as the Arsacids had done for centuries. Shapur, in his victory inscription from Naqsh-e Rustam, claims both that Philip became his tributary and that he was made to pay an indemnity of half a million gold aurei, a seemingly impossible sum, but at the very least an approximation of the scale: to get his army out of Persia safely, Philip mortgaged his throne. In all likelihood, along with acknowledging Sasanian hegemony in Armenian affairs, he also transferred the traditional supplementary payments for guarding the Caucasian passes against nomadic incursions from the Armenians to the Persians themselves, hence the shahanshah's willingness to claim that Philip was offering him tribute – and hence, too, the reason the Roman sources are silent on such details.

Philip, for his part, put as happy a face on things as he plausibly could. Back in Antioch, he struck antoniniani with the legend *pax fundata cum Persis* ('peace made with Persia'), took for himself the titles Parthicus and Persicus Maximus, and began to establish the dynastic image of his family. His wife, Marcia Otacilia Severa, was made augusta and named *mater castrorum*, a direct assertion of the regime's concern for its soldiers. Then, on two key frontiers, Philip installed relatives as his representatives: his brother Julius Priscus in Syria and their brother-in-law Severianus (Otacilia Severa's brother) on the Danube in Moesia. He himself returned to Rome as quickly as possible, taking the sea route up the coast of Asia Minor, reaching the imperial capital early in the summer of 244. Severianus's command shows the growing importance, in these years, of the Danubian armies by contrast to those of the Rhine frontier; it may also be an early sign of the increasingly assertive Roman self-consciousness in a region that was one of the last Latin-speaking parts of the empire to gain widespread access to the Roman citizenship – certainly men from the Danube would come to dominate politics in the latter half of the century.

The Syrian command of Julius Priscus, meanwhile, demonstrates Philip's determination to keep an eye on Persian developments and to maintain the family's close connections to their native east. The reconstruction of the dynastic home town of Shahba under the new name of Philippopolis was a truly massive endeavour, one financed in part by stricter financial exactions under the supervision of Priscus. Priscus's role is also significant: he was not merely the governor of Syria but also *corrector*, a nebulous word that signalled his precedence over other officials. He possessed, in other words, supra-regional jurisdiction over the other governors of the east, an important precedent for later third-century experiments in government. Priscus was, to all practical purposes, Philip's co-ruler in the east. Severianus probably disposed of a similar authority in the Balkans, though his title is not explicitly attested in the way that Priscus's is.

At the same time that Philip was securing his familial power in this way, he was also ensuring that he had no challenges to his own legitimacy – he had not forgotten how popular the young Gordian had been with the people of Rome, and so he put about word that Gordian had died of an illness and brought his body back to Rome, burying it with honours. He also asked the senate to approve the dead boy's consecration as Divus Gordianus, which it did, and though Tranquillina disappears from the historical record, she is likely to have enjoyed an honourable retirement, since she and Gordian had lacked any worrisome heirs. Philip's own son, born around 237/238 and thus five years old, was now made caesar. Because of the poor documentation for this period, we do not know how long this relative tranquillity lasted, or how popular Philip was in Rome itself. But trouble at the frontiers occupied the middle of his reign.

Just as the earlier 200s had seen upheavals among the barbarian polities of the upper Rhine and Danube, so the middle years of the century brought major cultural and political change beyond the lower Danube and the northern Black Sea coast. Scholars have traditionally associated these changes with the arrival in the region of Goths migrating from their former homes in what is now Poland. This narrative is shaped around what we find in the *Getica* of Jordanes, a tale of ethnic origins composed hundreds of years later, in sixth-century Constantinople, by a Latin-speaking Roman of Gothic descent. Archaeological evidence has been consistently distorted to fit a legendary saga of mass migration and Scandinavian origins. But this simplistic model is not well supported by the evidence.

It is true that a new and relatively homogeneous archaeological culture developed between the Carpathians and the Donets river in the second half of the third century, and that by the 320s this region was ruled by a number of tribal polities whose main language was Gothic and whose military elites are lumped together as 'Goths' in the Roman sources. This archaeological culture, which we call Sântana-de-Mures/Černjachov, is named for two cemeteries, one in modern Rumania, one in modern Ukraine, that share characteristic types of grave goods and burial ritual. New forms of settlement appear in this region during the second half of the third century as well, with farming villages clustered along the arable river valleys, large compounds for the elites dominating the landscape, a predilection for high-value Roman imports and a symbiotic relationship with nomadic pastoralists where agricultural lands bordered the grassy steppe. The decorative and dress styles revealed in the grave goods share some affinities with those found a century or so earlier in northern Poland, but they also show elements of central European origin, and quite a lot of influence from the nomadic art of the Eurasian steppe.

Rather than shoehorning this evidence into a narrative of mass migration from the north in order to fit our late literary evidence, responsible scholars recognise a local development, involving migration from both the steppes and parts of northern Europe, reshaping the more fragmented and less hierarchical agricultural societies that had preceded them. The formation of new, and often socially more complex, societies on the fringes of empires is well known from comparative evidence, both from antiquity – such as the Alamanni, discussed in chapter 8 – and from such modern examples as Tsarist Russia in its expansionist phase or the frontiers of the British Raj. The existence of the imperial power gave tribal military leaders a powerful structure against which to fight, but also something to learn from, and a supply of resources – either in loot, subsidy or trade – which they could distribute to increase their own power. Given time, and the consolidation of new tribal polities, a new and more or less uniform material culture developed out of numerous different antecedents, and a common language among the elite population in the form of Gothic.

Somewhat ironically, one of the first pieces of evidence we have for Goths and their relationship with the Roman empire is Shapur's monumental inscription at Naqsh-e Rustam, which lists Goths among the nations he defeated in Rome's armies and thus demonstrates that by the middle of the century the emperors were recruiting men from beyond the Danube into units that they could designate as Gothic. That said, the consolidation of the lower Danube and Black Sea regions under Gothic hegemony is really only apparent in the fourth century, when it was already complete. During the third century, all we see are its by-products – invasions from beyond the Danube and the Black Sea that were a constant problem for third-century emperors, whether led by assertive new rulers seeking plunder or their defeated opponents looking for greener pastures. In what follows, we will refer to the various third-century invaders from this region not as Goths but as 'Scythians', the generic word used in our Greek sources, rather than making presumptions about how they identified themselves or retrojecting Gothic hegemony into a period when it cannot be documented. These Danubian 'Scythians' joined the Persians and Alamanni as the most formidable of Rome's neighbours from Philip's reign onwards.

By mid 245, Philip had marched with an army to Dacia, and he is known to have been at Aquae in November of that year. Trajan's Dacian provinces had always been an experiment and Roman civic life never put down roots in Dacia, as it had begun to do south of the Danube from the time of Marcus Aurelius onwards. Pannonia and Moesia, and the Balkans more generally, began to look more and more like the rest of the Latin provinces as the later second century turned into the third. Civilian population followed in the wake of the huge military investment of the Marcomannic wars and three generations later, at mid third century, civilian life flourished both in the great military cities that led from the Alps to Asia and in rich villas where the topography was suitable to agriculture. Dacia, by contrast, had been built up hastily after Trajan's defeat of the last Dacian king Decebalus, with few monumental cities and a network of roads and way stations that primarily served a military presence needed to protect the mineral resources of the province.

Even though the Sarmatians and Carpi, whose territories neighboured the province to the west and east respectively, were relatively easy to control compared to the more powerful Alamanni, it does not seem that Roman-style living penetrated very deeply into the cultural fabric of the Dacian provinces, or that a civilian infrastructure developed save to cater for the direct needs of the military and the mines. Things might, of course, have changed – Pannonia and Moesia did not really start to develop into fully Romanised provinces until the time of Marcus, a hundred years or more after their conquest – but the upheaval to the east of Dacia, and in particular its challenge to the local hegemony of the Carpi, meant that the very real revenues from the Dacian mines can hardly have been worth the expense of keeping the region garrisoned.

Perhaps disturbed by events among the 'Scythians' north of the Black Sea, the Carpi began causing trouble on the Dacian frontier in 245, and Philip continued fighting there in 246, probably well beyond the imperial borders. Late in the summer of 247, he returned to Rome and celebrated a triumph, taking the official title Carpicus Maximus and perhaps also being hailed as Germanicus Maximus. The imperial family stayed in Rome for the winter of 247–8 and the following spring Philip celebrated the completion of the thousandth anniversary of Rome's history, on 21 April of that year. As we saw in the discussion in chapter 5 of the previous secular games, there was some confusion among the Romans themselves about their secular games, and so two rather different sequences of them developed. One was the supposedly archaic and Etruscan celebrations revived by Augustus in 17 BC, which were conducted every 110 years, supervised by the *quindecimviri* of the official priesthood and celebrated over a *triduum* from the nights of 31 May to 3 June. The others were centenary celebrations to commemorate centuries (*saecula*) since the foundation of Rome, which took place on her *dies natalis*, 21 April – the feast of the Parilia (or Natalis Urbis, as it was uniformly referred to in our period). In their different ways both sorts of 'secular' games publicly performed a link between the past and the present of the Roman state, asserting an essential continuity in Rome's identity over the years. Domitian and Septimius Severus had celebrated games in the Augustan sequence, Antoninus Pius in the second, and Philip's would continue that of Pius.

There can be no doubt that Philip's millennial games were even more symbolically significant for those purposes. We do not have an involved description of Philip's games, but one (not very reliable) source reports that he used the gladiators and animals that had been intended for the Persian victory of Gordian, a victory that of course never came. We do, however, have epigraphic attestations of the importance of these millennial games, and they are noted in the various strands of Greek and Latin chronicling from late antiquity. Philip's coinage is particularly rich in references to their celebration. Struck both in commemorative aurei and regular antoniniani and sestertii, in the name not just of Philip himself but also of the young Philip II and Otacilia Severa, they depict various animals killed in the Circus Maximus: lions, antelopes, hippopotami, ibexes, stags and gazelles, as well as pictures of a temple to Roma with her statue among the columns. We also see depictions of the chariot races – *ludi circenses* – that had been a regular part of the annual celebration of the Natalis Urbis since the time of Hadrian. But to the beast hunts and races, Philip added the rituals of the 'authentic' secular games in the Augustan sequence, with a *triduum* of theatrical spectacles on the Campus Martius, as well as singing competitions and other events whose victors are recorded in surviving inscriptions. This wide variety of attestation – particularly by contrast to the games of Antoninus Pius – is a marker of the celebration's millennial importance.

Perhaps the most surprising evidence of this is also the strangest: common *terra sigillata* – the red-slip tableware that graced every Roman table – decorated with medallions honouring Philip's games rather in the manner of today's painted place settings commemorating royal weddings or presidential inaugurations (and perhaps just as kitschy then as now). The pomp and circumstance of Philip's games was clearly felt out in distant provinces, but scholars remain divided about whether the sort of 'millennial fever' that was felt in Christian Europe around AD 1000 was there in Philip's time as well. The Latin sources are ambiguous at best, but there is one eastern source that does seem to make the case: a collection of Greek texts that came to be known as the *Oracula Sybillina*. These had nothing whatsoever to do with the original Sybilline oracles of the republican era, but were both a response to the crises of third-century politics and genuinely apocalyptic in outlook – in the Thirteenth Oracle, much the most famous in the collection, the millenarian expectations of Rome's thousandth anniversary meets with a fierce sense that the Roman empire needed to end.

Yet despite any such currents of unease, Philip's lavish celebrations seem to have been a propaganda success. The completion of one millennium could also be seen as the start of another, just as glorious: certainly successors of Philip continued to strike secular coins a full half decade after his games had been celebrated. In general, however, Philip's government was not faring well. In 248, in Cappadocia or Syria, a nobleman from Commagene named Iotapianus was proclaimed emperor, supposedly to protect the provinces from the heavy-handed exactions of Julius Priscus. There may also have been a revolt on the Rhine, led by one Marinus Silbanniccus, although the date of this revolt is uncertain and only two coins of the usurper are known to exist. More dangerously, the consular governor of Moesia, Claudius Marinus Pacatianus, was proclaimed emperor, possibly in April 248, probably at Viminacium where his coins were minted. But he was swiftly killed by his own soldiers when the neighbouring provincial governor led his army into Moesia.

It is possible that the senator Pacatianus represented the hostility of his order towards the junta of bureaucrats that surrounded Philip, one that resented the supra-regional commands awarded to men like Severianus and Priscus. It is also possible that Philip's celebration of the Roman millennium, with its heavy freighting of tradition, contributed to his decision to rise up. Regardless, Pacatianus's rebellion was put down. Unfortunately for Philip, the commander who suppressed him immediately allowed himself to be proclaimed emperor in turn. C. Messius Quintus Decius Valerinus was a senatorial commander in his mid-forties who came from the region, having been born near Sirmium. Under Severus Alexander he had governed both Moesia and Germania Inferior, while he held the prestigious command of Hispania Citerior under Maximinus and remained loyal to that emperor in the face of the senatorial revolt. In 249, he was serving as a legate of both Moesia and Pannonia, in one of the extraordinary commands that Philip so favoured. It was in Pannonia that his rebellion was declared, the mint at Viminacium striking issues in his name almost at once. He also changed his name to C. Messius Quintus Traianus Decius, reflecting the glory of the emperor Trajan who had conquered the Dacians, in what may have been a reference to Decius's own Balkan origins.

A bigger puzzle surrounds the whereabouts and actions of Philip himself. He was either still in Italy, where he mustered an army to personally confront this latest usurper, or he was deep in Thrace, marching eastwards to deal with the rebellion of Iotapianus, having thought it safe to leave Decius to deal with the Danube frontier. Either way, having suppressed a brief mutiny at Viminacium, Decius either advanced from Pannonia at the head of the Balkan legions, crossed the Julian Alps and defeated Philip at Verona in September 249, or else he marched down the main Balkan highway in the opposite direction and defeated Philip at Beroea in Thrace. Philip was killed by his own soldiers, the young Philip was put to death in Rome by the praetorians when news of his father's defeat reached them, and the emperor's other relatives are never heard from again.

After defeating Philip, wherever he did so, Decius advanced to Rome, and was by September recognised as *pontifex maximus* and *pater patriae*. He immediately launched a programme of great ambition. His ostentatious traditionalism was obvious from the outset, starting with his decision to change his name to include that of a conquering emperor remembered for his goodness as much as his prowess. The names he gave his children by the Roman matron Herennia Cupressenia Etruscilla are equally redolent of the past: Q. Herennius Etruscus Messius Decius and C. Valens Hostilianus Messius Quintus. Just as extraordinary were his numismatic initiatives. Coins were, of course, among the most widely seen and handled items to emanate from the imperial court and the emperor's circle. While we should not presume that emperors were personally responsible for every change and fillip in the numismatic iconography, when a major programmatic initiative in the coinage differs distinctly from what has gone before, we should take notice, as is the case with Decius.

After the new emperor had reached Italy, the mints at Milan and Rome began to issue not just the expected sorts of coins honouring Dacia, Pannonia and the *genius exercitum illyriciani* ('the genius of the Illyrian armies') but also an unprecedented series of antoniniani celebrating the deified emperors of Rome. These coins showed an altar on their reverse with the legend *consecratio*, while on their obverses there appeared a series of imperial portraits of the *divi*, beginning with Augustus and taking in Vespasian, Titus, Nerva, Trajan, Hadrian, Antoninus Pius and Marcus Aurelius. That imperial pantheon is standard and to be expected, but the selection of names that follows is more interesting: Commodus, Septimius Severus and Severus Alexander. No Pertinax and no *divus Gordianus*, the latter having been deified a mere five years previously. Now to be sure, false genealogies and the retrospective ascription of dynastic ties are something we have become used to already in this book – from Severus's shifting decisions about which 'ancestors' to honour, to the sedulously cultivated rumours of a filial connection between Caracalla and the two young cousins who succeeded him. Equally, Greek and Roman viewers were used to the periodic erasing of emperors from official memory, the physical chiselling away of names from monuments both effacing memories and simultaneously forcing remembrance, the better to damage the reputation of the one thus effaced. But the 'virtual' erasure of memory as we see it enacted here is something different and new. Because the remembrances with which it so visibly tampers were so recent, it can only be read as a deliberate rejection of the previous decade. Decius was asserting his direct succession to Severus Alexander and retaining none of the intervening emperors, not even the youngest Gordian whose *consecratio* was a matter of living and public knowledge. The miserable decade of invasion and civil war, it was meant to be clear, had ended.

In the end, Decius did not reign long. Yet he is one of the most famous emperors of the third century, not on account of his extraordinary coinage but for another measure altogether: an order for universal sacrifice to the gods, for the good of the Roman state. Like the new coin types, it was meant to signal a new beginning, the return of prosperity to the empire, but for it to work, everyone would need to sacrifice. The plan for carrying out the new emperor's order was modelled on the collection of taxes and registration for the census, and the evidence for it survives to a remarkable degree in the papyri of Egypt. These papyri are *libelli* that record a citizen's act of sacrifice to the 'ancestral gods' before public officials, who are named in the documents as having presided over the act of sacrifice and the consumption of sacrificial food. As with census registration for tax purposes, the inhabitants of each province were assigned a day on which they were required to appear before their municipal magistrates to perform sacrifice by burning incense to the gods, and were then issued with a chit proving that they had done so – with failure to comply carrying serious consequences. This devolution of imperial directives on to local authorities is entirely characteristic of the way regional administration worked in the early empire, but we know much more about Decius's edict than most others, for two reasons: one being the survival of the Egyptian *libelli*; the other being the impact it had on Christians.

Although the edict's wording was vague, and did not specify which or whose ancestral gods were being referred to, Christians seem to have interpreted the order as requiring them to sacrifice to the gods of the Roman state. Christian monotheism rejected any distinction between belief and cultic acts. Christians were prohibited from worshipping any gods but their own one god, and they regarded the many other gods they saw all around them as demons. Most Christians, that is to say, believed full well in the gods of the Roman state, knew them to be quite real, but regarded their reality as demonic rather than divine. An order to sacrifice along the lines of the Decian edict could not help but challenge them. Choosing to comply meant not just sinning, but exposing their souls to eternal damnation. Failure to comply, by contrast, meant exposing each one individually to the more immediate bodily vengeance of the Roman state. Thus, whether or not Decius had intended it as such, it was impossible for Christians to interpret his edict as anything other than a deliberate attack on them and their beliefs. Decius is duly remembered by Christians as the second of the great Roman persecutors after Nero, the scale of whose persecution is much exaggerated.

Decius's intentions have long provoked debate. Some elements of his plan are uncontroversial. He clearly believed that a single, unifying ritual act was necessary to please the gods and ensure the state's safety. Perhaps he was mainly concerned with shoring up his own rather weak claims to the purple. Perhaps he was responding to millenarianism provoked by Philip's celebration of Rome's thousandth anniversary. He may also have been influenced by the outbreak of a new and frightening disease that was taking hold in the eastern parts of the empire: beginning in 249 in Alexandria, a severely contagious illness that caused high fever and conjunctival bleeding had begun to spread across the empire. Fading away in high summer, it returned in autumn, reaching Rome and Carthage by 251 at the latest and recurring periodically for at least a decade thereafter. The precise virus responsible cannot be determined, but scholars have recently begun to recognise just how serious it was, affecting town and country, rich and poor, and killing off as much as two-thirds of the population in some cities, if our better sources are to be believed. Haemorrhagic fever similar to the Ebola virus has been hypothesised: the combination of seasonality with high morbidity and mortality makes a filovirus of that sort a likely candidate. As the recent Ebola outbreak shows, the sudden impact of a new epidemic can prompt hysteria and the demand that our leaders take drastic measures to save us. We should not be surprised if ancient people, lacking modern epidemiological knowledge, thought it necessary to propitiate angered divinities, and worried that those who habitually refused to honour the gods were responsible for their anger.

Whatever the admixture of foresight and reaction, or of reason and hysteria, that lay behind the Decian measure, we also need to understand it as an early fruit of the equestrianisation of the empire – the increasing dominance of men of equestrian rank with bureaucratic careers, and the type of 'governmentality' that went with that. Decius undoubtedly remembered Caracalla's citizenship edict, with its universalising rhetoric and still-more universalising impact in extending Roman law to the whole imperial population. Almost forty years after the Antonine constitution, a whole generation whose parents had been born as non-citizen *peregrini* was having to negotiate an adherence to Roman laws that were entirely outside the customary behaviours of their locales. Experienced administrators like Decius were aware of this before and after, and will have seen an ideological value in this universal conformity. We should thus think in terms of two governmental impulses, each functioning in parallel to the other: Caracalla's grandiose edict had made it possible to imagine the whole of the empire as a single world in which all could and should do things the same way; at the same time, equestrianisation and the relentless expansion of governmental routine made the aspiration to enforcing such uniformity seem both possible and achievable.

The ad hoc nature of early Roman government had stemmed from a recognition that ruling the empire could be done most cheaply, peacefully and efficiently if local customs and local ways of keeping the peace and extracting tribute were maintained – and also from the incapacity of a polity that had developed out of the *familia* and *clientela* of Augustus to administer an empire of such scale according to uniform rules. Two centuries of expanding government and structural stability had altered that picture, so that what was once both inconceivable and unnecessary could now seem both possible and worth having. Whatever else we see in Decius's edict to sacrifice – and it is clear that later emperors who ordered the deliberate persecution of Christians did see his edict as a model – we should also see it as an important stage in the development of a specifically late imperial approach to government, one that reached its fullest expression in the fourth century, and was thereafter sustained for a century or more in the west, and for a full three centuries in the east.

Decius's assertiveness extended to more than matters of religious practice or the power of the state. He seems also to have been intent upon asserting himself as a more effective military leader than Philip had been. We have already seen how changes north of the Black Sea and east of the Carpathians had seriously altered the balance of power there, with the imposition on a settled agricultural society of a new military elite whose culture combined elements of central European dress and language with fighting styles and decorative schemata from the steppe. By 249, Roman military planners were conscious enough of these changes that Decius sent soldiers to the Bosporus to report on developments, the rump of the Hellenistic Bosporan kingdom still hanging on as the world changed around it. Along the lower Danube, meanwhile, Philip had exacerbated an already bad situation by stopping traditional subsidies to the Carpi and campaigning against them, alleging that they had broken the peace with Rome. But the withdrawal of imperial subsidy was rarely a successful technique of frontier management: Decius had personally to lead an army to Moesia Inferior against barbarians who are variously called Carpi, Borani, Ourogundoi and Goths by sources with some limited claims to authenticity, and are generically known as Scythians by the contemporary classicising authors. The confusion of names attested in the sources is a fact of prime historical importance: contemporaries on both sides of the frontier had little real idea of what was going on. Only with hindsight can we understand these events as the by-product of a developing Gothic hegemony in the whole region, in consequence of which the barbarian polities along the fourth-century Danube bore little traceable relationship to those of the third.

We need to resist the temptation to paste our disconnected pieces of evidence into a single, neat narrative, but the one thing we can say with certainty is that Decius faced a truly disastrous situation when he led his army into Moesia Inferior, where an invading army of Scythians had placed Marcianopolis under siege. Newly discovered fragments of the Athenian historian Dexippus have confirmed details known from much later sources whose authenticity has been doubted, and it is now clear that several groups of Scythians were led by commanders named Ostrogotha and Cniva, and that they inflicted heavy losses on the emperor himself at Beroea. News of this debacle probably triggered a short-lived coup in Rome by the senator Iulius Valens Licinianus, but that appears to have been suppressed almost instantly, perhaps by the praetorians, for no coins were struck in Valens's name. Then, back in the Balkans at either the end of 250 or early in 251, Philippopolis did fall to Cniva's invaders, after a short-lived usurpation by the governor of Thrace, T. Julius Priscus, had taken place there. Finally, in the first half of June, Decius confronted the invaders at Abrittus, north-west of Marcianopolis, in a pitched battle that went disastrously wrong. His opponents had dug themselves in across treacherous, marshy terrain ill suited to the mass infantry engagements at which Roman armies generally excelled. In a monumentally foolish move, Decius personally led his forces into battle across the marsh, where they became entangled and were massacred. The emperor himself died, as did his son Herennius Etruscus, and his body was never recovered. Later Christian authors could gleefully imagine this as the condign fate that awaited persecutors: 'as an enemy of God deserved, he lay stripped and naked, food for the beasts and the carrion birds'.

News of the disaster reached Rome in mid June, as did word that the troops had raised C. Vibius Trebonianus Gallus, governor of Moesia Inferior, to the purple. He negotiated the withdrawal of the Scythians back across the Danube, though it appears that they took a large part of Decius' imperial treasury with them: what had been a silver-based economy north of the imperial frontiers was rapidly transformed into one based on gold, with aurei of Decius seized at Abrittus its primary model. As soon as the Scythians departed, Gallus returned to Rome with great haste, arriving there in late summer. Gallus was an Italian of high rank – that we even know the name of his father, whose career was underway during the reign of Septimius Severus, is rare enough in this period to mark the family's distinction. Despite ongoing trouble on the eastern front, Gallus's hasty journey to Rome was a wise idea: the symbolic conciliation of senate and plebs remained a necessary duty if an imperial acclamation was to win any long-lasting acceptance, and Gallus issued *adventus* coins to commemorate his arrival. The senate swiftly consecrated the dead emperor as *divus Decius*, and Gallus at first accepted the latter's younger son Hostilianus as a caesar alongside his own son Volusianus. It is unclear whether or for how long this situation lasted: there is some evidence that Decius suffered *damnatio memoriae* along with his sons, but it is not widespread enough for us to be sure and may instead reflect later Christian defacement of the hated persecutor's name. Certainly, the surviving son Hostilianus was either put to death or died of natural causes before the year was out. At any rate, before the middle of 251, only two emperors were recognised by the senate, C. Vibius Trebonianus Gallus and his son, C. Vibius Volusianus, the caesar and *princeps iuventutis*. Senatorial approval or acquiescence having been vouchsafed, however, more pressing matters needed attention.

The revolt of Iotapianus had been suppressed either at the end of Philip's reign or at the beginning of Decius's, in circumstances that remain unknown to us, but a new revolt had broken out led by an Antiochene notable with the Syrian name of Mariades. By the time imperial troops loyal to the Italian regime got properly involved, Mariades determined to flee to Persia and seek refuge with Shapur. Shapur, in his victory inscription, claims that Rome had violated the peace that Philip made in 244 by sheltering the Arsacid heir Tiridates of Armenia, who had sought refuge with the Romans after his father Khusrau II had been assassinated, probably at Shapur's instigation. In response, Shapur annexed Armenia, eliminating its Arsacid rulers and placing it under the rule of his son Ohrmazd.

Much more elaborate versions of these events survive in the Armenian tradition, with added folkloric elements of subversion, betrayal and massacre. One detail they preserve that may have some value is the extent to which the elder Tiridates and Khusrau had been irritants to Ardashir and then Shapur, promoting rebellions as far away as the Kushanshahr – which would help to explain the amount of time Shapur had to spend fighting in the east. Now, with the strategic mountain kingdom of Armenia in his possession and his eastern frontiers secure, Shapur again turned against the Romans, assisted by the rebel Mariades. In 252 or 253, the shahanshah attacked the Syrian provinces, not by the usual approach via Singara, Resaina and Carrhae, but by an unexpected route that caught by surprise the whole Roman garrison of Syria, which was being brought together in anticipation of a Persian campaign.

Shapur claimed that in this victory, at Barbalissos on the Euphrates, he defeated a full 60,000 Romans – a number that, even if wildly exaggerated, speaks to a major Persian victory. Antioch itself, along with other important Syrian cities like Hierapolis, were taken in this campaign or campaigns, Persian armies advanced as far as Cappadocia, and the Italian government of Trebonianus Gallus was powerless to do anything about it. Shapur deported a great many captives to Khuzistan, where he founded a new city that he called Veh Antiok Shapur ('Better than Antioch Has Shapur Founded This'), a name that was later corrupted into Gundeshapur, an important town in the zone between the Zagros and the Tigris. Shapur's motives went beyond military glory: Khuzistan was to become the economic engine of the Sasanian state, peppered with industrial centres, many populated by deported captives, specialising in production that enhanced the royal revenue and paid for further conquest. By suppressing older towns – perhaps most importantly Susa – with traditions of independent government and favouring instead royal centres governed directly by the imperial administration, Shapur inaugurated a long-standing policy that made the Sasanian dynasty the richest and most powerful of the ancient Near Eastern empires

In the third-century moment, however, the failure of the Roman emperors to act meant local easterners were compelled to take matters into their own hands. It may be at this time that Odaenathus, a nobleman from the flourishing caravan city of Palmyra, and an intermittently important figure in eastern affairs until his assassination in 267, came on the scene, but the chronology of events in this period is almost hopelessly tangled: some would attribute to this Odaenathus the defeat of a part of the Persian army that others attribute to one Uranius Antoninus of Emesa. That obscure figure's full titulature – Iulius Aurelius Sulpicius Severus Uranius

Antoninus – clearly proclaimed his kinship with the Severan house. He may have been a devotee and priest of Elagabal, the god of Emesa, and if so he was perhaps a relative of the family of Julia Domna. Given that he minted coins, which are the best evidence we have for his existence and his sphere of activity, it seems clear that Uranius was actively challenging Gallus's claim to the imperial throne. In the later romanticised version of John Malalas, a sixth-century author who related a great deal of local Antiochene lore of varying reliability, Shapur himself is said to have been killed in this Emesene encounter, although the usurper Uranius has been blotted out and replaced by a noble priest named Sampsigeramus. While the story is clearly fiction, Emesa is conspicuously missing from the list of cities Shapur claims to have conquered in his inscription at Naqsh-e Rustam, and it seems very likely that he suffered a substantial defeat there. The fact that it took place at the hands of a local ruler, rather than an army even putatively loyal to the legitimate emperor, reminds us of the ongoing difficulty western emperors faced in retaining control of the east, in part because of their inability to protect the eastern provinces from Persian threats: it was not that they did not want to act, but that other threats constrained them. Thus Trebonianus Gallus could not, in 253, have acted upon the devastating news from the east even if he had wanted to, because he was facing the threat of another rebellion, closer to home and thus more immediately dangerous.

This new challenge was triggered by events that should now be numbingly familiar to the reader: a general on the frontier wins a battle against some barbarians, takes the purple, marches against the reigning emperor, and both would rather allow the provincials to suffer than let their rival gather momentum. As so often, the state of the sources leaves us guessing about details, but it is pretty clear that although Gallus had neutralised the group of Scythians that had taken Philippopolis and killed Decius, these were just one small part of a larger problem: because there were as yet no organised polities beyond the Danube with whom to treat, no single ethnic or tribal group responsible for the problems the empire was facing, the suppression of one challenge meant nothing for the status of many others. Thus the Scythians with whom Gallus had dealt might very well have respected their treaty with him, but that left dozens of opportunistic raiders happy to take advantage of imperial distraction and weakness. So it was that in 252 there were major seaborne raids into the Aegean from the Black Sea, presumably by barbarians who had joined with, or conquered and seized the resources of, the remaining Bosporan Greeks. The raiders were successful and elusive and, although it is hard to gauge the actual level of damage, some of what they did was quite shocking to contemporary sensibilities, for instance, the burning of the temple of Artemis at Ephesus in Asia Minor, one of the most famous shrines of antiquity.

Then, in 253, Moesia Inferior was invaded by a different group of Scythians, who this time met with effective resistance from a general named Aemilius Aemilianus, about whom precious little is known. He was probably born in the first decade of the century, starting a career under Severus Alexander and rising through the ranks, but that is about all we can say. Now he demonstrated a fact that was becoming obvious to everyone – the loyalty of provincial armies to a distant emperor was impossible to guarantee. Aemilian's victorious troops declared him emperor and, though there was no way the Balkan frontier could yet be considered secure, he turned immediately to the march on Italy, necessary if he was to secure his hold on the purple. Crossing into Italy, he met and defeated Gallus at Interamna in Umbria. Gallus and the caesar Volusian were killed by their own troops and Aemilian won the recognition of the senate, who also acclaimed his wife Cornelia Supera the augusta. But Aemilian's reign was to prove a short one. As soon as Gallus received news of the uprising, he sent word to Gaul to summon support from Publius Licinius Valerianus, more generally known as Valerian. The latter heard of Gallus's death while still en route to Italy, and in Raetia he was proclaimed emperor in turn. In September 253, during the same campaigning season in which he had first been proclaimed, Aemilian was killed in battle with Valerian's army at Spoletium in central Italy. The rapid turnover of emperors had become bewildering. The reign of Valerian would last somewhat longer, but would be no less traumatic for the high politics of empire.

10

VALERIAN AND
THE GENERALS

The new emperor Valerian was an important man of long experience – it had been he who had brought the news of old Gordian's proclamation to Rome and brokered its acceptance in the senate. He was certainly of an old senatorial family, although the only source to give details of his parentage is plainly making them up. That said, we can be sure that he had held his first suffect consulship before 238 and was serving as some sort of military commander in Gaul when Aemilian rebelled against Gallus – he may have been a consular legate in one of the garrisoned provinces, but it is also possible that both Decius and Gallus had continued Philip's practice of appointing trusted men as *correctores* over large areas, as Valerian would certainly do. However, our uncertainty over what type of command Valerian was holding upon his acclamation reflects a phenomenon of these middle decades of the century – the disintegration of the empire's traditional military organisation, with its well-defined fighting units of legions and auxiliaries. In their place, we find multiple campaign armies, made up of detachments from a variety of units – a practice that becomes more regularised as the century progresses. In many ways, the reigns of Valerian and his son and successor Gallienus – poorly attested in the sources though they are – were the seedbeds of late third-century government and the late imperial state more generally.

In 253, almost as soon as he was acclaimed emperor, Valerian made his

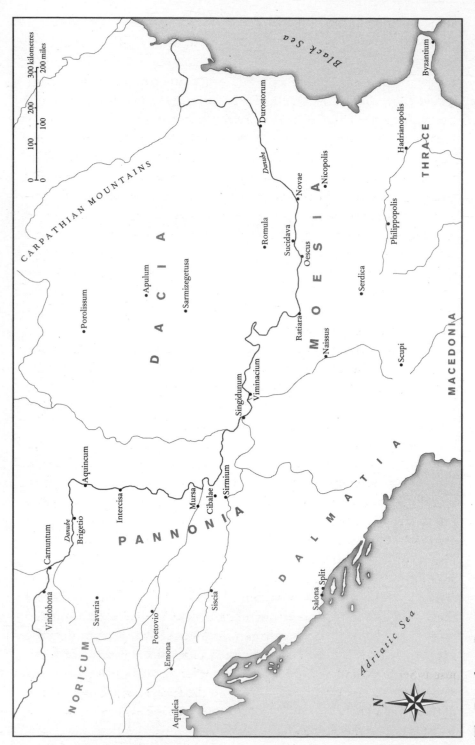

The Danubian Provinces

adult son P. Licinius Egnatius Gallienus his co-emperor. Gallienus was a man of about forty who already had a son, so in him Valerian could not only rely on a second adult ruler of equal authority but also the realistic prospect of dynastic continuity across several generations. In theory, that would allow the two emperors to deal with threats in different parts of the empire as they arose. The new rulers planned a flurry of activity. They spent the winter of 253–4 in Italy, establishing familial authority there. Valerian's late wife Egnatia Mariniana was deified as *diva Mariniana*, while Gallienus's wife Cornelia Salonina was made augusta and *mater castrorum* and their eldest son, Valerianus (Junior), was elevated to the rank of caesar and *princeps iuventutis*. However poorly recent attempts at dynasticism had gone, there remained a visceral sense that establishing a dynasty was essential to successful rule. As always for this period, the coinage is exceptionally instructive – Valerian abandoned the types favoured by Decius and Gallus, choosing instead to return to Severan reverses and legends, if not perhaps advertising continuity then at the very least suggesting his own preference for that now-vanished world.

With the passing of winter, the emperors began a period of frantic activity. Gallienus established himself in the Balkans, probably making Viminacium and Sirmium his main bases and foreshadowing those cities' great importance to the next 200 years of imperial history. They were among the cities founded by the Romans after Augustus had made the conquest and consolidation of the Balkans one of the main tasks of his principate. The rivers Sava, Drava, Morava and Danube were the main paths through the landscape of northern and western Illyricum, and the routes between them were dotted with towns that had begun life as way stations for Roman campaign armies. On the Drava, there were Poetovio (modern Ptuj) in Pannonia Superior and Mursa (modern Osijek) in Inferior just before the river flows into the Danube. Further south in Superior, on the Sava, there was Siscia (Sisak), and in Inferior Sirmium (Mitrovica) and Singidunum (Belgrade), where the Sava and the Danube meet. In Moesia Superior, there was Viminacium (Kostolac) on the Danube and Naissus (Nis) on the Nisava just before it meets the Morava. Naissus was the last of the great cities of the western Balkans, just as Serdica (modern Sofia), in Moesia Inferior, near the Iskar, was the gateway to the eastern Balkans and Thrace: the Succi Pass, just to the south of there, would become a military hinge between the eastern and western Balkans during the later empire.

Most of these cities were Julio-Claudian foundations, but the vast majority of the provincial populations in this region had only become citizens in 212 through the edict of Caracalla. It may be this unusually long gap between conquest, early imperial urbanisation and full enfranchisement that gave the region a peculiar sense of local citizenship. Whereas in most parts of the Roman empire, people were regarded as having their *patria*, or 'home town', in the legal centre of the *civitas*, in the Balkans the *vici* or villages within a *civitas* are regularly noted. This reckoning of regional identity, and the third-century prominence of men from the region in the government of the empire, may help us understand the growth of regional factions in fourth-century imperial government, a topic to which we will often return, in this volume and its sequel.

With his subordinate commanders overwhelmingly men of Balkan origin, Valerian headed to Syria overland via Cilicia, probably spending the winter of 254–5 in Antioch. The eastern frontier had been so disturbed, both by Shapur's invasions and the usurpations that they encouraged, that it would require more than just one winter's attention, but in 256, both Valerian and Gallienus moved to Colonia Agrippina (Cologne), where they campaigned against the Alamanni. Perhaps they judged it best for all corners of the empire to witness the emperors working effectively and in concert with one another, even if that meant gesturing towards problems rather than solving them. In the autumn of 256, the imperial pair travelled to Rome so that Gallienus could enter his first consulship on 1 January 257. Probably in that same year, or at the beginning of the next, Gallienus's elder son, the young Valerian Caesar, died and was consecrated as *divus Valerianus Caesar*, his place in the dynastic order being filled by his younger brother, Saloninus Gallienus, who was made *nobilissimus Caesar* and *princeps iuventutis* early in 258.

However, the mere fact of Valerian's residency in Antioch two years before had triggered a new Persian response. In 256 or 257 the south-easternmost Roman garrison on the Euphrates, at the long disputed fortress of Dura-Europos, fell to Persian forces. The site became a ghost town thereafter, thus leaving it for modern archaeologists to excavate as one of the most significant early imperial frontier sites (and a recent victim of Islamist vandalism). In response to this latest eastern setback, Valerian left Rome and made for Antioch, a journey from which he would never return. Events of the following years are hard to pin down with certainty: there was another Scythian attack in 257 or 258, this time into Pontus and

Cappadocia via the Black Sea coast. These invaders were now organised enough to deliberately target local mints, seizing dies that the Greek cities used to strike bronze coins, and using them to strike gold versions that are found north of the Black Sea. The army Valerian led to confront this invasion was ravaged by an illness that one source describes vaguely as 'plague', possibly a recurrence of the haemorrhagic fever of Decius's time, and it was this already depleted force that Valerian then took to confront yet another Persian invasion of Mesopotamia, in the spring of 260. The size, composition and routes of the respective armies are unknown, but whereas in 252/3 Shapur had achieved strategic surprise thanks to the help of Mariades, in 260 both Persians and Romans seem to have followed the well-worn military routes through the Mesopotamian steppe.

One can infer from its location – somewhere between Carrhae and Edessa – that the Persian shahanshah and the Roman emperor both personally led their armies into the decisive battle in which Valerian was taken prisoner. One of the most famous pieces of Sasanian art to survive from antiquity is a little cameo stone commemorating the battle. It shows the emperor and the shah cantering towards each other, the one in the military *paludamentum* of Rome, the other in the full chain armour of Persia, Shapur reaching out and grasping Valerian's wrist in the standard Persian iconography of capture. It is the same gesture we see on the reliefs of Naqsh-e Rustam and Bishapur, where Valerian the imperial captive stands alongside the dead Gordian and suppliant Philip. And, as had not been the case with Gordian, here there was no room for equivocation in the sources: a Roman emperor had been taken captive on the field of battle.

In Lactantius's lurid fourth-century account – Orientalism *avant la lettre* – the captive emperor lived out his days as the stool from which the shah would mount his horse and then, when he died, his flayed skin was dyed red and hung in a Mazdean fire temple. More plausible is the shahanshah's own account in the Naqsh-e Rustam inscription: he took the emperor captive – humiliation enough in itself – while his army, which surrendered in the face of so crushing a blow, was shipped to eastern Iran to build new cities for the Persians. There is architectural evidence for Roman legionary engineering in many Sasanian cities from this period, and the deportation of defeated enemies was a long-standing tradition in the ancient Near East, so this exploitation of the Roman prisoners as skilled labour makes more sense than does anything reported in the Roman sources.

In the face of the calamity, the eastern provinces fell into total disarray under their imperial officials or local dynasts and then, by April 260, news of Valerian's defeat reached the west and the chaos in the east was duplicated there. The only group to rejoice was the Christians. Before he set out from Rome at the end of 259, Valerian had issued an edict similar to that of Decius, in that it demanded universal sacrifice, but fundamentally different in that it deliberately and specifically targeted Christians, and left open considerable room for delation, denunciation and the settling of old scores. Under this edict, known leaders of the church – bishops but also Christian senators and other important laymen – were to be arrested and ordered to sacrifice. Rather than being banned from practising their religion, they were to be given the choice of adding this show of participation in the Roman state to their normal practices. Failure to do so would result in confiscation of their estates and the enslavement of those who were in imperial service at the time of their refusal; repeated recusancy would result in execution (and there were indeed some martyrs, including the bishop of Rome Xystus).

This persecuting edict – and unlike Decius's, this one was certainly a deliberate persecuting measure – had clearly not been widely trailed or expected. Indeed, the Roman senate asked Valerian to clarify whether the edict actually meant what it seemed to mean, and how it was to be enforced, which suggests the extent of de facto toleration among the Roman senatorial elite of Christianity in their midst. Christianity was no doubt viewed as eccentric – and in Roman terms, it *was* deeply eccentric – but it also seemed more threatening to an imperial bureaucracy with its aspirations to conformity and control than to the ruling classes of the empire as a whole. As if to confirm that interpretation, Gallienus restored freedom to the church, along with the extensive property rights it had formerly possessed, almost immediately after his father's capture. Valerian's fate, meanwhile, provided Christians with further gratifying evidence that their persecutors would meet a nasty end at the hands of their one true god.

Few others, however, can have welcomed something as unprecedented and horrifying as the captivity of a Roman emperor. Emperors fell in battle – sometimes even in battle against barbarians as Decius had done, though more often against pretenders and rivals. But captivity was worse, and what could it mean that foreign foes had destroyed two emperors within a decade? Suddenly, a world without a Roman empire must have looked possible. Equally, though, perhaps anyone could now be an emperor, since no measure of apparent legitimacy seemed to make any difference. Consequently, revolts broke out everywhere, or at least local initiatives that could look very much like revolt or usurpation when viewed from the centre.

In the east, a bureaucrat named Macrianus and an officer named Callistus rallied some opposition to the further advance of Shapur, but the self-help soon became usurpation: Macrianus's sons Macrianus and Quietus were proclaimed emperors in Syria in the summer of 260. Further south and east, Odaenathus of Palmyra took to calling himself the lord of Tadmor (the Syriac name of the city), a designation probably aimed more at Persia than Rome. In doing so, he was claiming an unprecedented authority in the region, where he won a substantial victory over Shapur as the latter's army was withdrawing from Roman territory. In the Balkans, when word of Valerian's capture spread, the provincial governors Ingenuus and Regalianus each in turn declared himself emperor, Ingenuus at Sirmium in Pannonia and Regalianus in Moesia, though his coinage was struck at the Pannonian city of Carnuntum. Both were defeated before the end of the year by Gallienus's crack cavalry commander, Aureolus. This Aureolus now emerges as the first of the great marshals of Gallienus whose careers (and imperial aspirations) would dominate the second half of the third century. Similarly encouraged by imperial disarray, another Scythian invasion penetrated deep into the peninsula. As the new Dexippus fragments show, a barbarian army assaulted Thessalonica in 261/2 and, when repulsed there, made for southern Greece. The senatorial governor of Achaea, one Marianus, organised the defence along with local Athenian and Boeotian officials and the pass at Thermopylae was fortified and defended by a makeshift army.

The ruling dynasty reacted as best it could. Gallienus's son Saloninus was raised from the rank of caesar and proclaimed augustus at Colonia Agrippina in the summer of 260, but by then he and his father were facing a usurpation even closer to home: the rebellion of the governor of Germania Inferior, Postumus. Gallienus had been in northern Italy or Raetia fighting a raid by the Iuthungi, one of the various Alamannic groups we met at the end of chapter 9, when he learned of Valerian's capture. These invaders, presumably taking with them great quantities of booty and many prisoners, were defeated by the emperor himself near Mediolanum (Milan). Perhaps Gallienus negotiated their withdrawal from the empire, perhaps his victory was rather less complete than our poor sources suggest, but more than a few of the Iuthungi survived the battle unscathed and in possession of their spoils. As they moved north through Raetia to withdraw beyond the upper Danube, they were attacked and slaughtered by units from Raetia and Germania Inferior, with the help of an unspecified militia. This success, which apparently freed many thousands of Italian captives, led the successful army or armies to proclaim Postumus, one of their generals, emperor.

It would make sense if Saloninus's proclamation at Colonia in his father's absence was a direct response to the usurpation of Postumus, orchestrated by the praetorian prefect Silvanus, who was resident in the city to supervise the young caesar. For one reason or another – and in the confused state of the evidence it is impossible to say – the troops under the young emperor's direct command mutinied, preferring Postumus to Saloninus, and laid siege to Colonia. Taking the city by storm, they executed Saloninus and his prefect and, with that, the whole of the region north of the Loire and Alps was governed by the usurper. With the east likewise in the hands of usurpers, Gallienus's empire was reduced to Italy, the Balkans and Anatolia, as well as Egypt, North Africa and the better part of Spain. There was little Gallienus could do – he could not be in two places at once – but it is unsurprising that he had appalling press in the later imperial period.

It was not just his military failures, either. He and his father were anachronisms in the world in which they lived. Their Severan senatorial outlook had long-since failed, destroyed in the carnage of 238. One needs only look at Gallienus's portraiture to take the point – he is portrayed as a young Alexander, not so much heroised as feminised. For all that Alexander was a conqueror, his portraits are those of a young and beautiful but profoundly Hellenic figure. Compared to the bearded soldiers who were coming into their own, Gallienus was from another world, in which those born into the empire's elite were meant to be good at anything they turned their hand to, simply because of who they were. Senators were deracinated by their status, adepts of a common Graeco-Roman culture that we can call *paideia* by its Greek name or *humanitas* by its Latin. They were fitted to lead as required – governing provinces meant entertaining sophists, leading armies and dispensing justice. Some, of course, would be better soldiers than others, and one could not require juristic brilliance from each and every senator, but the civilian, anti-specialist affect of the early imperial senate was never in question; as an ideal, at least, it survived the equestrianisation of government under the earlier Severans, and as an ideal it was put into practice, disastrously, by the Gordians and *vigintiviri*. Each of the men in the vigintivirate, with the exception of the benighted Pupienus and Balbinus, went on to prosperous careers, and the families of that senatorial inner circle consolidated their hold on wealth and status. But by Valerian's time, the age in which such men had actually run the Roman empire was over. The new emperors' failure was not to realise as much.

It was not that Gallienus or indeed Valerian tried to rule in the old way – they could no more reverse the structural changes to the imperial system than they could turn back time. Valerian's edicts partook of the universalising practicality of the new equestrian mindset. Gallienus made innovative use of his armies, accelerating existing changes whereby the old combination of legion and auxiliary was replaced by a more versatile campaign army patched together from detachments of larger units, and by a growing importance of cavalry on the battlefield. But neither emperor was prepared for the breakdown of hierarchy that equestrianisation implied, the possibility that birth might not fit one to command, and that, whatever the value of family, of patronage, of position – and value they retained – talent, system, specialisation and experience might count for more. The great families might still have a hold on the proconsulships of Asia, Africa and Achaea, and have a good claim to command other relatively peaceful provinces in Spain. But wherever power was actually concentrated, it was the equestrian marshals who led the way and birth did not come into it. There is a historical irony that the last imperial dynasty with any claim to a genuine connection with the Antonine and Severan senatorial aristocracy should have been the one to usher in the triumph of equestrian military rule. But that is what happened, and it was men forged in the ranks, their careers made by the endless wars of Gallienus's desperate reign, who embodied the future. With their stubbly beards and born in circumstances of the deepest obscurity, the Gallienan officer corps was the crucible of late imperial rulership – which makes it quite amusing that Gallienus, the last senatorial emperor, should have been remembered in the fourth century as the man who excluded the senate from government.

The whole of Gallienus's reign played out as a series of attempts to keep control of imperial territory and bind it together in the face of repeated challenges and no certain loyalty anywhere. In 261, the Syrian proclamation of Macrianus, initially a response to the campaigns of Shapur, became more dangerous, as the two Macriani crossed from Asia Minor into Europe, seeking to establish the dynasty at Rome in the usual way. Aureolus, already victorious over Ingenuus and Regalianus, now defeated the Macriani and put them to death. It was lucky for Gallienus – and in light of recent history somewhat surprising – that Aureolus's consistent successes did not prompt him into his own revolt. But nor was he sent east to deal with Quietus and Callistus. Instead, Gallienus entered an alliance with Odaenathus of Palmyra, granting him the title *corrector totius orientis*, on the model of the command that Julius Priscus had held under Philip in the same region. The reliance on such supra-provincial commanders, outranking any provincial governor, is a further sign of the breakdown of the old governing system, but it was a logical response to persistent instability. Odaenathus at once marched on Emesa, where the soldiery mutinied and killed Quietus and Callistus without taking the field against the Palmyrene.

This was the first act with which Odaenathus proved himself a powerful and reliable ally to the central emperor. He accepted Gallienus's provincial appointees without demur, but he was also, to all intents and purposes, the independent ruler of an eastern Roman empire. In the west, in the same year 261 that saw the suppression of the Macriani, Postumus achieved the major success of bringing Spain and Britain under his control. Postumus's emperorship is an interesting phenomenon, one that bears no relationship to the symbolic subordination but de facto hegemony of the Palmyrene leader in the east. Postumus, after all, claimed the imperial title. His full titulature was Imperator Caesar M. Cassianius Latinius Postumus, pius felix invictus Augustus, pontifex maximus, pater patriae, proconsul.

Postumus had declared himself consul at his accession in 260 and he entered a second consulate in 261, the year that all the provinces west of Italy recognised him not as *a* legitimate emperor, but as *the* legitimate emperor, a sole legitimacy which his titulature also asserted. His was a usurpation like any other, but with one major difference – successful usurpers, like the Macriani for a time, understood that the rules of the game were to secure one's rear and then march on the reigning emperor in order to defeat him, because there could only be one emperor at a time. In the face of such a putsch, the reigning emperor was obliged to eliminate the challenge, and would inevitably make that a priority over any other threat he might face – or so it had invariably played out in the past. Postumus, uniquely in Roman history, neither attacked the Italian territories of Gallienus nor sought to legitimise his position as his co-emperor, in the way that Clodius Albinus and Septimius Severus had in the 190s and would become normal practice in the fourth century. Rather, he contented himself with ruling the provinces that had declared for him in 260 and 261, safe behind the Alps, Vosges and Schwarzwald. Gallienus was constrained to regard him as an enemy and an existential challenge simply because of his imperial claim, but he did so without any active provocation from Postumus.

As a result, it is normal to talk of a separate 'Gallic empire' created by Postumus and sustained under several successors until suppressed in the 270s by Aurelian. There are problems with that view, however, inasmuch as it implies a sense of separatism – the German term for the regime, the *gallisches Sonderreich* ('Gallic splinter empire'), makes the point even more clearly. But evidence for separatism is hard to find. In ideological terms, Postumus and his successors at Colonia Agrippina ignored the existence of Gallienus as an imperial rival, and refused to follow the political script and pursue his defeat and destruction, but by the same token they never claimed to be anything other than *Roman* emperors. They simply didn't bother to try to control Rome. The de facto result was two imperial polities in Europe, both of which regarded themselves as *the* Roman empire. Only one, however, viewed the other as an existential challenge, and thus Gallienus would make several attempts to eliminate the Gallic emperor in the next years of his reign.

The most significant of these was in 265. Gallienus had by that point settled matters in the Balkans to his satisfaction, touring Achaea and holding the archonship of Athens in 264, and also acknowledging the heroism of the local population in resisting the Scythian invasion of two years earlier. That done, he was able to concentrate his manpower on challenging Postumus. He personally commanded the army that crossed the Alps and won a victory over Postumus, who fled to an unknown city where his rival besieged him. During the siege, Gallienus was wounded by the defenders and called off the attack. Postumus's regime was granted a long reprieve but, as a result of the campaign, the Spanish governors returned their allegiance to Gallienus. The year 266 is almost undocumented, but events in the east took a surprising turn in the autumn of 267, when Odaenathus, on campaign northwards to Heracleia Pontica, was murdered, possibly at Emesa. His son Herodianus, whom he had raised to co-rulership, was likewise killed. The motives and identities of their murderers are impossible to sort out from the confused sources, but it was clearly a family affair of some bitterness. The immediate beneficiary of the murders was Odaenathus's widow, Zenobia, who was the mother of several of his children, but not the older and favoured Herodian. Under the nominal rule of her son Vaballathus, Zenobia launched a conquest of the Roman east that went beyond the classic model of usurpation, not least in its success.

That took a couple of years to prepare, and we must be careful not to romanticise what is obviously an almost unique regime. Zenobia was born Julia Aurelia Zenobia, or Bath-Zabbai in the Syriac, to the Palmyrene nobleman Julius Aurelius Zenobius. She had built up a strong power base during the lifetime of her husband, but was no doubt displeased at the pre-eminence given Herodian, the offspring of a previous marriage, over her own sons, Septimius Hairanes and Septimius Vaballathus. With Odaenathus's death, the 7-year-old Vaballathus was given his father's titles of *rex regum* (the Latin for shahanshah, 'king of kings') and *corrector totius Orientis*, but there is no evidence that Gallienus accepted this succession from competent and loyal father to pre-adolescent boy. Zenobia, for her part, began to call herself Septimia Zenobia and queen. Her regime was much aided by the disarray of Shapur's late reign, when he faced disputes among his own heirs and a chaotic new situation on his eastern frontiers which we will look at later in this chapter. As a result, however, Shapur was unable to capitalise on the disruption in Syria as he would certainly once have done, and Zenobia's hands were almost entirely free.

We cannot know what Gallienus's response to these eastern events might have been, for he never got the chance to make one. In 268, the Balkans descended into violence once again, with a 'Scythian' invasion (this time the invaders are named as Heruli, a group well known in later history), again by ship, into Asia Minor and peninsular Greece. At the same time, Gallienus's great marshal Aureolus revolted, clearly on his own behalf, though claiming to be doing so as an ally of Postumus and striking coins in the latter's name at Mediolanum. It may be that Aureolus was at the time commanding a field army in preparation for another Balkan or Gallic campaign. Mediolanum would long be a centre from which to launch such ventures, commanding as it did all the key roads through the North Italian plain. Aureolus did not move swiftly enough to meet Gallienus in battle and found himself besieged in the city. What happened next is poorly documented and the sources give conflicting versions of how Gallienus came to be murdered while conducting the siege. Between them, the different accounts manage to blame almost every one of the prime movers of the next few years of imperial history: Gallienus's praetorian prefect Aurelius Heraclianus; the generals Marcianus, Marcus Aurelius Claudius and Aurelius Aurelianus; and a regimental commander called Cecropius, otherwise unknown. Practically the only great marshal of Gallienus's not named in one story or another is Marcus Aurelius Probus. One version has them being tricked into conspiracy by Aureolus; another has Gallienus being tricked into exposing himself to danger by Herodianus; others strive to exculpate one or another of the key players. There is no way to sort claim from counterclaim, no argument can be probative one way or another and, as with the murder of Odaenathus, we can either admit ignorance or let the question of *cui bono* guide our choice. If we do that, then regardless of who orchestrated the actual murder, the chief plotter will have been Claudius, because after Gallienus's death, the army acclaimed him emperor at the gates of Mediolanum.

Aureolus died in battle shortly afterwards, and the successful Claudius made a show of honouring his predecessor, sending his body back to Rome and interring it in the family's mausoleum on the Appian Way. He also prevailed upon the senate to have Gallienus deified. Before going to Rome himself, however, he marched north and won a victory at Lake Garda, in northern Italy, against some Alamanni who had launched an opportunistic invasion when the renewed Roman civil war offered them the chance. Claudius probably spent the winter of 268–9 in Rome, where he entered his first consulship in the company of a long-time senatorial supporter of Gallienus, Aspasius Paternus: whether from conviction or necessity, some of Rome's senatorial grandees were content to make their peace with this new regime of the marshals.

For Claudius, there was no question but that the year 269 would bring heavy fighting. His only choice was whether to favour an internal or an external foe. The Balkans were still being devastated, whether by the Herulian raiders of the previous year or by further incursions from across the Danube – instability at the centre always encouraged such activity at the frontiers, and we also happen to learn that there was a substantial nomadic attack on the African province of Cyrenaica at just this time. Athens, too, was sacked some time in this year, perhaps in the springtime. Claudius sent his fellow general Julius Placidianus to invade southern Gaul, assigning him some sort of extraordinary command. Claudius himself set out for the Balkans, while his fellow conspirator Heraclianus went east, perhaps to deal with Zenobia. Although the sources do not say so explicitly, we should discern in all this activity the work of a military junta determined to confront the multiple threats that faced it: in a coordinated strategy, three of Gallienus's marshals, who had in all likelihood shared in plotting his death, now each took charge of one of the three fronts with which Gallienus had been unable to deal. Outcomes, however, did not meet expectations.

Placidianus faced a confusing situation in Gaul, where one of Postumus's officials, Ulpius Cornelianus Laelianus, had rebelled, taking the imperial title for himself at Moguntiacum in Germania Superior. Postumus rapidly defeated Laelianus, but when he prevented his troops from sacking the city, he immediately faced a mutiny. His own troops murdered Postumus and declared one Marcus Aurelius Marius emperor in his place. Marius was in turn attacked and killed by Postumus's praetorian prefect, Marcus Piavonius Victorinus – probably a Gallic nobleman, to judge by his name. Victorinus had shared the consulship of 268 with Postumus and he now managed to hold things together longer than had his very short-lived predecessors. The invasion of Claudius's colleague Pacatianus advanced as far as the village of Cularo (later the fourth-century town of Gratianopolis, thus modern Grenoble), but no further. Perhaps inspired by the tide of the Claudian advance, the city of Augustodunum (Autun) revolted against Victorinus but, without support from Pacatianus, it was besieged and sacked by Victorinus and this once-prosperous Gallic town lost much of its importance thereafter. Despite these losses, Victorinus was able to enter a second consulship undisturbed in 270.

Meanwhile, at Naissus in the Balkans, Claudius won a dramatic victory over the Scythians that earned him the title Gothicus maximus, joining the Germanicus maximus that he had taken the year before to celebrate his victory over the Alamanni. We do not know where in the Balkans Claudius wintered in 269–70, but the next year opened with mopping-up operations against the Scythians whom we can now for convenience begin to call Goths – the victory title Gothicus demonstrates that this is how the Romans were beginning to identify the people they were fighting beyond the lower Danube.

In the east, Zenobia reacted violently to the arrival of Heraclianus. She had been claiming the title *corrector totius Orientis* for Vaballathus ever since the death of Odaenathus, as if it were a hereditary designation. She now began to mint coins in the name of Vaballathus, an act that could only be construed as rebellion, usurpation and treason. An obscure legend on coins may suggest that Vaballathus began to be styled *vir consularis* [or *clarissimus*], *rex, imperator* (*et*) *dux Romanorum*. If so, it was almost a claim to the imperial throne, but just enough short to be deniable – every title in the formulation could be explained in a relatively innocent way. What could not be explained away was the invasion of Arabia and Egypt, which Zenobia's army, under the command of one Zabdas, undertook in 270. The prefect of Egypt, Tenagino Probus, was defeated and killed defending his province against this invasion. Zenobia appointed his deputy prefect, Julius Marcellinus, as his successor, and Egypt now fell under Palmyrene hegemony for nearly half a decade.

Heraclianus proved powerless to dent Palmyrene control over the core territories in Syria and Arabia, and Zenobia's supporters felt emboldened to push into Anatolia. Meanwhile, in the Balkans, Claudius's recent victory over the Goths could not save his army from devastation by a more formidable enemy: plague broke out among the soldiers during the winter months, carrying off many of them – and then the emperor himself. There is a certain poignancy in the fact that the only emperor in decades not to die by the sword should have reigned so very briefly. But death saved his reputation – when the fourth century remembered the dark years before Diocletian and Constantine, Claudius was the only emperor to be well regarded by every different historical tradition, so much so that it could seem worth fabricating a fictional descent from him. Not since Severus and Caracalla had there been an emperor whose memory held that much credit.

With Claudius dead, his brother Quintillus claimed the throne at Aquileia in northern Italy as a bequest from the late emperor, but without much success. An imperial army on campaign could not exist without an emperor to lead it and Claudius's Balkan legions were much the strongest force in the empire. They were not about to accept any choice but their own, and so they elected Marcus Aurelius Aurelianus, the *dux equitum* of the dead Claudius, who, like him, was implicated in the putsch that unseated Gallienus. Aurelian began the march back to Italy and Quintillus, having reigned a mere seventeen days without leaving Aquileia, was killed (or perhaps committed suicide), thus averting yet another civil war.

Aurelian continued into Italy, basing himself at Mediolanum, where he repelled an attack of the Iuthungi in late 270, and one by Vandals in the winter of 270–71. In spring 271, another Iuthungian invasion followed. It seems clear that consolidation of authority within the Alamannic regions, and perhaps the withdrawal of Roman administration from the Agri Decumates beyond the Rhine–Danube salient, had made some of them much bolder in seeking out profit inside the Roman frontiers. The Vandals, however, are something new: Aurelian's brief campaign marks the first time that they appear in our sources as anything more than an indistinct ethnonym from central Europe, beyond real historical ken. Unlike the Goths, who were to all intents and purposes a creation of the Roman frontier zone, these Vandals seem to have been migrants from east-central Germany – or perhaps a particularly bold and successful war band that had managed to travel a good 400 miles or so in search of loot. It would be many decades before we hear of Vandals making a sustained impact on Roman history and for many decades the Quadi and Sarmatians remained the main cause of concern for the Roman military on the middle Danube.

Unlike the Vandals, the Iuthungi continued to be a threat. Whereas the campaign of 270 had gone smoothly, that of 271 began appallingly for Aurelian, with a major defeat near Placentia (modern Piacenza). The emperor pursued the victorious raiders and forced them to battle at Fanum and then at Ticinum (Pavia), where he crushed the invaders: we hear nothing of Iuthungi for decades thereafter. Moving south to Rome, however, Aurelian was greeted by rebellion – the workers at the imperial mint rose up, with grievances that go unspecified in the sources, and suppressing them was a messy afair that left thousands of Romans dead in the streets. It is a reminder of how militarised the Roman civil service was becoming that skilled craftsmen like the mint workers should be able to organise rioting just as effectively as a mutinous army unit.

After this rising had been suppressed, Aurelian conciliated the people of Rome by adding subsidised distributions of pork to the oil and bread that were already supplied to the plebs of the city by the imperial *annona*. The senate was conciliated with high offices: a great Roman aristocrat, Pomponius Bassus, was made Aurelian's colleague as consul in 271, and the emperor designated two other Roman grandees for the consulate of 272. Although senators had not been deliberately excluded from the consulship by Aurelian's predecessors, the frequent turnover of emperors and proliferation of dynasties, who had at a minimum to hold the consulship with their potential heirs in their first year in power, meant that very few non-imperial consulships had been available. Equally, the expansion of equestrian positions in provincial administration came at the expense of consular ones, which in turn meant that providing enough men of consular status to staff the provincial commands was no longer necessary for administrative reasons, as had still been the case in the Antonine and Severan periods. The suffect consulship, in consequence, more or less disappeared, while the ordinary consulship grew in status, as fewer and fewer opportunities for holding it lay open to the civilian elites of Rome. Aurelian understood the value of the consulship for such men and though he, like all the later third-century emperors, stemmed from a lowly military background, he knew he could not govern without some support from the old aristocracy.

While still in Rome, Aurelian also initiated a building project of unprecedented scale: a gigantic new wall around the city, as much a monument to his own ambition as a working defensive construction. The walls would take the whole of his reign to complete, but by 275 the circuit enclosed all the hills of Rome, as well as the Campus Martius and parts of the city on the other bank of the Tiber, including much of the Janiculum and modern Trastevere – almost twelve miles in circumference all told. Ten feet thick, made of concrete faced with brick, and with a square tower every hundred feet, the wall imposed itself on the landscape, as it still does today wherever its circuit survives. To be sure, given how few troops were actually stationed in Rome and also given the impossibility of defending twelve miles of wall, it could never withstand an actual siege. But it was not meant to. Aurelian's wall was built to discourage attack and overawe attackers, and to provide psychic comfort for an Italian population that had recently suffered the unaccustomed and unwelcome attention of peninsular invasion, not by a usurper but by barbarian armies.

To augment the propaganda victory of Aurelian's wall-building project, the news from Gaul was good – Victorinus had been killed in a coup by another Gallic nobleman, Gaius Esuvius Tetricus, who showed no more inclination to attack Italy than had any of his Gallic predecessors. With Italy also quiet, the emperor was free to plan his destruction of Vaballathus and Zenobia, whose assertions of imperial authority, and still more their conquest of Egypt, could not be tolerated now they no longer had to be. Marching a campaign army through the Balkans and taking the opportunity to repel another barbarian raid, probably by Goths, Aurelian also evacuated the Roman administration from the provinces of Dacia.

This may have been a sensible manoeuvre, in that it made more troops available to him at a critical moment before the eastern campaign, but it was also ideologically risky – giving up provinces was not something

Roman emperors did often or admitted to doing. Dacia, however, had never been worth the money it cost to maintain, as most studies have shown both archaeologically and historically, and in the shifting circumstances of the middle and lower Danube frontiers it is not at all certain that the Carpathian basin was really defensible any longer. Nevertheless, to provide some cover for a potentially unpopular move, Aurelian created two new provinces under the names Dacia Superior and Dacia Inferior, splitting up the old Moesia Inferior in order to do so. The inhabitants of Dacia do not seem to have been evacuated, merely the imperial administrative superstructure around them. None the less, over time the Roman cultural base of the region withered away. Unlike Moesia, or still more Pannonia, Dacia had never developed the civilian infrastructure to accompany its military, administrative and mining apparatus. Whatever part of the Roman population chose not to emigrate lacked the ability or desire to keep up a provincial Roman culture and was absorbed into the emerging archaeological culture that we call Sântana-de-Mureş/ Černjachov and associate with the beginnings of true Gothic hegemony in the region.

With Dacia's government evacuated and his army reinforced, the emperor could move east. Zenobia and Vaballathus now prepared for full-scale war, and the coins they minted finally drop the dual images of Aurelian on one side and Vaballathus on the other. De facto usurpation had become an open claim of imperial rivalry. News of Aurelian's boundless energy and his signal battlefield successes must have gone before him, as too did word of the ruthlessness for which he was long and rightly famed – imperial officials who had clearly sided with Zenobia and Vaballathus in 269 and 270 now came over to Aurelian. Among them were Virius Lupus, the governor of Asia, who would go on to share a consulship with the emperor Probus and serve as urban prefect in the years between 278 and 280, and Statilius Aemilianus, who returned Egypt to Aurelian's allegiance without demur and continued in his role as prefect of the province as a reward, even while a certain Firmus – clearly an equestrian official of some sort – was named provincial *corrector* over him. Aurelian met no resistance until he reached Tyana in Cappadocia, which closed its gates to him – and where it is claimed that he saw a vision of the wonder-working holy man Apollonius that stopped his laying the town waste and massacring its citizens.

The hostility of Tyana does not appear to have been matched by other cities in the region, and Aurelian's forces made it through the Cilician gates and into Syria without further opposition. In Syria, however, there was a major battle against Zenobia's generals in the Antiochene suburb of Daphne, which would soon become one of the swankiest addresses in the fourth- and fifth-century east. Moving south and east, Aurelian won a second battle at Emesa, whose cult Zenobia had honoured for its well-known Severan connections. She had, for that matter, been a generally prolific sponsor of the east's religious melting pot – from the Sarpedonion of Cilician Seleucia, to the Christian bishop of Samosata, to the Persian prophet Mani, whose revelation was being preached at this time. None were of much use to her now – the god Elagabal appeared to have sided with Aurelian, and the string of coins honouring Sol Invictus, the unconquered sun, which Aurelian began to issue at this time would suggest as much.

From Emesa, the conqueror marched on Palmyra itself, capturing the city during the summer of 272. A few key supporters of Zenobia and Vaballathus were executed, but for the most part the city and its inhabitants were spared. Zenobia was taken captive to be brought back to Rome in triumph. Unlike Cleopatra VII, to whom she had compared herself in her propaganda, Zenobia chose captivity over death. The victorious Aurelian took the titles Parthicus maximus and Persicus maximus, though his campaigns had not engaged the Sasanians in any way: under the short-lived shahs Ohrmazd I (r. 272–3) and Varahran I (r. 273–6), the Sasanian court was occupied in a power struggle of its own over how much prominence the Zoroastrian priesthood, in particular its dominant figure, Kardir, should have in the state, and how much or how little other religions like Christianity and Manichaeism should be tolerated.

Despite the momentary Sasanian weakness, however, Aurelian chose not to fight that particular battle. Instead, with one usurper – or breakaway regime – suppressed, he turned his attention to another one, in Gaul. Thinking the eastern reconquest complete, Aurelian started to march west. He had crossed to Byzantium on the European side of the Bosporus when news reached him from Palmyra – the city had rebelled. Just as bad, the riot-prone Egyptian city of Alexandria had erupted again, presumably finding the reimposition of central control by Firmus less agreeable than the rule of Statilius Aemilianus had been.

In January 273, Aurelian marched right back across Asia Minor and into Syria, where this time he put Palmyra to the sack. The great caravan city of the high empire became in the next century a down-at-heel posting for detachments of Rome's Syrian garrison. But the end of the Palmyrene regime actually meant more than that in terms of Eurasian history: in the course of just thirty years, three of the most important cities of the Syrian and Mesopotamian steppe – Hatra, Dura-Europos and Palmyra – had either been destroyed or comprehensively degraded. Neither the Roman nor the Sasanian polities, however often their respective armies might campaign across the region, were equipped to take over the role that those cities' indigenous elites had played in them. The result, over the course of several centuries, was the rise of newly assertive Arab confederacies further south in the Arabian desert. In the years after this book's narrative concludes, these Arabs would become a constant feature in the relations between Byzantium and Persia, from which would arise the last great religious movement of antiquity and the Islamic caliphate its adherents created. In the short term, by contrast, it looked as if forty years of eastern torment had finally been ended by Aurelian.

THE LAST OF THE
SOLDIER EMPERORS

After the destruction of Palmyra, 273 was quiet, and Aurelian used the rest of the year to make clear his intention of dealing with Tetricus in Gaul now that the east seemed pacified. In 274, he marched an army into Gaul, where Tetricus decided to surrender. He did so after his army had already drawn up for battle in modern Champagne, in the Catalaunian fields that are now more famous for a different battle that took place there almost two centuries later, in which Attila the Hun suffered a crushing defeat. This third-century battle of the Catalaunian fields was equally devastating, but for the Gallic legions, who were massacred by Aurelian's troops. Given their long-standing habit of rebellion, this may have been a sensible move. With Gaul under control, Aurelian returned to Rome and celebrated a lavish triumph, which both Tetricus and Zenobia graced. Unlike the *victi* of the republican period, they were not executed at triumph's end. Quite the reverse. Zenobia married into the Roman aristocracy, and was proudly claimed as an ancestor by a fourth-century scion of her house. Tetricus, for his part, was honoured with a minor governorship in the south of Italy that kept him safely out of the way.

Aurelian's success really did look absolute and it had been decades since a single emperor had ruled unopposed. Aurelian had accomplished that with relative ease and comparatively limited bloodshed. More importantly, no new military challengers had risen up in the wake of the suppression of the regimes in Gaul and Palmyra. After his triumph, in a city that was being enclosed in a wall of great magnificence, another symbolic *coup de théâtre* would follow. The revolt of the imperial mint workers in Rome had been one of the first challenges of Aurelian's reign and, though there is no reason to connect that fact to his next initiative, it is interesting that the men who produced Rome's currency should have had so prominent a place for a second time in a relatively short reign: having welded the whole empire back together, Aurelian in 274 launched a new currency, replacing the old-fashioned gold aureus that had been in use for centuries with a new one. While the old aureus had circulated with varying weights and purities, it had always been consistently tariffed against the silver denarius at 1:25 and had maintained that ratio throughout fluctuations in weight and purity which might also cause some aurei, in some places, to be traded as bullion rather than coins. Aurelian's new aureus was by contrast of extreme fineness and clearly intended to drive other, less fine, coins from the market. It was also no longer formally tariffed against silver at all, but was, in effect, stamped gold bullion. In and of itself, that might not have had any dramatic effect, but it was not the limit of Aurelian's monetary activity. In place of the supposedly silver antoninianus, which at this point had virtually no silver content left in it, he minted a new silver coin at a standard 5 per cent fineness. The new Aurelianic antoniniani were marked with a XXI or XX, which presumably means they were tariffed at 1:21 or 1:20 against the copper token coinage. The emperor's intent must have been to replace all the coins of his predecessors and their rivals then in circulation with a new coinage of his own, advertising to the whole world his achievement in restoring the unity of the empire.

Sadly, the impact of his move was disastrous, and came close to demonetising a Roman economy that was already suffering from the effects of epidemic disease. The debasement of the silver currency – from about 40 per cent fineness to less than 5 per cent in 270 – that had characterised the whole of the third century had not (amazingly, according to modern economic theory) had much of an impact on the economic stability of the empire. That is to say, there is no evidence of widespread inflation in response to the falling intrinsic value of the silver coinage year in and year out since the introduction of the antoninianus as a (theoretically) double sestertius under Caracalla. The imperial image on the coins, as well as their familiar tariffing, meant that they survived as a fiduciary currency – and as such were hoarded in troubled times, especially in the 250s and 260s, during which a hugely disproportionate number of known coin hoards were deposited – even when their intrinsic value had effectively disappeared. Aurelian's reform – and it is clear that he did mean it as a reform to unify the minting of a newly reunited empire – changed all that, and very painfully. Where debasement had caused no reliably measurable inflation, Aurelian's decoupling of gold from the fiduciary system of early imperial silver and base metal currencies did. Prices began to soar. The one place we can measure this is Egypt, where the papyri are able to track the almost instantaneous damage done by the decoupling of currencies. As Aurelian's new coinage was exported from Rome and entered into circulation in the various provinces, it seems certain that the same process repeated itself, though that is harder to document.

Aurelian's new coinage did drive many of the older currencies of various regions out of circulation, but it could not do so completely, if only because he could not supply demand fast enough. Worse, the floating of the relationship of gold and silver made nonsense of the link between silver and the intrinsically worthless copper currency. Without buyers and sellers sharing the faith that a handful of slugs of base metal bearing the imperial image and name were, somewhere in the universe, worth a set amount of gold, the fiduciary system collapsed. The sophisticated banking system of the early empire went with it. Coins were now worth what local markets thought they were worth, and that was always a great deal less than the tariffed price. It would be two decades before an effort was made to control the chaos that the Aurelianic reforms had unleashed, during which time payment in kind became a driving engine of the Roman economy for the first time in almost half a millennium – so much so that the next great reforming emperor, Diocletian (r. 284–305), was forced to build payment in kind into his administrative system. It is ironic that the empire began to face widespread economic problems only as the political situation seemed to have changed definitively for the better. But, as things turned out, Aurelian lived to see the impact of neither his military successes nor his economic reforms.

In 275, he ventured into Gaul, presumably to the Rhineland and the region of Colonia Agrippina, to reassert his presence in a region that had not seen an Italian emperor in decades. He then travelled with his army to the Balkans via Raetia, where he dealt with a minor Iuthungian raid. We do not know what Aurelian was doing in the Balkans, where there is no evidence of 'Scythian' or Gothic trouble; he may have been heading to the eastern provinces for a kind of 'beating of the bounds' along the lines of the Gallic trip. Regardless, in late summer or early autumn 275, at the imperial postal station at Caenophrurium, on the road between Perinthus and Byzantium, he fell victim to a putsch similar to the one that had unthroned Gallienus. It seems certain that the army as a whole was genuinely happy with their emperor's leadership, and that the murder was an unpleasant accident: a court official, for reasons of his own, forged a letter suggesting that the emperor had ordered the execution of some junior officers, who proceeded to murder him – a Thracian guardsman named Mucapor is named as the killer. His action cannot have been popular, for neither he nor anyone else on the spot claimed Aurelian's throne. That suggests frustration among an officer corps that had not, for a change, wanted to see their emperor dead. The man who did in the end succeed Aurelian – Claudius Tacitus – is an enigmatic figure, because the very few extant sources veil his succession in a bizarrely romantic fiction.

There are only two points of fact. Presumably because of internal disagreements, there was a six-week interregnum, with diplomatic twists and turns among rival factions that are now irrecoverable. At the end of it, Tacitus was invited to become emperor, left retirement in Campania in southern Italy and took up the purple in Rome. Because his name recalled that of the famous early imperial historian, the fourth-century author of the *Historia Augusta* concocted a purely imaginary mishmash: the army defers to the senate, which defers to the army, which again defers to the senate, so that a distant descendant of the historian takes the throne as the last senatorial emperor and includes among his edicts one that requires the copying and reproduction of his forefather's works. (If only this fairy tale were true, the tenuous thread on which hangs the preservation of Tacitus's extant writings – most of it from a single manuscript, more of it lost for ever – would be more robust.) The charms of this happy story are such that even Gibbon was deceived, and more recent commentators have not refrained from buying into one or another part of it. But the prosaic reality is that Tacitus was just another general from the Danube, older than most and now retired, hence a safe compromise candidate; he was quite possibly another marshal of Gallienus of whom we happen to lack a prior record. Clearly he was a known quantity, trusted by the Balkan soldiers, but so far away from the scene of Aurelian's murder that he could not possibly have had anything to do with it. That explanation at least fits our tiny residue of reliable evidence, which suggests that after six weeks there was universal agreement that Tacitus should become emperor and could make his way out to the Balkan armies. The most remarkable thing about the entire episode is that no other frontier army ventured to set up an emperor of its own while Aurelian's Balkan forces sat paralysed. That must be a measure of just how honoured – and also feared – Aurelian had been.

Tacitus crossed into Asia in command of the late emperor's field army, dealing en route with a naval attack from north of the Black Sea by Scythians, perhaps Goths or perhaps the same Heruli attested in that role half a decade earlier. His explicit aim was to catch and chastise Aurelian's murderers, some of whom had fled east. The Thracian Mucapor who had killed Aurelian, otherwise unknown, was captured and tortured to death. Tacitus then sent a relative named Maximinus to Antioch, intending to return to the west himself, but this Maximinus made himself so hated that the leading Antiochenes plotted with the surviving murderers of Aurelian to kill him. They then raised a force to pursue Tacitus and killed him as well, at Tyana, a city not long previously spared by Aurelian despite its support for Zenobia. It is possible, if speculative, that we are witnessing in this episode the vengeance of the Antiochene upper classes for the damage wrought on Daphne by Aurelian's victory there in 272 – the villain was dead, but his self-declared avenger could still be killed. Aurelian's army – having briefly been Tacitus's army – now chose the latter's half-brother, the praetorian prefect M. Annius Florianus, as his successor. But the Syrian army, presumably complicit in the Antiochene opposition to Tacitus, elected Marcus Aurelius Probus instead.

Probus was another of the old marshals of Gallienus, and matters appeared to be returning to the dreadfully familiar status quo of a decade previously – coup and counter-coup, putsch and push-back balancing each other out with no one the long-term winner. Florianus, about whom we know virtually nothing, began to lead his army towards Syria to confront his challenger, but had to call a halt at Tarsus in Cilicia when plague struck. Perhaps lacking the will to fight in their stricken condition, the army mutinied and declared for Probus rather than pursue the war. Florianus abdicated, but was promptly murdered, accused of plotting to retake the throne. With Florianus dead, Probus then executed the surviving murderers of Aurelian at a banquet.

Despite this promising start, Probus had nothing like Aurelian's force of personality. His reign, which is the worst documented half decade in all of imperial Roman history, seems to have been a series of constant revolts from one end of the empire to the other. Indeed, the biggest surprise is that he managed to hold his throne for a full six years without being assassinated. Chronology is imprecise at best, but the reign opened with the Egyptian communities of the Thebaid joining with the pastoralist Blemmyes, who lived at the desert edge of the province, to attack the city of Coptos. This reflects the peculiar political and social world of southern Upper Egypt, hundreds of miles upriver from the main centres of the province and confined to a relatively narrow strip of land along the upper Nile, ending with the garrison town of Elephantine just below the river's first cataract. Coptos was the southernmost of the really prosperous Nilotic towns and it was also the station at which the military road across steppe and desert from the Red Sea port of Berenike reached the Nile corridor. As such, it was an attractive target for periodic nomadic predation, but what is interesting here, and not fully explicable, is the participation of local provincials alongside the nomads in attacking a major town. Whether our evidence is a stray glimpse of a local feud that just happens to survive, or whether it represents something more systemic is unclear: perhaps it is a sign of the disruption and disturbance that Aurelian's currency reform had generated even in far off corners of the empire.

There was also fighting on the Danube against Goths and Sarmatians, but this had become a chronic rather than an acute problem, and one that would take many years to deal with effectively. Indeed, the renewed threat to the Balkan provinces from the Sarmatians is almost certainly a consequence of Gothic expansion, inasmuch as they had proved relatively biddable neighbours over many previous decades. While Probus was campaigning on the Danube, the governor of Syria, Saturninus, revolted, claiming the purple for himself, before his own men turned on him and killed him at Apamea. Then there was an uprising at Cremna in Pisidia, led by a local worthy named Lydios, and the town withstood a major siege operation at the hands of the governor, Terentius Marcianus, before surrendering (the surviving remains of the siegeworks are some of the best evidence we have for Roman military engineering).

Perhaps at the same time, the Rhine armies acclaimed Proculus and Bonosus in turn as their emperors at Colonia Agrippina. The soldiers had good reason to be dissatisfied, for it seems that Gaul and Germany had been badly mauled by raiding since the collapse of the Gallic regime and had received little or no help from the imperial centre. On the other hand, some argue that Probus fought a series of campaigns in Germany, before returning to the Balkans, and that the usurpations followed his departure. The sources are too fragmentary to tell us. Finally, the governor of Britain, whose name is unknown, was also acclaimed by his troops – which was unusual in that it was a province that had generally been at peace throughout the century. In all these cases, and most unusually, there are no coins, which suggests the extent to which Aurelian's monetary reforms had ruined the money economy.

Be that as it may, Aurelian had at least enforced unity and a certain peace on the empire. All that now looked as if it was disappearing. Probus could strike gold coins depicting the labours of Hercules, but he was not up to the Herculean challenges he faced. With the chronic frontier warfare, which fed a cycle of civil violence, the gap between the militarised parts of the empire and those that were generally at peace widened, and so too did the swathe of territory that was permanently exposed to the passage of imperial armies and the quartering of soldiers on them. And these soldiers, as the events of Probus's reign just described show, were terribly prone to violent rebellion. Probus himself discovered as much in the end, despite having hung on to power for longer even than Aurelian. But, as with so many of his predecessors, the hostility of a cabal of senior officers would prove fatal. Probus celebrated a triumph at Rome in 281 and then returned to the east in the following year, reaching Sirmium in Pannonia before he was murdered, having just learned that his praetorian prefect M. Aurelius Carus had been proclaimed emperor.

Carus is interesting if only because he is the only emperor in the long sequence of third-century soldier claimants not to have a Danubian background – he was, instead, from Narbonensis in the south of Gaul, and the nature of his connection to the world of senior command is unclear. We lack any sense of his power base or how he was able to succeed in a highly competitive environment that seems to have excluded men of his regional background. If the reasons for and circumstances of his accession are obscure, Carus at least had a family with dynastic potential: there was an adult son, Carinus, and a younger one, Numerianus, as well as a grandson, Carinus's son Nigrinianus. The family's dynastic ambitions were clear from the start: while Carinus campaigned against the Quadi in Pannonia, celebrating a triumph at Mediolanum in 282, Carus sought to enhance his personal prestige by leading Probus's campaign army into a Persian war. The timing was propitious, for the ruling Sasanian dynasty had collapsed into the sort of civil war that had afflicted the Roman state for decades. Shapur I had intensified his father Ardashir's practice of setting up his various sons as kings of the various parts of his empire. The eldest son, Ohrmazd, had been imposed on Armenia, but other sons ruled Mesene, at the head of the Persian Gulf; Sind, Seistan and Turan in the deserts of present-day Baluchistan; Gilan in the mountainous south-west of the Caspian; and in Kerman and Adiabene. That left plenty of rivals who might hope to succeed Shapur when he died, as he finally did in 272. The fact that he had never capitalised on his defeat and capture of Valerian was the result of his taking much more serious account of his multiple frontiers than did Valerian's Roman successors, all of whom would immediately privilege the eastern frontier over any other, and prioritise a usurper's challenge over any possible damage their provincials might be suffering.

Shapur, like his father Ardashir and for reasons that the absence of Sasanian literary sources makes it impossible for us to analyse, seems to have sought prestige and ideological legitimation among his core sup-porters in Fars by appropriating the necropolis of the Achaemenids and advertising far and wide the way he had humbled three different Roman emperors. But in pragmatic strategic terms, he focused more time and military attention on Central Asia: Sogdiana, which the Sasanians were never fully able to control; Margiana and Bactria, which fell to Persia during his reign; and beyond the Hindu Kush, in Kabul, Gandhara and Swat, where the Sasanians displaced the last of the Kushans. Thereafter, the Kushanshahr became a client of the main Sasanian line, usually ruled by one of its cadet branches, occasionally acting as a launching pad for rebellions, and striking a currency we know as Kushano-Sasanian (because it was minted on the Kushan gold standard rather than the silver drachms of Iran proper). As fourth-century history will show us once again, it is the numismatic evidence that often gives us information that we lack from any other source. In terms of the Sasanian conquest of the Central Asian and north-west Indian hinterland, which used to be dated as much as a hundred years later, new coin finds and in particular the proper identi-fication of mints, including travelling mints, have definitively shown the conquest to be the work of Shapur I: the royal silver coinage is increasingly struck in the Far East during the latter part of Shapur's reign, some of it by engravers from the Iranian heartland, which must indicate travelling mints created in order to pay multiple armies on campaign.

After Shapur's death in 272, his eldest son Ohrmazd I succeeded him, and is recorded fighting campaigns in Central Asia. Ohrmazd, however, reigned for just one year. His successors were all children, their courts dominated by the Mazdean priest Kardir, who had risen to prominence in the last years of Shapur and whose priority seems to have been to solidify the status of Zoroastrianism and the worship of Ohrmazd as the official cult of the Sasanian state. Although he was himself a convinced believer in the truth of his Zoroastrian religion, Shapur had been tolerant of other religions. There was room in the Zoroastrian worldview for non-believers, as indeed there had to be because its practice was so tightly connected to an Iranian ethnic identity. Christians and Jews in particular could contribute to the eternal fight of good against evil by cultivating their own, legitimate but inferior, faiths in their own way. They could not seek converts among the Iranian nobility, and the leaders of their communities were expected to play a similar role to the Magian priesthood in organising the economic affairs of their own communities and ensuring that their taxes were paid. Shapur's tolerance had gone further; he even encouraged the new revelations of the prophet Mani, whose gnostic and dualist beliefs would go on to play a divisive role in Roman society. Some have suggested that Shapur saw in Mani's revelation a belief system that would resonate, more than would his own Mazdaism, with the many non-Iranians of his empire, from Christians and Jews in Mesopotamia to Buddhists in the east and north-east.

Then, with Shapur's death, the Zoroastrian priesthood seized its chance to stifle what it saw as a potent threat to its social and religious dominance. The minorities of Varahran I (273–6) and Varahran II (276–93) seem to have been dominated by the Mazdean priesthood on the one hand and the Persian nobility on the other. It is during these reigns that we find the otherwise unknown phenomenon of a non-royal figure (Kardir again) inscribing his exploits in a public and royal context. It was also now that Mani was arrested and left to die in prison, perhaps in 276. Then, in the 280s, there was a civil war between supporters of Varahran II and those of his cousin Ohrmazd. The latter relied upon nomadic Sakas and levies from the Kushanshahr for support, minted his own coinage and may have even taken the title of Kushanshah. The war between the cousins also divided the empire's upper nobility, and the great families of both Persian and Parthian background now began to demonstrate an attitude they would maintain right until the collapse of the Sasanian dynasty: while the right of the Sasanian family to rule went unchallenged, the nobility reserved their right to choose among potential royal claimants, and depose one Sasanian in favour of another should that seem necessary. For the first, but not last, time in the history of the two empires, a combination of internal religious ferment and external distraction on Persia's eastern frontiers made the 270s and 280s a period during which Rome had little to fear from the armies of its imperial rival.

Perhaps realising this – though with the caveat that Roman military intelligence on Persian affairs was never very comprehensive – Carus marched into Mesopotamia in the summer of 283, straight down the Euphrates to the capital at Ctesiphon. The campaign went so well that word was put about that Ctesiphon had actually fallen to the emperor, and one strand of sources preserves that story. But Seleucia-on-Tigris, by then a suburb of Ctesiphon, was indeed sacked, as attested by Ammianus Marcellinus, a good fourth-century source, who had inspected the ruins with his own eyes when serving on the emperor Julian's Persian campaign.

Carus's military success was not rewarded by his army's loyalty: he was murdered, like so many of his predecessors, though there is also a story, surely legendary, that his tent was struck by lightning. His murder left the army stranded deep inside Persia, and the first order of business was to extricate it. Whoever was responsible for Carus's death, no one claimed his title, which passed to his sons Carinus and Numerian, the latter a young boy who had accompanied his father's campaign army into Persia. Carus's brother-in-law Aper, who had succeeded him as praetorian prefect, probably took de facto control of affairs until the army was back in Syria. Disarray among the Persians had helped them to extract the army intact and largely unscathed – Aper and his officers were lucky that no new Shapur emerged to harass them on their retreat.

The Roman forces reached Emesa in Syria by March 284, and Cyzicus and Nicomedia in Bithynia later in the year. There, in November, Aper announced the death of Numerian. Although the boy had been ill, his death was almost certainly murder. There was now just one emperor, Carinus back in the west, but Carus's campaign army was not likely to accept its subordination to a western rival. As Carus's brother-in-law, Aper believed he should succeed to the throne, but the army did not concur. Instead, its choice landed on a relatively junior officer, C. Valerius Diocles, a man of about forty who was the *comes domesticorum*, commander of the main guard unit which travelled with the emperor. Diocles accepted his acclamation, and renamed himself Diocletianus, a more Latinate-sounding name than his obviously Greek (and low-born) original. At a meeting of the whole army, he personally executed Aper in full public view, claiming thereby to avenge the murder of Numerian. He then proclaimed himself consul prior, along with L. Caesonius Bassus, a member of the Roman senatorial aristocracy. The truth of what happened can never be known. Numerian may have died naturally, with both Aper and Diocletian seeking to profit by his death, or one of them may have killed him. (We do not need to believe the story that, for some time after his murder, his corpse had been carried alongside the army in a litter in order to disguise it, word being put about about that he was suffering from a disease of the eyes.) A child emperor with no protector was a victim awaiting the slaughter, his death a foregone conclusion, but Diocletian's acclamation at Nicomedia necessarily meant civil war. Carus's remaining son, the emperor Carinus, could not be expected to acquiesce in the eastern army's presumption and, by taking the consular title for himself and appointing a colleague, Diocletian effectively declared war on Carinus.

Diocletian overwintered in Asia, before crossing into the Balkans, with an eye on attacking Carinus. The latter marched east from Rome, knowing that he would need to face Diocletian in the Balkans, but he had none of the personal authority his father Carus had commanded, and he had no dynastic prospects as his son Nigrinianus had died. The praetorian prefect Sabinus Iulianus, left behind by Carus to watch over his son, now revolted, presumably viewing him as unlikely to survive a war with the seasoned army of Diocletian. This revolt was put down at Verona, but then the *corrector Venetiae*, Marcus Aurelius Julianus, revolted in Pannonia, striking coins at Siscia before being defeated by Carinus early in 285 as he marched to the Balkans. There, at the Margus river, his army faced its more formidable rival, and Carinus's newly appointed praetorian prefect, Tiberius Claudius Aurelius Aristobulus, promptly betrayed him as well. So too did M. Flavius Constantius, who was then serving in an extended military command over Dalmatia and the Balkan interior. Constantius had probably previously served as a tribune of the *domestici* under Diocletian; he would go on to be a major prop of the latter's new regime. As we have seen many times, third-century soldiers were quick to desert a commander whose prospects looked dim, so Carinus was promptly assassinated by his own men. He and his wife Magnia Urbica suffered *damnatio memoriae*, as did Carus and Numerian, their names being chiselled from inscriptions.

The battle of the Margus ended in a relatively easy victory for Diocletian, but the past decades had shown that initial success counted for very little without persistent labour. Diocletian marched his army into northern Italy and took up residence at Mediolanum. There he made another general of no great pedigree his colleague as caesar, on 25 July 285. This general was Marcus Aurelius Maximianus, the son of a shopkeeper from very near Sirmium whose family had gained citizenship only with the edict of Caracalla. Diocletian and Maximian had come up through the ranks together and both had been present on Carus's Persian campaign. Neither man troubled to go to Rome at this point – there were too many problems on the northern frontiers. By the autumn of 285, Maximian was campaigning in Gaul, where the death of Carinus had prompted a revolt by a man named Amandus, who proclaimed himself augustus. Carus was from Narbonensis and Amandus may have been a relative; later sources also name one Aelianus as a part of the revolt, but he remains a mystery, as no authentic coins in his name have survived, only modern fakes. Maximian seems to have suppressed the revolt fairly efficiently, and later tradition reinvented Amandus and Aelianus as rustic brigands rather than the provincial notables they were. Still, their uprising prompted the usual uncertainty on the frontier, and Maximian also fought against Franci or Alamanni from across the Rhine. Diocletian, at the same time, was fighting against Sarmatians on the Danube bend, now a perpetual sore point trapped between the empire and what we infer was Gothic power expanding up the Danube and in the former province of Dacia. We do not know where Diocletian overwintered in 285–6, but he was back in Asia Minor in March of 286. Gaul was far too unsettled for Maximian to leave it.

The expedient of having an augustus in one place and a caesar of similar age and experience in another was a novelty. No one, least of all his soldiers, could have expected Maximian to remain in a subordinate role for ever. On 1 April 286, he was duly proclaimed augustus, without Diocletian being present, but with his full, stated approval. The cynical interpretation would be that Diocletian gave his old comrade something he would obviously have wanted before he took it for himself and thereby sparked a civil war; the loftier and more noble reading would have Diocletian and Maximian embarking on a bold experiment in power-sharing, the better for each to hang on to the imperial thrones they had won. What is certain is that they, or Diocletian, now began to concoct an elaborate ideological system to explain what everyone could see was an unprecedented relationship. Diocletian began to style himself as the child or companion of that most Roman of gods, Jupiter, the chief of the Capitoline triad, and thus the greatest god in the Roman pantheon. Maximian, for his part, was to be Hercules, Jupiter's son and loyal subordinate. Both emperors were equally augusti, both augusti were equally divine, but Diocletian was the senior, as Jupiter was senior to Hercules. This articulated a traditional Roman paternalism but injected the issue of divine election into the question of who could be emperor. Here we can see how far things had changed since the Antonine age: a hundred years before Diocletian, Commodus had been mercilessly ridiculed for his self-assimilation to Hercules; fifty years earlier, Elagabalus's belief in his own divine incarnation led directly to his assassination. By contrast, when Aurelian advertised his personal relationship with the unconquered sun it was accepted as perfectly reasonable, as, so it seems, was Diocletian and Maximian's identification with Jupiter and Hercules.

It remained to be seen whether this bold experiment in power-sharing between two men with no dynastic connection would work, especially because Maximian had a son on the threshold of adulthood, while Diocletian had only daughters. The presence of a presumptive heir to the junior augustus must have complicated expectations about both the present and the future balance of power. In the moment, though, both men had plenty of work to do.

In 286, a general named Carausius revolted in Britain, declared himself augustus and began minting coins. A Menapian by birth, from the territory between the Rhine and Scheldt, he had been the commander of the Channel fleet, protecting the coastline from Saxon and Frankish pirates. His revolt was a serious concern: not only the armies of Britain, but also many stationed in Gaul itself took his side, and he began striking coins at Rotomagus (modern Rouen) as well. Maximian was too busy fighting on the frontiers of eastern Gaul throughout the later 280s to do anything about this revolt, which is surprising given that usurpations almost axiomatically trumped barbarian incursions on the scale of imperial threats. The fact that Maximian divided his time among the main cities of the Rhineland – Trier, Moguntiacum and Colonia Agrippina – may suggest that he doubted his ability to challenge the usurper successfully, and it may be that a wide tranche of western Gaul recognised Carausius rather than the new regime of Diocletian and Maximian. Rather than face the usurpation outright, Maximian launched a police action on the frontier to shore up his authority, crossing the Rhine, sowing terror among the barbarians and installing a king named Gennobaudes among some of the Franci there. The victory emboldened him and, in 288, he led an army against Carausius, winning a battle at Rotomagus and regaining control over north-western Gaul. He then began to construct a fleet, taking the better part of a year to do so, only to see it destroyed in a North Sea gale before he could launch an invasion. Carausius promptly retook the Gallic towns he had recently lost to Maximian. It must have seemed like the fatal rhythm of the mid third century was returning.

While Maximian was in Gaul, Diocletian was fighting in the Balkans, with journeys to Syria in 286 and 287 to observe developments in Persia, which had been ignored for more than a decade apart from the brief campaign of Carus. Aurelian's destruction of rebellious Palmyra had destabilised politics on the Syrian frontier, for in 289–90 we find Diocletian at the old caravan city fighting the desert tribes and also visiting the important Severan site of Emesa. Further north, Shapur's weak successors had lost control of Armenia, and Diocletian was able to install as king the Arsacid Tiridates III, who had fled to the Romans as a child decades earlier.

On the whole, Diocletian had been having much greater success in his sphere of activity than Maximian in his. In 290, Diocletian inspected the field armies in the Balkans, en route to northern Italy, where he met Maximian in the winter of 290–91. Whatever else it may have been – and there was no love lost between the two augusti, however much they might need one another – the meeting at Mediolanum was a show of unity. The two received embassies from the cities of the west and from the senate at Rome. This reaffirmed the tradition by which earlier soldier emperors had coopted the support of the imperial capital's aristocracy, although neither Diocletian nor Maximian showed the slightest inclination to go there. Despite the symbolic power that Rome and its senate still commanded, sometime in the quarter century between Gallienus and Diocletian, the traditional link between emperor and eternal city had been comprehensively broken. In fact, there was no longer really an imperial capital, just a series of residences of greater or lesser importance: Trier, Mediolanum, Nicomedia and Sirmium were the most important at this stage in Diocletian and Maximian's joint reign, but there would be others. The outlines of the old, high imperial world were growing very blurred, and we – with the full benefit of hindsight – can see a new late imperial order beginning to take shape.

Shortly after the meeting in Milan, Maximian resigned the command against Carausius. It was taken over by a subordinate general, the same Flavius Constantius whose timely betrayal of Carinus eased Diocletian's path to power in 284 – and who had already been rewarded by marriage to Maximian's daughter Theodora in 289. The events of later 291 and all of 292 are obscure in the extreme, almost as opaque to the historian as the reign of Probus, but when the sources resume in 293, it is with a series of momentous, indeed unprecedented, reforms. Perhaps these were agreed upon at Mediolanum in 291; perhaps Diocletian spent the intervening years working out how he might shore up a regime that remained shaky even with two cooperative joint rulers at its head. What emerged at the start of 293 was nothing short of extraordinary – having discovered that even two emperors were not enough to secure a stable regime, and having quite unaccountably survived longer than any emperor since Gallienus, Diocletian and his colleague overhauled the shape of imperial government – from the currency to the army, to the administration of the provinces and even to the imperial office itself. On 1 March 293, two new caesars were appointed, and the shared emperorship of Diocletian and Maximian became an imperial college of four members, two senior augusti and two junior caesars. With the creation of this tetrarchy, a new stage in Roman history begins, one that reinvented the very nature of the empire.

I2

DIOCLETIAN, CONSTANTINE AND THE CREATION OF THE LATER ROMAN EMPIRE

※

The quickest way to make sense of the tetrarchy is to look at its coins. As the third century progressed, and claimant followed claimant with increasing speed, the portraiture of the coinage declined in both complexity and representational specificity. At mid-century, and especially on the bronze sestertii, the portraits of emperors like Decius show the sort of individuality that we can trace all the way back to the Hellenistic tradition of naturalistic coin portraiture, but already before that, the silver-washed antoniniani of Caracalla and Severus Alexander look more schematic and stylised; by the time of Claudius, Aurelian and Probus, sestertii had disappeared and portraits on the antoniniani no longer look as if they are meant to depict real people, but are instead stylised statements of rulership. The stylisation changes slightly from reign to reign, but with their beards, helmets and armour, they remain little more than abstract images of imperial power and authority. Much the same can be said of the early portraits of Diocletian. But then, in 293, he and Maximian not only took on two new junior emperors, they also reformed the mints and introduced an entirely new type of coin, whose ancient name is unknown, but which we call the follis. This medium-sized bronze type – at around 10 grams, double the weight of an antoninianus and half that of an old sestertius – was minted across the empire, in a whole series of new mints and in a variety of provinces. On these folles, the four emperors – the augusti Diocletian and Maximian and the caesars Constantius and Galerius – are indistinguishable. In some types they appear in military garb, in others in civilian, but their portraits are all the same: short full beard and moustache in the typical military fashion; heavyset, even jowly, faces; eyes fixed on the middle distance with no attempt at portraiture; and necks more like those of bulls than human beings. As an image of the unity and ubiquity of imperial purpose, tetrarchic coinage would be hard to better.

But these new coins were just one small part of a much larger Diocletianic programme of reform implemented by the tetrarchy. These reforms were an ongoing response to the political traumas the tetrarchs had experienced working their way up through the fractious military hierarchy of the post-Gallienan decades, a response that Diocletian was imaginative enough to modify when something seemed not to be working. The first element in the new tetrarchic programme, with which we ended chapter 11, was the multiplication of the imperial office and the creation of what we can call a college of emperors. Flavius Constantius, who had served as Maximian's praetorian prefect and had been married into his family since 289, was made caesar on 1 March 293, probably at Mediolanum. He immediately launched an assault on Carausius's Gallic strongholds and routed him, even taking the naval stronghold of Bononia (modern Boulogne), the main staging post for sailing to Britain. On the same day in March 293, probably at Sirmium in the Balkans, Diocletian proclaimed C. Galerius Maximianus as caesar in a parallel move, marrying him to his own daughter Valeria in June. Constantius would be the senior caesar, as Diocletian was the senior augustus, and the fiction of divine kinship already established for Diocletian and Maximian was extended further, with Constantius joining the 'Jovian' line of Diocletian and Galerius the 'Herculean' line of Maximian. Both caesars added a new nomen, Valerius, to their titulature, confirming their relationship to Diocletian. This division of government, with its publicly legible ideology, would make it easier to put an emperor on the spot wherever one might be needed. The eastern pair would begin to move against Persia, the western would continue to stabilise the frontiers and suppress usurpers, of whom Carausius had not been the last. Indeed, the defeat of Carausius in battle led to his murder by a man named Allectus, of whom very little is known save that he assumed Carausius's imperial title and began to mint coins in his own name.

Crushing usurpations as they sprang up would never, in itself, be enough to ensure stability, and Diocletian realised that. His new tetrarchic dispensation was meant to make such attempts much more difficult to stage in future than they had been in the past. A key move in that direction was redrawing provincial boundaries and thereby multiplying the number of imperial administrators, with a view towards both improving oversight and weakening the capacity of any one governor to cause trouble or win for himself a power base with which to challenge the ruling emperor. As we saw throughout chapter 11, the military side of imperial government had become more and more prominent, and likewise more specialised, as the third century progressed. The Julio-Claudian and Antonine high imperial model, in which all members of the governing class were at least theoretically able to serve both as civil administrators and military commanders, had given way to a system in which military commands went to career soldiers, many of them risen through the ranks, and more often than not promoted on the basis of ability rather than birth. That was the background of all the emperors after Gallienus. At least three of the tetrarchs – Diocletian, Maximian and Constantius – had come up through precisely that career path, and though little certain is known of Galerius save his parentage (his parents were peasants from near Romulianum on the Danube and his name at birth was Maximinus), he had undoubtedly served in the army.

So predominant was this career trajectory that fourth-century writers could imagine a moment in the third century when someone had made a conscious decision to exclude senators from high office (they attributed the choice to Gallienus, an irony given that he more than any other emperor of the period had portrayed himself in a traditionally senatorial vein). In fact, of course, the process was a natural one that grew out of the need to deal with the various short-term crises of the third century. Diocletian, understanding the value of a professional army, formalised some of the trends that had been emerging over the previous decades. He began by separating military from civilian commands altogether, thus marking off a divide between career paths through the officer corps and career paths in civil administration. The immediate value of this was not merely to confirm the professional skills of the relevant commanders, but also to ensure that those who commanded troops in battle would not at the same time be responsible for paying them their salaries. By separating these two functions, and relying on rivalry between soldiers and bureaucrats, Diocletian reckoned that any would-be usurper would have a hard time paying an army; and since an unpaid army was not a loyal one, the perennial third-century threat of usurpation would be severely limited.

Important as that move was, there was more. Diocletian radically revised the imperial administrative map, chopping the old Severan provinces up into more than a hundred much smaller provinces (as an example, Gallia Lugdunensis and Gallia Belgica were both split in half, doubling the number of provinces in that region of north central Gaul). These were administered by civilian governors of differing rank, the prestige accruing to each province developing into a very definite hierarchy over time. The idea was to provide greater oversight of regional affairs and stronger direct connections to the imperial government than had been possible in the old Augustan – or even the Severan – provincial system, with its enormous provinces and imperial government relying almost entirely upon local municipalities and local big men to mediate its interests. Where necessary, these provinces were assigned separate military commanders of middling rank, known as *duces*, further separating military from civilian governance. Sometime between 297 and 305, these new provinces were grouped into larger units for the purposes of fiscal administration and taxation by both the palatine treasuries and the staff of the praetorian prefects. These groups of provinces were known as dioceses and seem to have been supervised on an ad hoc basis, by the prefect himself or by a deputy, until, by 314 at the latest, each was put under its own official, who was known as a *vicarius*.

The prefects, too, multiplied under the Diocletianic system, as was necessary given the multiplication of the emperors. But they also now lost most of their military functions, becoming instead the most senior administrators in a civilian hierarchy, a process that became final in the second decade of the fourth century. A prefect was assigned to each augustus, and perhaps to each caesar, and travelled with his imperial court. Because these courts were so mobile, a prefect's sphere of activity was coterminous with that of the augustus (or caesar) he served and was not territorially fixed. By keeping the highest ranking administrators with them, but then fixing groups of provinces into dioceses that could be supervised by lesser officials on the prefects' behalf, the tetrarchs maintained the flexibility and adaptability of their collegiate emperorship but also provided for hierarchical and territorial supervision.

Change in other government bureaus accelerated as well. We have already mentioned the importance of jurists and lawyers in the period after Caracalla's citizenship edict, as Roman law was extended to people who had no practical tradition of using it. Even in the darkest days of rapid imperial turnover, the quotidian labour of instructing citizens on how they could and could not use the new laws to which they had become subject went on. Over time, the imperial bureaus into which such questions filtered, and by which they were answered, had changed. By the time of Carus, if not before, the old Antonine officials *ab epistulis* and *a libellis* had come to be known as *magistri epistularum* and *magistri libellorum*, and it was the occupants of these offices who had the most interest in regularising the application of Roman civil law across the empire.

Early in the tetrarchic decade, several of these *magistri* undertook major efforts to codify the laws that had been issued by the emperors of the previous century or more. The so-called *codices Gregorianus* and *Hermogenianus*, named after *magistri libellorum* of Maximian and Diocletian respectively, collected and organised imperial rescripts in coherent volumes. Their goal was to provide a more comprehensible statement of the standing law of the land than could be gleaned from the random consultation of whatever documents happened to be available in a given time or place. The Gregorian code collected rescripts of pre-tetrarchic emperors that its compiler believed to still have the force of law in 291, the date of its issue. A few years later, the Hermogenian code collected the rescripts of Diocletian, some of which had clearly been drafted by Hermogenianus himself. The dissemination of these codes was quite wide at the time, though only the Gregorian code survives – in seventeen small parchment fragments of the fifth century, recovered from the binding of a medieval book. Instead, for the most part, the rescripts collected in both codes survive in the great sixth-century code of the emperor Justinian that eventually supplanted them and rendered their further preservation otiose.

Change in the legal bureaus of the imperial government was matched by changes in the financial administration. The old separation of *aerarium* and *fiscus* had long since ceased to work in any regular fashion, and the capture of Decius' treasury at Abrittus must have accelerated their dysfunction. Instead, two new bureaus, the *res privata* and the *sacrae largitiones*,

1. Hadrian's Wall

2. Ribchester Helmet

3. Ludovisi Battle Sarcophagus

4. A Sarmatian Horseman

5. Library of Celsus

6. *Theatre of Leptis Magna*

7. *Roman Military Diploma*

8. *Herodes Atticus*

9. Mithras

10. A Parthian Noble

11. Fulvius Plautianus

12. Septimius Severus

13. The Severan Tondo

14. The Licinius Cameo

16. Pupienus

17. Balbinus

15. Maximinus

18. A Roman Tunic

19. Lamp in the shape of a Nubian

20. Kushan Fresco

21. Kushan (Gandharan) Buddha

22. *Palace of Ardashir at Firuzabad*

23. *Victory of Shapur, Naqsh-e Rustam*

24. *The Aurelian Wall of Rome*

25. *Deeds of the Priest Kardir, Naqsh-e Rajab*

26. Maximian

27. Edict on Maximum Prices

28. Fausta

29. The Tetrarchs

30. Shapur II Hunting Boar

31. Sasanian Royal Bust

32. Constantius II

33. Julian

34. Porphyry Sarcophagus of Helena

35. The Judgement of Paris (detail)
from the Atrium House, Antioch

PLATE CAPTIONS

1. Hadrian's Wall

With the Colosseum and the Roman forum, Hadrian's Wall is one of the most recognisable monuments of the Roman world, and certainly the most famous Roman monument in Britain. Stretching more than seventy miles from Wallsend at the mouth of the Tyne to Bowness on the Solway Firth, the wall is now a Unesco World Heritage Site. Working in the 120s AD, Roman military engineers made as much use as possible of natural terrain features, and enhanced them with turf, timber and stone fortifications as necessary. The wall was designed to function like other, less famous, Roman frontier systems – the German *Limes*, which enclosed the salient of the upper Rhine and Danube until the later third century, the *fossatum* deep in the pre-desert of North Africa, the late imperial *Strata Diocletiana* in the Syrian desert, and the chains of *quadriburgia* towers and forward posts along the lower Danube. A wall stretching across so much territory, even one with hundreds of watchtowers dotting its length and large garrison camps at strategic points, could not actually prevent the movement of people determined to cross it. But it could channel that movement, and provide the Roman military a vantage point for surveillance and oversight of potentially hostile populations beyond the wall, in what is now the Scottish Lowlands, and a potentially rebellious population inside it: the northern British tribes of Cumbria and the Pennines remained prone to revolt many generations after the Roman conquest.

2. Ribchester Helmet

Discovered at Ribchester, Lancashire, in the eighteenth century as part of a small hoard of metal items, and now in the British Museum, the Ribchester helmet is one of several distinct helmet types that Roman cavalrymen wore during military exercises. Weighing almost three pounds and made out of bronze that was sometimes heavily silvered, such helmets were of little practical use on the battlefield. But they would have made a dashing impression on parade, with their stylised face masks stripping the horsemen of their individuality and turning them into pure symbols of Roman military proficiency. Helmets like these would have been worn during parades and ceremonies, and also when the emperor appeared to inspect the troops, for instance at the North African garrison town of Lambaesis where the emperor Hadrian observed cavalry exercises early in the second century and made comments about them that survive to this day inscribed on stone (chapter 2).

3. Ludovisi Battle Sarcophagus
In the second and third centuries AD, highly elaborate battle-scenes were in vogue for the decoration of the sarcophagi of elite Romans. Gladiatorial games had long been a feature of Roman funeral rites, but the imagery of Roman armies violently subjugating the bodies of stereotyped barbarians is a specifically high imperial fashion in funerary decoration, and one that drew on artistic motifs popularised on Hellenistic victory monuments. The Ludovisi sarcophagus, discovered near Porta Tiburtina in Rome in 1621 and now in the Museo Nazionale there, is one of roughly two dozen second- and third-century battle sarcophagi known, all of them carved by highly skilled sculptors in Roman workshops. In this detail of the composition, one gets a sense of the depth and fluidity that could be achieved by deeply undercutting the figures so that some are virtually standing free of the main block of marble. The effect is to contrast the writhing collapse and abjection of Rome's enemies with the still, commanding calm of the Roman general on the right (he is perhaps one of the third-century soldier emperors, but no attempted identification has been truly convincing). As well as an exceptional piece of art, the sarcophagus underscores a timeless Roman sense of imperial military superiority that was, with rare exceptions like the battle of Abrittus (chapter 9), all too real for the agricultural peoples who dwelled along and beyond Rome's northern frontiers and experienced the depradations of Roman imperialism.

4. A Sarmatian Horseman
The Sarmatians were a group of loosely related and semi-nomadic warriors who initially dwelt north of the Black Sea. From there, different clans formed shifting states throughout antiquity and right into the fourth century AD, when Rome's most important Sarmatian opponents were found in the Great Hungarian Plain (the puszta or Alföld) between the Danube and the Carpathians. The Sarmatians were the only military aristocracy in Europe to depend primarily on the type of heavily armoured cavalry that was also characteristic of the Iranian nobility of Persia. This rather crude fresco, discovered in 1872, comes from a tomb in Kerch on the Crimean Bosporus where the Black Sea and the Sea of Azov meet. The coasts of the Black Sea had been dotted with Greek settlements for many centuries, and a Hellenistic kingdom flourished in the city of Panticapaeum (within modern Kerch) until the mid-third century, surviving well into the fourth. The fresco depicts a Bosporan infantryman standing his ground against a charging Sarmatian wearing full chainmail body armour and carrying a long lance – a heroic stand against a fearsome opponent.

5. Library of Celsus

The city of Ephesus, now a Unesco World Heritage Site, was once a major port city on the Ionian coast of Asia Minor. Already important in the Archaic period, it was one of many Greek cities to experience a renaissance under Roman rule: across Asia Minor, local elites in Greek cities used the freedom and peace of the Roman period to create a sort of facsimile of the classical *polis*, competing for local office and patronising the arts on a grand scale. The Library of Celsus reflects the type of local patriotic enthusiasm indulged by leading Greeks who prospered under Roman rule and became Roman citizens. It was built by Gaius Julius Aquila (consul in the year 110) in honour of his father Tiberius Celsus Polemaeanus (consul in 92), who had been one of the very first Greeks to exercise his rights as a Roman citizen to pursue a senatorial career, serving as proconsular governor of Asia (105–107) under the emperor Trajan. The Library was meant to do many things – as a gift to the citizens of Ephesus it would house thousands of scrolls containing treasures of Greek literature; as a mausoleum, it would house the remains of the great man in a crypt below the main structure; and as a public monument it would commemorate the name of Celsus and do credit to his living heirs, ensuring their ongoing importance to the life of the city. The façade illustrated here is the product of archaeological work in the 1970s, which rebuilt fallen remains that had lain in ruins since an eleventh-century earthquake. No full archaeological context existed for many of the architectural elements, which means that this reconstruction may not accurately reflect the original façade of the building despite its being an iconic image of Greek culture under Roman rule.

6. Theatre of Leptis Magna

Leptis Magna was the main city in the North African province of Tripolitania, the easternmost of the Latin-speaking African provinces (chapter 5). It was originally a Punic foundation, and the city had been a Roman ally long before the region was incorporated into the empire. It was made a *municipium* (a legal status with special rights during early imperial times) in the first century AD, and raised to the status of citizen *colonia* by Trajan. During the reign of Hadrian, Leptis produced its first senators, and its leading citizens – men like the grandfathers of Septimius Severus and Fulvius Plautianus – by then owned property in Italy. The city was rich, its urban fabric lavishly appointed. Here one can see the city's theatre, looking out from the stands past the colonnaded backdrop (*scaena frons*) of the stage, to the Mediterranean. Built in AD 1 or 2, it was repeatedly embellished right through the second century, and could seat at least 30,000 spectators. Because the city was not continuously occupied after antiquity, its imperial townscape was unusually well preserved, and seems thus far to have been spared by the current chaos in Libya.

7. Roman Military Diploma

Hundreds of discharge diplomas are known from the Roman empire, dating from between the reign of Claudius and the third century. The vast majority of these were issued to members of the *auxilia*, troops recruited from the non-Roman population of the empire. Before the third century, the imperial military establishment was made up of legions recruited from the Roman citizen population on the one hand, and auxiliaries from non-citizens (who were known as *peregrini* and formed the majority of the population in most provinces). Service in the *auxilia* was one of the main routes to citizenship and the social capital that it promised non-citizen provincials: after twenty-five years in the *auxilia*, honourable discharge brought with it the grant of Roman citizenship and the various legal privileges that entailed. To mark the occasion, newly enfranchised veterans were issued with a bronze diploma documenting their service, and providing proof of their new legal status that would stand up in court from one end of the empire to the other. Hundreds of diplomas issued to auxiliaries survive, either complete or in fragments, but the diploma illustrated here (in the collection of the Rheinisches Landesmuseum in Bonn) is more unusual. Though in shape and size similar to an auxiliary's discharge diploma, this third-century document records the honourable discharge of a legionary soldier, Septimius Bubas, and was issued by the governor of Germania Inferior. When the abbreviations in the Latin text are expanded, it reads *Aufidius Coresnius Marcellus, legatus Augusti pro praetore, dedi honestam missionem Septimio Bubati, militi legionis I*

Minerviae Severiane Alexsandrianae candidato ... before breaking off, which translates as 'Aufidius Coresnius Marcellus, the emperor's propraetorian legate, grants honourable discharge to Septimius Bubas, soldier of the Legio I Minerviae of Severus Alexander; he was a candidate ...' We do not know how to account for the relative scarcity of legionary diplomas by comparison with those of auxiliary soldiers: perhaps they were only ever issued in special circumstances, or perhaps their use was confined to a very short historical period.

8. Herodes Atticus

Herodes Atticus was the son of Claudius Atticus, one of the wealthiest men in early second-century Athens (chapter 1). By that point, Athens had become a sort of museum of ancient Hellenism, a site to which lovers of Greek culture flocked to bask in the glory reflected by centuries of history. Athens was also a thoroughly Roman city, its elites keeping one foot in their traditional past, the other in the political life of the larger empire, with the most prominent among them joining the *ordo senatorius*. The emperor Hadrian, who developed a well-earned reputation as a Hellenophile, had spent time in Athens as a guest of Claudius Atticus when he was a young man, before he was recognised as Trajan's heir. When he returned to the city as emperor in 124, he made use of the imperial prerogative to bestow senatorial status on individuals (*adlectio* – literally 'reading into the roll') to adlect Herodes Atticus into the senate. This meant Herodes had all the privileges of a junior senator (which is to say one who had served as quaestor, the lowest-ranking magistrate in the senatorial hierarchy), without his having had to serve in the minor qualifying offices that young men of the senatorial class normally pursued. He would go on to be an influential figure in the second-century cultural world, and even became consul in 143 under Antoninus Pius. The portrait bust shows him wearing the Greek *himation* rather than the much bulkier Roman toga, with the neatly cropped beard that had long been the norm among Greek males.

9. Mithras

The cult of Mithras centred on the mystery of a divine salvation and revelation. Though the god Mithras was based on the Zoroastrian divinity Mitra, the religion we now know as Mithraism developed within the frontiers of the Roman empire and was particularly popular with Roman soldiers. No systematic account of Mithraic mythology or theology survives, and quite possiby none ever existed, but stray literary references, a huge number of inscriptions by the god's devotees, and a remarkably uniform and consistent archaeological record provide a great deal of insight into his cult. The iconography of the god's underground temples (*mithraea*) all centre on an image of the tauroctony (the scene of Mithras, dressed in his Phrygian cap, slaying a sacred bull) like the one illustrated here. Several other iconic images of Mithras' deeds survive (his birth from a rock, the banqueting of his worshippers), but the appeal of the religion appears to have been its emphasis on secret meetings of devotees, who were ordered into various ranks of initiation, and able to recognise each other all across the empire and participate in the salvation that Mithras brought. This 'internationalism' made the religion especially appealing to soldiers and other servants of empire who travelled constantly.

10. A Parthian Noble

The Parthian empire dominated the Iranian and Mesopotamian world for hundreds of years on either side of the millennium, stretching from the edge of the Syrian desert to modern Turkmenistan and Afghanistan. The written record of Parthian history is disappointingly slender but art and archaeology show that the Parthian ruling elites, originally semi-nomadic steppe warriors, swiftly adopted the habits of the sedentary cultures they conquered. Along with the Persian military ethos and the elaborate governmental traditions of Mesopotamia, the Parthians also discovered a strong taste for Hellenistic court life. Throughout the centuries, however, the royal family of the Arsacids and their closest retainers hung on to an ideological connection with the steppe from which they haled. That connection is visible in this statue of a Parthian dynast or nobleman, dressed in trousers and a short, tight-fitted jacket, rather than the cloaks and tunics worn by the majority of the empire's population. While the frontality and rigidity of the statue are in keeping with traditional Near

Eastern figural art, the moulding of the flowing robes and the naturalistic depiction of hair and facial features is evidence of Hellenistic influence.

11/12. Fulvius Plautianus and Septimius Severus

These two sons of Leptis Magna in Tripolitania conquered the empire together in the 190s. Coming from the only important city in the backwater province of Tripolitania, Severus pursued a senatorial career while Plautianus remained an equestrian. When Severus declared himself emperor after the murder of Pertinax, Plautianus was at his side and became his praetorian prefect after Italy was won. They were, effectively, partners in empire, and Plautianus' daughter Fulvia Plautilla married Severus' son Caracalla. But Severus was jealous of his prerogatives, and when Plautianus' statues were displayed at Leptis on equal terms with those of the emperor, a rift opened between the two men that ended in Plautianus' execution in 205 (Chapter 6). These two portraits are typical of Severan style, with deeply moulded facial hair and their gaze turned away from the viewer; a similarly intense characterisation would be used in sculpture throughout the early and middle decades of the third century, giving way to increasingly abstract and impersonal imagery by the era of the tetrarchy.

13. The Severan Tondo

One of the most famous pieces of Roman art, this is one of very few pieces of tempera-on-wood panel painting to survive from the Roman world. Held in the Staatliche Museum in Berlin, its origins are unclear, and it has probably been cut down from a differently shaped, and perhaps larger, composition. The tondo depicts the imperial family of Septimius Severus, the emperor on the right and the augusta Julia Domna on the left, with their two sons Caracalla and Geta. Geta, who once stood on the left below Julia, has had his features erased, following his murder by Caracalla and posthumous condemnation (*damnatio memoriae*). *Damnatio memoriae* was a common imperial strategy for dealing with enemies of the regime, real or imagined. Effacing the name and image of the condemned from inscriptions and public monuments both erased them from the official record of the past and simultaneously created a permanent reminder that the fact that they had once actually existed could not be admitted as truth. Lacking the apparatus of a modern security state, imperial authorities could never succeed in as total an expunction of an individual's record as they would in theory have liked to, but the *damnatio* of Geta was carried through with unusual thoroughness: many surviving coins that once bore the joint images of Caracalla and Geta have had Geta's portrait chiseled off, and he has become a ghostly non-presence within the composition of this painting (Chapters 6–7).

14. The Licinius Cameo

This sardonyx cameo, mounted in gold enamel, was already in the French royal collections in the sixteenth century, and has been in the Bibliothèque

Nationale since 1851. Commonly known as the 'Triumph of Licinius' or Licinius Cameo, it depicts a fourth-century Roman emperor in a triumphal procession, though whether he is actually Licinius or not is open to question. Regardless, the cameo displays every aspect of the imagery used in the formal celebration of Roman triumphs. The emperor rides in a four-horse chariot, holding an orb and sceptre, six enemies trampelled underfoot. He is flanked by two winged victories, the one on the left holding a trophy (a suit of armour seized from the vanquished), the one on the right a military ensign depicting the busts of two emperors. Above and behind the emperor on the left, Sol (the Sun) with his crown and torch, offers the emperor a celestial globe, while on the right Luna (the Moon) does the same. Every time the emperor entered a city, the event (called an *adventus*) was greeted with much public solemnity, but a formal triumph, the protocols for which reached back to the republican period, was an affair of an entirely different magnitude.

15/16/17. Maximinus, Pupienus, Balbinus

C. Julius Verus Maximinus was proclaimed emperor in March 235 when the legions in Germania mutinied, killing the emperor Severus Alexander (chapter 7). He had risen from obscure origins through the ranks of the army and become an equestrian, and though the senate and armies recognised him and legitimised his accession, his rule never generated much enthusiasm among his subjects. Some senators in Africa

Proconsularis raised a rebellion against him in 238 under the patronage of the proconsul M. Antonius Gordianus, but though this Gordian and his son were rapidly suppressed, the senate in Rome recognised them and declared Maximinus a public enemy. In a strange and quixotic gesture towards a very old tradition of senatorial oligarchy, they appointed a board of twenty senators (the *vigintiviri*) to lead the state against him; two of these *vigintiviri*, the wealthy patrician Clodius Balbinus and the career soldier Caelius Pupienus, were jointly proclaimed emperor. Maximinus invaded Italy, but was killed in a mutiny, while at Rome the praetorian guard rose up and murdered Balbinus and Pupienus, proclaiming the grandson of Gordian emperor. Portraits of the three rivals are a study in contrasts, as in the statue and coins illustrated here: Maximinus is brooding, stubbly, every inch a soldier; Balbinus is fat, jowly, both civilian and old-fashionedly civil; Pupienus, bearded and stern but clothed like a republican magistrate, sits uneasily halfway between the two. The differing portraiture can almost serve as a metaphor for the changing Severan empire: Balbinus and the old senatorial nobility increasingly eclipsed by military men like Pupienus who had been favoured by the regime of Septimius Severus, but the real future lying with common soldiers like Maximinus, who had come to power by means of long service, talent and a healthy dose of luck.

18. A Roman Tunic

This fourth- or fifth-century tunic

from Egypt, now in the State Pushkin Museum of Visual Art, Moscow, is a rare complete example of late Roman clothing. Although Romans had a variety of types of clothing for different special occasions, from the high empire onwards, simple tunics, belted and worn over trousers, were what most people wore from day to day. This is a fairly costly example, made of wool and linen, and embroidered with decorations on common classical themes – Artemis, Apollo, satyrs and maenads.

19. Lamp in the shape of a Nubian

Scholars disagree about the extent of the Romans' awareness of what we now think of as race. They were certainly conscious of ethnic distinctions, and there was a general feeling that people's character and physiognomy were shaped by the climate of their home region; they were, moreover, well aware that people's skin colours differed dramatically, that sub-Saharan Africans, whom they called Nubians, were very dark, and that northern Europeans, whom they called Celts or Germans, tended to be very fair-skinned. There is not, however, consistent evidence that the ancient world associated skin colour with race in the modern western manner. That said, images of exotic peoples were a basic part of the Roman artistic repertoire. This oil lamp, found in the Athenian agora and probably dating to the second century, takes the shape of a seated African, with exaggeratedly pronounced nose and lips, curly hair, and the hooded cloak (*cucullus*) characteristic of the Roman working classes.

20. Kushan Fresco

The Kushan empire was the crossroads of Eurasia between the first and fourth centuries AD, when it took in large swathes of Bactria, Gandhara and Sind in modern Afghanistan, Pakistan, and the former Soviet republics of Central Asia. Poised between the cultures of Iran, the Eurasian steppe, India and China, the Kushan empire became a melting pot of different traditions, not least the Hellenistic legacy of Alexander the Great and his Macedonian successors in Bactria and India. This third-century wall-painting, now in the Metropolitan Museum in New York, can stand as a metaphor for Kushan culture as a whole: in the Iranian fashion, a god and a worshipper are depicted at identical scales, standing side by side in a composition without any additional figures in it. The bearded god on the left can be identified variously as the Greek Zeus, the syncretic Hellenistic deity Serapis, or Ohrmazd (Ahura Mazda), the supreme god in Iranian cosmology. On the right, the worshipper wears the short Iranian tunic and clasps his hands in respect, while the god, dressed in South Asian style, raises his fingers in a gesture familiar from Indian iconography. Yet both god and worshipper are depicted naturalistically, their clothes unstylised and draping realistically, their gestures those of actual human bodies in motion – a representative style that is entirely Hellenistic and distinct from the static poses of Iranian tradition.

21. Kushan (Gandharan) Buddha

The chronology of early Buddhism is a controversial topic, but there can be no doubt that the religion was well established in what is now Pakistan and the northwest of India by the first century AD. Buddhist art produced under Kushan rule in the region is generally called 'Gandharan', after the city of Gandhara near modern Peshawar. It is characterised, as in this example, by South and East Asian religious themes rendered in a distinctly Hellenistic fashion – facial features and gestures are naturalistic, and the sculpted clothes fall realistically on the body of the human figure. The harmonious blending of multiple Eurasian traditions is characteristic of Kushan culture and also explains why the Kushan empire could act as a sort of gateway through which goods and ideas penetrated from east to west and vice versa.

22. Palace of Ardashir at Firuzabad

This Sasanian palace stood opposite a fortified stronghold and near the city of Firuzabad, which was one of the sites from which the Sasanians launched their rebellion against the Arsacids (chapter 8). The palace itself was not meant to be a defensible site, but rather a grand meeting place, sumptuously decorated in stucco that imitated the ancient city of Persepolis, and with the large reflecting pools that were typical of a much older Persian architecture. The giant arched assembly hall in the picture is at the northeastern edge of the site, and would once have overlooked the reflecting pool. The city of Firuzabad, which remained an important site throughout the Sasanian period, has not been excavated, leaving the palace of Ardashir the most

significant of extant monuments from the dynasty's earliest years. Indeed, we might imagine the king negotiating here with other senior families of the Iranian nobility to cement his takeover of the empire from the ruling dynasty.

23. Victory of Shapur, Naqsh-e Rustam

Shapur I, son and successor of Ardashir, cemented the dynasty's hold on power, conquering vast territories in Central and South Asia, incorporating large parts of the Kushanshahr, and subjugating remaining challengers among the Arabs of the Syrian desert. In his monumental displays, however, he was primarily interested in demonstrating his superiority over the Romans, whom he defeated on several occasions (chapters 9–10). Appropriating for himself the Achaemenid sanctuary at Naqsh-e Rustam, he had inscribed a record of his great deeds and conquests, as well as this rock-cut image of his triumph over two Roman emperors – Philip kneeling in supplication before him, Valerian standing with his wrist grasped by Shapur in a traditional gesture of capture. A more elaborate version of this same relief was put up at Bishapur and additionally shows the dead Gordian III under the feet of Shapur's horse.

24. The Aurelian Wall of Rome

In the 270s, when Italy itself had experienced foreign invasion for the first time in centuries, the emperor Aurelian ordered the construction of a huge wall around the city of Rome (chapter 11). The wall would enclose not just the traditional hills of Rome, but also the Campus Martius and, on the other side of the Tiber, the Janiculum and parts of modern Trastevere. Twelve miles in circumference, made of brick-faced concrete ten feet thick, and with a projecting tower every hundred feet, the project was designed to overawe potential attackers and reassure the citizens of Rome that their emperor was looking out for them. That said, a wall of such length could not actually be defended for any length of time, no matter how large the garrison. Its main point was its symbolism, and throughout the rest of antiquity, if an invading army was not stopped at the Alps or in the north Italian plain, the rest of the peninsula lay wide open.

25. Deeds of the Priest Kardir, Naqsh-e Rajab

The Zoroastrian priest Kardir was the only non-Sasanian to erect a monumental inscription during the period of that dynasty's hegemony (chapter 12). He had risen to power during the reign of Shapur I, and accompanied him on his various travels, but the tolerant king was not willing to enforce the type of strict orthodoxy that Kardir favoured. After Shapur's death, however, Kardir became much more influential and was appointed mobad mobadan ('priest of priests', on the model of shahanshah or 'king of kings'). As he tells the viewer in this inscription, erected under Varahran II, the fourth of the four kings he served, Kardir had worked tirelessly to found fire temples and support the priesthood so that the good god Ohrmazd would

be served and the evil god Ahriman harmed. To this end, among other things, he enforced the subordination of non-Zoroastrians like Christians and Jews who had a role to play in the divine order, but he persecuted Mani, who had thrived under Shapur, and also those Zoroastrians whose practices he believed to be heretical.

26. Maximian

This impressive portrait of the tetrarchic augustus Maximian comes from the villa complex at Chiragan, along the Garonne river about thirty miles southwest of Toulouse. Discovered in the seventeenth century and excavated in the nineteenth, the villa contained an enormous collection of sculpture, making it one of the most impressive rural sites known from the Roman west. Alongside a fairly standard repertoire of Roman copies of famous Greek sculptures, Chiragan was decorated with an elaborate program of bas-reliefs depicting the labours of Hercules, and with one of the largest collection of imperial portrait busts ever discovered. This portrait of Maximian, now in the Musée Saint-Raymond in Toulouse, is probably the least stylised image of him to survive – compare the abstract, stereotyped image on the coins (pl. 29) – and doesn't conform to a standard tetrarchic model that attempts to make all the tetrarchs resemble one another as closely as possible. Here, despite the damage to the nose, one sees Maximian depicted as a third-century soldier emperor, heavily muscled and large, with a full but not long beard. His features are also deliberately intended to recall traditional images of Hercules, whose labours are one of the villa's main decorative schemes and who was the emperor's patron deity and supposed divine father.

27. Edict on Maximum Prices

Diocletian's Edict on Maximum Prices, issued in November or December 301, was an attempt to curb the rampant inflation that he had inadvertently set off in his attempt to reform the currency and restore some semblance of order after the chaos of the 270s, when the emperor Aurelian had re-tariffed money already in circulation and more or less accidentally demonetised the Roman economy (chapters 11–12). The Edict attempted to set a maximum price on a breathtaking number of goods and services, and it was promulgated very widely in the eastern provinces of the empire, though much less so in the Latin west – and perhaps not at all in the Gallic administrative region controlled by Constantius. However fervently Diocletian may have wished to put a cap on prices, and restrict the arbitrage and speculation that he saw as being detrimental to the Roman state, there was no way for him to control the actual behaviour of buyers and sellers, and the Edict was a dead letter almost from the moment of its issue. Despite that, numerous fragmentary copies survive from the eastern provinces of the empire, and between them allow us to reconstruct an almost complete text of the legislation. The illustration shows one of four fragments preserved as a result of being re-used in the church of John Chrysostom at Geraki, Greece, this one as part of a door-jamb.

28. Fausta

The frown and piercing gaze of this portrait belongs to an imperial princess of the late tetrarchic or Constantinian era (note the stylistic similarities with the portrait of Constantius II, pl. 32). She is traditionally identified as Fausta, daughter of Maximian and second wife of Constantine. Betrothed to Constantine as a little girl when he and her father struck up an alliance of convenience, she was raised at her future husband's court until old enough for the marriage to be consummated, surviving the disgrace and death of Maximian. She became the mother of three future emperors, but was either executed or forced to commit suicide in 326. The circumstances of her downfall are obscure, but she was clearly implicated in the conspiracy that brought down Crispus, Constantine's eldest son by his first wife Minervina, and by the later 310s his caesar (deputy emperor). It may be that Fausta and Crispus had begun a liaison, being of much the same age, or that Crispus had plotted to challenge his father for the throne with her connivance. The truth cannot be recovered, and Crispus' memory was never rehabilitated, though Fausta was restored to posthumous honour when her sons Constantinus, Constantius II and Constans split the empire between themselves in 337.

29. The Tetrarchs

Imperial coin portraits had degenerated to the vaguest suggestion of individuality from the later 250s onwards, but Diocletian and his fellow rulers took this trend much further and made a virtue of the disappearance of highly artistic die-engravers (*celatores*): the homogeneity of their coin portraiture emphasised their fraternal closeness, their common purpose, and the inseparability of their collegial rule. Coins, after all, were perhaps the most ubiquitous manifestation of imperial government, handled in tens of thousands every day by people all over the empire. Whether consciously or unconsciously, people absorbed the messages that coins sent. Looking at these portraits, one is not meant to see Diocletian or Maximian, Constantius or Galerius. One is meant to see a single imperial power, omnipresent and united against all its enemies. Only the legends tell us which emperor is depicted on which coin (clockwise from top left, Diocletian, Maximian, Galerius, Constantius). Stylistically we can distinguish tetrarchic coins only by the mint at which they were struck, not by the emperor whose portrait they bear. For more than thirty years, tetrarchic-style coin portraits were the norm across the Roman world, until Constantine established a new model of abstract, idealised portraits: youthful and clean-shaven in place of this mature, bearded military image of the tetrarchs.

30. Shapur II Hunting Boar

Sasanian silverwork is one of the glories of that civilisation and reached extraordinary levels of complexity. Scenes of the hunt, long associated with royal prerogative and majesty in ancient near eastern cultures, are a dominant theme in the large number of plates that survive, and here the mounted Shapur II (recognisable by his crown) brings down wild boar with a bow. While simpler plates were made of two sheets of silver, one for the base, one for the repoussé relief, this example was made of nineteen separate pieces, some of them fire-gilt (in which a mixture of mercury and gold leaves behind an iridescent gilding that seeps around the edges of the fire-gilt chasing), while the missing haunch of the lower boar demonstrates how other pieces around it were applied. Strangely, a lot of Sasanian silver made its way to the distant northeast of Russia, probably traded by raiders from the Caucasus to the Siberian tribes, loot from Persia serving as a means to acquire northern furs. This example, now in the Smithsonian, was in the collection of the Stroganov family in the nineteenth century and reached the United States after they fled the Revolution of 1917.

31. Sasanian Royal Bust

Now in the Metropolitan Museum in New York, and of unknown provenance, this silver portrait head may be a free-standing piece or may once have formed part of a larger statue. Hammered from a single sheet of silver and chased with gold, it is one of the finest examples of Sasanian metalwork to survive. Though often said to represent Shapur II (chapters 17–18), that identification is not at all certain. Normally, we distinguish Sasanian royal portraits by the iconography of the ruler's crown, which was different in every reign. Here, however, the crescent and orb on the crown have no parallels in the coin evidence which could provide a firm identification. It is possible, then, that this composition was meant to be a generic representation of royal majesty, rather than a specific Sasanian ruler.

32. Constantius II

Though one would not know it from the number that survive, bronze sculptures once stood everywhere in Greek and Roman public spaces – the vast majority were melted down for other purposes, either in antiquity or since. This portrait, recovered in the fifteenth century and now in the Capitoline Museum in Rome, is one of the best likenesses of Constantius II to survive. In it, one can see the basic resemblance to all Constantinian portraiture – the distinctive nose, the fixed gaze, the clean-shaven contrast with the beards of the tetrarchs. Portraits of Constantius (chapters 16–18) are readily identifiable by his distinctive ringleted fringe.

33. Julian

This statue of Julian, now in the Louvre, depicts him in the traditional manner of a philosopher, a pose he favoured throughout his life (chapters 17–18). He holds his Greek *himation* around him in the formal manner of a speaker about to begin a disquisition, with his arm raised awkwardly in its folds. In deliberate contrast to the rest of the clean-shaven Constantinian dynasty, he grew out his beard, not close-cropped in the tetrarchic manner, but instead the full, unkempt facial hair of a philosopher too unworldly to care about his appearance. Julian's own writings, which survive in quantity, demonstrate that this was no mere

pose: he took himself very seriously, to the point that many contemporaries found him slightly ridiculous.

34. Porphyry Sarcophagus of Helena

This porphyry sarcophagus has long been associated with Helena, first wife of Constantius I, and mother of Constantine. Held in the the Museo Pio-Clementino in the Vatican since the eighteenth century, it was taken there from an extramural mausoleum on the Via Labicana. We cannot be entirely certain that this was in fact the sarcophagus assigned to Helena herself, but it was certainly meant for a member of the imperial family: in ancient times, the reddish purple stone porphyry was quarried at great expense from a single site in the Eastern desert of Egypt, whence it was brought along the so-called Via Porphyrites to Maximianopolis (modern Qena) on the Nile (Qena remains the main road through the eastern desert to the tourist sites on the Red Sea). Because of its rarity, and the association of the colour purple with royalty, it was used almost exclusively for imperial monuments during the imperial period. Because porphyry is so hard a stone, it is much more difficult to work than marble, so the extraordinary detail of the high-relief figures on this sarcophagus represents craftsmanship of the highest order available to the fourth century. While it is thematically not dissimilar to the Ludovisi battle sarcophagus (pl. 3), its symbolism is more abstract, its action seeming to take place on a plane outside both time and space.

35. The Judgement of Paris (detail) from the Atrium House, Antioch
Throughout the Roman world, the rural and suburban villas and the urban townhouses of Graeco-Roman elites were covered in mosaic floors, hundreds upon hundreds of thousands of them, from one end of the empire to the other. Many a middling household could manage the cost of a mosaic or two in simple geometric patterns, but the rich could pave room after room with exquisite figural compositions. This image is a detail of a much larger mosaic of Paris judging a beauty contest among three Olympian goddesses that inadvertently sparks the Trojan War. Here we see Hera, queen of the Olympian gods, seated in the centre, with helmeted Athena, goddess of wisdom and war, on the left and Aphrodite, goddess of love, disporting herself confidently on a rock. Now in the Louvre, it comes from a house (the so-called Atrium House) in Antioch, the second largest city in the eastern Mediterranean and one of the very richest. The mosaic dates to the second century and decorated the house's *triclinium*, the reception hall in which host and guests would dine, reclining on couches and contemplating the artwork at their feet.

were created, though whether they developed to their fullest form before the end of the tetrarchy is open to dispute. The *sacrae largitiones*, whose staff travelled with the imperial courts, administered mining operations throughout the empire and paid soldiers their salaries and any extraordinary donative payments; they levied taxes on precious metals and oversaw the imperial arms and clothing factories. The *res privata*, into which the old *aerarium* and *fiscus* were merged, oversaw imperial estates throughout the empire, managed their leases and collected their rents; they also monitored properties that for one reason or another were forfeited to the emperor.

As we saw at the start of the chapter, the money these officials worked with had undergone thoroughgoing reform alongside the rest of the government's functions, and this new coinage was struck at a large number of mints. In the high empire the mint at Rome provided the official coinage for the entire empire; supplementary economic needs were met by the local civic coinages that continued to be minted in the eastern provinces right into the last decades of the third century. Thus, imperial coinage minted anywhere but the city of Rome was almost always a sign of usurpation or political crisis. Both those phenomena, of course, multiplied during the third century and many legitimate emperors, not just local usurpers, struck official imperial coinage at regional capitals like Antioch, Siscia or Viminacium as circumstances required. The multiplication of imperial mints thus became somewhat normalised and the distribution of tetrarchic mints is striking: Londinium, Trier, Lugdunum, Arelate, Ticinum, Rome, Carthage, Aquileia, Siscia, Heracleia, Thessalonica, Cyzicus, Nicomedia, Antioch and Alexandria, with Sirmium joining the list in the immediately post-tetrarchic period. Not every one of these mints struck coins in every currency, and not every tetrarchic mint survived the tetrarchic period, but many that were established under Diocletian continued to operate into the fifth century and beyond. They were meant to allow for tighter control of the money supply and the taxation that it was meant to bring in.

It is therefore no surprise that in 296 Diocletian conceived, and by 297 had created, a new census system that was meant to be uniform across the empire. It was to run on a 5-year cycle, with registered persons being assessed for taxation as uniform units of people and land (*caput* and *iugum*, poll tax and property tax respectively). Three tax cycles of five years made up an 'indiction' of fifteen, and this 15-year tax cycle in turn became a calendrical system that long outlived Roman government in large parts of the Latin west. Taxation had always been one of the most visible ways in which imperial government interacted with its subjects, and it now became less random and far more predictable. It also became more uniform, and the new fiscal regime had very distinct long-term effects in the east and the west that we will consider in chapter 15.

In many ways, the Diocletianic reforms were the culmination of the process of equestrianisation that we have seen evolve in earlier chapters. They involved an aspiration to greater control and oversight, a sense that system was not only desirable but also necessary, and most importantly that system was achievable. We shall see this theme repeated in later tetrarchic history, in fiscal contexts attempting to harmonise taxation and fix prices, and in attempts to impose uniformity on religious practice, if not belief. As with so many of Diocletian's reforms, we can scour earlier reigns for precedents and find them, particularly in the third century, but those were expedients meant to deal with the exigencies of specific moments. What makes Diocletian's experiment so surprising, and gives it its enduring interest, is the way it aimed to create a total system, one that could account for most possibilities and allow a response to every contingency to originate close to its source, even if that response had then to make its way up to one of the prefects or an emperor for decision. This aspiration to totality provided real flexibility, but it also brought in an increasingly totalising rhetoric of the state and its power, one that was articulated as a series of good/bad binaries. Heated rhetoric and exclusionary language is intensely characteristic of the fourth-century empire, and it is quite clear that this language often shaped the actions of those who used it. As a cultural propensity it was exaggerated still further after the emperor Constantine's conversion to Christianity, but its origins lie here, in the far-ranging reforms of Diocletian.

It would take years for the full implications of Diocletian's many changes to make themselves felt. The immediate effect was not social and cultural but political: it revolutionised tetrarchic activity, allowing for multiple actions on multiple fronts. Thus, having won his victory over Carausius immediately upon his promotion, Constantius began to do what Maximian had earlier failed to do – build a fleet that could spearhead an invasion of Britain and suppress Carausius's murderer and successor Allectus. That this project took the better part of two years shows how difficult seaborne warfare could be in antiquity, and is also a reminder that Roman control of Britain was always a greater challenge than anticipated.

By 296, Constantius had readied two fleets, one of which he commanded personally, the other sailed under the command of his praetorian prefect Asclepiodotus, who seems to have done for Constantius what Constantius had once done for Maximian. Asclepiodotus's fleet landed in Hampshire, Constantius's probably in Essex or Kent, and, while the emperor made for the provincial capital at Londinium, Asclepiodotus brought Allectus to battle and routed his forces, leaving the usurper dead on the battlefield – becoming in the process the last praetorian prefect on record to hold a military command. Constantius and Asclepiodotus were then able to impose the tetrarchic model of provincial division on Britain, creating four provinces where in the Severan system there had been only two. Although we know the names of the four British provinces (Britannia I, Britannia II, Flavia Caesariensis and Maxima Caesariensis), we know neither their boundaries nor their respective locations. Despite that ignorance, we can see the way in which the tetrarchic model responded to circumstance, imposing new ways of doing things as the four rulers extended control and stable governance to new areas. In a nicely symbolic manner, the sole extant inscription of Carausius is a milestone from near Lugovalium (modern Carlisle), which in 297 was turned upside down and re-engraved in the name of Constantius Caesar.

Maximian, the least militarily successful of the tetrarchs, spent most of the years after 293 in Italy and North Africa, and the administrative pairing of those dioceses would become increasingly characteristic of the fourth- and early fifth-century empire. Africa had been relatively neglected by the third-century emperors, but it had also been relatively untouched by military crises. Prior to Caracalla's enfranchisement of the whole imperial population, Africa had been more than usually a patchwork of communities of differing status, the colonial, municipal and peregrine rubbing up against one another at much closer quarters than was the case in the other urbanised parts of the empire, such as Spain or southern Gaul. During the third century, formerly less privileged or unprivileged communities in Africa raced to bring themselves into line with such long-standing citizen colonies as Carthage and Hippo Regius. By the time of the tetrarchy, urban and enfranchised Africa Proconsularis was increasingly matched by similar landscapes in Mauretania, Numidia and in the fertile enclave of Tripolitania, where the desert came closer to the Mediterranean than it did elsewhere in North Africa. In the west, the Rif remained a virtually insuperable barrier to communication. Tingitania – the tip of modern Morocco – remained much closer to Spain across the straits of Gibraltar than it did to the rest of North Africa, and Diocletian made it a part of the Spanish, not the African, diocese. But the new Diocletianic provinces of the African diocese – from west to east, Mauretania Caesariensis, Mauretania Sitifensis, Numidia, Proconsularis, Byzacena and Tripolitania – would be one of the intellectual and economic powerhouses of the coming century.

As often happened along Rome's less populous frontiers, however, this thriving Roman civilisation created imitative and competitive impulses along its edges. Just as we have seen increasing sophistication and organisation among the Alamanni, Franci and Goths along the northern frontiers, so along the African pre-desert and desert frontiers, tribes of Mauri that had not been incorporated into the imperial governmental system, but who had all sorts of informal relations with the urban world nearer the coast, become more active in the later third and the fourth centuries. At the same time that Constantius was reconquering Britain for the tetrarchic government, Maximian was to be found in Africa, fighting against unspecified Mauri, perhaps the Quinquegentanae (a tribe that is also attested in an unreliable source as having supported a usurper named Julianus who most likely did not exist). A better source is a fragmentary poem, preserved in a single papyrus, that seems to have been an epic account of Maximian's Moorish campaigns. However, like most of Rome's frontier wars, what the poets make into epic was just one of many endlessly repeated police actions. Except in rare circumstances (almost always the imperial army's distraction in civil war), the tribal polities of the Rhine, Danube and African pre-desert could never muster organised forces on a scale to threaten a Roman campaign army in the field.

The eastern frontier was altogether different. There, the Sasanian kings, when not distracted by internal challengers or attacks on their northeastern satrapies, could frequently best Roman armies in the field, using a combination of the Iranian nobility's heavily armoured cavalry, massed archers drawn from subject tribes, mounted archers from the steppe and peasant levies from the agricultural regions. The reigns of Probus and Carus, and the early reign of Diocletian, had seen the Persian state deeply divided against itself. As we saw in chapter 11, Shapur I's eldest son Ohrmazd I had ruled for only one year, and his successor Varahran I for only three. The latter's son, Varahran II (r. 276–93), was just a child when he acceded to the throne and his reign was never secure. Openly challenged by his cousin Ohrmazd, based in the eastern satrapies, he was also permanently threatened by the resentment of his uncle Narseh. The latter was the last surviving son of old Shapur and a one-time king of Armenia: he rankled at the sight of an untested boy on his father's throne. For a time, however, enough of the great feudal lords supported the young Varahran to render the question moot, and the power of the Mazdean priesthood in the state is the dominant theme of the 280s. Kardir, Varahran's *mobad mobadan* ('priest of priests') – modelled on the title shahanshah ('king of kings') – was the dominant figure in his regime.

We met Kardir in chapter 11, but we need to consider him more closely here, because the manner in which he persecuted non-Zoroastrian believers in the Persian empire is directly relevant to the course of events in Rome. Temple priests had a tradition of wielding great power in the Near East from very early in Mesopotamian history. The Iranian world had long since adopted these Mesopotamian traditions, vesting many functions of imperial administration in the priesthood since the time of the Achaemenids. Ardashir and Shapur, though the latter was himself relatively tolerant, had carefully nurtured the Mazdean priesthood, which accumulated ever greater wealth and control of royal decision-making as Shapur aged. Kardir, remarkably, was the only non-royal figure to inscribe his image and an account of his deeds on the monuments at Naqsh-e Rustam, where he boasts of having protected Zoroastrians in the lands of the Romans. With Shapur dead, he used his personal dominance at Varahran's court to impose a policy of persecution on Persia's Christians and other non-Zoroastrians, most particularly the Manichaeans.

One of the most interesting religious cocktails of later antiquity, Manichaeism was the creation of a single man's bizarre inspiration. Mani was born in 216 at Mardinu in Mesopotamia, though both of his parents were Persians and probably devotees of the gnostic Mandaean religion. He experienced a revelation at the age of twelve, when a heavenly 'twin' appeared, urging him to leave the community into which he was born, and he experienced this same vision again, in 240, when he was twenty-four. From that moment, he devoted himself to spreading the newly revealed truth, continuing to experience revelations through the year, when he began to preach, just at the end of Ardashir's reign. His first destination was the Kushanshahr, where he encountered the Buddhist art and texts of Gandhara, before returning to Fars and converting Shapur's own brother Mirshah to his new faith. In the fourth year of Shapur's reign, Mani had an audience with the shahanshah himself, and thereafter preached widely in the empire's western provinces. Though the Mazdean priesthood was infuriated at it, Shapur authorised this proselytising and made Mani a member of his court; he would go on to accompany the king in his wars in Rome's eastern provinces. Mani sent one of his chief followers to the Mesopotamian cities to convert Christians, another into eastern Iran, whence Manichaeism would spread widely in Central Asia. When Shapur died in 273 and his successor Ohrmazd shortly thereafter, the Mazdean priesthood saw its chance for revenge and pounced. While he was in Mesopotamia, Mani was summoned to the court of Varahran and there interrogated by the king himself, who accused him of all sorts of anti-social behaviours. Bound in chains early in 276, he died of hunger and exhaustion after a month of imprisonment.

His teachings, however, would not die out. Their appeal, like that of many other salvific faiths, was the access they gave believers to the possibility of being saved by the secret wisdom that belief imparted. Written mainly in Syriac (some in Parthian), his teachings try to explain the dualist world of 'two principles', good and evil, within which man must live. This resembles the Mazdean belief in a perpetual struggle of Ohrmazd and Ahriman, but incorporates elements of pantheism and a very elaborate mythology of the fall of man that resembles Christianity – something that made Mani's teachings particularly attractive to Christians whose worldview was already prepared for many features of Mani's cosmology. Ultimately, through the practice of asceticism and the coming of revelation, the fallen human can be reunited with his higher self and rise up into the realm of light. Mani granted that Buddha, Zarathustra and Jesus were all his predecessors, but that he had surpassed them because he wrote his own revelation.

His followers were divided between the 'elect' and the 'hearers'. The elect led much stricter lives than did the hearers: they had to keep pure in thought and word, maintain a strict vegetarianism and do no harm to animals, and abstain completely from sex. This staunch asceticism and self-denial is what gave Manichaean divines their appeal, much like Christian holy men. Hearers, to maintain their position in the faith, were required to fast every Sunday, and undergo a full month of fasting once a year. It was the combination of ostentatious other-worldliness with the promise of salvation that set Mani's revelation apart from Zoroastrianism, while the secret, gnostic elements in his system, and the hierarchical promise of reaching a place among the elect, was a powerful attraction to many Christians. We will see that Roman emperors saw Mani's revelation as being just as threatening as did the Mazdean priesthood, but the hostility of neither could suppress the spread and elaboration of Manichaean theology from one end of Eurasia to another, in time reaching as far as China, where many otherwise lost Manichaean texts are now preserved in Chinese translation.

Yet though it helped entrench the role of the Mazdean priesthood in Sasanian political life, Mani's death did not make Varahran's hold on his throne materially more stable. In fact, the disarray within the Persian ruling elites only subsided somewhat in the early 290s, when the rival regime of Varahran's cousin Ohrmazd was finally suppressed. Varahran now styled himself shah of Seistan along with his other titles, indicating the submission of the eastern part of the empire. He died, naturally so far as we know, in 293. If Varahran's rival Ohrmazd had in fact survived his defeat, it was now that he ruled, however briefly, in his own right, but only in the central part of the empire. Meanwhile, the claims of Varahran's very young son were pressed by a faction of the Persian nobility, led by a certain Vahunam. The boy's accession as Varahran III, however, angered as much of the nobility as it pleased. It may be that they foresaw the continued dominance of Kardir and his priests, or it may be that the essential function of the shahanshah – leadership in the martial virtues which defined his ability to rule – could simply not be exercised by so young a boy. In consequence, they exercised their prerogative of choosing among Sasanian claimants and looked around for an alternative.

In another of the remarkable inscriptions to survive from ancient Iran – this one from Paikuli – the monarch who overthrew the young Varahran III explains how he came to power. That monarch was none other than Narseh, the former king of Armenia and the last surviving son of Shapur the Great, by now a man in late middle age. Narseh's inscription is not the triumphal account that we found in Shapur's Naqsh-e Rustam text. It is instead an explanation for his actions in seizing the throne, or rather an extended apologia assuring his audience that his act of usurpation was in fact entirely legitimate. The location of the inscription speaks almost as loudly as do its words, for Paikuli is in Asuristan, the Parthian and Persian province of the lower Euphrates and the heart of urbanised Mesopotamia, where the vast majority of the shahanshah's subjects lived. (Although etymologically derived from 'Assyria', Asuristan was the ancient Babylonia far to the south of the old Assyrian heartland, which was known in late antiquity as Adiabene.) Although written in Middle Persian, rather than Parthian or Greek, the inscription was clearly meant to justify Narseh's reign to the widest possible audience.

The text is quite fragmentary, and has been reconstructed in various ways that pre-occupy and divide specialists, but the gist of the story is clear. Narseh records how a delegation of the nobility came to him in Armenia and begged him to take the throne that was his due. Those he lists are an interesting array, for they clearly represent the fringes of the Sasanian realm, rather than its centre: we find among them Gilan on the south-western coast of the Caspian and all of the easternmost regions that had until recently supported Ohrmazd against Varahran II. The great Parthian hereditary houses go unmentioned, as do the core regions of Fars, Khuzistan and Asuristan. Even behind the studied ambiguity, we can presume that the child Varahran III was the candidate of a powerful court faction, while Narseh offered an appealing alternative for men who had been excluded from power under Varahran II.

It seems that Narseh marched out of Armenia into Iran and then led an army into Asuristan. There, at Paikuli, where he later set up his inscription, many of the great lords 'both Persian and Parthian' came over to his side, including members of the Varez, Karen and Suren clans, as did the *mobad mobadan* Kardir. Varahran III's support melted away, Narseh marched on Ctesiphon, where Vahunam was defeated in battle and Varahran was himself killed. Narseh, aged though he was, had proved vigorous. He seems to have received the submission of all the provinces and satrapies of the empire – the inscription mentions regions as distant as the Kushanshahr, Turan and Khwarezm on the Amu Darya, as well as the Lakhmids of Arabia – but in truth the internal history of the Sasanian empire is a blank for most of Narseh's reign. Not so his frontier with Rome, however, for two years after his victory at Ctesiphon and secure now on his throne, he launched an attack on the empire.

Narseh began by invading Armenia in 295 or early 296, driving out the Arsacid Tiridates whom Diocletian had installed half a decade before. He then marched south into Roman Mesopotamia. There, late in 296 or early in 297, he was met by a tetrarchic army under the direct command of the caesar Galerius, who had been in the region since 295. Details are scant, but it is clear that Galerius was completely routed and Narseh took control of the lands between the upper Tigris and Euphrates that had been in Roman hands for decades. Galerius's defeat was a bad one, a point Diocletian hastened to drive home: meeting his defeated caesar upon his return to Antioch, he staged a procession in front of his own and Galerius's campaign armies, riding in the imperial coach while Galerius, clad in his full imperial regalia, trod the course before him on foot. It is a testimony to Diocletian's authority over both his soldiers and his caesars that a man as proud and dangerous as Galerius would later prove permitted himself to suffer such treatment and that his soldiers would tolerate it. But Diocletian attached no blame to the army for its defeat – the emperors were universal, universally powerful, and if the young Herculius had failed the elder Jovius, then in good Roman fashion he would receive the punishment his divine father meted out.

Galerius now conceived a well-concealed hatred for Diocletian, and would in time repay him for his humiliation. But in the short term, the message of unity was clear and the defeated caesar redoubled his efforts, collecting another army on the Danube in 297 and preparing to launch a new campaign against Narseh in the following year. His fellow tetrarchs were similarly busy. As we mentioned above, part of Diocletian's reform plans included the introduction of a new system of taxation with uniform poll and land taxes. To collect them first required a new census, which was highly disruptive of the old ways of doing things in many parts of the empire. One such place was Egypt, where the new census procedures led directly to usurpation. One L. Domitius Domitianus claimed the purple between August and December 297, minting both local Alexandrian tetradrachms and folles on the Diocletianic imperial model. Diocletian led his army against the usurper and, although Domitianus himself was dead by the end of 297, one of his *correctores*, Aurelius Achilleus, carried on the revolt in Alexandria. He must have done so in Domitianus's name, for he minted no coins of his own, but he held out against a siege in Alexandria until late spring 298.

While Diocletian campaigned in Egypt in 298, Galerius resumed the Persian war. He invaded Armenia and then carried on down the course of the Tigris through Media and Adiabene into Asuristan. There was heavy fighting throughout the campaign, and at least two pitched battles against Narseh in which the Romans were victorious. In the second, Galerius actually captured the shahanshah's camp, taking his harem and some of his family, along with a great deal of treasure. The king's wife was escorted back to Daphne, in the Antiochene suburbs, and treated with the dignity due to a queen. Narseh retreated to Ctesiphon to rally support and regroup, and it is a measure of his surprising authority that even so major a defeat did not lead to a coup against him.

Rather than continue to fight, Narseh opened negotiations with the

Romans, wintering in Mesopotamia in 298–9. In the spring of 299, he was met in Adiabene by Diocletian himself. Peace talks were conducted on behalf of the Romans by Sicorius Probus, who occupied a new palatine office created by Diocletian, that of *magister memoriae*. This *magister* supervised a bureau (or *scrinium*) of scribes who handled the responses to any requests and petitions in which the emperor took a specific personal interest, while other *magistri* supervised the more routine business of government. On the Persian side, the negotiators were Narseh's close adviser Apharban, and Hargbed, one of the great Iranian nobles. They argued that the Roman and Persian empires were the two lamps of humankind: 'as with two eyes, each should be adorned by the brightness of the other and not forever be seeking the other's destruction'.

As a statement of political theory that might have been accepted as true, but the treaty that Sicorius negotiated was heavily one-sided. Narseh received back his wife and family, but few other concessions. Rome got back its long-standing prerogative of appointing the Armenian king, this time yet another Tiridates. The treaty also required Narseh to surrender a great deal of territory that had been contested between Persia and Rome since the Severan age – not just the Mesopotamian steppe between the Tigris and the Euphrates, but also the mountain regions of Sophanene, Arzanene, Corduene, Zabdicene and Ingilene that commanded access into Armenia. Nisibis was to be the sole point of commercial contact for traders between the two empires, and its prosperity in the following half century is well known. Not all of these provinces would remain in Roman hands for long, but the Mesopotamian steppe became the focus of Roman military defence and was transformed into a chain of fortress cities, from Edessa and Carrhae just beyond the Euphrates, via Resaina on the Khabur, Amida and Nisibis, to Singara. For much of the fourth century, confrontations between Romans and Persians were concentrated on this broad stretch of strategic land, Rome relying upon the great cities to stop Persian armies and bog them down in debilitating sieges. Those confrontations lay in the future: Galerius's victory led to a forty-year peace between the two great powers of the world.

Further to the south, in the Syrian desert, Diocletian created an elaborate fortification system known as the Strata Diocletiana, along a military road running from Resafa on the Euphrates down past Palmyra (the latter a shadow of its former self) and into the northern Arabian desert. The earliest Arabic inscription yet known is from the city of Bostra in north-western Arabia, along the Strata Diocletiana, and is from about this time. Entirely by chance, it reveals another consequence of the victory of Galerius over Narseh: the Lakhmid king of Hira, Imru'ulqais, changed sides. Having long served Shapur and his successors, he now joined the Romans and moved his seat of power westwards, to Bostra. Hira itself remained a Persian client under other Lakhmids, but the habitual allegiance of some Arabs to Rome and some to Persia would become one of the main political dynamics of later antiquity.

At the end of the third century, and in the aftermath of Galerius's momentous victory, it must have seemed as if the tetrarchic experiment had fulfilled most, if not all, of its explicit goals: although Diocletian's ambitions had not gone unchallenged, his grand project to harmonise and make uniform the administration of empire looked not just feasible, but very nearly accomplished. And yet it is clear that Diocletian did not think he had gone far enough. On the contrary, still more centralising regulations, for the economy and for the state religion, issued from the court right at the turn of the century.

The extent of Diocletian's ambitious reshaping of Roman government becomes clearer when one looks at four measures he took between 301 and 303, each written in the bombastic style that the professional jurists at his court were now coming to perfect. In September 301, he retariffed the coinage, as is demonstrated by a fragmentary inscription from Aphrodisias in Caria, an important and well-excavated city in Asia Minor. The edict that enacts this measure states that the imperial coinage would, from 1 September of the year, be worth double its face value; consequently, debts to the imperial treasury contracted prior to that date could be repaid at the old prices, while those contracted since would have to be paid at the new tariff. So far, so good, and presumably a measure meant to combat the inflation that the economy seems to have been suffering at this time. The second part of Diocletian's plan, however, was both more original and more problematic. In late November or early December 301, he issued a far-reaching measure that we call the Edict on Maximum Prices, which happens to be the best attested Latin document from the Greek east. The law it preserves was an attempt – an almost demented attempt, as it proved – to revolutionise the imperial economy. With the hyperbole that is the standard currency of late Roman edicts, the Edict on Maximum Prices sets out to regulate the price of an extraordinary range of goods of all sorts, and at different and precise stages of manufacture. It does so because the greed of nefarious individuals had damaged the very people whose job it was to protect them, the servants of the state and the soldiers. That is, we have here yet another tetrarchic attempt at regularising and regulating the affairs of the empire in a single, systematic way across the length and breadth of an amazingly diverse polity. Some such attempts succeeded, others did not. The impact of this one was catastrophic.

Local conditions had long made some goods cheaper in one part of the empire than in another. This was inevitable, given how much the costs of transport, particularly transport by land, added to the end value of goods. That meant that many things were intrinsically more valuable in one place than another, with the exception of highly perishable items such as fresh foodstuffs, the range of which was limited by the threat of spoilage in those pre-refrigeration days. Opportunities for profitable arbitrage were thus ubiquitous. Demanding that there be a universal maximum price for every item in the empire, as Diocletian's edict did, was a practical impossibility, not least because where we can calculate actual prices and compare them to the prices set out in the edict – which is to say, mainly in Egypt – the prices in the edict are much lower. We can of course explain this in terms of the government trying to save itself money on the many things it had constantly to buy for its own use, though that is perhaps to give too much credit for rational economic thinking to a regime that so prized uniformity for its own sake. And, whatever the motive, the attempt ended in failure. The price edict survives in numerous epigraphic copies, some complete, some fragmentary, but we have only one literary source – the Christian Lactantius, whose loathing of Diocletian was total – that mentions it at all. For what his hostile testimony is worth, Lactantius claims that the edict caused violence over 'small and cheap things' and led to a continued rise in prices. We may well believe that it did worsen inflation and spark widespread rioting but, despite Lactantius, it is hard to know how widely any attempt was made to enforce the edict. In theory, tetrarchic laws were issued in the name of all four emperors and valid across the whole empire; in practice they depended upon the willingness of the different members of the imperial college to endorse one another's measures, and even more on provincial governors' willingness to enforce them. That means that, despite its breadth of dissemination, the Edict on Maximum Prices may well have been a dead letter the moment it was issued, and there is some ambiguous evidence that the edict was repealed without fanfare within the year. But the damage it had done, and the chaos it had introduced, was lasting. The imperial economy, and indeed the value of the imperial currency itself, took several decades to stabilise.

The Edict on Maximum Prices is revealing of the tetrarchy's aspirations to total control, but another such measure was still more significant. Diocletian, famously, launched the last empire-wide persecution of Christians, known fittingly enough as the Great Persecution. Ever since Gallienus offered toleration to Christians after his father's defeat in Persia, adherence to Christian beliefs had undergone a very dramatic expansion. Numbers are impossible to come by, though they are bandied about freely by scholars, and the evidence is fragile enough to make controversy endless and irresolvable. Probably, Christians represented a majority population in parts of the Greek-speaking empire and formed substantial minorities in a few urbanised regions of the Latin west. By the early 300s, there is evidence of communities self-segregating in the east, with some villages entirely Christian, others entirely pagan, in the manner of modern American suburbanites self-segregating by race and party political taste.

Within Christian communities, a clear hierarchy of clerical grades was beginning to emerge, and the bishops who led each Christian community corresponded widely with one another across the empire. Shortly before the year 300, the first council of bishops whose rulings ('canons') are preserved met at Elvira in southern Spain, passing judgement on all sorts of issues that arose when Christians needed to get along in a world of many other religions. Among the empire's educated population, Christianity was just one option among many, and was certainly not the religion of the majority even though monotheism of one sort or another was now the elite norm. That said, the evidence does not support the once commonly held belief that Christianity was predominantly confined to the lower echelons of society. Indeed, Christianity was widely enough practised that both the army and the civil service included numbers of open Christians, and it is reported that Diocletian's wife and daughter were among their sympathisers. It was precisely that visibility that incited persecution.

Beginning with an incident at court in 299, Diocletian enacted increasingly harsh penalties against Christians in government, spurred on by his caesar Galerius. These ended in an edict imposing universal sacrifice to the gods of the state and specifically outlawing Christian worship. The actual causes of the anti-Christian hysteria – for that is clearly what it was – at the courts of Antioch and Nicomedia are hard to disentangle, given the weight of later Christian apologetic and the wholesale destruction of anti-Christian books from the reign of Constantine onwards. Neverthe-less, we know that Diocletian's court, like that of many earlier emperors, was a place of learning in which Christian and non-Christian intellectu-als mingled and taught, and in which the patronage of such men was a signal part of the emperor's duties. Elsewhere in the empire, at Antioch, Alexandria, Caesarea and Rome, imperial officials took part in the soirées of celebrity thinkers, enjoying their debates as entertainment suitable to men of their social status. Philosophical and religious debate was at one level cultured entertainment, but at another it was deadly serious, particu-larly where the philosophical and the religious overlapped. When sincere beliefs are also a cause for rivalry among intellectuals, the poison native to academic debate could seep into more perilous contexts, accidentally but suddenly turning political. Ever since the Julio-Claudian and Flavian periods, when Stoic philosophy and opposition to autocracy were equated, philosophers and theologians could, occasionally, influence government or draw down its wrath.

The tetrarchic persecutions may in part have been triggered by just this sort of politically charged intellectual debate. The basic story of how the persecution began is simple. During a ritual haruspicy in the *praetorium* at Antioch in 299, Christian officials had crossed themselves and the haruspex proved unable to take the auspices from the entrails of the sacrifical animal. Galerius himself was present at this event, after which an oracle of Apollo at Daphne issued the statement that the 'righteous', or Christians, were forcing him to compose false oracles. Galerius was enraged, and he was already an enemy of Christians. Diocletian's immediate response was to order the flogging of any courtier who refused to sacrifice to the gods. Early in 300, the order was extended to take in the whole of the eastern army. Other anti-Christian oracles – Zeus of Dodona and several theurgic oracles of Hecate – also began to circulate, playing upon the fears of an emperor who believed, like everyone, that the safety of the state was in the hands of the divine. Galerius continued to expend considerable energy on convincing Diocletian to mount a full-scale persecution, but it was not until 303, when the oracle of Apollo at Didyma issued another anti-Christian pronounce-ment, that Diocletian was convinced. That February, he ordered Christians to 'return to the institutions of their ancestors'. By placing braziers and altars in all courts of law, Diocletian hoped to ensure that all inhabitants of the empire, Christians included, participated in sacrifices to the gods by burning incense on their altars. Those who did not would be punished.

That raw chronology does not get to the intellectual background of events. It is clear that during the 290s, Christian apologists were deeply exercised in defending themselves against philosophical attacks on their beliefs, the tenor of which is recorded in some sources. Eusebius of Caesarea, in particular, quotes hostile pagan writers who asked, given Christian atheism and apostasy from the gods of the state and their ancestors, 'to what kind of punishments would they *not* be justly subjected'? The author of the lines quoted by Eusebius is certainly the Neoplatonist Porphyry, a man who positioned himself among Greek intellectuals as the true heir to the philosopher Plotinus, universally acknowledged as the most brilliant Greek thinker of the third century. Plotinus was a Neoplatonist, and late Platonic philosophy, unlike most post-Classical philosophical schools, had always had a dogmatic side that could conceive of there being just one single path to truth. Porphyry's attacks, both on rival philosophers claiming similar pedigree and on Christians, were widely read and seem to have circulated among the more cultured officials of the eastern civil service, some of whom became strong supporters of persecution. We know that, before the outbreak of the Great Persecution of 303, the imperial official Sossianus Hierocles (his actual post at the time is unclear) and a philosopher who may have been Porphyry himself argued the case against the Christians before Diocletian.

Galerius, for his part, had every reason to stoke Diocletian's fears and worries, for Constantius, his fellow caesar on the other side of the empire, was if not himself a Christian then at least quite sympathetic to their presence in his court and family. Constantius had a daughter named Anastasia, which is diagnostically a Christian name, and if we could be certain that the name was given to her at birth, we would have much greater certainty about Constantius's own predilections. Regardless, Constantius implemented only the mildest clauses of the persecuting edict in his territory. Attacking Christianity might usefully undermine Constantius, which was very much in Galerius's interest, because while he and Diocletian had no sons, both Maximian and Constantius did. These, respectively named Maxentius and Constantinus (though we will call him Constantine henceforth, as is conventional), were being groomed for the succession, so that if one of the augusti were to die, Constantius would, as the senior caesar, succeed him and then promote one of the two heirs apparent – presumably his own son Constantine – to the vacant caesarship, leaving Galerius in that lower rank himself. But if Christians were ejected from public roles then both Constantius and his son would be out of contention, opening the way for Galerius. Fears for the safety of the state, philosophical disagreements, the petty rivalry of intellectuals and the deadly serious politics of imperial succession thus prepared a toxic miasma of hatred, misunderstanding and wilful misrepresentation.

The edict that resulted – promulgated at Nicomedia at the end of February 303, in much of the east in March, and by May in Africa and elsewhere in the west – was nothing if not damning. It ordered Christian churches to be pulled down and Christian scriptures burnt, condemned Christian imperial freedmen to slavery, and stripped Christian civil servants of their rank, thus opening them up to consequences that would be just as dire. In legal matters, Christians lost any recourse in actions taken against them, nor could they initiate prosecutions against their assailants. In sum, the edict was designed to make being a Christian intolerable, rendering Christians defenceless against charges and inviting neighbour to prey upon neighbour, in the way that delatory regimes have always done. Denunciation became profitable, and that was one point of the decree. Indeed, with a sort of malign glee, the initial edict was promulgated on the feast of the Terminalia, a festival celebrating the boundaries that kept the Roman state safe, that was traditionally marked by the sacrifice of a black lamb – a macabre joke at the expense of a religion whose central figure was often represented in the form of a shepherd or indeed a lamb.

As always, the success of this edict depended upon its enforcement by imperial officials, which varied widely across the empire. The caesar Constantius did the bare minimum possible to keep up the appearance of participating in his senior colleague's initiative, tearing down churches, but burning no scriptures and enforcing no other bans. In Maximian's territory, only in North Africa did the efforts of local officials ensure serious attention to enforcement. In the east, by contrast, enforcement was vigorous and violent, all the more so after Christians tore down the edict in Nicomedia as soon as it was posted and then set fire to the imperial residence. That arson prompted a second edict, ordering the arrest of the church's leaders, but this was only promulgated in the east – it was entirely ignored in the west.

There were victims everywhere, of course, and the few genuine martyr acts that survive illustrate both enthusiastic and utterly indifferent prosecution by imperial administrators. Some municipal officials made sure that Christians in their midst would be forced to declare themselves; others did their best to let Christians get away with the form rather than the substance of compliance, for instance by accepting for the pyre any book handed them by a known Christian without verifying its content. Where officials cared to enforce the law strictly, there were many deaths. Palestine and Syria, where Galerius was nearby and men loyal to him in charge, saw something of a bloodbath, enough so that parts of Syria and Commagene may have erupted in open rebellion. North Africa, where the governor C. Annius Anullinus harboured anti-Christian sentiments as virulent as those of Galerius, suffered badly and the behaviour of North African Christians in the face of persecution would fuel a schism in their church that dragged on for more than a century. In Italy, by contrast, the deadlier side of the edict could be evaded, while in Britain, Gaul and much of Spain, the loss of corporate property certainly exceeded that of life and limb.

Although undoubtedly the most numerous, Christians were not the only group targeted for persecution under the tetrarchy: on 1 March 302, Diocletian issued an edict against the Manichees, a measure that was not merely about conformity, but about xenophobia as well. This law is preserved intact, with all its rhetorical preamble, whereas most laws of this period survive only in edited forms in later codes. A work known since the sixteenth century as the *Collatio legum Mosaicarum et Romanarum* ('Comparison of Roman and Jewish Law') but properly entitled the *Lex dei quam praecepit dominus ad Moysen* ('The Law of God Which the Lord Taught to Moses') is an early fourth-century Jewish text that juxtaposes passages from the Torah with Roman law from second- and third-century juristic texts and imperial edicts from the Gregorian code. One of its sections, on astrologers, magicians and Manichees, preserves the Diocletianic edict condemning Manichaeism.

Mani's faith was a product of the cultural diversity of the eastern Persian world, and of the support that a prince like Shapur had been willing to give it. Narseh, when he became shahanshah, ruled in a similarly tolerant vein when it came to religious matters, and allowed followers of Mani to practise their religion freely after the years of persecution by Kardir and the Mazdean priesthood. This meant that, in Roman minds, Manichaeism seemed not just foreign, but specifically Persian – an enemy religion in a literal sense – and Mani's followers could be seen as fifth columnists of the Persian kings and their 'depraved' religion a threat to the Roman state. In Diocletian's edict, that connection is made explicit: Manichaeism is referred to as a new religion, 'recently sprung up from the Persian people, our enemy', bringing the 'accursed laws and customs of the Persians' to innocent Romans. The governor Julianus, to whom the law is addressed, should burn Manichaean leaders alive along with their holy books, their followers should suffer capital punishment and the confiscation of their estates, while Manichees in imperial service are condemned to the Phaenensian or Proconessan mines, the equivalent of a death sentence. So far as we know, this edict was never revoked, and occasional persecution of Manichees continued throughout the fourth century, under both pagan and Christian emperors.

Although many Romans continued to flirt with the religion, whose dualism and salvific promise was as mystical and attractive as Christianity, imperial law never ceased to view Manichees, like practitioners of black magic, as an inherent threat to the state.

It is tempting for the modern historian to downplay the religious side of the tetrarchic persecutions and see in it a cynical political manoeuvre on the part of Galerius, or a passing storm exaggerated in retrospect by Christian writers. But that would be wrong. Galerius really did hate Christianity, while Diocletian, more than many emperors, had a heavy ideological investment in the traditional religion of the state. Yet both in the end reluctantly ceased persecution, having realised that Christianity really was too widespread, and Christians too widely represented among the powerful, to eliminate. It is not that Galerius and Diocletian were on the wrong side of history, though some confessional historians would to this day argue that point. Rather, Christianity was simply too large a phenomenon to submit to their totalising mania. Late in 303, amnesty was declared throughout the empire, no doubt to the displeasure of the more committed persecutors. But there was a festival to celebrate: blood would not be shed during the *vicennalia* of the augusti.

Late in 303, with the persecution of Christianity in abeyance across the empire, Diocletian and his court travelled to the territory of his fellow augustus Maximian. The two then progressed together to the city of Rome and on 20 November 303 celebrated their *vicennalia*, the twentieth anniversary of their joint reign: in a rewriting of past history typical of the later empire, Maximian and Diocletian shared the same regnal reckoning, despite Maximian's actually having become augustus a full year after Diocletian. It was meant to be a happy occasion, and no doubt for many there it was: the tetrarchs had imposed a stability on the empire such as had not been seen for two generations. What went on in Rome between the two augusti is unclear, but decisions were certainly made for the future. Although there have been many modern discussions about a tetrarchic 'theory of government', all rely on inference from later events that may have owed more to chance than design. What is clear is that for some time, perhaps since 293, there was an understanding among the tetrarchs that at some point the augusti would retire, to be succeeded as such by the caesars, and that two new caesars would then be appointed.

We cannot know if a retirement date had long been anticipated, or whether in 302 or 303 Diocletian decided that the time had come and that Maximian now needed to be told as much. But that there had been retirement plans in the works for some time is made clear by the massive palaces that the tetrarchs were building. The best preserved and under-stood of these is Diocletian's at Split in Dalmatia, which must have been designed as a retirement residence, given its distance from the main centres of imperial government. Galerius's palace at Romuliana, now Gamzigrad in Serbia, was on a similar scale. A third tetrarchic palace has been excavated in Spain under the high-speed rail station in modern Córdoba (Corduba), which destroyed most of the remains, although its speculative attribution to Maximian is dubious. It had thus long been intended that a new college of emperors would continue to run the empire from Antioch, Nicomedia, Sirmium, Mediolanum and Trier, while their former colleagues lived out an honourable but discreet retirement far enough away to cause no trouble. Diocletian's plan for systematic retirements would guard against the unexpected and disruptive death of an augustus, but it implies no formal theory of government or, as is sometimes claimed, a hostility to dynastic succession.

Diocletian was too smart a man to believe that competent male heirs, if such existed, could be passed over; they would surely try to seize what they were not given. The plan was thus that Maximian's adult son Maxentius and Constantius's adult son Constantine would become the new caesars once Diocletian and Maximian stepped down as augusti and Constantius and Galerius became the senior pair, so both Constantine and Maxentius spent much of the 290s at Diocletian's court, being groomed for power. But when the imperial retirements were announced rather more than a year after the *vicennalia*, on 1 May 305, the succession plan had changed – wholly to the benefit of Galerius.

Events are obscure, but during the celebrations of the *vicennalia* at Rome, Diocletian fell badly ill. He left Rome on 20 December 303, his second and last visit to the eternal city. Marching back to the Balkans via Ravenna, he met Galerius, who had not gone to Rome for the ceremonies. In the spring, Diocletian was evidently well enough to take joint command of a punitive war against the Carpi along the lower Danube. Maximian likewise made a journey to the Balkans a few months later, after Diocletian had departed for Asia, and met Galerius at Sirmium. The two men argued violently, which may suggest that Maximian had learned of the plan to alter the succession and disliked it. Constantius, throughout all this, had been studiously silent, which bespeaks either deep political wisdom or later whitewashing by his victorious son. Regardless, the western caesar would be present beside his divine father Maximian on the fateful day in May 305. The latter had returned to Rome after his angry encounter with Galerius, and there celebrated the secular games in 304. Diocletian was in Nicomedia by August of the same year but, those facts apart, little is known of this period – save that a fourth persecuting edict was issued in the east, ordering all subjects to sacrifice, in a return to the policy that had been abandoned for the sake of the *vicennalia*.

The renewed persecution was probably the work of Galerius, who gained an ascendancy over Diocletian after the latter's illness. He stood beside Diocletian on 1 May 305 outside Nicomedia, where the army had been gathered to hear a very special announcement. On a dais, in front of a column honouring Jupiter, Diocletian announced his retirement with tears in his eyes, pleading age and exhaustion. He would leave the direction of affairs to others, and appoint new caesars. Constantius's son Constantine was there, too, and the gathered crowd must have expected his proclamation to be the next step. Instead, Diocletian proclaimed as caesars Severus and Maximinus, relatives and cronies of Galerius. Maximinus, likewise present at Nicomedia, was brought forward and took off his civilian cloak before Diocletian garbed him in his own purple mantle, effectively resigning the imperial office and handing it to another. In Mediolanum, on the same day, a parallel scene was playing out, in which Maximian and Constantius garbed Severus in the purple and Maximian stepped down into retirement. Nothing like this had happened before in Roman history, a voluntary resignation and peaceful handover of power between rulers. It is impossible to exaggerate the strangeness of it all.

13

THE FAILURE OF
THE TETRARCHY

Having achieved so much, a peaceful transition of power was to have been Diocletian's crowning glory. Perhaps unsurprisingly, it did not happen. The exclusion of Constantine and Maxentius was an act of folly, and Galerius – as he had done before in his Persian campaign and as he would do repeatedly over the next five years – fatally overestimated his own ability to control events. But for a brief time, imperial politics slowed, reeling, as it were, from the shock to its system. Diocletian left the army gathered outside Nicomedia and processed in the imperial cart back to the palace. He went thence into retirement in Dalmatia, determined to stay out of politics ever after. Galerius moved his residence to the Balkans, chiefly Sirmium, leaving Maximinus to govern the east. Constantius, now senior augustus, left Mediolanum for Gaul, planning a campaign in northern Britain against the Pictish tribes. Severus, who seems to have been something of a non-entity, stayed behind in Mediolanum.

Below the surface, however, all was not well. The new augusti entered into what can only be called a cold war. Galerius arrogated to himself the rights of a senior augustus and issued edicts for parts of the empire outside his sphere; Constantius ignored him altogether and treated Constantine as his de facto caesar. Constantine had left the east quite rapidly, possibly immediately after the succession of Severus and Maximinus was announced in late spring. He joined his father at Bononia and accompanied him to

Britain. Maxentius, who had probably been at Diocletian's court at the same time, returned to Rome, where we next meet him in late 306. In Britain, Constantius and Constantine together won a victory in Pictish territory, beyond Hadrian's Wall, before the end of the year. Then, on 25 July 306, Constantius died at Eboracum and the army acclaimed his son as emperor.

Something like this had been inevitable from the moment Diocletian abrogated the original plan for the succession, but it was accelerated by Constantius's unexpected death. Had he and Galerius been on better terms, Constantine's acclamation might have looked rather less like a usurpation than it did. Surprisingly, Galerius did not immediately declare war and, even more surprisingly, Constantine was able to convert himself into a legitimate member of the imperial college. That is a reminder that Constantine is one of history's most extraordinary figures: no matter how much revisionist effort has been put into showing the many ways in which he acted like any other post-Severan emperor – and there were many ways in which he did – the scale and sweep of his capabilities continue to astonish. Like Julius Caesar's heir Augustus, he had an extraordinary capacity for being what the occasion required him to be – showing a pragmatism, even cynicism, that was quite compatible with always truly believing himself to be right. Also like Augustus, his continuous effort at rewriting his own past as circumstances dictated is only partly traceable in the historical record. Unfortunately, the one place where the comparison between Constantine and Augustus fails is in the quality of the extant sources: we know much less about the life, actions and even the bare chronology of Constantine's reign than we do of his exalted predecessor. As a result, we are often left guessing as to how precisely he managed to accomplish everything that he did.

The late Constantius had been a typical product of the Severan empire. A man from the Balkans, his parentage totally obscure, he rose from the ranks and probably entered the officer corps around the time of the coup that brought down Gallienus. Any connection to the family of the short-lived emperor Claudius is a later fabrication of Constantine's, but Constantius was certainly a *protector* (one of the emperor's personal guardsmen) in the main field army attached to Aurelian and Probus in the 270s, and probably then tribune of a guard unit. Under Carus, he became the governor of a middling province (*praeses* of Dalmatia). Familiar since late adolescence with the treachery and betrayals of the Severan officer class, he proved agile enough to switch sides just before Diocletian defeated Carinus, and his career prospered quietly under Diocletian and Maximian, with an uneventful tenure as the latter's praetorian prefect, before his elevation to the rank of caesar in 293. Divorce and remarriage accompanied his rising fortunes, and he became the son-in-law of Maximian in 288 or so. This marriage to Theodora would produce a large family of half-brothers and -sisters for Constantine, who was already a grown man when Constantius divorced his mother Helena in favour of the imperial connection.

The parentage of Constantine was much mythologised by the emperor himself once he was in a position to do so. The humility of his mother Helena was exaggerated, the actual status of her marriage to Constantius called into question, her saintly role in 'discovering' the Christian topography of the Holy Land embellished from almost the moment of her death; her legend has persisted ever since, inspiring Evelyn Waugh to produce his only humourless novel, *Helena* (1950). The truth about Constantine, insofar as we can extract it from the fog of his own propaganda, is much simpler. Helena was not the humble stable girl of legend, but rather the daughter of a *stabularius*, that is, the manager of an imperial relay post or *mansio* in Asia Minor. Constantius no doubt met her en route to the Palmyrene campaigns of Aurelian; for a junior guardsman, it was a good enough match, tying him into the class of minor functionaries that dotted the third-century empire. The son born to them at Naissus in Moesia, probably in 273, received a proper education – a symptom of his father's growing success in the military hierarchy – and became passably bilingual in Greek as well as Latin.

As the son of an officer, Constantine was destined for a good military career, early entry into one of the elite guard units and swift promotion to command – prospects that need not have changed dramatically after Constantius's promotion to the praetorian prefecture and marriage to Theodora. It was a different matter when Constantius became caesar. The tetrarchs, as we have seen, were pragmatic and ambitious men. They preferred to share power rather than squander it in ceaseless, self-defeating battles. But that did not mean they liked or trusted one another. Constantius was a tremendous asset to Maximian, but as the demonstrably better general he was also a potential rival. That he, like Maximian, had an adult son whose ambitions would inevitably be stoked by paternal successes, was another risk. And so Constantine, instead of pursuing a conventional military career, found himself sent for further education at the court of Diocletian, part privileged heir apparent, part hostage for his father's loyalty.

Diocletian's main residence was at Nicomedia, one of the great cities of Bithynia, the homeland of Constantine's mother, to which she probably retired when her son moved to the eastern court. He served at court for the better part of a decade, no doubt mixing in its intellectual circles, where the Christian scholar Lactantius was a teacher and the Neoplatonist philosopher Porphyry an active speaker. The idea that Constantine was educated at the court, however, is a retrospective myth, the future emperor later revising his true age downwards by fifteen years. In truth, Constantine continued his military career, serving in various commands as a tribune, fighting on the Danube alongside Diocletian and deep in Persian territory on Galerius's successful campaign against Ctesiphon. It was in this period that he married Minervina, with whom he had a son, the future caesar Crispus. About Minervina nothing is known, although it has been conjectured that she was a relative of Diocletian, perhaps the daughter of a sister or an in-law.

We do not know what Constantine did after the Persian campaign, but his succession had been universally expected before the shocking announcements of 305. His proclamation at Eboracum came as a surprise to no one. The way he handled his next steps, however, was remarkable: he refused to style himself augustus, accepting his soldiers' acclamation, but claimed for himself only the rank of caesar. This ostentatious humility made it hard for Galerius to brand him a usurper, and Constantine put it about that Constantius had designated him as caesar on his deathbed – which as senior augustus he would have been indisputably within his rights to do. Galerius, the new senior augustus, could find no workable objection to this strategy and accepted the imperial portraits that Constantine sent him. The latter could now claim legitimate imperial status in not one but two ways – designation by the then-senior augustus on his deathbed, and designation by the new senior augustus, Galerius, upon receipt of the imperial portraits. The role of the army, so crucial in the moment in July 306, was played down, and the Diocletianic insistence on the exclusive right of the senior augustus to determine the composition of the imperial college was reaffirmed.

Constantine moved to Gaul and set himself up in his father's old residence of Trier, patiently waiting on events, but already showing signs of the independent thinking that would in time transform the tetrarchic model of governance for good. At Trier, in 307, he ordered the restoration of Christian property confiscated during the brief year in which Constantius had enforced some of the measures of the Great Persecution. Working through the stages by which Constantine rewrote his past is a thankless task – the Christian polemicist Lactantius is the earliest witness, and though his *De mortibus persecutorum* contains Constantinian propaganda, it is at least early Constantinian propaganda: and it suggests that already in 306 Constantine was changing the story of his father's last months. Whereas in reality the two had campaigned together for the better part of a year, Constantine now began to claim that, fearing for his life, he had fled Galerius's court and raced to his father's deathbed, hamstringing the post horses as he went to evade pursuit. A good story, but nonsense. More secure evidence is the coin portraits that testify to the new emperor's plans. The mint at Rome, under the control of Severus at the time, struck coins in the name of Constantine as caesar that reflected the standard tetrarchic image – thick-necked, grim and bearded. But the Trier mint, which along with Londinium was the only mint under direct Constantinian control, introduced a new type, in which the hooked nose that Constantius had sported on some of his more distinctive coins is paired to an entirely non-tetrarchic image. Gone is the tetrarchic beard, gone is the thick neck, the heavy features. In its place is a strikingly youthful portrait, clean-shaven and angular. Only the fixed stare of the eyes remains the same. Constantine was showing that he could respect parts of the tetrarchic model as long as it suited him and helped his claim to legitimacy, but would disregard it freely when he chose.

A similar flexibility was to be shown by the other spurned heir apparent, Maxentius. Not surprisingly, the success of Constantine galled him, for he too had been meant to become emperor. So he staged a coup. On 28 October 306, the urban prefect Annius Anullinus, an aristocrat of Rome, secured the support of the senate. At the same time, in the camp of the praetorian guard, Maxentius assumed the purple with the connivance of several tribunes and had the *vicarius* of Italy, a partisan of Severus, put to death. The praetorians, as we have seen, rarely needed a reason to revolt, but they had gone quiet in recent years. Now they were angered at Galerius and his regime for reducing their numbers, and they reckoned – correctly – that they would find support among the Italian populace, who had even more reason to hate the new order: Galerius had reduced Italy to the state of a normal province.

He did so by including Italy alongside the other provinces when, in early 306, he ordered a general census of the imperial population as the basis on which to set rates for the next tax cycle. This was both a revenue-generating mechanism and, probably, a deliberate provocation aimed at Constantius, who should, as senior augustus, have been the only one issuing edicts. For many centuries, since 167 BC, Italy had been exempted from poll and land taxes. In the late republican and early imperial periods, this was a logical consequence of the fact that the Romans ruled an empire made up mostly of non-Romans but explicitly for the benefit of Romans. Even as the provinces became more Romanised in legal and cultural terms, and a smaller percentage of provincial wealth was siphoned off for the good of Italy, the peninsula retained its old privileges. Emperors, as we have seen, had long been in the habit of making straight for Italy upon their acclamation, lavishing honours and benefits as they went. To strip Italy of its special status was inconceivable. But by the mid third century, rival claimants ceased to go to Rome straightaway. Some did not bother to go at all. By century's end, Rome and much of the peninsula had lost their structural importance. Galerius's edict, which effectively provincialised Italy, is only comprehensible in the light of that recent history – in the newly remade Diocletianic empire, Italy really was just another province, with an important imperial residence at Milan and a symbolic capital in Rome that – alone in the peninsula – would retain its privileges.

Maxentius offered a prospect of restoring Italy's importance and his usurpation – for that is what it clearly was – would find wide support. Severus, who had become the legitimate augustus in the west upon Constantius's death, marched south from Mediolanum as soon as he learned of Maxentius's rebellion, but he did so at the head of a field army that had been under the command of Maxentius's father Maximian until just a year or so before. Perhaps unsurprisingly, they refused to fight against their old leader's son, especially when they learned that Maximian had emerged from retirement in Lucania and gone to Rome – Maxentius had sent him the imperial purple and reinvested him as *bis Augustus*, 'emperor for the second time'. Some units deserted Severus in favour of the rebels. Severus attempted to retreat but ended up surrendering to Maximian at Ravenna, returning to him the purple cloak with which Maximian had invested him not even two years before. Severus was imprisoned south of Rome on the via Appia, where he would remain until he was executed a year later.

Galerius was now forced to deal with the consequences of having changed Diocletian's succession plan to his own advantage. Severus, the man he recognised as his legitimate fellow augustus, was being held in captivity. Constantine, an enemy who had outmanoeuvred him politically, was consolidating his authority in the western dioceses of Britain, Spain and Gaul. And now Italy and Africa were in the hands of another challenger, backed by a former augustus. While Constantine had allowed Galerius to save face and retain the fiction of senior authority, nothing so decorous would work in Italy. There was no vacancy in the imperial college when Maxentius was proclaimed – he was a usurper from day one and would in fact never be acknowledged as legitimate by Galerius. In the short term, though, his success was troubling. Maxentius's sister Theodora had been married to Constantius in 293, establishing a family connection and producing the half-siblings of Constantine. Theodora was dead by 306, but Maximian had in the meantime had more children, and so a daughter named Fausta, probably only eight years old, was offered to Constantine in marriage. Constantine divorced Minervina and, in August 307, with Severus still languishing in jail and Galerius occupied in the Balkans, Maximian processed north to Trier with Fausta.

A panegyric to Maximian and Constantine, delivered to celebrate the marriage in late August or early September, struggles to cast events in a legitimate light. It implies that Maximian had never really abdicated and that it was Maximian, not Galerius, who had appointed Constantine as caesar, a role that he had also rightfully inherited from his father Constantius. And now, at Trier, Maximian made Constantine augustus, just as if he had become the senior emperor upon Diocletian's abdication. To make clear this point, Constantine began to recognise Maximian as consul prior of the year in place of Galerius. Such were the ideological contortions necessary to make sense of the reality on the ground. And yet it is not those contortions that surprise so much as the fact that the tetrarchic model, and its vocabulary for describing legitimate rulership, had taken such deep hold of imperial governance that it could not simply be abandoned in favour of the much older, more immediately legible narrative of hereditary succession. In fact, the Diocletianic concept of legitimate imperial rule would never be abandoned – the fourth century would eliminate many aspects of tetrarchic government, but the notion of an imperial college, access to which was in the gift of the senior emperor, never disappeared.

The wedding over, and the little girl Fausta presumably being brought up in the imperial residence of Trier until she came of an age for the marriage to be consummated, Maximian returned to Rome. There, Maxentius had embarked upon an ambitious scheme of public building that would bring the massive architectural style of the tetrarchy to the imperial capital. He also extended toleration of Christians to Italy and Africa, as Constantine had already done in the lands he controlled, but he did not yet go so far as to order the restoration of confiscated Christian property. In the east, meanwhile, Galerius and Maximinus were continuing to enforce the persecution of Christians, the latter most vigorously of all. The dismantling of persecution in the west was one of the major distinctions between the eastern and western regimes and it contributed to their mutual hostility. Galerius had already made it clear that he would not compromise with the Italian regime, so Maximian and Maxentius knew a war was coming: when it did, in September 307, Galerius invaded Italy, marching unopposed as far as Interamna near Rome, where his army, like that of Severus, showed itself disinclined to fight. Galerius was a better commander than Severus, however, and, rather than face mutiny, he retreated to Illyricum, allowing his soldiers to loot the Italian countryside as they went, thus ensuring their loyalty and goodwill. In response to the invasion, Maxentius had Severus killed. A return to the pre-tetrarchic problem of endlessly repeated warfare now seemed likely, but Galerius then played a trump card.

The new year opened (in the east, at least) with Galerius and Diocletian holding the consulship. By bringing Diocletian out of retirement, Galerius was reminding all of the major participants that he, and no one else, was the successor to the role Diocletian had invented. The fact that Constantine had appointed his own consuls in his own part of the empire was neither here nor there: Diocletian could force compromise on all involved, except perhaps Maxentius, who early in the year fell out with his father Maximian. The latter had been pushing for a negotiated settlement of the issue, no doubt spurred to this by Diocletian, who had studiously avoided taking any action in the previous years: if his old benefactor and chief had had enough of the mess, then Maximian was ready to listen. Perhaps realising that with Maxentius in power, a settlement was nigh impossible, Maximian tried to depose his son, but the Italian army, which Maximian had once delivered into his son's hands, would not tolerate this coup attempt. Maximian fled to his son-in-law Constantine in Trier.

In November 308, now on behalf of Constantine rather than Maxentius, Maximian journeyed to the military headquarters of Carnuntum on the

Danube near modern Vienna. By 11 November, a deal had been reached, presumably brokered by Diocletian, who showed no signs of wanting to resume power in the manner of his former colleague. Maximian and Diocletian acknowledged their status as retired augusti, Maximian again laying down the purple and thus allowing Galerius to appoint another ally as augustus in succession to the dead Severus: this was Valerius Licinianus Licinius, an experienced general who proved to have considerably more ability and staying power than either of Galerius's original choices. From Carnuntum, Galerius returned to Sirmium, Maximian retired to Gaul and Diocletian went back to his palace at Split, this time removing himself from imperial politics for good. In the new dispensation, Galerius and Licinius would be senior and junior augusti, while Constantine and Maximinus would remain caesars, receiving the new title 'sons of the augusti'. Maxentius remained unrecognised. The solution was far from perfect, but it had at least the potential to work.

A certain equilibrium had been reached and so the next year was occupied with the frontier campaigns that were always necessary after bouts of imperial instability. Hammering the barbarians was an easy way for emperors whose authority had been shaken to reassert their fitness to command. So in 307 Constantine attacked some of the Franci along the lower Rhine, even throwing two of their kings to the beasts in the arena at Trier, and in 308 he invaded Francia again, in the same year that Galerius battered the Carpi on the Danube. The next two years are barely documented in the sources – Constantine built a permanent bridge across the Rhine at Colonia Agrippina in 310, Licinius campaigned on the Danube in 309 and 310, and the victory titulature of Carpicus becomes repetitive. In Africa in 308, the governor of Numidia, L. Domitius Alexander, proclaimed himself emperor, forcing Maxentius into an expedition against him and then, after his suppression, against the tribes of the desert further south in 309. Maximinus spent 310 fighting on the Persian frontier, though the details are extremely sketchy and in general the Persian peace held up very well. All were ensuring their personal authority over their troops and making a show of defending their provincials.

The relative political calm did not last. Constantine's preoccupation with the Rhine gave Maximian ideas – chronically lacking in Diocletian's restraint, he found retirement insupportable and decided to do something about it. In southern Gaul, where he had based himself since the Carnuntum conference, he called together some troops while Constantine was off fighting beyond the Rhine. He claimed that Constantine had been killed and that he, Maximian, was now emperor. He took Massilia (modern Marseilles) as his base, but the city was indefensible and when Constantine, hearing of the revolt, marched south to suppress it, any soldiers whom Maximian had convinced to support him deserted. He was dead within days.

Two versions of his death survive, both clearly a product of Constantinian image-management. In the first, Maximian committed suicide when he realised that the truth behind his lies would be found out. In the second, Maximian besought the forgiveness of his loving son-in-law, who offered it with great magnanimity, even allowing him to live in his own chambers in the palace, until the good son-in-law was betrayed by the vile old plotter. Maximian, it was said, crept into Constantine's quarters planning to kill him, but because Constantine had been forewarned, he found a slave in the emperor's bed; caught red-handed he hanged himself in despair there and then. Over the next three decades, Constantine demonstrated a similar penchant for concocted stories of betrayals miraculously averted, using them to explain his own ruthless elimination of relatives and rivals. But Maximian could never have been permitted to outlive a second coup and, with the old man's death, Constantine's uneasy détente with Maxentius could be reconsidered as well.

14

CONSTANTINE AND LICINIUS

The first problem Constantine faced was that, although he and Maxentius might be brothers-in-law, they could no longer both be sons of Maximian. Constantine also needed to obscure the fact that Maximian had been the one who had promoted him from caesar to augustus, and so a new myth appeared: ancestral descent from Claudius II, the only third-century soldier emperor with an untarnished posthumous reputation. We first discover this story in a panegyric delivered at Trier not long after the death of Maximian, and Constantine never discarded this element in his self-fashioned ancestry. It contained an implicit rejection of the tetrarchic model in which appointment by the senior augustus was the core of legitimacy, and instead claimed inheritance down the generations as the proper guarantor of legitimate power. The appeal to Claudius had an additional valence, and a menacing one. By the early fourth century, Claudius's name was deeply associated with the defeat of 'the Goths' – as the varied and diverse people whom the third century had known as 'Scythians' were now generally called. By claiming descent from the emperor who defeated the Goths, Constantine was also claiming the Balkan provinces as his rightful inheritance.

That, however, was a project for the future. The immediate aftermath of Maximian's coup was another Frankish campaign, or perhaps a return to the one Constantine had been fighting when news of Maximian's revolt reached him. The journey north would have striking consequences. As the panegyric of 310 also reveals, while en route back to the Rhineland, Constantine had stopped at the shrine of Apollo Grannus in the town of Andesina, now the village of Grand in the Vosges. There he had a vision of the god himself, accompanied by Victory, presenting him with laurel wreaths. Constantine may have induced this vision by incubation in the temple, but he thereafter formed a persistent habit of explaining his actions by appeal to miraculous revelations. Presumably, the panegyrist echoed a theme that he knew to be circulating at Constantine's court, and it is no coincidence that Constantine's mints began to strike coins honouring Sol Invictus, a sun god like Apollo, and a favourite of earlier soldier emperors like Aurelian. The cult of the sun had strong monotheistic tendencies and could thus seem compatible with the Christianity to which Constantine was also attracted, even if he was not yet a practising Christian. Both Christian and pagan priests travelled in his entourage and he was clearly willing to consider their conflicting interpretations of events, particularly if these seemed to promise him future glories, as Apollo had done.

He was also taking practical steps to improve his position, encouraged by developments in the east. In 310, Maximinus unilaterally arrogated to himself the title of Augustus, precipitating an open breach with Galerius. But the latter then fell extremely ill with the bowel cancer that would kill him. We can very rarely pinpoint the precise cause of natural deaths in antiquity but, thanks to Lactantius's gruesome delight in Galerius's suffering, we can diagnose metastatic cancer of the bowel, so advanced that it ate away a good part of his lower intestines before infection set in and he died in agony. Lactantius's point was that God will punish persecutors with fittingly obscene deaths – even when, like Galerius, they repent. For it was none other than the ailing Galerius who repealed the persecuting edicts and extended toleration to Christians in the east. Since Lactantius quotes this document verbatim, it reveals Galerius's true motives: persecution had failed, Christianity had not been eliminated. Worse, from his statist and pagan point of view, many 'persevered with their own way of life and ... neither offered proper worship and cult to the gods or to the god of the Christians'. The state was thereby deprived not just of the support that proper and true worship should bring, but also of whatever help might come from the clearly deluded Christians. Just as the persecuting edicts were issued for the good of the state, so too they were now revoked for the good of the state. There is real logic here, peculiar though it seems.

Lactantius will, of course, remain uncharitable, but we should recognise Galerius's edict of toleration as an act of genuine statesmanship. For all his faults, chief among them a fatal capacity for overestimating his own strength, Galerius was a much better steward of the Diocletianic legacy than he is usually given credit for. His insistence on appointing Severus and Maximinus as caesars had, in the end, proved to be a miscalculation but, once that fact became clear to him, he strove very hard to avoid the kind of civil war that would lead the state back to the third century. It is as if he had come to understand that the ideological ambition to universal conformity, central as it was to tetrarchic ideology, should when necessary be subordinated to the pragmatic goal of de facto control. That Maximinus had made himself augustus against Galerius's will in 310 was a problem, but one that could be negotiated if necessary, for there was never any doubt about Maximinus's basic legitimacy, any more than there was with that of Constantine. The latter had proven himself formidable beyond any reasonable expectations. By extending toleration to a religion that Constantine was known to favour, Galerius took away one of the main differences between government in east and west. It meant that Constantine would have one fewer reason for dispute with Galerius's friend and chosen partner Licinius, the man who had been chosen as his Maximian to Galerius's Diocletian. Both Diocletian and Galerius had proved over and over again that the endurance of the new tetrarchic regime mattered more to them than did its individual personnel. If toleration lessened the likelihood of civil war, it would have been worth it.

It failed to have that effect. Maximinus, ensconced in the diocese of Oriens beyond the Propontis, had at least some claim to be an augustus, despite Licinius having been appointed directly to that rank in 308 over Maximinus's head. Since 310, Maximinus had been styling himself augustus, although neither Galerius nor Licinius would ever acknowledge his right to the title, and he had deliberately accelerated the persecution of Christians in his territory in protest at Galerius's edict of toleration. He did so in a way that allowed him to deny that he was doing any such thing.

The tetrarchs still operated within a traditional imperial system of petition and response, however much they aspired to universalising control. Maximinus therefore began to encourage petitions from non-Christians who wished to expel Christians from their villages or towns, petitions to which he could reply with a favourable rescript. Two epigraphic versions of such petitions survive and their fragments authenticate the version of

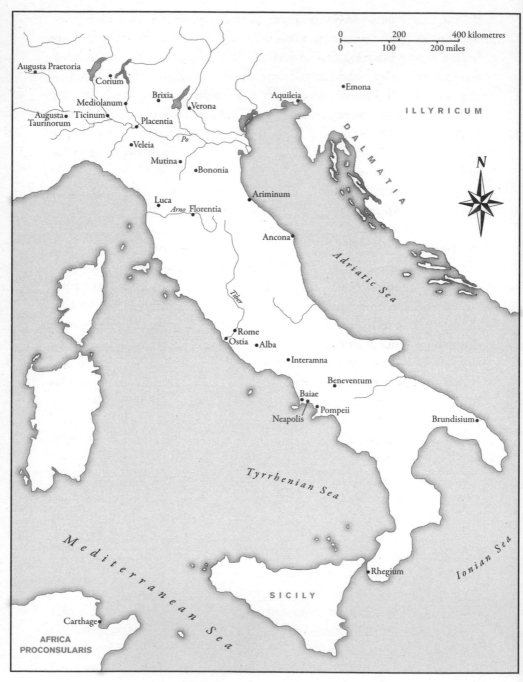

Italy

the document preserved verbatim in the ecclesiastical history of Eusebius. The wording of the rescripts is so homogeneous that there must have been a model petition, probably drafted by Maximinus's *magister libellorum*, for use by communities wishing to act against their Christian neighbours. Maximinus could thus carry on persecuting while claiming not to do so. Imperial encouragement of local petitions in order to enact a favoured policy would later be used by Constantine to carry out an explicitly Christian agenda, though only after he had already assured his political ascendancy. But in 312 that was still a good way off.

In 312, Licinius looked like the direct inheritor of the Diocletianic legacy, appointed augustus by the man himself in 308 at the instance of Diocletian's truest heir, Galerius. And yet Licinius faced a difficult political scene. He held Pannonia, the Moesias and Greece – the well-garrisoned crossroads of the empire and the highway between west and east. And yet, important as these regions were, and even though they had produced the empire's military leadership for more than half a century, they were not self-sustaining. Unlike the empire's other heavily militarised zones – northern Italy and Raetia, which had Africa to feed them; the Rhineland, which had southern Gaul and Spain; or Syria, which had Egypt and its own fertile valleys – there was no rich and peaceful agrarian hinterland in the Balkans large enough to sustain the disproportionate size of its civilian and military administrations. To make matters worse for Licinius, neither Constantine, Maxentius nor Maximinus suffered any such structural constraint – they could all feed themselves if worst came to worst. The court of Licinius was not tranquil either: for reasons so obscure that our sources make no sense at all, Galerius's widow Valeria and their son Candidianus fled to Maximinus rather than remain in the territory of Licinius. Once there, they were treated very badly indeed, but old Diocletian was powerless to help his own daughter and grandchild (he would die, without emerging from his palace in Split, either later in 311 or perhaps as late as 313 – our ignorance on this point is itself quite telling). If we can infer anything from Valeria's flight to the east, it is that some factions in the Balkan army and palatine administration favoured Galerius's young heir Candidianus over his appointee Licinius. But having got rid of the dynastic threat, Licinius needed to decide how best to hold on to power and, with Maximinus an almost open enemy, Constantine seemed the best option available.

The sources are vague, but it appears that Licinius and Constantine

Gaul and Spain

devised a plan to share the empire between them, with Constantine supporting Licinius against Maximinus and Licinius supporting Constantine against Maxentius. The enforcement of Galerius's edict of toleration may have played a part in their negotiations, for it would emerge within the year as a key concern of Constantine's. Maxentius now looked to Maximinus for support, but Constantine was well ahead of him, showing the preternatural sense of timing that was his hallmark. In 312, he invaded Italy with a crack force of cavalry, descending from the Alps via Segusio and then turning to Augusta Taurinorum (modern Susa and Turin, respectively), crushing two separate field armies sent against him by Maxentius. Fighting must have been quite widespread, for military graveyards from exactly these years are scattered across the North Italian plain and probably reflect skirmishes and minor battles that go unrecorded in the written evidence. Maxentius's third field army, under the command of his praetorian prefect Ruricius Pompeianus, had been stationed at Aquileia to guard against an assault by Licinius, who may have feinted towards the Italian frontier to prevent Maxentius from concentrating his forces. Constantine met this Pompeianus at Brixia (Brescia) near Verona, crushing his army, too. And, as had long been the case, if an invading army was not stopped in the North Italian plain, the rest of the peninsula was effectively indefensible. Maxentius, his field armies left in ruins by the Constantinian advance, had little choice but to await events with the praetorians and his *protectores* at Rome.

On 28 October 312, he marched out to meet the Constantinian advance. We are told that he had consulted the Sybilline oracles, gaining new confidence when they revealed that an enemy of the Roman people would die that very day. If that story is anything more than Constantinian propaganda, then the joke was on Maxentius. Constantine's army was as successful against Maxentius's palatine troops as it had been against his field armies and Maxentius himself drowned in the Tiber. Though much was and still is made of this victory at the Milvian Bridge, it was something of a sham: Maxentius had lost the war the moment the third of his field armies was beaten. That said, sham victories can have real ideological power, and that is true of the Milvian Bridge, which Constantine claimed to owe to direct contact from the Christian god. The reported versions changed over the years, sometimes deliberately, sometimes because Constantine's psychological understanding of his own experience changed as well. More disturbingly, for the empirically minded historian, is that the number of times Constantine claimed to have experienced divine revelation changed, as did the nature of the decisive vision, and the number of people who witnessed it.

The most reductively positivist reading is the following: while returning to the Rhineland from Marseilles in 310, after suppressing Maximian's uprising and before ending the Frankish campaign, Constantine and part of his army witnessed a rare celestial phenomenon known as a solar halo that can, in the right atmospheric conditions, look vaguely like a cross with stars hanging from it. This vision, which was seen by many others besides Constantine, was clearly perceived as a portent of the emperor's future victories and helps account for the unwavering loyalty of his soldiers. Its meaning, however, like that of all celestial signs, was not transparent and required expert interpretation. One was solar or Apollonian, hence the incubation and vision of Apollo at his temple in Andesina; another was Christian. In the latter analysis, the celestial phenomenon was real, everyone agreed there had been a portent, and Constantine eventually came to favour the Christian explanation over others – so by the time of the Italian campaign, Constantine remembered the vision in explicitly Christian terms, and then dreamed of an encounter with the Christian god that led him to send his army into battle under Christian banners.

This simple analysis is in many ways the best but the number of alternative analyses is almost limitless: Constantine used Christian imagery to curry favour with the Christians whom he knew to be a major force in Rome; or (postmodernity to the fore) there were either no dreams and visions or there were many dreams and visions, but what mattered was the emperor's discursive play on religious tropes to convince listeners that he was favoured by whatever divinity *they* wanted to believe in. One can understand why scholars keep at it, but we cannot really get inside the mind of Constantine no matter how hard we try and, at one level, that doesn't matter at all. We can content ourselves with the fact – and it is a fact – that after 312 Constantine considered himself a Christian, conducted himself as a Christian according to his own lights, and did a great deal to promote Christianity in the territories he controlled, while insisting on toleration of Christians in those he did not. And his decision to act in that way is one of the most important decisions in western history, for it made an exclusivist and extremely prescriptive faith the privileged – and in time, official – religion of the largest polity the world had yet known. What Constantine believed, when he experienced his 'conversion', and whether there were multiple 'conversions' along the way, is beside the point in terms of historical consequences. It only matters if we want to infer human motives from evidence that renders them invisible to us.

Be that as it may, in the immediate aftermath of Maxentius's defeat, there was no clarity as to what Constantine did or did not believe, only that he had won, and won decisively. The point is made by the triumphal arch erected to him by the senate and people of Rome at the edge of the Forum Romanum, the oldest and most sacred part of the imperial city – a senate led by the very same aristocrats who had held high office in the regime of Maxentius. Pagans to a man, these senators mattered enough that Constantine was happy to keep them in office despite their having served a 'tyrant' – a word that in Constantine's usage came to be redefined as 'usurper', a connotation it retained for the rest of antiquity. On his triumphal arch, the senators honour Constantine because he avenged the Roman *res publica* upon the 'tyrant', 'at the instance of the divinity, through the greatness of his intellect'. The victory, the inscription concludes, was just. It is significant that Constantine's guiding divinity is not named in the inscription, or in a nearly contemporary panegyric. People clearly knew that Constantine believed he was divinely inspired, but they had not yet understood that his was a specifically Christian version of divine inspiration. He, meanwhile, was sensible enough not to clarify these ambiguities too publicly right away, though Christians, at least, took the new emperor for one of their own, and rival Christian groups immediately began to compete for his recognition.

Christian communities were a fractious lot. That was partly an inheritance from the extreme sectarianism of late Second Temple Judaism that has been revealed by the strident polemics found among the Dead Sea scrolls from Qumran. But it was also the necessary consequence of a religion that cared more about what people thought and believed than about what they did. In traditional Roman religion, it did not matter what a person sacrificing to Jupiter Optimus Maximus for the safety of the emperor actually believed he was achieving; the very act of sacrifice was efficacious. For Christians, efficacy lay in belief. To believe the wrong thing was to forfeit the chance of salvation and those appointed or self-appointed as guardians of true belief were duty-bound to prevent their wards from suffering that fate. But, of course, being human, they disagreed on many things, and very few of their disputes could not be reconstituted as problems of salient belief. Thus, wherever there were Christian communities, there were likely to be schisms between, within or among them, and wherever there were schisms, there was an urgent need for one side to be proved right and the other wrong: the salvific efficacy of belief was at stake. Constantine, as a product of the tetrarchic age, understood instinctively that striving for universal conformity must be a good thing and, being a Christian as well, he was an ideal recruit to Christian partisan wranglings. Constantine also had a surprising confidence in his own capacity to understand the most abstruse questions, and so waded into intractable theological controversies with mind-boggling disregard for their complexity.

In 312, almost as soon as Maxentius was dead, Constantine found himself assailed by competing factions of African Christians, who were refusing to communicate with one another on the grounds that some of the men claiming positions of authority as priests or bishops had compromised with tetrarchic officials enforcing the persecuting edicts. At stake was whether churchmen who had handed over Christian scriptures to municipal or imperial authorities were still legitimate clerics: some groups of African Christians labelled them *traditores* (those who handed things over, etymologically the ancestor of our 'traitor') and denied that someone who had been a *traditor* could become a bishop in the newly tolerant empire of Constantine, or that the consecrations performed by a *traditor* were valid. Just before Constantine's victory over Maxentius, a new bishop had been elected at Carthage, one Caecilianus. His enemies maintained that Felix of Apthungi, the bishop who had consecrated Caecilianus, had been a *traditor*, and that Caecilianus could not be legitimately made bishop. The uncompromising party elected its own bishop, and then another one when the first died. This was Donatus, who pressed his claims against Caecilianus and eventually gave his name to the schism that split the African church into two rival successions for more than a century. Both sides appealed to an emperor who shared their faith and he in turn consulted the bishop of Rome, Miltiades, who ruled against the Donatists in 313. Refusing to accept this judgement, they again appealed and Constantine summoned a church council to meet at Arelate (Arles), in southern Gaul, in 314. This too ruled in favour of Caecilianus, and an angry Constantine ordered the suppression of the recalcitrant followers of Donatus who refused to accept Caecilianus's legitimacy.

There were some martyrdoms, and some exiles, but the imperial hierarchy always recognised the Caecilianist succession as the true bishops of Carthage. But oppression merely suspended controversy and did not resolve it. Conflict between Donatists and Caecilianists would flare up again later in Constantine's reign and remained an open wound in North African Christianity throughout the fourth and earlier fifth centuries, with many, if not most, towns having two rival bishops most of the time. Yet the schism's ramifications were for the most part safely confined to the African provinces, because few real theological issues were at stake: even the cleverest and most partisan North African churchmen had a hard time framing their conflict in terms that touched on the technicalities of true belief. So while Constantine took an interest in the Donatist controversy, his greater concern was with the east, where Maximinus had stepped up persecution in defiance of his rivals' tolerant policies. Constantine and Licinius, for both ideological and pragmatic reasons, wanted to put an end to the eastern regime in the same way Maxentius had been eliminated in the west.

Constantine left Rome in good order, the city's aristocracy conciliated and firmly in charge of local affairs. Although he would long be absent from the city, and indeed from the west, he invested a great deal in its urban fabric, remodelling parts of the Roman forum, putting up a new portico in the Campus Martius, building new baths beside those of Diocletian, and converting the great basilica of Maxentius into what was effectively a monument to his own triumph; the colossal head of Constantine, now in Rome's Capitoline Museum and famous from a million photographs, crowned a similarly colossal statue that sat in his disgraced predecessor's most dramatic creation. But while Constantine stuck to a traditionally imperial giganticism in the city centre, on the periphery he began to patronise Christian churches, and would soon launch into the building of St Peter's. In a parallel gesture of control, he suppressed the praetorian guard, eliminating it as a separate military unit after more than 300 years in existence. The guard's support for Maxentius provided the excuse, but the measure was also realistic in the same way that Galerius's imposition of a census and provincial tax on Italy had been realistic: Rome might still matter, but it mattered in an altogether different way than it had a hundred years before. With the city no longer even an occasional imperial residence, a standing garrison at Rome ceased to be a necessity and became if anything a liability. The emperor's guard would henceforth be confined to those palatine units that travelled with him. These *protectores domestici*, whose third-century origins are obscure, now emerge not as part of the military chain of command, but under the palatine command of the *magister officiorum* rather than a praetorian prefect. Here, as in many another instance, Constantine's reign would regularise and make permanent the ad hoc arrangements and experiments of his third-century predecessors and the tetrarchs.

Late in 312, with Rome secure, Constantine and Licinius met at Mediolanum. There they agreed that Constantine's Christian half-sister Constantia would marry Licinius, and soon thereafter Licinius sent a letter to Maximinus ordering him to end persecutions in his territories. Maximinus, as we saw, could deny he was engaged in any such persecution, but was merely responding to the petitions of non-Christian communities to suppress the Christians in their midst. In point of fact, there had been considerable persecution of Christians thanks to the licence his rescripts gave local provincial officials, and martyrs had been made from Galatia in Asia Minor to Alexandria in Egypt, where the bishop Peter was executed. Indeed, this last phase of eastern persecution would always be remembered as the most vicious of them all.

In April 313 Maximinus attempted to take Licinius by surprise, floating an army across the Hellespont into Thrace from Asia Minor, but Licinius was ready for him, awaiting his advance at Adrianopolis in the Thracian plain. A personal meeting between the two commanders went badly and Licinius sent his troops into battle on 30 April after having them recite a monotheistic prayer that Lactantius, for one, thought was Christian. Maximinus's army was crushed and he hastily fled the battlefield with just a few men. Gathering up his family, whom he had left at Nicomedia, he retreated towards the diocese of Oriens beyond the Taurus. He also issued his own version of Galerius's toleration edict, to the existence of which he made no reference, but none the less revoking the persecuting edicts of Diocletian's era and ordering the restoration of property stolen from Christians during the persecution. With Licinius's army hot on his heels, he committed suicide at Tarsus in Cilicia; his wife drowned herself in the Orontes.

The victorious Licinius, having crossed into Asia Minor and paused at Nicomedia, then sent a letter to the provincial governors of the east, reminding them of the need to tolerate Christian and non-Christian alike and stating that the emperors were under the protection of the Christian god. This edict enacted nothing that was not already the law of the land across the whole of the empire, and was thus, in both legal and practical terms, entirely otiose. Yet ironically, this Licinian document, preserved verbatim in Lactantius, is to this day often attributed to Constantine, referred to as the Edict of Milan and dated to the year 312. But just as the Holy Roman Empire was neither holy, nor Roman, nor an empire, the so-called Edict of Milan was not an edict, was not issued at Milan, and did not date to 312. Rather, the agreement Licinius and Constantine had reached to enforce the (Galerian) law of the land ending persecution could be enforced de facto with the defeats of Maxentius and Maximinus. Nothing in Licinius's act, famous and famously misnamed though it is, had the slightest thing to do with it.

At Nicomedia in June 313, Licinius also condemned Maximinus and ordered his *damnatio memoriae*, executing those of his top officials who were most closely identified with persecution. Then it was a matter of tying up loose ends, and ensuring that the only tetrarchic dynasties left standing were those of Constantine and Licinius himself. Galerius's son Candidianus was executed, as were Severus's son Severianus, Maximinus's two children and, a year later, after her capture, Diocletian's daughter Valeria, the widow of Galerius. That Licinius and Constantine both intended to found dynasties, and thus to in part do away with the tetrarchic system of government, is abundantly clear. But in this Constantine had the clear advantage. Licinius was still without a male heir in 313, but Constantine's son Crispus, a product of the emperor's first marriage to Minervina rather than his later dynastic marriage to Fausta, was being groomed for the throne much as Constantine himself had once been; given his age, he would surely be the first heir to succeed, and in 315–16 he was based in Trier, campaigning against the Franci and Alamanni and collecting the victory titles that were a vital part of the imperial image.

But then, in 315, Constantia gave birth to a son named Licinianus, who might one day challenge Constantine's family for predominance. This also provoked further dynastic bloodshed in the west. Having already done away with a father-in-law, Constantine next turned the same technique against his brother-in-law in 316. Bassianus was the husband of Constantine's half-sister Anastasia, and had been a long-time ally of Constantine. In 315, as a response to the birth of Licinianus, Constantine made both Bassianus and Crispus caesars. Doing so was a form of dynastic insurance, bringing closer a relative by marriage who might become dangerous if aggrieved. When, however, Fausta gave birth on 7 August 316 to a son named Constantinus, the situation changed radically. Bassianus was no longer an ambiguous asset but an undoubted liability who was best used to provoke Licinius. Word was spread that Licinius had suborned Bassianus's brother Senecio, that Senecio had in turn roped his brother into a conspiracy against Constantine, and that Bassianus was executed when caught trying to kill his imperial brother-in-law while Senecio fled to Licinius. The account is so similar to the tale of Maximian's final hours, and both are so implausible, that we must again be looking at the typically Constantinian combination of character assassination and judicial murder.

The execution of Bassianus also gave Constantine the excuse he needed to attack Licinius, who had refused to hand over Senecio and allowed statues of Constantine to be overturned at Emona (Ljubljana), at the very frontier of the two rulers' territories. He promptly invaded Licinius's territory in a war often known as the war of Cibalae (Vincovki in Croatia). At Cibalae, on 8 October 316, Constantine won the first of two major battles against Licinius, each emperor personally commanding his own armies. Licinius then raised one of his better officers, Valens, to the rank of augustus and the pair fought a second battle against Constantine at Adrianopolis in Thrace that also went Constantine's way. Licinius then withdrew to the south-west, threatening to cut off Constantine's overextended supply lines and chance of retreat. As a result, the two met at Serdica and renewed their alliance in March 317. They divided the empire again, more to Constantine's advantage, with a new boundary set at the frontiers of the province of Thrace. Licinius thereby ceded almost the whole of Europe to Constantine, retaining control of the Bosporan straits and the Hellespont, but little more land than modern European Turkey. It was an extraordinary admission of weakness on Licinius's part, though he was able to save some face through the recognition of his dynastic ambitions – his young son Licinianus, still no more than a small child, was elevated to the rank of caesar, as was Constantine's still younger son by Fausta, Constantinus, joining the adult Crispus in that rank. The hapless Valens was executed as reward for his services.

The years that follow the treaty of Serdica are terribly documented even by period standards, but the fact that Constantine based himself firmly in Sirmium suggests that he was keeping a close eye on his chances in the east. The defence of the west was left to Crispus, who remained there the whole time, and to Fausta, who supervised the rearing of Crispus's half-brothers in Rome; this inaugurated a tradition maintained right into the fifth century whereby a female relative of the emperor usually resided in the city to mediate the absent emperor's dynastic relations with the senate and people. That Constantine's ambition was to rule the whole empire seems certain, and he kept up a small string of continuous irritations to Licinius.

As time went on, and Fausta continued to prove fertile, relations between Constantine and Licinius worsened. In 321, Constantine deliberately provoked his fellow emperor by refusing to acknowledge the imperial consulship proclaimed in the east in the names of Licinius and Licinianus, instead proclaiming himself consul along with the caesar Crispus. Neither augustus would recognise the other's consuls until the final breach came in 323. In that year, Constantine defeated a Sarmatian king named Rausimod at Campona, just inside the Pannonian province of Valeria, and then won a second victory at the confluence of the Danube and the Morava rivers in Moesia Superior. He issued a victory coinage with the legend *Sarmatia devicta* and took the title Sarmaticus, celebrating the triumph with some new gladiatorial games, the *ludi Sarmatici*. This rather over-the-top commemoration of a commonplace piece of imperial frontier management was again meant to annoy Licinius, all the more so because, in his pursuit of the Sarmatians, Constantine had violated Licinius's territory. Predictably, the latter refused to allow the *Sarmatia devicta* coinage to circulate in his part of the empire.

It may be that Constantine was genuinely worried by developments beyond the Danube frontier. If the region had coalesced under Gothic leadership during the late third century, it was only now that Gothic royal dynasties were beginning to form. After Licinius won a Gothic victory in 315, Goths had served in his army as part of the conditions for peace. That sort of thing was a standard part of regulating client kings along the imperial frontiers, but it seems to have strengthened the hand of competent leaders among the Goths, whereas the Carpi and Sarmatians had long been deeply ineffectual. And it gave Constantine – who was of course recruiting support beyond the frontiers in exactly the same manner as Licinius had done – an excuse to claim that he was defending the empire when Licinius failed or refused to do so. War was certain and Constantine wintered in Thessalonica rather than Sirmium in the expectation of conflict.

It came in 324. On 3 July, Constantine defeated Licinius, again at Adrianopolis, and the eastern emperor retreated to Byzantium, where he awaited the outcome of a brief naval campaign between Crispus and his own admiral Amandus. When Amandus was outmanoeuvred and defeated, Licinius became vulnerable by both land and sea. Holding Byzantium was no longer tenable, and he slipped across the Bosporus to Chalcedon on the Asian side. Pursued there by Constantine, he brought the rest of his army to the field at Chrysopolis on 18 September, again suffering a crushing defeat. Licinius's army surrendered and he fled to Nicomedia (Izmit). His wife Constantia went and pleaded with her half-brother for her husband's safety. Constantine agreed to accept the unconditional surrender of his enemy, and promised his sister that Licinius and Licinianus would be allowed to live out their lives under house arrest. They were sent to Thessalonica for safe-keeping, but within the year Constantine reprised his standard tactic – accused of plotting against the emperor's life, both Licinius and Licinianus were executed.

In 324, the Constantinian triumph was total. Licinius's legacy was recast as that of a tyrant, and all his laws and statutes annulled – too hastily, in fact, as provincials seized the opportunity to overturn perfectly routine legal decisions for their own benefit. Constantine's image likewise underwent another transformation. Gone is the severe youth on the coinage, replaced by an ageless, smooth-skinned hero, eyes gazing upwards as if to god or gods – for this is not a straightforwardly Christian portrait and could mean different things to different viewers. More, the emperor now wears a diadem, a feature not of Roman but of Greek rulership, while, in Greek style, only the emperor's head and neck are shown, rather than a full bust in the traditional Roman manner. Here there is less ambiguity than in the upwards gaze – Constantine is a Hellenistic king, a successor of Alexander, and the sole master of the Roman world.

Constantine would soon find that the pressures of governing the east were more complex than they had been in the west and, if anything, his methods for handling them became more extreme. But he had already transformed the Roman empire. Much of the tetrarchic infrastructure survived, but it was utterly remade by Constantine's insistence on one-man rule. The forty years that separated Diocletian's coup d'état in 284 and the beginning of Constantine's sole rule in 324 were the culmination of changes in Roman government since the time of Severus. The sole reign of Constantine – and even more so, if also more obscurely, that of his middle son Constantius II – were the foundations of a new Roman empire that would in time bequeath its heritage to Byzantium, to the first Islamic caliphate, and to the kingdoms of the medieval west.

15

THE STRUCTURE OF
EMPIRE BEFORE AND
AFTER CONSTANTINE

Constantine's victory over Licinius left him in possession of the part of the empire in which his formative years had been spent, but where he had not set foot since 305. He now determined to make it his home and mark that fact with a new foundation, a city in his name and in his own image – Constantinople. Built on the site of ancient Byzantium, at the crossroads of Europe and Asia, the ceremonial foundation and ground-breaking for the new city took place on 8 November 324: as so often, the emperor wasted no time once he knew what he wanted to do. He claimed to have had a vision directing him where to build the city and a divinity also helped him lay out its boundaries. It would be six years before the city was habitable (the dedication was on 11 May 330), and its status as a second Rome was not cemented for many decades thereafter. But by the end of the fourth century, Constantinople was indisputably the capital of the eastern empire.

At the same time as he dedicated his new city, Constantine proclaimed as caesar his second son by Fausta, named Constantius after his paternal grandfather, adding him to the caesars Crispus and Constantinus in the imperial college. Constantius would prove the longest-lived of all Constantine's sons, and the one who most clearly cemented his father's legacy

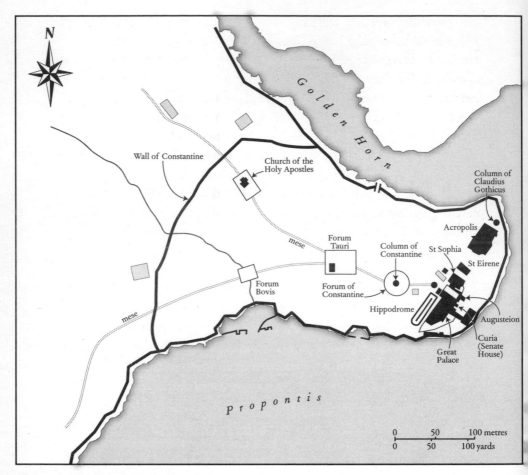

Plan 2 Constantinople in the Fourth Century

as the founder of a very different Roman empire than the one Augustus or Trajan or Severus had ruled. Before returning to the narrative of Constantine's sole reign, it is worth understanding the structures of the empire he created, for they are the foundations for understanding the political narrative of the remaining chapters and also this volume's sequel.

That Constantine created a new Roman empire has never been in doubt. A hundred years ago, before the concept of late antiquity as a period with a historical dynamic all its own had really taken root, it was commonplace to mark the divide between the ancient and medieval worlds as the year 312. Nowadays, we mark that divide less sharply, and place it much later, but that question of periodisation has not diminished our assessment of Constantine's role in transforming how the empire was governed. He built directly upon foundations laid by the tetrarchs, and it is not always easy for us to distinguish Constantinian initiatives from those of Diocletian, Galerius and Licinius, or from those of his son Constantius II, who systematised and standardised many of his father's more ad hoc measures. This chapter will sketch the chief differences in the administration of the empire from the Antonine world in which our story began to the emergent late imperial state of the Constantinian empire.

In many ways, the late empire can be understood as the natural outcome of the long process of equestrianisation that we have encountered so many times in the course of our narrative; the ways in which practice and ideologies of government were transformed by bureaucrats and bureaucratic methods. These meant that governmental uniformity could be envisaged as a real possibility in a way that it could not in the second century or before. And then the juridical Romanisation of the empire that followed Caracalla's universal citizenship grant of 212 made uniformity seem that much more desirable. The degree to which the late empire's ideological outlook depends upon the high imperial *ordo equester* follows from the second-century change in the balance between senators and equestrians.

Under the republic, there had been a very fluid boundary between those men who possessed the equestrian census of 400,000 sestertii but chose not to pursue public office and those who did so. Augustus created the legal basis for distinguishing the *ordines*, first by raising the minimum senatorial fortune from the ancient equestrian census of 400,000 sestertii to the more substantial million sestertii (not in itself a huge fortune when a moderately rich man might have an annual income larger than that), but also by making senatorial status heritable within a family down to the third generation. Along with the new property requirements, Augustus stabilised the number of senators at around 600 men, revised the *leges annales* (the age at which the different magistracies could be held), and formalised the rules according to which the senate met. With those measures, it became possible not only to maintain the basic *cursus honorum* of the old republican magistracies, but to build on them and accommodate them to a new world in which power flowed from a single man, and where senators could not leave Italy without imperial permission.

The Augustan reform established the basic size and shape of the senatorial order that it would more or less preserve until the merging of the two *ordines* in the fourth century. Throughout the early imperial period, and certainly under Hadrian where our story began, the number of available senators was only ever minimally sufficient to fulfil the many tasks that were expected of them. Even with the annual influx of the sons and grandsons of senators from the twenty minor magistracies (the vigintivirate) and into the quaestorship, the natural tendency of senatorial families to die out had to be countered, either by the imperial adlection of experienced men directly into the higher ranks of the *ordo*, or by the adlection of the sons of successful equestrian officials *in amplissimum ordinem*, which allowed them to seek office as if they had been born into the *ordo senatorius*. The pressure on senatorial numbers was the result of both the individual roles senators had to play and the number of functions the body had to serve as a collective institution. For centuries after the inception of imperial rule, the senate continued to serve as the primary legislative and juridical body of the empire, which meant that a substantial quorum of senators had to be permanently in place in Rome. At the same time, the expanding empire needed senators – former praetors and consuls – to run it. The reason that additional 'suffect' consuls were appointed at intervals during the course of the year, after the 'ordinary' consuls had taken office on 1 January, was to provide sufficient ex-consuls to staff offices of consular rank in the imperial administration.

In the ten 'public' provinces, proconsuls continued to be chosen by lot and to serve for a single year, in a formalised version of the old republican promagistracy, with responsibility for jurisdiction, administration and peacekeeping with whatever auxiliary troops were stationed in the province (legions were not stationed in public provinces). Yet almost every imperial province needed a senatorial governor as well, serving as *legatus*

Augusti pro praetore for a period of time limited only by the imperial pleasure. Additional legionary legates were needed in provinces with more than one legion, because a single governor would have a dangerous level of power if he were allowed complete control of several armies. Each of these posts required men of at least praetorian, and more usually consular, rank; in the largest consular commands – Tarraconensis, Cappadocia – an additional praetorian *iuridicus*, or legal officer, was needed to supplement the consular legate's limited time for dispensing justice to Roman citizens in the province. Augustus and Tiberius had also created a whole series of new senatorial posts for Rome and Italy, including the urban prefecture – always the preserve of a distinguished and particularly honoured consular – and a variety of other *praefecti* and *curatores* for financial and judicial positions. Below the praetorian and consular ranks, junior senators were needed as *adiutores*, 'assistants', to more senior magistrates throughout the empire, both in public and imperial provinces.

From the end of the first century, the pressure of business in the Greek provinces, many of which consisted of numerous independent and semi-autonomous communities, required the frequent appointment of special officials known as *correctores* to oversee a city or region's local affairs. Already at the end of the Julio-Claudian period, at least 145 senatorial officials were needed annually, a number that had risen to more than 160 by the accession of Marcus Aurelius in the year 161. Moreover, the tendency of eastern senators to have purely eastern careers affected available manpower right through the third century. There was, in other words, a constant tension between a need to maintain the dignity of the senate by keeping its membership fairly restricted and the need to administer the empire effectively.

That was a need that never slackened, since by the second century the empire covered roughly 2 million square miles and there was sometimes just one senatorial (or senior equestrian) official per 350,000–400,000 inhabitants. As a result, the first emperors leant heavily both on the *familia Caesaris*, particularly their own most trusted freedmen, and on the *ordo equester*. As the imperial system expanded, so too did the number of positions needed to manage it. These could not easily be filled by senators, even had enough of them been available: the new offices lacked sufficient prestige, because they were personally dependent on the emperor in a way that was less obviously true of the old republican magistracies, and they therefore offended against the polite fiction that the empire was not actually an autocracy. Initially, moreover, some of the tasks entrusted to equestrians (the *praefectura annonae*, for instance) required long tenures of office which would have interfered with a senator's progress through the traditional *cursus*, something that men of high status could not be asked to tolerate. The careful balancing act of the early empire, in which monarchy was disguised behind the facade of republican institutions, was therefore made easier by using equestrians to staff new posts as they were created. Normal Roman conservatism ensured that posts that had been filled by men of a particular rank for any length of time would usually continue to be so. So while nearly all the most prestigious offices in imperial government remained in the hands of senators for centuries, much of the actual machinery of government fell to the *ordo equester*.

Under the republic, young aspirants to the senate, who necessarily possessed the equestrian census, began their careers as junior officers in a legion, generally as military tribunes. However, after the creation of the new *ordo senatorius* under Augustus and Tiberius, the vast majority of the military tribunates and all the prefectures of auxiliary units were reserved to equestrians; under Claudius, the so-called *tres militiae* of an early equestrian career (*praefectus cohortis, praefectus alae, tribunus militum*) were formally codified. Such posts served as training grounds for men who would go on to staff an ever-expanding imperial hierarchy, and by the middle of the second century there were as many as 550 junior commands available to *equites* in the army. The two praetorian prefects had been equestrians since the office was created, and that prefecture remained, with the prefecture of Egypt, the most senior equestrian post until the *ordo* itself disappeared.

We have encountered many of the other, more junior, equestrian offices in the course of our narrative. In the immediate orbit of the emperor, there were officials responsible for imperial correspondence (the *ab epistulis*), dealing with the embassies of Greek cities (*ad legationes et responsa Graeca*), replying to petitions (*a libellis*), investigating legal cases in which an imperial interest was required (*a cognitionibus*), the administration of imperial finances (*a rationibus*), these including private estates (*patrimonium*) and mints (*moneta*), the inheritances due to the emperor (*procurator hereditatium*) and the various indirect customs tolls known collectively as *portoria*. In the second century, a new entry-level post of *advocatus fisci* allowed equestrians to enter the financial bureaus without having held a junior military command first, and also allowed the rhetors and other members of the eastern educated classes to share in the honours of Roman government, even if it was the sole office they ever held. Some of the tasks previously undertaken by a single official were split at this time as well – for instance, that of *ab epistulis*, which was split into Latin and Greek divisions, thereby giving the educated classes of the main Greek cities a direct route into imperial government. Under Hadrian or Pius, the whole new bureau of the *res privata* was created to distinguish the personal property of the imperial family from the *patrimonium* that had, since the end of the Julio-Claudian dynasty, come to be associated with the imperial purple rather than the man who wore it. This new *patrimonium privatum* or *res privata* was thenceforth staffed by its own hierarchy of equestrian officials in Italy and the provinces, and exploded in size after the confiscations that followed on the defeats of Pescennius Niger and Clodius Albinus during the civil wars of 193–7.

The city of Rome also fed the growth of the *ordo equester*. Leaving aside the praetorian prefects, the most important equestrian officials were the *praefectus annonae*, in charge of the food supply, and the *praefectus vigilum*, used for firefighting and occasional policing when the praetorians proved recalcitrant or insufficient. Equestrians were also employed as administrators of the imperial gladiatorial schools (*procuratores ludi*), head librarians of the imperial library (*a bibliothecis*), transport chiefs (*praefectus vehiculorum*) and as procurators responsible for collecting the taxes on inheritance and on the emancipation of slaves (*procuratores vicesimae hereditatium* and *vicesimae libertatis*) and collating the data from provincial censuses that were vital to the collection of those taxes (*a censibus*).

The senatorial *curatores* for temples and for the aqueducts (*curatores aedium sacrarum* and *aquarum*) had equestrian chiefs of staff by the second century. In the provinces, the prefect of Egypt had been an equestrian since the reign of Augustus, holding an *imperium* equal to that of a proconsul and taking over wholesale the administrative structure put in place by the Ptolemies, which was likewise now staffed mainly by equestrians. Many small provinces had equestrian procurators playing the role that a senatorial *praeses* would fill elsewhere, although whenever such provinces developed real military importance, they were transferred to the command of senatorial legates, as happened at various times to Judaea, Cappadocia, Thracia, Noricum and Raetia. The prefects of the Tyrrhenian and Adriatic fleets, stationed at Misenum (now Bacoli on the bay of Naples) and Ravenna respectively, were equestrians, as were at least seven attested provincial fleet commanders serving under the provincial governors. More pervasively, a dozen financial procurators in the imperial provinces and another ten or more financial procurators administered the imperial patrimony in the public provinces. As mining became an important source of imperial revenue in the second century, so it became necessary to appoint procurators to supervise the imperial revenues from it in Dalmatia, Pannonia and eventually in Dacia as well, though in other provinces imperial freedmen might still undertake the task.

Then, as the second century progressed and Roman citizenship became ever more widespread, a number of tasks that had previously been unnecessary, or so rarely necessary that they could be handled by a governor's staff, now required the extension into the provinces of equestrian bureaus previously active only in Italy; this was most visibly the case with the procuratorial staffs responsible for the taxes on inheritance and emancipation that only citizens paid. Equally, as is the natural tendency of bureaucracies, many of these hierarchies developed increasing complexity and required multiplications of effort, so we find growing numbers of *subpraefecti* and *subprocuratores* from the early second century onwards. The procuratorial service alone doubled in size between the Trajanic and Severan eras. Moreover, imperial procurators increasingly took on the financial roles in public provinces that had formerly been the work of senatorial quaestors, and sometimes intervened in affairs that had nothing to do with the administration of either the imperial patrimony or the taxation of the province.

Unsurprisingly, as such equestrian posts multiplied, they began to form a *cursus honorum* comparable to the senatorial *cursus*. Though much more flexible, because not dependent on the old hierarchy of the republican magistracies for its structure, the equestrian *cursus* had certainly hardened into a recognisable hierarchy by the time of Commodus, when equestrian offices were organised according to their pay grades as *sexagenarii*, *centenarii*, *ducenarii* and *trecenarii*, which is to say, offices to which were attached salaries of 60,000 and 100,000, 200,000 or 300,000 sestertii per annum. Again, just as a senator was a *vir clarissimus*, so was an equestrian a *vir egregius* (*ho krátistos* in Greek), or, from the time of Marcus, a still more prominent *vir perfectissimus* (*ho diasemótatos*).

The growth of equestrian offices, though clearly taking place on a very large scale throughout the first and second centuries, is difficult to trace in detail because our literary evidence is heavily biased towards the activities of senate and emperor, and because epigraphic and papyro-logical evidence is not enough to fill the gaps. Thus the first attestation of an equestrian post may come decades after it was actually created, which distorts our understanding of chronological details without altering the overall picture of ever-expanding equestrian responsibilities. This expansion had an impact on the horizons and the outlook of elite society across the empire. The *ordo senatorius* was in the first instance a hereditary caste, even when it became more common to adlect men, especially those who were already an emperor's trusted allies, directly into its ranks. Senate membership implied a personal relationship to the emperor right through the Antonine period, whether a senator was the scion of an old family whose offspring had to be taken into account or a man who had come to the emperor's attention and been adlected into the *ordo*: once adlected, the legal requirement that senators transfer a large proportion of their wealth to Italy and take up residence there kept these new families locked in the imperial orbit. Indeed, throughout the principate, and even after Marcus loosened the strictness with which Italian residency was enforced, a senatorial posting came in a codicil signed by the emperor himself and perhaps even written out in his own hand.

The *ordo equester*, by contrast, always remained an economic class, dis-tinguished by its gold rings as clearly as were senators by the *latus clavus* on their togas. Entry to an equestrian career in imperial service could come at a much greater physical and social distance from the person of the emperor than could a senatorial career – as is illustrated by the fact that appointment to lower equestrian posts came via *epistulae* from the bureau *ab epistulis*, rather than via an imperial codicil. At the lower end of the equestrian order were men who had risen from the ranks of the common soldiery, ex-centurions who had held the senior non-commissioned post in their unit (the *primipilarii*) and for whom an equestrian office was the culmination of a long career. At the uppermost end, the wealthiest and best-connected members of the *ordo* could expect, or aspire to, adlection to the senate, or at least permission to pursue a senatorial career late in life after admission to the vigintivirate.

The vast majority of equestrians fell somewhere in between, as the census requirement which remained the only qualification for equestrian rank was never ruinously high. Partly for that reason, many *equites* never left the municipal world of their *origo* or entered imperial service; even so, if they came to the notice of the right person, their sons might be granted the *latus clavus* and with it the right to start on the senatorial *cursus*. But in the simplest, most practical way, the need for personal contact with the emperor shaped and circumscribed the senatorial order, which was much less diverse geographically as a result. High imperial senators tended to cluster in distinct regions within distinct provinces – southern Hispania and Narbonensis from the time of Nero; Asia, Achaea and Bithynia et Pontus after Vespasian; proconsular Africa and far eastern provinces like Cappadocia from the time of Marcus Aurelius. The equestrian *ordo* was spread more thickly on the ground throughout the 'civilised' provinces of the empire and even beyond them, numbering perhaps in the tens of thousands. In part because of this geographical diversity and physical distance from the imperial court, members of the *ordo equester* were more dependent on vertical relations of patronage, often at several removes from the emperor, for advancement and preferment. While the Roman upper-class ideology of the *ordo senatorius*, dating back to republican precedents, downplayed the necessity of experience or special skills as prerequisite for office, the *ordo equester* became relatively more professionalised thanks to its numbers and geographical diversity, with promotion at least plausibly on the basis of merit rather than simply on birth.

Birth did remain the primary factor in access to power for a long time: the *ordo senatorius* retained its lock on the most senior and the most prestigious of imperial posts through to the very end of the second century. The most powerful *equites* might be honoured with consular symbols – *consularibus ornamentis ornati*, as it was put – but they did not themselves hold even the suffect consulship. Only in the reign of Severus do we begin to see changes that laid the groundwork for the later empire. One of the main things that separates the Severan empire from the Antonine is the unembarrassed acknowledgement of an equestrian elite as the chief ministers of state. That was perhaps a natural result of brutal civil wars that had divided and depleted the senate, and of the purges that accompanied the Severan victory. Yet it is also clear that Severus never really trusted his fellow senators; the Severan empire witnesses a real sea change in the balance of senators and equestrians at the highest levels of government. Severus massively expanded the old *res privata* in order to handle mass confiscations from former followers of Niger and Albinus and, before long, this *res privata* subsumed the old *patrimonium* and became the most important financial bureau in the third-century state, its staff entirely equestrian. In the public provinces, where the census had formerly been the prerogative of the local communities, the use of equestrian *procuratores ad census accipiendos* was extended from the imperial provinces. More and more often, as inscriptions in particular make clear, it was minor imperial officials – or soldiers seconded from their units, acting for and reporting back to the financial bureaus – who collected taxes in cash and in kind, replacing both tax farmers and local councils.

If this expansion of the financial administration reached deepest into provincial life, changes to military commands were equally dramatic. The first legions to have permanent equestrian *praefecti* rather than senatorial *legati* from the time of their formation were the I, II and III Parthica, which had been raised to prosecute Severus's wars. His new province of Mesopotamia was organised on the Egyptian model, with an equestrian *praeses* and equestrian prefects for its legions. As we have seen, minor provinces had always been governed by procurators of equestrian rank, but Severus began to extend the practice to major military provinces as well, doing so with the polite fiction that such directly appointed equestrians were merely 'acting' (*vice agens*) for an absent legate. Caracalla was blunter, promoting large numbers of *equites* to the senatorial order and thus qualifying them for senatorial offices, even when they lacked any experience of, or feel for, the senatorial *cursus*. Before long, even official sources started to use the title *praeses* indiscriminately for the governors of both imperial and public provinces.

As these early Severan precedents took hold and were imitated by the precarious successors to his dynasty, the number of senatorial families with very recent equestrian roots continued to rise, while the Augustan and Flavian aristocracies all but disappeared from the consular *fasti*. Within the single generation that separated Macrinus's failed reign from the death of Gordian III, an *eques* like Philip could look like a plausibly imperial figure. In the course of the same generation, the administrative fiction of governors '*vice agens*' was discarded and the status of provinces could change as equestrian *praesides* replaced senatorial *legati*. By the second half of the third century, Arabia, Baetica, Dalmatia, Numidia, Pontus-Bithynia and Germania Superior had all been transferred to equestrian control, while only one of the provinces created in the third century – Phrygia-Caria in 249/50 – was entrusted to a senatorial *legatus* and only a few of the large old provinces like Hispania Tarraconensis continued to be governed by *legati*.

After the otherwise unremarkable Vitulasius Laetinianus and C. Iulius

Sallustius Saturninus Fortunatianus, who served in the reign of Gallienus, we can identify no *legatus legionis* of senatorial background. The new mobile cavalry units that became central to the military system under Gallienus were all commanded by equestrian *praepositi*. Likewise, by the time of Gallienus, holders of the highest equestrian offices, which brought with them the rank of *eminentissimus*, might frequently reach the consulship, thereby changing their rank to that of the senatorial *clarissimus* without their having held any post in the senatorial *cursus*. Such men almost never went on to further office after attaining the clarissimate, but it was nevertheless impossible for such changes not to cause some confusion of the senatorial and equestrian *cursus*, and eventually of the senatorial and equestrian *ordines*.

As the senatorial and equestrian *cursus* became blurred, civilian and military careers overlapped less and less, in a way that foreshadowed the explicit Constantinian division of civilian from military *cursus*. Right into the reign of Severus Alexander, men who had reached the pinnacle of a career in the ranks were then drafted into the equestrian civil service, but as the third century progressed that became rarer and rarer: soldiers who rose to be *primipilarii* ceased to become civilian procurators, the last one known to have done so being Aurelius Sabinianus, who served during the reign of Valerian and Gallienus. Gallienus, more even than his early third-century predecessors, had a habit of placing junior equestrian officers straight into legionary commands that would once have been held by *legati legionis*, with the title of prefect and the rank of *viri egregii*, and of naming similar men *duces* – a new generic title for a field commander holding great discretionary powers.

The officer corps that was created in this half-accidental manner finally brought Gallienus down, for all the senior officers who plotted his overthrow – Aureolus, Heraclianus, Marcianus, Claudius, Aurelian – derived from precisely this background, as later did Diocletian's senior caesar, Constantius I. It is quite clear that the military crises on several fronts that so affected the middle years of the century required experiment and expedient measures, and it may also be true that Gallienus – remembered as the scourge of the senate in the fourth century – could make so pragmatic a use of equestrians in senatorial positions precisely because his own senatorial background was beyond reproach. Of the other third-century emperors, however, only Trajan Decius had followed a senatorial *cursus*, while the rest, where we can ascertain anything of their early careers, had risen through the army to an equestrian command before acceding to – or seizing – the purple.

The multiplication of equestrian experts in government brought with it a new sense that it was possible to manage things in fundamentally reproducible and impersonal ways across provinces, and without the ad-hoc-ery that had characterised republican and early imperial govern- ance of the provinces. By the reign of Severus Alexander, reproducible, universal practices were beginning to homogenise the vagaries of provincial governance, in part because the enfranchisement of the whole popula- tion by Caracalla meant that Roman law had to be extended to regions where it was previously barely known. At the end of the third century, Diocletian and his co-emperors saw the systematic value of bringing practical, managerial aspirations of governance together with an ideologi- cal uniformity. By the end of the tetrarchy, the last remnants of an early imperial system that distinguished between the emperor as *privatus*, the emperor as *princeps* and the Roman state he led had disappeared. With them went most of the vestigial trappings of the republic that Augustus had deliberately enshrined. The minor senatorial offices had already started to disappear earlier in the third century: the vigintivirate, the tribunate of the plebs and the plebeian aedileship are all unattested after the time of Gallienus, after which a token quaestorship marked the beginnings of a senatorial *cursus*. Under the tetrarchy, the quaestorship became little more than a hidden tax allowing the sons of senators to formally enrol in the *ordo senatorius*, as it remained after Constantine suppressed the equestrian *ordo* and replaced it with a hierarchy of senatorial ranks.

Another legacy of the third century was the reduction in the number of praetorships, made redundant by mid-century, when all the formerly praetorian governorships had become equestrian. In this period, we likewise cease to hear of the old senatorial *correctores* and *iuridici* in Italy, those honourable ad hoc appointments that had, in the first and second centuries, provided senatorial administration throughout the peninsula's districts. In their stead, a new and permanent breed of *corrector* is first attested under Probus, implying a provincialisation of Italy that would be formalised by the second tetrarchy of Galerius. Under the tetrarchs, the last consular provinces – Tarraconensis, Phrygia and Syria–Phoenice – became equestrian as well, while the remaining public provinces of Achaea, Crete and Cyprus were transferred to full imperial appointments, following on the transfer of Macedonia and Lycia-Pamphylia under Probus and Carus.

Constantine thus inherited a vastly altered landscape, one that had already made permanent many of the ad hoc experiments of the third century. His own reforms cemented the extensive and coercive state that the tetrarchy had begun to systematise. Whereas the tetrarchic model had dispersed power among first two and then four emperors in order to bring third-century political violence back under control, Constantine ensured that his own hold on power was absolute. He kept in place the tetrarchs' increasingly intrusive hierarchy of state government, its voice bombastic, its ceremonial simultaneously inclusive and distancing. But he also recognised the value of the older, Antonine model of an emperor who communicated with such subjects as could get near him, responding to their petitions with grace and magnanimity. For that reason, whereas Diocletian's governing voice had insisted on the centrality of officialdom to the care of the empire, Constantine inaugurated a hectoring style that promised to protect his subjects from the very officials he himself had set to govern them. He inflicted harsh and exemplary punishments on officials who offended against his subjects and preyed upon them, treating such offences as attacks upon his own dignity. He thus sought to appeal directly to his subjects in a way that Diocletian had not, while doing so in the heightened emotional style that Diocletian and his lawyers had pioneered. For Constantine, it was the deliberate gesture of a charismatic ruler, one who used the apparatus bequeathed him by the tetrarchy to govern, but who addressed his subjects directly as their champion and protector. This ostentatious distancing of himself from the very officials who governed the state that he embodied was in part a function of the constant expansion of that state, an expansion that is the single most visible feature of his reign and of those that followed.

At the base of the fourth-century system there was provincial government, the Severan provinces that had been split up and multiplied under Diocletian. The main evidence for these provinces is a bureaucratic document from early in the joint reign of Constantine and Licinius known as the Verona List (*Laterculus Veronensis*), which lists the more than 100 provinces into which the empire was divided. Provincial governors had different titles – proconsul, *consularis*, *corrector* – and they came to signify a hierarchy of rank and prestige among different provincial commands. As heirs of the oldest senatorial provinces of the republic, the proconsuls of Africa Proconsularis, Asia and Achaea were marked out by the special legal privilege of reporting directly to the emperor, rather than to a higher official like the prefect. For the most part, the governors all had similar functions, the whole civilian administration of their province, including both the legal system and the province's obligation to the various financial bureaus of the state. The outline and number of provinces was relatively fungible, with new ones created over the course of the fourth and fifth centuries and various changes made in their status and provincial boundaries.

The dioceses – those larger units into which provinces were grouped by the tetrarchs – tended to be much more stable. Their primary function seems at first to have been fiscal, placing together regions that were subject to the same hierarchy of tax officials. They were initially governed by subordinates of the praetorian prefects, often acting as vice-prefects or plenipotentiary representatives. By the time of Constantine, however, diocesan governance had become more systematic, under officials called *vicarii*, who had the authority to judge legal cases *vice sacra*, that is to say, in the imperial stead. The goal of this was both to provide better justice to a solicitous emperor's beloved provincials and to ensure that different layers of increasingly complex appellate jurisdiction would overlap one another, and thus provide surveillance of both the officials and provincials. It was probably the same need for greater and more coherent oversight that caused Constantine to split Diocletian's Moesian diocese into Dacia and Macedonia, and Valens, late in the fourth century, to separate Egypt from Oriens under its own vicar, known as the *praefectus Augustalis* (the vicar of Oriens was also uniquely styled, as *comes* rather than *vicarius Orientis*). Throughout the fourth and well into the fifth century, the dioceses remained the building blocks of empire, the administrative level at which divisions between different emperors' spheres of influence were marked. Despite that, *vicarii* never gained inappellate legal powers: just as a provincial governor's decision might be appealed to a *vicarius* or a prefect, so too a vicar's judgement could be appealed before the emperor or the praetorian prefect.

These late imperial prefects were the direct descendants of the early imperial officials we have seen throughout our story. Quite early in the fourth century, they did indeed come to have inappellate judicial powers, their judgements standing as unchallengeable as an emperor's. Under the tetrarchy, each emperor had had his own praetorian prefect, and that practice continued as Constantine gave his children subordinate courts in different parts of the empire. The prefects had lost their vestigial military powers after Constantine suppressed the praetorian guard in 312, but they remained the most powerful officials in the imperial state, judging in the stead of the emperor, collecting and disbursing the revenues of the dioceses under their authority and hearing appeals against lower ranking regional officials. Their financial responsibilities were enormous, because they were responsible for the *annona* – all the pay and rations of the imperial civil service and the army. Because the late empire as much as the early empire was essentially a machine that redistributed tax from the provinces back out as pay, in cash or kind, to the emperor's servants and soldiers, the officials in primary charge of that machine could not help but have a preponderance of power and responsibility. Along with their basic responsibility for the redistribution of wealth, the prefects oversaw the upkeep of the imperial infrastructure, maintained the public postal system and the private shipping networks that were paid to carry the *annona* and levied taxes in cash, in kind or in conscription of unpaid labour to see that those functions were fulfilled.

By the time of Constantine's death, the de facto territorialisation of the prefects' jurisdiction is noticeable in the sources, and quite clearly so in the reign of his son Constantius II. Though the dioceses that pertained to the prefectures might shift at times (and did so frequently in the later fourth and early fifth centuries, thanks to civil wars and invasions), four relatively stable prefectures grew up by around 350: a prefecture of Gallia, generally administered from Trier and taking in Britannia, the two Gallic dioceses and Hispania; a prefecture of Italy and Africa, taking in Italy, Latin-speaking Africa west of Cyrene, the Alpine provinces and sometimes Pannonia; a prefecture of Illyricum that was sometimes administered jointly with Italy and Africa, and taking in Macedonia, Dacia and often Pannonia as well; and a prefecture of the east, taking in Thrace, Asia Minor, the Levant and Mesopotamia and Egypt. The provinces of Achaea, Asia and Africa Proconsularis were not subject to the prefect's authority, though in practice they needed to work with his administration in financial matters. Nor was Rome (or, after 359, Constantinople), which was governed by the *praefectus urbi*, a highly prestigious senatorial post, and the *praefectus annonae*, generally a lower-ranking official with connections to the prefectural system.

Along with the provincial governors, *vicarii* and prefects, each of whom required scores or even hundreds of lesser officials, there were the bureaus that surrounded the person of the emperor, the so-called *comitatus*, or government that travelled with him. In nearest proximity was the emperor's household staff, the *cubicularii* under a *praepositus sacri cubiculi*, or 'head of the sacred bedchamber'. These *praepositi*, as well as most of their staff, were made up of eunuchs, generally from the borderlands between Rome and Persia. They supervised the imperial accounts, attended to the personal and intimate needs of the emperor and his wife, and supervised a staff of teachers, clerks and servants of various sorts, collectively known as *ministeriales* or *curae palatiorum*. The other main palatine offices dealt with the public activities in which emperors needed to engage. The *magister officiorum* was probably the most powerful of the bureau chiefs in the *comitatus*, in charge of the various *scrinia* required to cover the emperor's public roles: his staff of three junior *magistri* – *memoriae*, *libellorum* and *epistularum* – handled imperial correspondence, received the appeals and petitions addressed to the emperor and the *relationes* (reports) of provincial administrators, and then drafted responses to them.

The bureau maintained a corps of translators for diplomatic purposes, and the *magister officiorum* also controlled the confidential courier system of imperial government, which was assigned to the care of men known as *agentes in rebus* ('doers of things') or *magistrianoi* in Greek. Numbering perhaps a thousand at any one time and with their own precise hierarchy of rank, these *agentes* would start their careers as messengers, but very frequently end them as highly confidential spies, secret agents or assassins, doing the sort of ad hoc duties that could not be safely regularised, but that the emperor often needed to have done in short order and with minimal publicity. Perhaps surprisingly, the *magister officiorum* was the only civilian official to retain a substantial military role during and after the reign of Constantine, being the titular commander of the household troop units, the *scholae palatinae*, though each of these had as field officer a tribune chosen by the emperor himself.

The functions of the *magisterium officiorum* were to some large degree duplicated by those of another palatine office, the corps of notaries. This staff was responsible for keeping track of official appointments across the length and breadth of the empire, and for issuing the commissions that came from the emperor to all officials in his service. The head of the bureau was a *primicerius notariorum* who kept the master list, the *laterculum maius*, of every imperial officer, and who issued the codicils by which officials were informed of their appointment. This required a large staff of *notarii*, technically clerks, but just as often in charge of all sorts of special business, sometimes working as administrators without portfolio and doing whatever the emperor needed to be done at a given time, even when it was shifty or illegal.

Though the praetorian prefects oversaw the largest sums of money circulating through the state system, Diocletian's new financial bureaus grew throughout the reign of Constantine and thereafter, and the *comites* who supervised them were always senior members of the *comitatus*. The *res privata* had swallowed up the old *patrimonium* well before Constantine's reign, and the *comes rei privatae* travelled with the senior emperor, supervising five different *scrinia*, or departments, dedicated to different elements in the management of imperial property, from taxation and rent to sales and escheats. The bureau of the *res privata* was thus represented throughout every province, with regional and provincial levels of administration.

The bureau of the *sacrae largitiones* ('sacred largesses') controlled the mints, including new Constantinian mints at Sirmium and Serdica, as well as those tetrarchic sites that continued minting. It also supervised the gold and silver mines that belonged to the state, and the *fabricae*, or state factories, where weapons and armour for the officer corps were made and adorned with precious metals. Finally, the bureau was the destination for all taxes collected in silver or gold: these included various tolls and harbour taxes of very long standing; the *aurum tironicum* (a tax that commuted a levy of military conscripts into gold); the *aurum coronarium* (the 'voluntary' donation of urban jurisdictions to an emperor at his accession and on each 5-year anniversary); the *aurum oblaticium* (paid by senators, on the same calendar); the *collatio glebalis* (an annual fee paid by senators); the *collatio lustralis* or *chrysárgyron* in Greek (a tax on all businessmen, levied every five years, originally in gold or silver, later only in gold). There were fully ten *scrinia* in the bureau of the *comes sacrarum largitionum* and, as with the *res privata*, these were frequently duplicated at provincial as well as palatine level.

Constantine separated the military hierarchy of the empire from the civilian once and for all, save for the anomaly of the *magister officiorum* and his command of palatine units. The military command, at the empire-wide level, was rather simpler than the civilian hierarchy. A distinction was gradually drawn between units of the field army, the *comitatenses*, and the provincial armies on the frontiers, the *limitanei* or *ripenses*. While there is some evidence for differences in the fighting quality of the two types of troops, there was definitely no fixed hierarchy of first- and second-class soldiers. The field army was commanded by two senior generals, generally serving in the emperor's *comitatus* and thus known as *magistri militum praesentales*. The senior commander was the *magister peditum praesentalis*, the junior the *magister equitum praesentalis*, and, though one finds those titles translated into English as Master of Infantry and Master of Horse, each of them commanded forces of mixed infantry and cavalry and were generically known as *magistri militum*, 'masters of soldiers'. If several emperors were ruling in an imperial college, these commands would be duplicated in each *comitatus*, although over time – and in parallel to the development of regional prefectures – there came to be regional command establishments for the *comitatenses*.

Along with the praesental *magistri*, there tended by the mid fourth century to be a *magister per Gallias*, one *per Illyricum* and one *per Orientem*, each with a more or less stable core of *comitatenses* that might fluctuate depending upon military conditions in the region. The permanent garrison armies on the frontiers were commanded by *comites* or *duces* with various units of *limitanei* at their disposal, although these were sometimes dispersed widely throughout a province and often functioned as much as policemen and frontier administrators as soldiers. A corps of *protectores domestici*, drawn from the privileged and well-connected children of civil servants and the military hierarchy, attended the emperor's personal military commands and served as an officer's training corps for the men of very diverse background who joined the late imperial officer class. These *protectores domestici* served under a *comes domesticorum* who was a senior member of the *comitatus*, and need to be distinguished from the regular *protectores* who were promoted from the ranks of the field or frontier armies late in their careers and then assigned various special supervisory tasks, often in distant provinces, as a reward for long and distinguished service. As we have noted, the palatine *scholae* fell outside the command of the praesental *magistri militum*, instead being subject to the *magister officiorum*. From the ranks of these special *scholae*, the emperor drew his personal bodyguards, who were called *candidati* because their uniforms were white (*candidus*, 'shining'). Each palatine *schola* was about 500 soldiers strong, and commanded by a *tribunus* who was selected by the emperor himself.

Thanks to the history of Ammianus Marcellinus, a *protector domesticus* from an Antiochene military family who went into retirement in the mid fourth century and penned the last great Latin history to survive in any bulk, we have an unprecedented insight into how the massively complicated administrative system we have sketched in this chapter operated in practice. The Constantinian empire, with its military and civilian hierarchies, its overlapping of palatine, provincial, financial and managerial bureaus, was a world away from the Antonine world in which our story began. Then, a relatively thin layer of imperial authorities sat atop a regional and provincial landscape that was in some places very little changed from how it looked before the territory had been brought into the Roman empire. By the time of Constantine's death, the entire empire was integrated into a system of government that functioned – often creakingly, often redundantly – irrespective of who happened to be emperor, carried on the shoulders of an imperial elite that justified its existence not by senatorial birth, but by the roles it served in perpetuating the machinery of state. Constantine had, in fact, given birth to an entirely new Roman empire.

16

THE CONSTANTINIAN EMPIRE

Constantine, in 324, enjoyed total control over his empire. The victory over Licinius meant that no viable challengers remained, unless they were to come from his own family. It also gave Constantine control of the frontier with Sasanian Persia, and a new and still wider horizon for his expansionary imagination to contemplate. It was an interesting time in Persia, for the young shahanshah Shapur II was just attaining his majority. Though he would go on to prove as formidable a ruler as his third-century namesake, the years of his minority had not been easy. Narseh had died in 302 or 303 and was succeeded by his son, Ohrmazd II (r. 302–9/10). We know very little about Persia under Ohrmazd, since the late Arabic sources contain little reliable information. Upon his death, and probably after a rebellion, he was succeeded by Shapur II (309/10–79), who was in 309/10 only an infant. His accession looks like a coup on the part of some of the nobility and priesthood against the older sons of Ohrmazd. Although the 310s are something of a blank in Persian history, by the early 320s Shapur had begun to assert his own authority. Around 324 or 325 his brother Ohrmazd (Hormisdas, to the Romans) went into exile at the court of Constantine, and probably shortly thereafter Shapur personally led an army deep into Arabia, disciplining Sasanian clients there, and perhaps seeking to undermine Roman control of trade routes to the Far East. During that expedition, or at least probably related to it, there were skirmishes between Persians and Romans along Rome's Arabian *limes* (the Strata Diocletiana discussed in chapter 12), seemingly with real Roman losses. For the most part, Shapur first concentrated on consolidating his power in the satrapies of his empire, but in time he and Constantine would enter into a conflict that was sustained for more than a generation.

Constantine found in the east a very different world than the western empire he had left behind. Beyond the obvious contrast of Greek and Latin cultures, the two regions had had entirely different experiences of persecution in the previous decade. Not only had there been many more Christians in the east than in the west, but they had suffered more and for longer. What is more, Greek Christianity was much more complex than Latin Christianity. In part this was a matter of language – Greek is capable of much greater subtlety than Latin and can produce almost infinite variations of meaning through the coining of new words out of existing morphological elements. Latin, with a smaller vocabulary and a greater resistance to neologism, was far less suited to theological or philosophical nuance, the same words often doing duty for many different things. For that reason, even native Latin speakers had often chosen to write in Greek when they turned to philosophical topics in the early imperial period – we saw this with the emperor Marcus Aurelius in his Stoic notes to himself. For the same reason, Greek thinkers rarely felt a need to learn Latin. But this linguistic complexity had consequences for Greek Christanity.

Constantine's new faith, as we have seen, was predicated on belief more than practice, and failure to work out right belief compromised salvation. Abstruse problems of definition – things that would have been a matter of heated and competitive debate among philosophers, even dogmatic Platonists – became for Christian theologians matters of life and death, because they might mean the death of Christian souls, and the subtlety with which Greek could create variation of meaning provided almost limitless space for alternative propositions. Right belief was not, of course, something out there waiting to be discovered, but rather a construct forged in the hurly-burly of theological argument. Formulations that lost in this battle of ideas would be condemned as heresy, wrong belief, but there were problems: not only might one churchman's heresy be another's orthodoxy, but the moment a formula was accepted as orthodox or a question appeared to be settled, the settlement would produce new questions and with them new, and often equally divisive, formulae.

When Constantine defeated Licinius and took over the east, he found himself in the midst of one of these theological controversies. The problem revolved around the relationship of the three persons of the Christian trinity – the father, son and holy spirit – and in particular the way God the father was related to God the son. The contested ideas had been proposed by an Egyptian priest named Arius, and the long theological battle that ensued is now universally known as the Arian controversy. Unlike his rather limited engagement with the Donatists of North Africa, Constantine's intervention in the Arian controversy was shockingly bold and, briefly, decisive; it would have momentous consequences for the future of the Roman empire, both politically and culturally.

Egypt and its main episcopal see at Alexandria had experienced similar problems to those that created the Donatist schism in Africa – who could be admitted to communion with the church after having made some accommodation to the Roman state during the Great Persecution. But in Egypt, unlike in Africa, the problem of the *traditores* was linked – opportunistically by one party to the controversy – to a genuine theological problem. Arius, who had studied at Antioch, objected to the views of the Alexandrian bishop Alexander on the likeness of God the father and God the son in the Christian trinity. If, Arius argued, God the father had 'begotten' God the son, then there must have been a time when God the son had not existed, and in consequence they could not share the same substance, but rather God the son must be both different from, and subordinate to, God the father. Alexander exiled and sequestered Arius in response to this challenge, which he considered not just insubordinate but heretical, but Arius searched out and found powerful political supporters in other churches of the east.

Once the intellectual question of who was right in his description of the relationship between the father and the son in the trinity became politicised, it did so not merely in pure intellectual terms, but also according to who knew whom along the networks of friendship and patronage that influence thinking in any society. These networks each besieged Constantine's court from the moment he defeated Licinius, knowing not only that he could be asked to render an enforceable judgement, but that as a member of their faith he would feel obliged to do so. Leaning on the same conciliar solution with which he had tried to settle the Donatist controversy in the west, came, in the east, to exacerbate both the intellectual problem and its political dimension, because it enshrined a technique of constructing orthodoxy that was intrinsically fraught with dangers: it asked groups of bishops, men who were used to dominating their own communities, to seek compromise on questions where the stakes were as high as they could be. Free rein was thereby given to jealousy, vanity and status hierarchy among clever and ambitious men who could claim, and generally believed, that other people's souls depended on their being right. In theory, a council's decisions were not just binding, but divinely inspired. In practice, they were political as much as theological, and attended by the bitterness and recrimination that a process with plenty of losing parties will always produce. In the three centuries during which Christians were either ignored or persecuted by the Roman state, conciliar or episcopal decisions could be enforced only by mutual consensus among communities of believers. Constantine's conversion, and his decision to put the full weight of the Roman state behind conciliar decisions, instantly sharpened the edge of church politics.

We see this with the council of Nicaea, called to address the controversy over the teachings of Arius. Constantine had long taken advice from bishop Hosius (or Ossius) of Corduba in Spain, in all likelihood the person who had convinced him that his visions in Gaul were a Christian not an Apollonian portent. Faced with the rivalry of bishops who favoured and those who opposed Arius, Hosius advised the calling of a council, to which all the bishops of the empire were to be invited. It was held at Nicaea, in Asia Minor, a location convenient for the bishops of most of the east. The number of bishops who attended is canonically accepted to have been 318, but the true number is impossible to come by. Eusebius of Caesarea, who would write the first history of the church, which culminated, in its later editions, with Nicaea, is not just one of our foremost sources, but one of the dozens of important bishops we know to have been present. These included both senior Christian leaders who bore the scars of the Diocletianic persecution and the representatives of the holiest sees of the east: Alexandria and Antioch. Though Eustathius of Antioch attended in person, Alexander of Alexandria sent a young deacon, Athanasius, as his representative, pleading old age. Given that the main controversy the council was meant to address concerned Alexander's own priest Arius, the decision to leave matters in the hands of a young and politically vicious subordinate would prove to have major consequences.

Constantine and Hosius, however, were clearly trying to achieve both unanimity and the establishment of the true faith, and they cast the net wide: western bishops took part – from Gaul, Hispania, Africa, Dalmatia and Italy – as did bishop Eusebius of Nicomedia, whose importance rested both on his seniority and on his tenure of the episcopate in the main imperial residence in Asia Minor. Eusebius was one of the supporters of Arius, having shared a teacher with him, and, although they were in the clear minority at Nicaea, they put up a vigorous argument in the presence of the emperor himself: Constantine insisted on debating as an equal among the assembled bishops, an audacious but characteristic move.

There is no need to go into the details of the theological debates that took place at Nicaea, in part because reconstructing them with precision and a lack of confessional *partis pris* has been the work of centuries. But that said, we should simultaneously stress their importance, for even deeply devout believers in the twenty-first century are hard-pressed to conjure the significance that late ancient Christians placed on precise theological accuracy. It will suffice to say that, after considerable debate, airings of intellectual positions and callings-in of political favours, Arius's contention that God the son was the first creation of God the father and thus different in 'being' or 'substance' (*ousia* and *substantia* in the respective Greek and Latin) of God the father, was rejected. In its place was mandated a formula by which God the father and God the son were – in Greek – *homoousios*, or identical in being or substance (*homoousios* is a compound of the Greek words for sameness and being). This Nicene formula absolutely excluded the possibility of 'substantial' difference between the persons of the father and the son, despite the creation of the one by the other, and if the reader suspects a paradox, a leap of faith will surely be needed to overcome it. That said, the formula was a success in the moment: it satisfied those who believed Arius was irredeemably unorthodox and who wanted to ensure a settled theological solution he could not possibly subscribe to; it also satisfied those who wanted merely to please the new eastern emperor and emerge from the contest unscathed, since the new emperor clearly thought the Nicene creed was a winning proposition; and even those who thought that the homoousian formula was intellectually indefensible – Eusebius of Nicomedia chief among them – found it good enough for the needs of the moment. In that they proved right. All but three bishops subscribed to the conciliar creed produced, Arius and the other recalcitrants went into exile, and there the matter was meant to rest.

Of course, like the Donatist schism in North Africa, it did not. Not only those who genuinely agreed with Arius found the Nicene formula discomfiting. There were many who thought Arius quite wrong, but who also thought the homoousian solution equally, if differently, wrong. That was a recipe for ongoing conflict, and conflict was what it generated. Athanasius of Alexandria and those on the winning side who agreed with him had a deep political investment in maintaining the Nicene formula against all challenges. When Athanasius succeeded Alexander as bishop of the Egyptian metropolis in 328, the stage was set for perpetual trouble. Eusebius of Nicomedia, in particular, was very close to the emperor, becoming closer to him as Constantine aged. As the reign progressed he did his best to ensure that others sympathetic to the views of Arius filled eastern bishoprics. These bishops – derisively called Arians by their opponents, but better styled 'homoians' for the formula they advocated – suggested that instead of father and son having an identical substance, they were actually alike in substance, *homoios*. By the time of Constantine's death, the emperor himself had come to see Athanasius and those who followed him as not merely more wrong than their opponents in theological terms, but more dangerously obstructive as well.

We could fill several pages here with an account of the machinations, political and theological, that followed from Nicaea, and it is true that theological controversy is one of the dominant themes of late ancient history and of the literary sources it has left us. But the point that is at present crucial for us is structural. Nicaea and its aftermath made the emperor and his officials responsible for enforcing conformity with one form of Christian belief against another. This was very different from the enforcement of sacrifice under Decius, for instance, where the goal was to enforce conformity of practice, not of belief. What Constantine had committed himself and his officials to enforce was something not susceptible of proof. Christian controversialists understood this, and seized upon it for its political utility. In the long run, the state was forced to expend vast resources on defining and enforcing what people should profess to believe, a process that created entire classes of people who were excluded from the state and its protections because they would not conform to the formulation of Christian belief endorsed by the emperor.

The discovery and enforcement of orthodoxy was not the only measure Constantine took in favour of the church. Throughout the east, Constantine sent officials out to catalogue and plunder the treasuries of pagan temples. Temples were huge repositories of wealth, having long served the Greek world as a combination of banks and museums; many of them held gifts going back 500, 600 and 700 years. Constantine took all of this gold and other treasure to finance two of his most ambitious projects: the construction of Constantinople and the monetary reform that we will consider later in this chapter. The confiscations were not intentionally planned as means of suppressing pagan belief. If they had been, Constantine would not have placed a leading pagan, the Eleusinian hierophant Nicagoras of Athens, in charge of seeking out precious monuments from Egypt. Nevertheless, the sudden impoverishment of many great temples did more damage to traditional Hellenistic religions than did any other measure Constantine took against them. One of these other measures is a source of great controversy because it is surprisingly difficult to document: it is quite probable that Constantine banned pagan sacrifice in public, not just blood sacrifice, but also the symbolic lighting of incense at the shrines of the gods. No contemporary source unequivocally attests such a ban, but a pagan Greek poem alludes to altars which no longer smoke, and a law issued by Constantine's son Constans in 341 bans public sacrifice and claims that Constantine had already done so in the past. The balance of probability does therefore suggest that Constantine banned public sacrifice, but equally suggests that the ban was not very strictly enforced – rather like the Great Persecution, it must have depended largely on the attitudes of officials on the spot. In another manifestation of his Christian beliefs, in 324 Constantine invented the weekend by declaring that no public business should be conducted on the day sacred to the sun. (Only agricultural labourers continued to be required to work every day of the week – an interesting persistence of the old Graeco-Roman sense that only men who lived in a politically defined and urban place were fully human.)

Among these varying signs of favour towards Christians, Nicaea clearly remains the pivot on which the story of Constantine turns, not just because of its importance, but because of the distribution of surviving evidence: after the closing of the council, the narrative history of the reign becomes difficult to plot apart from intermittent glimpses. The most dramatic moment was the execution of the caesar Crispus and the disappearance or execution of Fausta. Crispus was killed at Pola in May 326, having been summoned there to answer unspecified charges. Because Constantine was so consummate a manipulator of his own reputation, there is no way of knowing what actually happened. A late fourth-century pagan source, Eunapius (as transmitted in the still later *Historia Nova* of the pagan Zosimus), suggests that Crispus and Fausta had an affair and that, after Crispus's execution, Constantine's grief drove him to kill Fausta as well.

Another version had her go into exile and die a few years after Crispus. It seems that contemporaries knew very little, and as a result we know still less. A liaison between Crispus and Fausta is by no means impossible – they were much the same age – but Constantine's fear of a coup is more likely. Crispus had done well in the war against Licinius and he had been groomed for power for a decade as the face of imperial government in the west. To westerners dissatisfied with a distant and perhaps radically Christian Constantine, Crispus might have looked like an attractive alternative. Constantine may have been right to suspect his son of dangerous ambition, or he may have been duped into killing a loyal lieutenant. What is certain is that Constantine was in Rome in July and August 326 when Crispus was executed at Pola. The caesar's memory was never rehabilitated, but Fausta's name was eventually restored to the imperial ancestry after her sons succeeded to their father's throne.

Constantine's movements in the later 320s can be traced in the places from which he issued laws. He spent the winter of 326–7 in the Balkans, and then, in late spring 327, travelled to Asia Minor via Thessalonica and Constantinople, presumably to check on the progress of his new city. During December 327 and January 328 he took part in a church council at Nicomedia that worked out the further consequences of Nicaea's rulings. While doing so he probably refounded the city of Drepanum, a Bithynian *polis* near Nicomedia, as Helenopolis, in honour of his mother Helena, who had by now taken on a prominent public role as a patron of Christianity. By May, however, he had left Asia Minor for the Balkans: we find him at Serdica in the middle of that month, then moving on to Oescus (a town, now uninhabited, north-west of Pleven in Bulgaria), before making a journey to the Rhineland that autumn, presumably to placate local elites who regretted the death of Crispus. He overwintered in Trier, but also did some campaigning beyond the Rhine, presumably against one or another group of Franci. In March he was back in the Balkans and he spent almost three years there, including a full year in his new residence of Constantinople after its formal dedication on 11 May 330. He shuttled between Constantinople and Nicomedia in 331, mainly addressing ecclesiastical issues, but in early 332 he returned to the Danube, where he launched a war that would have large consequences for future events.

We know more about Constantine's Gothic campaign than we do about most late imperial frontier actions, but what we know is in some ways more tantalising than informative. By the later 320s the land from what the ancients called Lake Maeotis (and we call the Sea of Azov) to the Carpathians was under the hegemony of Goths, people who both identified themselves and were identified by Romans in that way. Even the mention of non-Gothic polities disappears in the region after the last tetrarchic war against the Carpi, although that does not mean that most of the regional population was 'Gothic'. Goths seem to have been the dominant group in a society that included a lot of subjects who were not recognised as Gothic, though they all shared the distinctive material culture known as Sântana-de-Mureș/Černjachov. The older populations – Carpi, Dacians, former Roman provincials, Sarmatians – did not disappear, but were now ruled by Goths, whom Roman sources divide into two main groups, the Tervingi and the Greuthungi. As we have seen, these Goths were not ethnically homogeneous migrants from elsewhere, but a product of the Roman frontier and the various peripheral cultures that mingled there. The real proof of growing Gothic strength in this period is the terminal decay of the Bosporan Greek kingdom towards the end of Constantine's reign, and its final disappearance in the mid fourth century. No wonder we find the left bank of the Danube called the *ripa Gothica* ('the Gothic bank') at just this time.

It is not at all clear what prompted Constantine's Gothic war in the 330s. He may have intended to punish the Goths for fighting on the side of Licinius in their final civil war, or he may have become alarmed at the way tetrarchic support for the Goths against Carpi and Sarmatians had allowed the Tervingi to consolidate power so quickly. Constantinian building projects, the financing of which is evidenced by a dramatic increase in the region's supply of bronze coinage in the late 320s, included a major wall system in the valley of the Porecka near the Iron Gates and an ambitious new bridge over the Danube from Oescus to Sucidava, completed in 328. The base at Sucidava established an imperial bridgehead on the *ripa Gothica* and continued a tetrarchic project to fortify the Danube frontier with so-called *quadriburgia*. These were small forts, enclosing less than two and a half acres, with a tower at each of their four corners. They were built both in the Roman provinces of Moesia Secunda and Scythia as well as on the other side of the river, and Constantine erected a new *quadriburgium* at Daphne, opposite Transmarisca (Tutrakan). Campaigning on the left bank is attested in 328 and 329.

Then, in 330, some Taifali – a minor group identified in the sources as being 'Goths' – invaded the Balkan provinces, perhaps fleeing from the

Tervingi, because there soon followed an embassy from the Sarmatians, requesting imperial aid against the latter. Constantine's Gothic campaign followed 'in the lands of the Sarmatians', conducted by his eldest surviving son Constantinus, Crispus's successor as senior caesar. The campaign ended in a major imperial victory, with the Goths handing over hostages that included the son of a Tervingian king named Ariaric, who clearly ruled a substantial polity and who may have been the grandfather of the Gothic king Athanaric who would fight the emperor Valens to a standstill in the 360s. The Romans followed up this victory with a campaign against their Sarmatian allies, who had supposedly proved unfaithful to their agreements with the emperor. Even two decades later, Constantinus's victory was remembered as particularly dramatic and it ensured peace on the Danube for more than thirty years.

Scholars have built elaborate hypotheses upon the extremely poor fourth-century evidence for the peace treaty's terms, often retrojecting sixth-century evidence with no relevance to 332. For contemporaries, 'the Goths finally learned to serve the Romans'. They offered tribute to the emperor, provided a reservoir of recruits for imperial campaigns, and the Danube frontier was opened to trade all along its length. This was unusual given Rome's long history of restricting the export of Roman technology, but the large quantities of bronze coinage from the 330s to the 360s found on both banks of the river suggest that commerce surged and Gothia became well integrated into the Roman monetary economy. Roman diplomatic connections with the Gothic elite, meanwhile, are attested by large quantities of silver coins, normally found in small hoards distributed across the whole of Gothic territory. Since silver had by now ceased to play any meaningful role in the Roman economy itself, these may have been minted as bullion for gift subsidies to Gothic chieftains, or as discharge packages for Gothic soldiers serving in the Roman army: silver would have been useful as a means of exchange eastwards into the steppe and Sasanian worlds, where the economy was entirely silver-based. If so, it is evidence for the ways Rome could accommodate its practices to a Eurasian context.

A final consequence of Constantine's interest in the Goths was the spread of Christianity beyond the frontier. Inside the empire, Constantine took various measures against paganism but did nothing to actively encourage conversion. Outside it, he was a busy proselytiser. He saw himself as a bishop to those outside the empire, called to evangelise the *gentes* beyond the frontier, but also making conversion a tool for diplomacy binding the faithful to the empire and its emperor's personal religion. Predictably enough, however, this activity made Christians look rather like a fifth column in non-Roman territory, and not just among the Goths. Constantine supported Christian missions to a variety of kingdoms beyond the empire. During the reign of Licinius, in 313 or 314, the Armenian king Tiridates III had converted to Christianity, inspired by the bishop of Cappadocia, Gregory (known as the Illuminator). Armenian influence probably led to the spectacular conversion of Caucasian Iberia, along the eastern coast of the Black Sea south of Lazica, as the old Hellenistic kingdom of Colchis was now called.

Unlike Armenia, which was always torn between the Roman and the Persian worlds, Iberia had long been firmly in the Iranian orbit, its ruling elite generally subscribing to the Zoroastrianism of the neighbouring Arsacids and Sasanians. Then, a wonder-working Christian holy woman converted the Iberian king – perhaps Meribanes (Mirian) III, a staunch Roman ally – and he set out to convert his kingdom: an embassy to Constantine was met with great approval and the emperor began to subsidise missionary work and church-building projects in Iberia that would lead to conflict with Persia later in the fourth century. The Iberian alliance was important for another reason as well, for it is almost certainly in Iberia that a hitherto unknown source of very fine gold was discovered in the last decade of Constantine's reign or shortly thereafter; that new eastern gold had a profound impact on the fourth-century economy, and on the respective fates of the eastern and western empires in the fifth.

Another mission field for the zealous emperor was Axum, ancient Ethiopia. Recent research has shown how the Red Sea zone – including Axum on the one hand and Himyar, now Yemen, on the other – was much more closely connected to the Roman and Persian worlds than was previously thought. Indeed, a long-lasting Jewish kingdom in Himyar is of great significance for the later rise of Islam and the end of the ancient world. In the Constantinian period, however, the conversion of Axum closely paralleled that of Iberia: two Christian slaves belonging to a travelling philosopher named Meropius found themselves in Axum, where they were freed, one of them entering the service of the king, the other returning to the Roman empire and becoming bishop of Tyre while maintaining connections with his old companion. This companion, Frumentarius, converted king Ezana, and Christians from the empire were then granted privileged access to Axumite trade.

Athanasius of Alexandria, the expert controversialist whom we met at Nicaea earlier in this chapter, claimed responsibility for policing the orthodoxy of the Axumites. Orthodoxy, as Constantine's intervention at Nicaea had demonstrated, was a matter for imperial politics. In the same way that the rise of the Sasanians had gradually brought the Roman empire into contact with wider Eurasian history, so too did the replacement of the pragmatic cult of the early empire with an aggressive imperial Christianity extend the imperial gaze out to wherever there were Christians to protect or regulate.

The stories of both Iberia and Axum's conversion are filtered to us through layers of pious fiction and the kind of legendary distortion that infects all Graeco-Roman accounts of distant lands that were known mainly through a mixture of merchants' tales, very rare diplomatic embassies and the overlay of Classical mythology and Hellenistic romance. By contrast, the Gothic conversion is fairly well attested: the treaty of 332 did not impose Christianity on Ariaric's Goths but, by the time of his death, Constantine had sponsored the mission of a Gothic bishop named Ulfila, sometimes called Wulfila or Ulfilas. Our information on the life of Ulfila derives from two sources: a letter written by one of his disciples, Auxentius, and a heavily abbreviated version of Philostorgius's fifth-century *Ecclesiastical History*. Ulfila was descended from Cappadocians taken captive in the Scythian raids of Gallienus's reign, though he himself bore a Gothic name. He came from Gothia on an embassy to the emperor – probably Constantine, perhaps Constantius II – and was consecrated in either *c.* 336 or *c.* 341 by Eusebius of Nicomedia and other bishops. Eusebius, as we have seen, was an adherent of the post-Nicene homoian theology, towards which Constantine was increasingly inclined in his later years. It is clear from the bishops who consecrated him that Ulfila was a member of the homoian party, and so the earliest evangelism among the Goths brought Christianity in its homoian form. Gothic homoianism was later heavily re-enforced in the reign of Valens, and homoian doctrine and a liturgy in the Gothic language would remain a distinguishing factor between Romans and Goths until the sixth century.

After his consecration, Ulfila was meant to serve as bishop to all the Christians in the land of the Goths, but we have no idea how many such people there were, how many were, like Ulfila, descended from Roman captives and how many were converts won beyond the frontier. But within a decade of Ulfila's arrival, Gothic leaders were becoming worried at the growing number of Christians and began their persecution. We will look at the consequences of Gothic conversion in the sequel to this volume, but here we can understand the story of Ulfila in the context of the missions to Axum, Armenia and Iberia. All are symptoms of a new phenomenon in fourth-century imperial history: elites from regions not actually administered as provinces becoming integrated into the imperial elite, participating in its governance in much the same way as did provincial elites from regions subject to imperial administration. We will have more than one occasion to consider this structural change in imperial politics, inaugurated by Constantine, which meant that later in the century Franci and Alamanni, Mauri from the North African steppe, Iberians and Saracens, exiled Persian royals and Goths – all could make good careers in imperial government, some retiring back to their homelands beyond the frontier, others settling down as honoured grandees inside the empire. It is all a world away from the senatorial elite of the Antonine period with whom our story began.

To return to our fragmentary narrative of Constantine's last decade, the short-term consequence of the emperor's Gothic victory was merely to shift the focus of confrontation to a new set of barbarian enemies. In 334, as we saw, Constantine campaigned against the Sarmatians, probably those that had asked for his help against the Goths in the first place. We are told that the servile population of the Sarmatian lands rebelled against their masters, and that many Sarmatians – 30,000, according to one source – fled into Roman service. Once inside Roman territory, they were divided among the Balkan and Italian provinces. That is a reminder of just how effective the Roman state remained at managing the mass relocation of large populations, although it involved keeping an eye on, and preparing for, the upset of old power hierarchies in the *barbaricum*. We should understand this Sarmatian relocation as the last major consequence of rising Gothic power during the tetrarchic period. In fact, it was not until the 370s that the lands beyond the Danube were again similarly disrupted.

After the 334 campaign, Constantine took the victory title Sarmaticus maximus to accompany his multiple acclamations as Gothicus maximus. He also took the title Dacicus maximus, which probably represents a claim to have restored Trajan's province of Dacia. The Carpathian lands of the old province were certainly not reannexed and subjected to Roman administration, but new garrisons in trans-Danubian *quadriburgia* and other small forts justified the claims. Constantine was a familiar and frightening force beyond the *limes*, as is illustrated by the large number of barbarian ambassadors present in 335 at the celebration of his *tricennalia*, his thirtieth anniversary on the throne, which is described to us by Eusebius of Caesarea, an eyewitness. Here we find not just the expected Goths and Sarmatians, but also Blemmyes, from south of the Roman frontier in Upper Egypt, as well as Ethiopians and Indians. This latter testimony is not as far-fetched as some might think, for as we shall see India was much on the mind of the Constantinian court towards the end of the reign.

The *tricennalia* was a major event, for it had been a very long time since any emperor had lived long enough to reach a thirtieth anniversary. During the celebrations, Constantine and Fausta's middle son, Constantius, was wedded to a daughter of Julius Constantius, Constantine's half-brother, with great pomp and circumstance. Perhaps the most significant thing to note, however, is where the celebration took place: Constantinople. Even Diocletian and Maximian, whose interest in the city of Rome was minimal, had felt it essential to travel there to celebrate their *vicennalia* in 303. Now, only just over thirty years later, Constantine felt no such compulsion. Constantinople would not be recognised officially as *the* new Rome until the 380s, but few things make clearer its status as the second city of the empire than the fact that Constantine chose to celebrate so momentous an occasion there.

Constantine would rule for just two years after his *tricennalia* and these were spent planning for the succession and plotting another war against Persia. War had been brewing since 324, when Constantine received the brother of the Persian king Shapur II (r. 309–79) under his protection when the latter fled to Roman territory. This Hormisdas (Ohrmazd), as he was known to Greeks and Romans, was a major figure at the eastern court for many years after that, but harbouring a competent adult pretender was an affront that Shapur felt strongly – not least because Constantine took in Hormisdas at more or less the same moment that the shah had written to congratulate him for his victory over Licinius and to welcome him into the fellowship of monarchs. Constantine's reply had hectored Shapur about the need to protect his Christian subjects, and had also denounced the Mazdaism of the Persian court as a false religion. The conversion of Iberia to Christianity was another incursion into the Persian zone of influence, fuelling Shapur's resentment, but it was an Armenian succession crisis that, as so many times in the past, led directly to the war with Persia.

The Christian Tiridates III died in 330 and his only son was a minor. The Armenian nobility, which played a decisive role in many successions, was divided along pro-Roman and pro-Persian lines, with various family jealousies playing their part as well. Unsurprisingly, those nobles who favoured the Roman side chose Tiridates' young son Arsaces, but others sent to Shapur asking him to give them a king. Civil war broke out in Armenia, Arsaces fled to Constantine and Shapur invaded the kingdom and raided the easternmost imperial provinces. Constantine gave Arsaces shelter, but did not try to restore him to his throne; instead he proclaimed Hannibalianus, the younger son of his half-brother Flavius Dalmatius, as 'king of kings and of the kingdom of Pontus'. This proclamation was the proximate cause of war but, in the wake of the *tricennalia* and its show of universal rulership, it was also said that Shapur had stolen the gifts sent by the rulers of India to acknowledge Constantine as their ruler of thirty years. Even discounting the characteristically Constantinian propaganda in that rumour, we should not doubt that he thought he could conquer Persia. Constantine shared with many a Roman emperor the fantasy of surpassing Alexander, of taking his conquests as far as the eastern sea – wherever that was – and he had won so many battles that he might justifiably think himself capable of making the fantasy real. He chose as his excuse the fate of Christians in Shapur's realm, which was as convenient as any other, and the dynastic arrangements adumbrated at the *tricennalia* of 335 telegraphed his ambitions: the appropriation of the title 'king of kings' for Hannibalianus (his *rex regum* in the Latin calqued from the Persian 'shahanshah') was as provocative as it was speculative.

Along with the marriage of Constantius, which cemented Constantine's lineage to the cadet branch of his half-siblings, the *tricennalia* made clear the settlement that the emperor wanted to bequeath posterity. At least since the execution of Crispus, the three sons of Constantine by Fausta had been groomed for the succession as Constantine had been four decades earlier. Constantinus was permitted to cover himself in glory in the Gothic wars of the early 330s, and in 335 Constantius was very nearly old enough to be entrusted with a political role. Constans remained too young to command armies, but it was now he who represented the face of the dynasty to the Italian nobility, residing at Mediolanum and betrothed to Olympias, daughter of Constantine's powerful praetorian prefect, Flavius Ablabius.

By contrast with the children of Fausta, Constantine's half-siblings and their offspring – the sons, daughters and grandchildren of Constantius I and Theodora – were kept in the shadows. They seem, wisely, to have supported their victorious half-brother while keeping out of his way, until the *tricennalia* changed the political calculus. Whether through megalomania or mere realistic ambition, Constantine had determined that nothing short of world conquest would suit; his three surviving sons were too few to make that happen, and his father's collateral offspring had to be made an asset if they were not to be a threat. Not until the *tricennalia* did the extent of the plan become clear: as we have seen, Hannibalianus, the son of Constantine's half-brother Flavius Dalmatius, was proclaimed king of kings, but he was also married to Constantine's daughter Constantina. Flavius Dalmatius's other son, like his father called Dalmatius and until 335 still a schoolboy under the famous Gallic rhetor Exsuperius of Narbo, was now raised to the rank of caesar. He and his brother were thereby given parity of rank with Constantine's own sons, and the younger Dalmatius was probably, if not certainly, married to Constantine's youngest daughter Helena. To drive home the point of the succession plan, each of Constantine's four caesars was assigned his own residence and his own praetorian prefect: Constantinus at Trier, Constans at Mediolanum, Dalmatius probably at Sirmium, and Constantius at Antioch. Constantius would oversee the muster of a campaign army, while Constantine travelled to Palaestina to receive baptism in the river Jordan en route to the conquests that would deliver Shapur's Persian throne to the young *rex regum* Hannibalianus.

It was early in 337 when Constantine set out from Constantinople for Antioch. He was expecting many more years of triumphs before the succession he had arranged with such theatrical splendour actually took effect, but expectations failed him: falling ill just after departing Nicomedia, he became too weak to travel. Prostrate in a *mansio* of the imperial postal service, he accepted baptism from his long-time episcopal favourite Eusebius of Nicomedia and died on 22 May. The emperor's middle son, Constantius, got word of what had happened and hurried as fast as he could from Antioch. Meanwhile, Constantine's body was embalmed and carried in state back to Constantinople for a massive funeral that took place as soon as Constantius had arrived.

Constantine was buried in the mausoleum of the Twelve Apostles, a monument he had himself commissioned in the city that bore his name: in his own mind, at least, he had been a thirteenth apostle. We do not know when the obsequies were finally concluded, or when the interment actually took place, but on 9 September Constantius, along with his elder brother Constantinus and his younger brother Constans, were proclaimed augusti. Their cousins Hannibalianus and Dalmatius did not share this happy outcome, or take up the inheritance promised them at their uncle's *tricennalia*: both were dead, murdered along with all their male relatives save two very small children, Gallus and Julian, one the full brother, the other the half-brother, of Constantius II's wife. The tripartite succession of Constantine and Fausta's sons meant that the late emperor's own plans had outlived him by less than three months. A new era was inaugurated by an orchestrated massacre that has correctly been described as a 'summer of blood'.

17

THE CHILDREN OF CONSTANTINE

Constantine had died in May 337. Until 9 September, he remained technically the ruling augustus, for none of his sons or generals proclaimed themselves augustus. What his sons did, they did as caesars. Constantine's will was concealed by the *praepositus sacri cubiculi*, head of the imperial household. This was Eusebius, a eunuch who was a long-standing and loyal partisan of the middle son, Constantius II. That meant in turn that Constantius more than any of his brothers could arrange the empire's affairs without reference to others. The power of the late emperor's sons was consolidated by the massacre of male kinsmen who were not, like them, born to Constantine and Fausta: Constantine's half-brothers Julius Constantius and Flavius Dalmatius died, as did the latter's sons Dalmatius and Hannibalianus. Gallus and Julian, sons of Julius Constantius by different mothers survived, but survival did not imply trust: both were confined under close house arrest in the imperial palace at Nicomedia, where they were to grow up under the watchful eye of the local bishop Eusebius, who had been with Constantine on his deathbed. There, Julian was trained by a eunuch grammarian named Mardonius (as possibly was Gallus as well) who inspired in the boy a love of the Classical Greek literature and mythology that would later blossom into an extraordinary conversion to traditional paganism.

Constantius II, Constantine's middle son by Fausta, was the main instigator of the great massacre, and in its aftermath he proved himself almost as adept at controlling a historical narrative as his father had been. Eusebius of Caesarea, who wrote a *Life* of his hero Constantine in 338, utterly effaces Dalmatius and Hannibalianus from the historical record, along with Constantine's half-brothers, going so far as to assert that Constantine had willed that his empire be ruled by his sons alone. The one major source even to mention the massacre is Aurelius Victor, who wrote his *De Caesaribus*, a heavily abbreviated history of the Roman emperors, while Constantius II was still alive. It spouts what must have been the official line: the army had insisted that only Constantine's children should rule and forced on them the execution of Dalmatius. Better still, and in typically Constantinian fashion, it suggests that Dalmatius and Hannibalianus had plotted against Constantine before his death and might even have been responsible for it. The truth has only been worked out by meticulous study of the coinage sequence. Constantius II had acted alone in ordering the massacre, even if he had his brothers' tacit approval, and after the three were declared augusti publicly in early September, they met at Viminacium in Moesia, in territory that would have gone to Dalmatius under their father's 335 settlement, to negotiate terms on which they could coexist. At least one eastern garrison had mutinied in response to the dynastic murders and Armenia was in open revolt after the loss of its putative king Hannibalianus, so the stability of the new arrangement remained in some doubt.

And of course the brothers could not trust one another. As such, neither Constantinus, Constantius nor Constans took the consulship of 338, handing it instead to Flavius Ursus and Flavius Polemius, two senior generals whose acquiescence in the coup helped calm the army. But that was symbolic, and real power would be kept in the family. Constantinus (or Constantine II, as he is sometimes known, especially among coin collectors) was the eldest, and he retained the western portion of the empire that had been assigned to him under the original Constantinian dispensation of 335. The youngest, Constans, had not yet reached his majority, but divided the share of Dalmatius with Constantius II, giving Thrace to the latter, while himself taking the dioceses of Pannonia, Macedonia and Dacia, the latter two having been split by Constantine out of the tetrarchic diocese of Moesia. The main beneficiary of this change was Constantius II, whose share brought with it both Constantine's new foundation at Constantinople and the whole of the east. His first action as emperor was to execute Flavius Ablabius, one of the main architects of Constantinian government, and praetorian prefect at the time of the old emperor's death in May 337. Ablabius, a Christian and an intimate of Constantine, had been prudent enough to retire to his huge estates in Bithynia when the emperor died, but – perhaps because of his proximity to the captive princes Gallus and Julian at Nicomedia, perhaps because of his own well-established power base – lying low was not enough. Ablabius's associates, and many others who might have favoured the settlement of 335 rather than that of Constantius II and his brothers, were purged as well.

Yet Constantius's ruthlessness was not enough to keep the peace. He may personally have been quite secure, but in the west the relationship of Constantinus and Constans was parlous, the elder brother attempting to treat young Constans more like a caesar than as an augustus in his own right and sending directives to Constans' officials in a way he dared not do to Constantius's. Obscure though events are, the regimes at Trier and Mediolanum were at odds from the moment the fraternal conference at Viminacium concluded. By 340, things had got so bad that Constantinus invaded Italy, on some pretext unknown to us. Constans' generals met the invaders at Aquileia and Constantinus was killed on the battlefield. There were now just two emperors, with Constantius very much the senior partner, even though Constans held a larger, and rather more secure, part of the empire.

For us, the story of the next decade is more one of ecclesiastical politics than might be imagined, though whether it was experienced as such by those who lived through it is another matter. Our perspective is forced on us by the sources, which record next to nothing about secular history until the dawning of the 350s. Thus the political history can be sketched very briefly indeed. The death of Constantinus left his western regime intact so that Constans, who was completely unknown to the Gallic establishment, had little choice but to work with Constantinus's advisers and supporters. He seems to have made every effort to do so, leaving Italy and the Balkans behind for the better part of three years, residing at Trier between 340 and 342, accompanying the army on at least two Frankish campaigns and touring the British armies. He divided the next two years between Trier and the Balkans, and then settled down where he was most comfortable, at Sirmium – a decision that exacerbated the existing rivalry between the Gallic and Balkan high commands. That particular rivalry would repeatedly have fatal consequences during the fourth century but, in the short term, Constans had to be in the Balkans to manage a fraught relationship with the regime of his brother Constantius.

The latter, after the dynastic slaughter of 337, faced a problem in Persia. Shapur had understood the scale of Constantine's bellicose intentions in 337 and was prepared to meet the army mustering at Antioch when Constantine died. Rather than await the Roman invasion, Shapur struck preemptively, attacking the fortified citadel of Nisibis in Mesopotamia. As would happen again more than once, the Persian army got bogged down in the siege of Nisibis, failing to take it by storm and withdrawing back to Persian territory early in 338. Rather than press the advantage, Constantius merely sent an army into Armenia to put down the revolt there and install a compliant Arsacid on the throne. He also concluded an alliance with some of the Arab tribes in the desert between Roman and Persian territory. Feints and border skirmishes followed on both sides – one source suggests that there were nine battles between Constantius and Shapur, two of them with the emperor himself commanding – until in 344 the Romans suffered terrible losses at Singara, where one of Shapur's sons was also killed. Deadly as the battle had been, it was not decisive, and the eastern provinces braced themselves for another Persian invasion. Indeed, fear of Shapur was the excuse used by many eastern bishops to stay away from a major church council, at Serdica in the Balkans, in 342. It was this council of Serdica that caused the first major crisis between the imperial brothers.

Religious controversy forms the largest part of what we know about the 340s, and that is appropriate inasmuch as Constantius II was personally very interested in theological questions. The difficulty both he and Constans faced was the failure of the Nicene settlement to stick: Arius had died in exile (on the toilet, of haemorrhagic diarrhoea, according to hostile witnesses), but bishops sympathetic to his formulation of the relationship between God the father and God the son reacted by working out a new terminology to counter the objections to Arius's original teaching as aired at Nicaea – that father and son were 'alike' or similar in all things, but not identical. These 'homoians', as they were labelled by their detractors, found a leader in Eusebius of Nicomedia, the favourite of Constantine and bishop of a Bithynian *polis* historically locked in rivalry with neighbouring Nicaea. Constantine, in his advancing years, clearly supported the homoian formulation, and it was, as we saw, Eusebius of Nicomedia who baptised him on his deathbed in 337. Nicene extremists, most notably the bishop of Alexandria, Athanasius, who had succeeded his patron Alexander in 328, argued that the creed of Eusebius and his fellow bishops was nothing more than Arianism in disguise, incompatible with the true Nicene faith – only total likeness of substance in the godhead, the homoousianism of 325, was acceptable.

One of the last religious controversies in which Constantine had been engaged was the trial and exile of Athanasius in 335. The Alexandrian bishop, a political operator of great skill, seized the opportunity presented by Constantine's death to return to Alexandria, where he openly challenged the rights of the incumbent bishop, Gregory of Cappadocia, who had been installed on the late emperor's orders upon Athanasius's exile. The city of Alexandria was of course notorious for its public disorders and had been for centuries, but Athanasius positively encouraged his supporters to riot and attack their opponents. It is a reminder of how easily, thanks to Constantine's open endorsement of Christianity, theological disagreements could be used as excuses for public violence; indeed, there is a level at which the 'sacred violence' of late antiquity was a sort of hooliganism that might well have found outlet in gangsterism or banditry, but was instead legitimised by religious rhetoric. In the fighting of 337, Athanasius and his supporters won, but the bishop had failed to reckon with attitudes of the new emperor, a character as bloody-minded as the Alexandrian bishop himself.

Constantius, more than his father, was a convinced homoian and he would expend a great deal of energy during his reign in trying to find some variation of a homoian formula that could unify all the bishops of the empire. Over the course of his long reign, he called putatively universal and ecumenically binding councils half a dozen times: at Antioch (341), Serdica (342), Sirmium (351), Arelate (353), Mediolanum (355), Ariminum and Seleucia (359) and Constantinople (360). In all of these, he personally intervened in the drafting of creeds he intended to be universally acceptable, and therefore universally enforced. He failed in this ambition every time, in part because the theological differences he was trying to paper over were too wide, in part because partisan politics was deeply entrenched in the post-Nicene episcopate. Yet part of the blame also lay with Constantius, who persecuted the extreme Nicene party without let-up and freely exiled bishops who refused to conform to his homoian line. One of his earliest moves was to replace Paul, the Nicene bishop of Constantinople, with Eusebius of Nicomedia. Paul was exiled to Pontus, but his arrest by imperial troops led to rioting in the streets, during which an imperial officer named Hermogenes was lynched. Constantius then turned on Athanasius.

The latter had been condemned by a council of hostile bishops called in Egypt after his return from exile in 337. When Athanasius refused to accept this local council's condemnation, his rivals appealed to the emperor, who agreed to meet with Athanasius in Caesarea. The Alexandrian bishop had mustered powerful support, not just from Greek sympathisers but also in the Latin west, a manoeuvre that would have fateful consequences for imperial politics. Constantius, however, remained hostile and summoned a council to meet at Antioch and judge the case: on 16 April 339, Athanasius was again condemned and sent into exile, this time at the court of Constans. The western emperor was disinclined to support his brother in religious matters and consistently backed the Nicene party throughout his reign. The brothers agreed to sponsor a council at Serdica in 342, not just to deal with Athanasius but to consider the trinitarian language of Nicaea yet again. Constans, however, permitted intransigently Nicene Latin bishops, led by the now ancient Hosius of Corduba, to head the western delegation. They refused even to be seated alongside the eastern bishops, and the council was a total failure. In its aftermath, Constans sent a menacing letter to his brother, demanding that he allow exiled bishops – for which read Athanasius of Alexandria – to return to their sees. Constantius refused, and in retaliation each emperor appointed different consuls for 344.

In 345, Constantius proclaimed a joint imperial consulship with Constans, with himself as senior partner, but the latter failed to recognise it until late summer, when Athanasius was allowed to return to Alexandria: only then, on 21 October, was the joint consulship proclaimed in the west as well as the east. What lay behind Constantius's change of heart is uncertain, but it may be that the endless fighting on the Persian frontier had left him with no stomach for a civil war. Patching up the situation with his brother would at least allow him to concentrate safely on Persia. Constans did nothing to help his brother pursue the Persian conflict, even though he commanded a far larger military establishment that could have accomplished a great deal on the eastern front. Instead, he continued to reside at Sirmium, ready for a potential confrontation. It was in these years, with Constans firmly based in the Balkans and Constantius on the eastern front, that a major administrative transition took place: where formerly the praetorian prefects accompanied the emperor, so that their prefectures were not fixed geographically, there now developed a system of regional prefects, who acted with executive authority in the emperor's stead.

This change was politically important, in part because it played a role in the downfall of Constans. The military and civilian establishments in Gaul had been catered to throughout the reigns of Constantine and Constantinus with a resident augustus or caesar. But with Constans far away in the Balkans, and clearly favourable to its rival high command, the Gallic establishment felt both neglected and resentful. Fabius Titianus, praetorian prefect of Gaul since 341 and thus one of the longest-serving holders of that office, formed the centre of a conspiracy that allied the civilian and military hierarchies of the western provinces against those of the Balkans. The conspirators included the senior western financial officer, the *comes rerum privatarum* Marcellinus, and a general high up in the Gallic field army, Flavius Magnentius, who would lead the planned coup. Titianus, whose long tenure speaks to the trust in which he was held, may have decided to go along with the conspirators out of enmity with Constans's *magister officiorum* Eugenius, who was, like Titianus, a long-serving minister but one firmly tied to the Danubian high command.

Towards the end of 349, Constans returned to Gaul, and it was then that the trap was sprung. On 18 January 350, while the emperor was off on a hunting trip, Magnentius was proclaimed emperor at a birthday party for the son of Marcellinus, to which he had arrived dressed in the imperial purple. Rather than confronting the threat, Constans tried to escape, but was tracked down by a *comes* named Gaiso towards the end of January and executed – the officer's reward would be a joint consulship with his emperor Magnentius in 351. Constans's body, some scholars believe, was recovered by loyalists and buried in an elaborate mausoleum at Centcelles, over the Pyrenees from the Gallic village of Helena where he had been killed.

There were loyalists elsewhere as well, and a distant cousin of the imperial brothers was proclaimed at Rome. This Roman coup was sponsored by Eutropia, a half-sister of Constantine who had survived the massacre of her male relatives. Her son, Julius Nepotianus, was clad in the purple and immediately began to mint coins in his own name. But his position was weak. Constantine's reforms had left no meaningful military force in Rome, and no praetorian guard who might sponsor a new emperor. Nepotianus had to rely upon a makeshift force of gladiators to back him and, without a field army, he was completely helpless when Magnentius sent troops over the Alps to suppress him. He and his supporters were massacred, though Eutropia was allowed to live. And that was not the only usurpation. Vetranio, Constans's *magister militum* in Moesia, also seized the purple in response to the Gallic coup.

The episode is baffling, and the sources almost certainly conceal the truth. We are told that Constantia, the sister of Constantius and Constans, encouraged Vetranio to take the purple when she learned of her brother's death and Magnentius's usurpation. Vetranio was an old and trusted associate of the family, the brother of Julius Constantius's first wife and thus a distant relative by marriage; he would protect the dynasty's interests, and he won the approval of Constans's loyal prefect of Illyricum, Vulcacius Rufinus. Rufinus personally carried a letter from Constantia to the eastern citadel of Edessa, where Constantius was in the midst of a Persian campaign. Constantius, as senior augustus, accepted Vetranio as his colleague and sent him a diadem. Or so we are told. It may all have happened, or the story may disguise a coup by the Balkan high command. We shall never know, but from Constantius's perspective, it was better if the field armies of Gaul and the Balkans served different masters than if Magnentius took control of Illyricum as well as Gaul and Italy.

The western usurper appointed his brother Decentius as caesar and left him to oversee the Rhine frontier while he himself took control of the government in Italy. Constantius could do nothing, for he found himself confronted with yet another Persian invasion, led by Shapur himself. Like previous ones, it foundered on a siege of Nisibis, which held out for four months before Shapur retreated. Only then could Constantius begin to consider the murky situation in the Balkans and a usurpation that clearly had the support of a wide variety of western elites. In 350, Constantius led his field army back to Europe and Vetranio went to meet him at Serdica in a clear gesture of reconciliation. Whatever had spurred the usurpation, and whatever was now worked out between them, the two appeared together at Naissus on 25 December 350, a day that was not yet given special significance as Christmas Day. Both the Balkan and eastern field armies were drawn up in full parade for the occasion and, as Constantius began to address the assembled soldiery, they began to chant for Vetranio's abdication. That was according to a pre-arranged plan and the old man duly obliged, humbly allowing Constantius to take the purple from his shoulders. It was an extraordinary, unprecedented and still inexplicable moment, but it saved the Constantinian dynasty. Vetranio retired to Prusa in Bithynia, a down-at-heel Hellenistic market town, where he lived on unmolested for another six years.

Constantius was now in command of two field armies to Magnentius's one, but the events of the past year had proved to him how dangerous the absence of sufficient dynastic oversight could be. The field armies, their officer corps now closely linked to the civilian establishments of the regional prefectures, would prefer to make an officer on-the-spot emperor rather than accept a sole ruler who was far away in another part of the empire. Constantius thus decided to recall Flavius Gallus from confinement in Nicomedia. Gallus was the elder son of Julius Constantius and of Galla, the late sister of the prefect Vulcacius Rufinus who had brokered the peace between Constantius and Vetranio. Gallus had been allowed to survive the massacre of 337 because his sister, now dead, had been Constantius II's first wife. Now, on 15 March 351, Constantius raised his half-cousin Gallus to the rank of caesar and sent him to Antioch to keep the dynasty visible and dissuade Persian advances by the very fact of his presence.

To solidify the relationship, the 25-year-old Gallus was married to Constantius's eldest sister Constantina, who was much older than the new caesar and had previously been married to Hannibalianus, one of the victims of 337. The plan was good in theory, but the imperial couple made themselves profoundly disliked in Antioch during the three years they resided there – and that despite the fact that the administration of the east remained firmly in the hands of officials personally loyal to Constantius, especially the praetorian prefect Thalassius.

In the short term, however, the appointment of a new caesar meant that Constantius could deal with Magnentius. He took the normal invasion route from the Balkans across the Julian Alps via Emona and Aquileia, but Magnentius was able to stop the invaders there and deny them a free run of the North Italian plain. As Constantius's army retired to regroup, Magnentius pursued it into Pannonia. Although some of Magnentius's commanders went over to Constantius – among them the general Silvanus, who would later be made *magister militum per Gallias* and fall victim to the emperor's paranoid fear of conspiracy – the two armies took the field at Mursa (now Osijek in Croatia), just beyond Cibalae on the highway to Sirmium. The battle was remembered as the worst in fourth-century history, with unspeakable losses on both sides. None the less, it was the eastern troops who emerged victorious: though nearly half their number lay dead on the field, two-thirds of Magnentius's field army had been wiped out and the usurper himself was forced to retreat to Italy. The mauling suffered by the victorious army encouraged trouble on the Danubian border and Constantius had to launch a punitive campaign against the Sarmatians to remind them of imperial potency.

After that, in 352, the emperor crossed the Julian Alps, this time without opposition, and took control of the North Italian plain. The rest of the peninsula was in his hands by early autumn. He overwintered in Italy, then crossed the Alps into Gaul at the start of the campaigning season in 353. In a battle at Mons Seleucus (today in the French Alps) Magnentius was defeated again, and committed suicide shortly thereafter on 10 August. His brother Decentius hanged himself at Senonia (Sens). As luck would have it, this was the year of Constantius's *tricennalia*, thirty years since he had been raised to the rank of caesar. Like his father before him, he did not trouble to go to Rome to celebrate it. Instead, the ceremonies took place at Arelate, the sometime residence of Constantine. It was a city now entering the height of its good fortune, in an era when the southern Gallic aristocracy was enjoying an unprecedented flowering of talent and artistic ascendancy in Latin literature. The Gallic poet Ausonius, later famous as both a writer and a statesman, was just now beginning a career that would one day celebrate Arelate as *Gallula Roma*, 'the little Rome of Gaul'.

Southern Gaul would go on to play a pivotal role in the history of the western empire, and another recurrent feature of late imperial politics first becomes visible with the defeat of Magnentius: though just another failed usurper, he was recast as a barbarian invader. The sources make much of his having been the son of a Frankish father and a British mother, implying that he was not actually a Roman but a foreign foe. Of course, no one had noticed any of that while Magnentius was alive, and his background was not a problem for the impeccably aristocratic Gallo-Romans who supported his regime. Even today, there are authors who make Magnentius's parentage evidence for the barbarisation of the Roman elite, but they are missing the point: the ruling class of the fourth century was so diverse that regional and ethnic origins were noticed, but were not in themselves markers of either barbarism or 'Roman-ness'. And in the same way that an emperor's memory had long been subject to public erasure – *damnatio memoriae* – a usurper could be retrospectively 'barbarised' after his political failure, reimagined as a permanent outsider to the Roman state.

Our insight into the process is possible in part because, with Constantius's victory over Magnentius, we are suddenly much better informed about the empire's political history than we have been for the earlier fourth century, thanks to the survival of the *Res Gestae* of Ammianus Marcellinus, one of the last great classicising works of Latin history, and the last to survive in any bulk. Ammianus was a Greek from one of the prominent Syrian cities, probably Antioch. He came from a good family that had been excused from its obligation to serve in the local town council and was instead closely linked to the larger imperial administration. He was, in other words, a typical product of his era: well connected, ambitious and owing his social distinction to the family's participation in the state apparatus. As a young man, Ammianus served as *protector domesticus*, one of that elite group of soldiers who carried out a variety of special functions and often operated in the close vicinity of the emperor himself.

The institution can be seen as a sort of officer training academy, socialising young men from diverse backgrounds, with little common linguistic or cultural ground, into a shared military ethos: in the *protectores*, an educated urbanite like Ammianus learned to work not just with others like himself, but with men only a generation removed from labour in the fields and with favoured nobles from Francia, Alamannia or Iberia. They all learned to communicate in a standard military Latin, and were taught a basic, stereotyped version of Roman and Greek history so that those who lacked a proper education could still navigate elite society as officers. Thus prepared for life in the camps, palaces and towns, *protectores* usually moved on to command units of active service troops in later life. For the same reason, close proximity to the imperial person and the military high command meant that more than one former *protector* went on to become emperor himself.

Ammianus, for those reasons, was personally involved in a number of high-profile missions, and ultimately joined the invasion of Persia launched in 363 by Julian, Constantius's successor. But his promising career came to a sudden halt when Julian was killed and he chose to pursue the research that would inform his history of the Roman empire – a gift to posterity on which we will never cease to rely. We know that he travelled widely, and that he moved from his native Greek east to Rome. He wrote much of his history there, perhaps under the patronage of one of the great senatorial families. It was probably finished within a year or so of 390 and Ammianus may have died soon afterwards. His *Res Gestae* intermixes a political history of the empire with all sorts of learned digressions and, most unusually for an ancient historian, with Ammianus's personal reminiscences. It ran, originally, from the reign of the emperor Nerva (r. 96–8) to that of Valens (r. 364–78), but much of it was lost in antiquity and the surviving text begins with the events of summer 353. The whole of the *Res Gestae* is shaped by the catastrophe that befell the emperor Valens at Adrianople in 378, when much of the eastern field army was destroyed in a single afternoon. The whole narrative is filtered through that battle's retrospective significance and a sense of penetrating gloom, but, thanks to its survival, we can study the years between 353 and 378 in greater detail than we can any other phase of Roman imperial history after Tacitus's *Historiae* break off in AD 68.

When the extant text of Ammianus picks up, it is 353 and we are plunged into the aftermath of Magnentius's defeat and suicide. Constantius has put a fearsome magistrate named Paulus Catena – Paul 'the Chain' – in charge of hunting down and extirpating the usurper's followers (we know few details, only that the *magister militum* Gratianus, father of the future emperors Valentinian and Valens, went into retirement at this moment and was lucky to survive it). Paul was a *notarius*, on the staff of the *primicerius notariorum*: technically, then, he was a shorthand-writer and part of the palace secretariat but, like the *agentes in rebus*, who served under the *magister officiorum* as a secret police, *notarii* were often selected to undertake disparate and distasteful tasks. That was because *notarii* and *agentes* (who were technically in charge of the imperial post) tended to come to the attention of the emperor's most intimate officials for their discretion, their loyalty and their willingness to do unpleasant things, which meant that they were regularly seconded to sensitive or specialist duties. With their ill-defined jobs and wide-ranging practical power, *notarii* were naturally disliked by most other sections of the government.

Paul, in Ammianus's account, struck fear into all those he investigated because of his relentlessness and brutality. He was, for Ammianus, typical of the creatures Constantius favoured, and the historian paints a chilling picture of the emperor: morose and paranoid, terrified of plots swirling in the background, convinced that anyone he trusted would betray him. The vigour with which Paul the Chain was encouraged to root out those who had sympathised with, or just acquiesced in, Magnentius's usurpation shows, for Ammianus, the perversity with which Constantius ruled the empire.

What Ammianus never says outright, but clearly believed, is that Constantius wasted enormous energy on Christianity: the number of church councils Constantius sponsored are contemptuously denounced as a drain on time and resources, clogging up the imperial postal service and public roads as bishops were shipped from council to council at public expense. There is something in this, actually. We have already seen the efforts that the emperor made to impose a homoian creed on those parts of the empire under his direct control, and the extent to which that had poisoned relations with his brother Constans. Thus in 351, immediately after Mursa, Constantius not only regrouped to continue fighting, but also immediately summoned a council at Sirmium to work out a creed that would be acceptable to both eastern and western bishops. It failed to do so, but the mere attempt tells us a lot about Constantius's priorities. Again in 353, while Paul the Chain was hunting down rebels, Constantius was calling a church council at Arelate to compel recalcitrant western Nicenes to subscribe to the creed of Sirmium. Some, like Hilarius, bishop of Pictavium (Poitiers), refused and were sent into exile; others conformed with ill grace. The credal controversies of the reign were far from over.

In the east, meanwhile, Constantius's paranoia was being fed by the behaviour of the caesar Gallus, whose appointment the emperor had swiftly come to regret. Constantius could not bear the thought of his caesar exercising actual power – he and the emperor's sister Constantina were meant to represent the dynasty, not act for it. But Gallus got a taste of actual responsibility in 352, when an abortive rising in favour of Magnentius by someone named Orphitus needed to be put down. He also suppressed a Jewish revolt in the same year. Then, in 353, Gallus collided with the eastern administrators Constantius had appointed, and the officials got the better of him. Ammianus makes much of Gallus's oppressiveness and irascibility, and it is clear that Gallus did in fact order the execution of a *bouletes*, or town councillor, of Alexandria, and that the order was carried out by Clematius, the *comes Orientis*, the eastern official equivalent to *vicarii* elsewhere in the empire. Clematius was reprimanded by the eastern praetorian prefect Thalassius, who reported directly to Constantius. Gallus already resented Thalassius, but now they fell out completely. The caesar tried to stir up the Antiochene mob against the civilian administration, insinuating that the provincial governor Theophilus was hoarding grain. Food shortages were an unfortunate but constant feature of Roman urban life, and never failed to bring mobs into the streets. Theophilus was duly lynched and Thalassius demanded that the emperor bring Gallus to heel.

When the prefect died suddenly, of natural causes, Gallus thought he had won, but he underestimated his imperial cousin's anger. Constantius sent Gallus a new prefect, Domitianus, carrying letters of reprimand that summoned the caesar back to court to answer for his conduct. Units of the *scholae palatinae* accompanied Domitianus, to serve as the caesar's escort. Gallus defied the order and there was a stand-off for much of 354, while Constantius campaigned across the Rhine from a base at Rauracum (now Augst, near Basel). Then, when Domitianus again tried to enforce the imperial orders, Gallus had his personal guardsmen kill the prefect. The senior *magister militum* in the east, Ursicinus, was then ordered to seize Gallus and deliver him to the western court. Constantina went ahead of them, hoping to calm her brother's fury, but she died of natural causes somewhere en route. Gallus dragged his heels on the long westward journey, lingering at Constantinople to watch the chariot races, doing so from Constantius's seats in the imperial box. With that presumption, he signed his own death warrant.

In autumn 354, having traversed the great military highway of the Balkans through Naissus, Siscia and Sirmium to Histria, he was arrested by his own guard captain, Barbatio, and stripped of the imperial robes that marked him as caesar. From there he was shipped to Pola, tried by a tribunal headed by Constantius's *cubicularius* Eusebius and executed along with three friends who were accused of having corrupted him. The complexity of the corporate government that is revealed in the Gallus episode reminds us that it was Constantius who completed the transformation of the imperial bureaucracy into a fully-formed state apparatus, building upon the innovations of his father and the tetrarchs. Equally noteworthy is the role of the *cubicularius* Eusebius in Gallus's trial. *Cubicularii* were heads of the emperor's household staff, but their proximity to the imperial person meant they would be entrusted with many other sensitive tasks. It was Eusebius who had concealed Constantine's will to Constantius's advantage, and he served his emperor throughout the latter's lifetime. *Cubicularii* were frequently eunuchs, as Eusebius was, and, because the emasculation of Roman citizens was banned, eunuchs were almost always foreigners, mainly from Persia or the Caucasus. That lent them a sinister air that would linger over the office of *cubicularius* even when it was not held by a eunuch, and it is part of the reason that Eusebius was as hated a member of Constantius's inner circle as Paul the Chain.

With Gallus dead, his associates had to be investigated, and Paul was again given the commission. Constantius himself spent the winter of 355 in Mediolanum and he is not attested outside of northern Italy again until the following year. While in Mediolanum, and no doubt anxious about developments on the Persian front, he found something else to worry about in Gaul. There, in 355, the *magister militum per Gallias*, a man named Silvanus, is said to have seized the purple. In fact, this so-called usurpation was no such thing, but rather a tragic deception, cooked up by rival factions in the palatine administration. Silvanus, like Ammianus Marcellinus among many others, had prospered as a young man because of his family's imperial service: his father, Bonitus, had served Constantine in the wars against Licinius and, again like Ammianus, Silvanus had begun his career young, we may presume in the corps of the *protectores domestici*. As his career flourished, he built up a network of support among the palatine and military administrations. From Ammianus, we have a very good general sense of how these fourth-century political networks worked, as a series of regional factions, with alliances threaded across the empire and its near frontiers, men from different groups favouring others from their own region and reaching out to build alliances in other regional networks. Even as we concentrate on the person and actions of the emperor, it is the background rumble of such factional rivalries that explains much of late imperial history. The case of Silvanus, which is so well known only because Ammianus took part in it personally, can stand as an example of how palatine factionalism claimed its victims.

What appears to have happened is this: Silvanus was still a relatively junior officer when Magnentius's coup presented him with an opportunity for promotion. In that, he was similar to a great many other Gallic and Frankish men in the western establishment who found themselves neglected by the Balkan regime of Constans. A tribune of a guard unit, Silvanus had cannily switched sides just before the bloodbath at Mursa, and as a reward he was promoted after the Constantian victory to the rank of *magister peditum per Gallias*. That made him the senior military commander in Gaul, taking charge of the western military establishment from his residence at Colonia Agrippina. Constantius was no fool. In choosing Silvanus, he reckoned on the fact that the Gallic establishment would respond better to one of its own than to someone who had marched west with Constantius. But that meant promoting Silvanus over the heads of Constantius's own more trusted supporters, and military men are sensitive to slights over rank and precedence.

Constantius's *magister equitum* Arbitio immediately began plotting against Silvanus, knowing just how easy it was to prey upon Constantius's paranoia. He suborned a junior officer name Dynamius to request a letter of reference from Silvanus; having done so, Dynamius erased the letter's contents, but kept the signature, and then redrafted it to suggest that Silvanus was plotting rebellion. Constantius's praetorian prefect at the time was C. Ceionius Rufius Volusianus *signo* Lampadius, a privileged member of the Italian aristocracy and an ally of Arbitio's (the *signum*, or nickname by which a man chose to be called, is a characteristic affectation of fourth-century aristocrats). Lampadius received the forged letter in confidence and presented it privately to the emperor, who became enraged and summoned his *consistorium*. There, in the presence of his senior officials, he denounced Silvanus and the conspirators named in Dynamius's forged letter, but two of the guard tribunes, Malarichus and Mallobaudes, both of them Franci, protested loudly that something was amiss, causing the emperor to stay his hand for a time. During that pause, Dynamius produced a second forged letter in which he tried to implicate Malarichus, and to insinuate that a Frankish court faction was plotting against the emperor. Malarichus learned what was going on, brought the forgery to the emperor's attention, and a commission of enquiry was empanelled to get to the bottom of the affair. It rapidly discovered that the letters were forgeries and Dynamius was duly punished. But what happened in Gaul was worse.

Because Ammianus was complicit in Gallic events, he had every reason to keep the ugly truth under wraps and so he peddles the official version at face value, contradictory and implausible as it is. According to our author, Apodemius, the same *agens in rebus* who had brought the news of Gallus's execution back to Constantius, was sent to Gaul to summon Silvanus to answer charges, but instead spread the word that the *magister militum* had already been condemned to death. Hearing that grim news – and believing it, given the emperor's personality – Silvanus proclaimed himself emperor. Now in open revolt, he awaited the arrival of the emperor's representative, his high-ranking peer Ursicinus, on whose staff Ammianus was serving. Ursicinus's orders were to suppress Silvanus, and that is what he did. The two generals commiserated, to be sure, both lamenting the fate of good men like themselves under an emperor such as Constantius. But that did not stop Ursicinus from doing his job: on Easter Sunday, when the pious Silvanus was leaving church and suspected nothing, Ursicinus's guard of *protectores*, Ammianus among them, set upon him and cut him down as a usurper.

Except he was not and the story is a lie. Silvanus may never have lifted a sword in anger against Constantius, and it is certain that he never seized the purple. There are no coins. The first thing a usurper always did was to strike coins in his own name: the most ephemeral emperors of the third century are known to us solely through their coinage, and even short-lived fourth-century pretenders like Domitius Alexander (311) or Nepotianus (350) have left a relative profusion of coins for the modern numismatist to ponder. For Silvanus, there is nothing, and it will not do to protest that being based at Colonia Agrippina he had no access to a mint in the few weeks of a short reign – the region had seen a profusion of irregular *Notmünzen* (as the Germans succinctly call unofficial emergency coinage) during the dying days of the Magnentian regime, the mint at Trier was close by, and makeshift mints had been available to every other usurper in late Roman history. Silvanus cannot have been uniquely handicapped in this respect, which means he never proclaimed himself Augustus. On the contrary, he was murdered by a crack force of imperial guardsmen, led by one of the emperor's most successful generals, and he was murdered because once the rumours about him had reached a certain pitch, it no longer mattered whether they were true: an emperor like Constantius would condemn a man for such charges, even if he knew them to be false, *pour décourager les autres*. Even so, that sort of emperor would not feel safe. Distance, jealousy, ambition were incubators for usurpation, and though both Gallus and Silvanus had been false alarms, at some point a real threat would arise. So, despite the precedent of Gallus, Constantius turned once again to a relative.

18

CONSTANTIUS, JULIAN AND THE EMPIRE TO COME

·───···───·

While Paul the Chain investigated the intimates of Silvanus and some Alamanni seized the opportunity to attack Colonia Agrippina, Constantius remained in Italy. There, at Mediolanum on 6 November 355, he elevated his sole remaining male relative – his cousin Julian, half-brother of the late Gallus, to the rank of caesar.

We last met Julian at Nicomedia, in 337, after the summer of blood. There, he would later remember, he enjoyed an idyllic boyhood in the care of the eunuch Mardonius, before an unwelcome transfer to the supervision of bishop George of Cappadocia, who kept him under the equivalent of house arrest on the large imperial estate of Macellum. It was not until 348 that Julian was set free and left to his own devices. These took him to Constantinople, where he studied with the pagans Nicocles and Themistius, the latter a very important figure in the reigns of four emperors, and the Christian Hecebolius; then to Pergamon, to learn from the philosopher Aedesius, an heir to the neo-Pythagorean sage Iamblichus; and finally to Athens, where the theurgist Maximus became his spiritual guide. It would later emerge that, over time, Julian had abandoned the Christian faith of his hated uncle Constantine and instead embraced a vivid and highly baroque form of traditional pagan ritualism. This he blended with an esoteric and heterogeneous stew of third-century mysticism and theosophism. In 355, he kept this profound conversion experience, and the anti-Christian fervour that accompanied it, deeply buried. Rather than the pagan zealot he would prove, Julian seemed like a somewhat wayward intellectual, unkempt and argumentative in the usual manner, but also the last surviving member of the dynasty on whom Constantius might perhaps rely – though the senior emperor did so with some reluctance, and even then only at the urging of his wife Eusebia.

In the end, Constantius summoned Julian from his studies at Athens and made him caesar at Mediolanum. After a month together, Constantius escorted Julian from the city and entrusted him with the care of Gaul. Like Gallus, Julian was expected to be a figurehead, and his officials would not be of his own choosing but of Constantius's alone. Unlike Gallus, he would be given some opportunity to act his part and learn to command an army, of which he had no experience, but only under the watchful eye of men the augustus trusted more than him. While Eusebia gave him a copy of Caesar's *Gallic War* to educate him about the lands to which he was heading, Constantius went so far as to write out in his own hand a memo documenting the subordinate position he expected his cousin to maintain. He permitted only one of Julian's intimate friends, and only four of his old servants, to accompany him – everyone else was a creature of Constantius. In time, as Julian became ever more successful, these restraints would poison relations between the two emperors, but in 355 the Roman world appeared to be at peace.

That being the case, Constantius turned once again to the enforcement of his doctrinal views. The refusal of many western bishops to sign up to the creed of Sirmium had been a source of maddening frustration to the emperor for a couple of years, but now, in 355, he had *agentes in rebus* out bullying bishops into adherence. The bishop of Rome, Liberius – not yet a 'pope' or head of the western church in the way his successors would become – was summoned to a personal audience with the emperor at Mediolanum, where he was browbeaten for his resistance to the acts of Sirmium. Liberius was a powerful figure in the city of Rome and also the first Roman bishop to articulate fully the idea that his place as the putative successor of the apostle Peter gave him particular claims to moral authority. Constantius had him exiled in 355.

More or less simultaneously, Athanasius of Alexandria was deposed and exiled for the umpteenth time, Constantius correctly perceiving him to be the figurehead of empire-wide resistance to the homoian creed of Sirmium. Constantius was willing to harass but not to execute church leaders, and he seems genuinely not to have understood why so few of those he wished to have cooperate with him were willing to do so. Compounding Constantius's frustration was the public and evident care he took to be a good Christian emperor – in some ways a better one than his father, though he could never replicate the latter's status as the deliverer of Christians from persecution. And yet Constantius tried. Early in 356 he promulgated an edict making sacrifice to the images of pagan gods a capital offence and, though he allowed pagan temples to remain standing and temple priests to maintain their properties, they could no longer carry out any cult acts to their gods. Constantius also explicitly demanded that all Romans abstain from sacrifice. His clear intention was to put an end to traditional cultic practice altogether.

In 357, he made a triumphal visit to Rome to celebrate his victories in Persia and Julian's in Gaul, entering the city on 28 April. Waspish contemporaries carped that his only real successes had come in wars against his fellow Romans, but if the eastern wars had been inconclusive, Julian's victories in Gaul were real enough. The narrative in which Ammianus Marcellinus recounts Constantius's entry into Rome is one of the great set pieces of late Classical literature, and Ammianus, despite his intense dislike of the emperor, could not help but admire the control and self-possession with which Constantius conducted himself, every inch the figure of the aloof and distant lord of the world. While in Rome, the emperor had both the altar and the statue of Victoria removed from the senate house at Rome, a gesture for his fellow Christians and a sign that he would not have the business of the Roman state conducted in a place where sacrifice might still be offered. That this action met with very little protest is a signal of the surprising speed with which the imperial government, and imperial magistrates, were becoming Christian.

Although he did not yet know it, Constantius's edict was a direct blow to his cousin Julian, whose pagan philosophical beliefs had continued to develop in Gaul. His fortunes had prospered as well, as he laid the groundwork for a massive campaign into Alamannia. In summer 356, Julian accompanied an army led by Constantius's generals Marcellus and Ursicinus and invaded Alamannia via Germania Prima, re-enforcing Colonia Agrippina en route. The army then retired to winter quarters, dispersed throughout northern Gaul, rather than base itself at a major imperial residence like Trier – it may be that the damage done by the civil war against Magnentius was such that a campaign army could not have been kept supplied in a single location. Julian wintered with his guard troops at Senonia, deep in the north Gallic interior, and nowhere near its military or administrative nerve centres. This may have been Julian's choosing to wilfully defy his cousin's generals, or else they may have been trying to keep him away from places where he might recruit sympathisers among soldiers and bureaucrats. One way or another, it was courting disaster, for the whole of northern Gaul remained insecure – the civil war had denuded its garrisons and Silvanus had not been given much of a chance to restore order on the frontiers. As a result, Julian found himself besieged in Senonia by a large Frankish war band, and had to hold out for several months behind the city walls. Julian blamed Ursicinus and Marcellus and convinced Constantius to replace them with a much less powerful figure, the *magister equitum* Severus.

But rather than allowing him to deal with the Franci, Constantius ordered Julian to carry out the invasion of Alamannia that had been planned since Julian became caesar. Severus, with Julian in tow, advanced across the Rhine into Alamannic territory, while Constantius's senior *magister peditum*, Barbatio, crossed the upper Danube in Raetia Secunda. The two armies, however, failed to make their planned rendezvous, Julian having stopped to win some minor engagements in the Rhineland rather than listening to Severus and executing the plan as intended. Barbatio withdrew from Alamannia as a result and, though Ammianus suggests he did so deliberately to endanger Julian, it showed good strategic sense once the Roman pincer movement had failed. Seeing that, the Alamannic king Chnodomarius turned on Julian and met him at Argentoratum (modern Strasbourg), where Julian found himself vastly outnumbered – supposedly 13,000 to 35,000, though the latter number is undoubtedly inflated. That the Roman triumph was total is a reminder of how rarely barbarian armies could win an open battle against a well-disciplined Roman force: Julian disposed his men on a narrow front, harassing the Alamannic infantry with his cavalry before launching an infantry advance that broke the Alamannic line and led to their total rout.

We say that Julian did this because the sources, not least his own account, tell us so. It is perhaps more likely that old Severus had done much of the actual planning, but after the victory Constantius began to allow Julian more latitude, even supporting the caesar against his own praetorian prefect in a dispute over whether to levy an extraordinary tax to cover a shortfall in 357. Seemingly to his own surprise, Constantius was finding Julian a useful partner. Though as augustus he properly took credit for the Gallic victories in his Roman triumph, he no longer felt obliged to police Julian as closely as he had once done. The latter overwintered in Lutetia (modern Paris), again demonstrating his preference for the interior provinces of the Lugdunenses over the traditional administrative centres in the Rhineland. By now he was almost certainly beginning to plot against his cousin, and the victory at Argentoratum had given him a new hold on his troops' personal loyalty. An easy victory in Francia, more a show of arms and a training exercise than a campaign, followed in 358, further cementing those bonds.

As yet, however, Constantius had no inkling of his cousin's evolving plans – or indeed of his secret paganism and continued interest in theurgy – and he had other problems to worry about. The Persian front was again unsettled as Shapur prepared for another assault on Roman territory, while Constantius's relationship with fractious western bishops had worsened still further. Latin churchmen had decisively rejected continued Greek hair-splitting over the terminology of *ousia* (or *substantia* in Latin), insisting that nothing could improve upon Nicaea. But Constantius remained insistent that all churchmen subscribe to an identical creed, even though he had finally learned that bringing eastern and western bishops together in a single council was not just pointless but actively counterproductive. He therefore determined to hold two councils, one at Ariminum (Rimini) in northern Italy and the other at Seleucia-on-the-Calycadnus (modern Silifke in southern Turkey), then the most important city in Isauria. The creed Constantius offered at Ariminum was presented by a trusted bishop from the Balkans, Valens of Mursa, and left out controversial words like *substantia*. Despite that, the Balkan bishops were much distrusted by their Italian and Gallic counterparts: they were too close to the emperor, doing his bidding rather than demonstrating proper episcopal independence. The westerners duly rejected the creed of Ariminum, reaffirmed the sufficiency of Nicaea alone, and excommunicated Valens and two of his supporters. Constantius himself was far away, off beyond the Danube fighting the Sarmatians, and the western bishops who travelled to Sirmium to inform him of the council's decision were forced to wait there for several months.

During this time, the other western bishops were detained at Ariminum by imperial troops, forbidden to return to their sees, which made a mockery of Constantius's supposed efforts at compromise. In the short term, however, the heavy-handedness seemed to pay off. Without reference to their fellow bishops back at Ariminum, those waiting at Sirmium for Constantius to return revoked the excommunications and accepted the creed of Ariminum, if only to allow themselves to go home. Constantius thus never met with the bishops who had come from the western council, instead taking the highway back to Constantinople as soon as his campaigns were finished. There he was met by not one but two delegations from the council at Seleucia in Isauria, which had failed as comprehensively as Ariminum had done. One faction, led by Basil, the powerful bishop of Ancyra in central Anatolia, insisted on a creed that not only discussed the fraught term *ousia* but did so in a way that could easily be described as neo-Arian. The imperial creed, sponsored in Latin by Valens of Mursa, had been pushed at Seleucia by Acacius of Caesarea, and both sides were so intransigent that they demanded adjudication by Constantius himself. Late in December 359, Constantius met in person with the competing delegations and extracted from Basil's party adherence to the creed of Ariminum. Early in 360, he summoned another council, to Constantinople, to proclaim the creed of Ariminum as the uniform creed of the empire. For the first time there was little demur and fewer than the usual number of exiles, but the sham consensus would not outlive the emperor, and the ripples of this theological controversy will occupy us time and again in the sequel to this volume.

While Constantius had been in Sarmatia, Julian had continued to fight on the Gallic frontier. Winter 358–9 was again spent in Lutetia, and at the start of the next campaigning season he crossed the Rhine at Moguntiacum (Mainz), inflicting a major defeat on several Alamannic kings and publicising their surrender widely. This self-promotion was more than Constantius, as suspicious as ever, could bear. He recalled Julian's most trusted officials, particularly his *quaestor sacri palatii* Salutius Secundus, and instead sent him a new set of court advisers – the hated Paul the Chain and two others, Pentadius and Gaudentius, the former of whom had been active in the downfall of Gallus in 354. This provocation led Julian from cautious ambition to open revolt. Constantius's young caesar timed his coup well. Had he acted any sooner, Constantius would have been free to leave the eastern provinces unattended and crush his errant relation. By 359, Persia was once again a problem.

Despite periodic blustering on both sides in the earlier 350s, the decisive war threatened by both Roman and Persian rulers had never materialised, largely because of disruptions on the distant Central Asian edge of Shapur II's empire. These were the result of huge changes to the dynamic of the empire still further east, in the Hexi corridor of north-western China, which we will consider at some length in the sequel to this volume. Broadly speaking, they represented far-ranging military actions on the part of various steppe nomads all claiming descent from the Xiongnu (or Huns). In the 350s, neither the Persians nor the Romans had any idea of what was going on in eastern Eurasia, but Shapur was kept occupied on his eastern frontier for much of the 350s. By 358, however, the most immediate challenges had been suppressed, and at least one Hunnic clan had allied itself to Shapur as his clients. The shahanshah immediately began to muster a campaign army to make good on earlier plans to attack the Roman frontier and retake long-disputed territories. Negotiations occupied much of 359, but Shapur refused to give up his demand that Constantius surrender the eastern Roman provinces to him. It is now, for the first time, that we have good evidence for a Sasanian ruler actually claiming to be the successor of the Achaemenids Darius and Xerxes and using the extent of Darius's empire as a justification for his demands.

Constantius reappointed Ursicinus to high command as *magister equitum*, placing him in charge of the preparations to meet the invasion. We know a great deal about this campaign because Ammianus Marcellinus took part in it and expounds in detail the hardships faced in the Persian siege of Amida. It is clear that the Roman field army had not been properly deployed when the invasion began, because Ursicinus himself was almost taken in an ambush by the Persian cavalry while inspecting some frontier defences. As so often, however, the great cities of Mesopotamia proved capable of stopping a Persian army in its tracks, when the garrison at Amida killed the son of Shapur's royal client Grumbates – a king of the 'Chionitae', according to Ammianus, though we cannot be sure which Hunnic clan he commanded – against whom Shapur had until recently been campaigning. To satisfy Grumbates, Shapur consented to a full-scale siege of the city, in the winter of 359–60, and the ability of the Amidan garrison to hold off the besiegers for a couple of months forced Shapur to withdraw and prepare another attack for the following year.

Julian would have known of the problems on the Persian front almost as soon as they began – a close friend of his, a philosopher named Eustathius with whom he had once studied at Pergamon, was part of the embassy that failed to avert the Persian invasion. Then, in February or March 360, while still in winter quarters at Lutetia, Julian received an order from Constantius demanding a levy of western troops to assist with the Persian campaign, and not a light one either: four entire infantry units and 300 men from every other unit in the Gallic army. It was a reasonable request, given the scale of the threat Constantius faced, but Julian used it as an excuse for his own imperial proclamation. This he had clearly planned in advance: for the first time since he went to Gaul, he had assigned units of the field army winter quarters at Lutetia, and not merely his own guardsmen. Julian would always claim, as was traditional, that he accepted the rank of augustus with deep reluctance and in response to his soldiers' spontaneous demand. But the fact that the whole Gallic army supported his move suggests that it had been prepared well before units had settled into their winter quarters, and that selected officers had been at work over the winter plotting the coup. Two elite units, the Celtae and the Petulantes, were the first to acclaim Julian Augustus at Lutetia, but the rest of the Gallic army fell into line at once.

Julian must have realised that Constantius's reaction would be hostile, but he did not immediately press the issue, instead bloodying his troops in punitive razzias through Francia. Constantius was cautious, too. He received an embassy from his cousin, which suggested that Julian should be augustus in the west but remain a mere caesar in the east – a proposal the emperor rejected, demanding that Julian renounce the title of augustus and content himself with caesar. By Constantian standards, it was a moderate reaction, but there was little more he could do because of the Persian situation.

Deprived as he had been of western levies, Constantius could not launch a counteroffensive against Shapur, whose armies took Singara and Bezabde on the extreme edge of Roman territory in summer 360 and razed the former city. In winter 360–61, Roman armies retook Bezabde, but there was no avoiding a full-scale war with the shahanshah. The question was when it would come, given that now civil war loomed, too. In November 360, Julian celebrated his *quinquennalia* at Vienna (modern Vienne in France), the capital of the important province of Viennensis. He did so in the full garb of an augustus and also minted coins with that title, knowing full well that Constantius would find that intolerable. The latter wintered at Edessa, vacillating between a Persian and a civil conflict.

In early 361 Julian mobilised his army, ostensibly for another raid into

Alamannia. There he captured a king named Vadomarius, known to be a personal client of Constantius, who – Julian now claimed – had ordered Vadomarius to attack Julian. This *casus belli* was undoubtedly spurious, but it was all Julian needed. He marched along the Danube into the Balkans in high summer, transhipping part of his force downriver in advance, and taking all the major cities as far as Sirmium by the end of summer. Nevitta, his *magister equitum* and most trusted general, took the main land route through Raetia and Noricum, down the Sava, into the central Balkans.

The plan was to occupy the western part of Illyricum and meet any advance by Constantius there, while sending a few units into Italy across the Julian Alps to seize the North Italian plain. Strategically it was an excellent plan, save that two of these units rebelled en route to Italy, suborned by agents of Constantius, and took up position in the stronghold of Aquileia. Julian might now face a war on two fronts, or have his supply lines to the loyal Gallic provinces cut off. He therefore halted at Sirmium to await events, while some of the units he had left behind in Gaul marched into northern Italy and occupied the garrison cities there. Julian occupied himself with composing letters to the public of the eastern cities, justifying his actions and accusing Constantius of all sorts of villainy. That left Constantius no choice but to leave the eastern front to its fate and deal with his rebel cousin. In October 361, he set out westwards at the head of his army, but he made it only as far as Cilicia when sickness overtook him. He died on 3 November and, in an act of great statesmanship, he named Julian his legitimate successor on his deathbed. There would be no rival proclamations, and Julian could inaugurate his sole reign as the last emperor of Constantine's dynasty.

The death of Constantius marks the end of this book's narrative, a hinge on which late imperial history turns. Constantius had more than anything else cemented the structural strengths, and political dynamics, of his father's revolutionary reign. After the tetrarchic experiments had rendered permanent the ad hoc experimentation of the third century, and brought to its culmination the gradual process of equestrianisation on which we have spent so much time, Constantine institutionalised a new, more expansive, more intrusive and more complex state than the Roman world had ever known. The long and surprisingly stable reign of Constantius ensured that there would be no counter-revolution, and that the bureaucratic state of the earlier fourth century would go from strength to strength in the decades to come. In religion, too, Constantius made permanent his father's legacy. Though Julian – famous to posterity as Julian the Apostate – attempted to unmake the imperial Christianity that his relatives had embraced and increasingly enforced, he could only imagine an anti-Christian empire and not a meaningful return to the religious landscape of the pre-Constantinian era. That he died very soon after his accession to sole rule meant, if anything, the further entrenchment of a Christian political and ecclesiastical establishment as the very heart of imperial legitimacy.

Julian, though a strangely bitter man, was also a starry-eyed idealist. His immediate impulse upon succeeding his cousin was a massive invasion of Persia that went disastrously wrong. The aftermath, which saw the imperial campaign army having to extract itself at great cost from enemy territory, showed how remarkably powerful the military high command, the palatine bureaus and the establishments of praetorian prefects had become: the later fourth century is a great age of collective government, regional and bureaucratic oligarchies tussling with one another while ensuring that those who became emperor – Jovian, Valentinian and Valens, and Theodosius – were junior officers unable to impose their will on events even when they were individually competent and authoritative. Other seeds planted in the reigns of Constantine and Constantius bore fruit in the course of the later fourth century. The ideological, political and economic power of the Christian church, the entrenchment of its priestly hierarchy, and its ever greater patterning on the geographies of the Roman state were all far advanced by the century's end, as too was a growing body of canon law meant to guide and bind Christian believers.

East and west diverged in this, as in many things, with Greek and Latin Christianity revealing ever more fundamental differences of thought and habit that have never been bridged since. The eastern and western empires became politically and economically more distinct from the 360s onwards as well. The growing dominance of Constantinople to the life of the Greek world is part of the story, but so too is the eastern empire's control of a source of new gold in the Caucasus to which the western empire had no access. One consequence of that was of tremendous significance:

the ruling elite of the east was far more closely bound to the structures of the imperial state, which monopolised the currency supply, than was the western elite, where society's uppermost strata could get along, if pressed, without much help from the structures of government. That, more than anything, explains the generation-long collapse of western imperial government in the middle of the fifth century, while the eastern government was left essentially unscathed. It also helps explain why the western empire was less able than the eastern to cope with changes to the much wider Eurasian landscape – a brief but consequential few decades in which various Xiongnu or Hun empires remade political boundaries from China to India to central Europe.

Two hundred and fifty years ago, Edward Gibbon began his story of Rome's decline and fall more or less where we began ours, in what he saw as a golden age of the Antonine emperors. So captivated was he by his tale of the 'barbarism and religion' that brought down the empire that he carried his narrative forward to the conquest of Constantinople by the Ottoman Mehmet II, over a millennium later. All of us who write on the later Roman empire, or more broadly on the cultural world of what we now call Late Antiquity, tread in Gibbon's footsteps and in the shadow of his intellect, his prose and his ambition. But no one today would attempt to match his scope. This volume and the one that follows cover a very specific set of stages in the journey from the early Roman empire to a Greek Roman empire in the east standing alongside a post-imperial west. We have moved from an empire ruled by Romans to an empire filled with Romans, and from a Rome whose horizons were those of a somewhat expanded Classical Mediterranean world to a Rome that was one of Eurasia's four great civilisations in an era of archaic globalisation.

The Roman empire of later Late Antiquity, which we will look at in our next volume, was unrecognisably different from the Roman empire of Hadrian, but it was recognisably heir to the empire Constantine had remade on the foundations laid first by Severus and then Diocletian – who could, strange though it is realise, at least imagine himself restoring a pristine Roman past that Hadrian would have recognised. We need not decide here the extent to which that vision corresponded to reality, any more than we need decide, in the next volume, how much the successors of Constantius and Julian knew that the empire they were slowly remaking was a product of Constantine and his revolutionary reign. Their ideas and their actions are story enough.

THE ROMAN EMPERORS FROM AUGUSTUS TO JULIAN

(omitting usurpers)

Augustus, r. 27 BC–AD 14

Tiberius, r. 14–37

Gaius (Caligula), r. 37–41

Claudius, r. 41–54

Nero, r. 54–68

Galba, r. 68–9

Otho, r. 69

Vitellius, r. 69

Vespasian, r. 69–79

Titus, r. 79–81

Domitian, r. 81–96

Nerva, r. 96–8

Trajan, r. 98–117

Hadrian, r. 117–38

Antoninus Pius, r. 138–61

Marcus Aurelius, r. 161–80

Lucius Verus, r. 161–9

Commodus, r. 177–92

Pertinax, r. 193

Didius Julianus, r. 193

Septimius Severus, r. 193–211

Caracalla, r. 198–217

Geta, r. 210–11

Macrinus, r. 217–18 (caesar
    Diadumenianus, r. 217–18)

Elagabalus, r. 218–22

Severus Alexander, r. 222–35

Maximinus 1, r. 235–8 (caesar Maximus,
    r. 236–8)

Gordian I, r. 238

Gordian II, r. 238

Pupienus and Balbinus, r. 238

Gordian III, r. 238–44

Philip I, r. 244–8 (co-augustus Philip II,
    r. 247–9)

Trajan Decius, r. 248–51 (co-augustus
    Herennius Etruscus, r. 251, caesar
    Hostilianus, r. 251)

Trebonianus Gallus, r. 251–3 (co-augustus
    Volusianus, r. 251–3)

Aemilianus, r. 253

Valerian, r. 253–60

Gallienus, r. 253–68 (co-augustus
    Saloninus, r. 260)

Claudius, r. 268–70

Quintillus, r. 270

Aurelian, r. 270–75

Tacitus, r. 275–6

Florianus, r. 276

Probus, r. 276–82

Carus, r. 282–3

Carinus, r. 282–5

Numerian, r. 283–4

Diocletian, r. 284–305

Maximian, r. 285–305; usurper 306–8, 310

Constantius I, r. 293–306

Galerius, r. 293–311

Severus II, r. 305–7

Constantine I, r. 306–37

Maximinus II, r. 305–13

Licinius, r. 308–24 (co-augustus Valens, r. 316–17)

Constantinus (Constantine II), r. 337–40

Constantius II, r. 337–61

Constans, r. 337–50

Julian, r. 361–3

PERSIAN KINGS FROM ARDASHIR TO SHAPUR II

⁂

Ardashir I, r. 222–42
Shapur I, r. 240–72
Ohrmazd I, r. 272–3
Varahran I, r. 273–6
Varahran II, r. 276–93
Varahran III, r. 293
Narseh, r. 293–302
Ohrmazd II, r. 302–9/10
Shapur II, r. 309–79

FURTHER READING

Original Literary Sources

Almost the whole canon of Graeco-Roman authors is available in the Loeb Classical Library, with facing page English translation. Readers should seek out recent copies of the relevant texts, which have with few exceptions been updated (and generally much improved) over their early twentieth-century originals. The Loeb series is less comprehensive from the late third century onwards, and includes very few Christian authors. Liverpool University Press's Translated Texts for Historians series fills many of those gaps with excellent annotated translations. Two other series, Fathers of the Church and Ancient Christian Writers, can also be consulted: translations in the latter series are almost uniformly good; those in the former are very variable. Coins are an essential primary source for Roman imperial history, and the basic reference remains the ten volumes of the Roman Imperial Coinage (London, 1923–). Alternatively, the research page of the Classical Numismatic Group's website (http://www.cngcoins.com) has colour illustrations of all but the very rarest coin types from antiquity.

Reference

There are two basic reference works that anyone really interested in Roman history should have on hand: the third and best edition of the *Oxford Classical Dictionary* (Oxford, 1996) and *The Barrington Atlas of the Greek and Roman World* (Princeton, 2000), edited by Richard Talbert and breathtaking in its coverage, its detail and the beauty of its maps.

General Histories

Many textbooks cover our period, though their intended classroom audience tends to render them rather lifeless. Much the best of these, aimed at American undergraduates, is Mary T. Boatwright, Daniel Gargola, Noel Lenski and Richard Talbert, *The Romans from Village to Empire* (2nd ed., New York, 2011). More entertaining are Mary Beard, *SPQR: A History of Ancient Rome* (London, 2015), which covers social history more comprehensively than the present book but ends with Caracalla, and Greg Woolf, *Rome: An Empire's Story* (Oxford, 2012). The old Fontana history of the ancient world, which the present series replaces, included a number of classic surveys, and Colin Wells, *The Roman Empire* (2nd ed., London, 1995) remains well worth reading. Giant handbooks, hypertrophied companions and diffuse dictionaries have proliferated in the past decade, as scholarly publishers chase library sales. I have counted more than forty that treat one or another aspect or author of our period (and I've missed some, I'm certain), and, while almost all include essays of real value, almost all are variable in quality and patchy in coverage – reader discretion is advised.

David Potter, *The Roman Empire at Bay, AD 180–395* (London, 2004) has excellent annotation and good coverage of intellectual and cultural history. Much of the really good work on the third-century empire continues to be published in French and German: there is, for example, no English equivalent to Michel Christol's wonderful *L'empire romain du IIIe siècle* (Paris, 1997). For the period after Diocletian, the foundational work remains (and always will remain) A. H. M. Jones, *The Later Roman Empire, 284–602* (4 vols., Oxford, 1964; 2 vols., Oxford, 1973). Several scholarly generations have been amazed and inspired by Peter Brown, *The World of Late Antiquity* (London, 1971), which remains magically compelling almost half a century on.

Primary and Secondary Reading by Period

From Hadrian to the Death of Commodus

The primary sources for this period are few. The *Historia Augusta* (available in the Loeb series under the title *Scriptores Historiae Augustae*) is a collection of imperial biographies from Hadrian to Carus and Carinus, compiled by a single author in the late fourth century, but purporting to be an early fourth-century collection written by six authors. For the legitimate augusti between Hadrian and Caracalla, it reproduces quite faithfully the work of a third-century biographer now lost. But its lives of caesars and usurpers are worthless, as is almost everything in it after Caracalla. The history of Cassius Dio (also in the Loeb series) is essential for this period, even where it is preserved only in fragments. Fourth-century abbreviated histories (the *Breviarium* of Eutropius, the *De Caesaribus* of Aurelius Victor, both in the Liverpool series) supply some basic information as well.

The period is rich in other non-historical literature, however (Aulus Gellius in Latin; Arrian, Athenaeus, Galen and others in Greek, many available in Loebs). For introductions to this Antonine cultural world, see: C. P. Jones, *The Roman World of Dio Chrysostom* (Cambridge, 1978); Leofranc Holford-Strevens, *Aulus Gellius: An Antonine Scholar and His Achievement* (revised edn., Oxford, 2005); D. A. Russell, ed., *Antonine Literature* (Oxford, 1990); and David Braund and John Wilkins, eds., *Athenaeus and His World* (Exeter, 2000). For the Greek rhetorical and philosophical movement known as the Second Sophistic, see: Glen W. Bowersock, *Greek Sophists in the Roman Empire* (Oxford, 1969); Graham Anderson, *Philostratus* (London, 1986) and E. Bowie and Jas Elsner, eds., *Philostratus* (Cambridge, 2009), for the thinker who coined the phrase; and Graham Anderson, *The Second Sophistic* (London, 1993) on the whole phenomenon. For imperial Roman art, which can be difficult to write about interestingly, see Jaś Elsner, *Imperial Rome and Christian Triumph* (Oxford, 1998), a triumph of exposition and analysis, and very accessible.

On the imperial governance and bureaucracy, Andrew Lintott, *Imperium Romanum:*

Politics and Administration (London, 1993) is the most readable introduction. The role of the emperor is still best treated in Fergus Millar, *The Emperor in the Roman World* (Ithaca, 1977), though nowadays scholars see the emperors as somewhat more interventionist and less reactive in their style of rulership than this classic study argues. The ideology of the period's ruling elite is sensitively probed in J. E. Lendon, *Empire of Honour* (Oxford, 1998), while the senate can be studied in exhaustive detail through Richard J. A. Talbert, *The Senate of Imperial Rome* (Princeton, 1984).

For Roman money, see David L. Vagi, *Coinage and History of the Roman Empire*, 2 vols. (Sidney, OH, 1999) – although aimed at the coin collector, not the historian or numismatist, it is probably the simplest and most accessible introduction to this important type of evidence. More scholarly, though still accessible, is Andrew Burnett, *Coinage in the Roman World* (London, 1987) and the numerous specialist studies listed in the bibliography.

For political history, imperial biography remains an attractive approach though not necessarily a fashionable one. There are several excellent biographies for this period, particularly Anthony R. Birley, *Hadrian: The Restless Emperor* (London, 1997) and the same author's *Marcus Aurelius* (2nd ed., New Haven, 1987). Olivier Hekster, *Commodus: An Emperor at the Crossroads* (Amsterdam, 2002) is provocative but not always convincing. Thorsten Opper, *Hadrian: Empire and Conflict* (Cambridge, MA, 2008) is a well-rounded introduction with superbly chosen illustrations.

On social and economic history, Peter Garnsey and Richard Saller, *The Roman Empire: Economy, Society, and Culture* (Berkeley, 1987) is showing its age but remains very readable and the best introduction overall. Walter Scheidel, Ian Morris and Richard Saller, eds., *The Cambridge Economic History of the Greco-Roman World* (Cambridge, 2007) is variable but up to date. For the Antonine plague and its impact, see essays in Elio Lo Cascio, ed., *L'impatto della 'peste antonina'* (Bari, 2012), a few of them in English. For the army before Gallienus, see: Roy Davies, *Service in the Roman Army* (New York, 1989); Hugh Elton, *Frontiers of the Roman Empire* (London, 1996); Ian Haynes, *Blood of the Provinces: The Roman Auxilia and the Making of Provincial Society from Augustus to the Severans* (Oxford, 2013), a superb book with a silly title; and Graham Webster, *The Roman Imperial Army* (3rd ed., New York, 1985). J. E. Lendon, *Soldiers and Ghosts: A History of Battle in Classical Antiquity* (New Haven, 2005) is an allusive and provocative study of ancient psychology and warfare; it bears careful reading, even if not all its conclusions are persuasive.

Provincial and regional studies that can appeal to a non-specialist audience include, on the eastern provinces: Warwick Ball, *Rome in the East: The Transformation of an Empire* (London, 2000); Simon Goldhill, ed., *Being Greek under Rome: Cultural Identity, the Second Sophistic and the Development of Empire* (Cambridge, 2001); William Horbury, *Jewish War under Trajan and Hadrian* (Cambridge, 2014); Benjamin Isaac, *The Limits of Empire: The Roman Army in the East.* (revised ed., Oxford, 1992); and Fergus Millar, *The Roman Near East, 31 BC–AD 337* (Cambridge, MA, 1993). On the western provinces, see the not very readable but important David Cherry, *Frontier and Society in Roman North Africa* (Oxford, 1998) and Greg Woolf, *Becoming Roman: The Origins of Provincial Civilization in Gaul* (Cambridge, 1998), much the best book ever written in English on the phenomenon of 'Romanisation'.

From the Death of Commodus to the Death of Maximinus I

The main primary sources for this period are Herodian and Cassius Dio, both available in Loeb translations. On Dio, see Fergus Millar, *A Study of Cassius Dio* (Oxford, 1964). There is an important collection of primary sources in Olivier Hekster, *Rome and Its Empire, AD 193–284* (Edinburgh, 2008). There are fewer imperial biographies for this period, but see Anthony R. Birley, *Septimius Severus: The African Emperor* (2nd ed., New Haven, 1988). The works of economic, military and provincial history noted in section 1 continue to be relevant here. For the literature of the period, see Simon Swain, Stephen Harrison and Jas Elsner, eds., *Severan Culture* (Cambridge, 2007). For law, see Tony Honoré, *Emperors and Lawyers* (2nd ed., Oxford, 1994) and *Ulpian: Pioneer of Human Rights* (2nd ed., Oxford, 2002), although the first editions of both books are sufficiently different to bear consideration in their own right.

On Eurasian developments, the literature is so vast and diverse that the following should be taken as a small sample. Edward A. Alpers, *The Indian Ocean in World History* (Oxford, 2014) is a good introductory summary. Rachel Mairs, *The Hellenistic Far East: Archaeology, Language, and Identity in Greek Central Asia* (Berkeley, 2014) and Grant Parker, *The Making of Roman India* (Cambridge, 2008) are more specialised, but fascinating. Steven E. Sidebotham, *Berenike and the Ancient Maritime Spice Route* (Berkeley, 2011) is much more accessible than its title suggests. There has been little reliable work in English on the Kushan empire since John M. Rosenfeld, *The Dynastic Arts of the Kushans* (Berkeley, 1967), but the historical introduction to David Jongeward and Joe Cribb, *Kushan, Kushano-Sasanian and Kidarite Coins: A Catalogue of the Coins from the American Numismatic Society* (New York, 2015) shows how far the field has progressed, mainly on the basis of new numismatic information. Vidula Jayaswal, ed., *Glory of the Kushans: Recent Discoveries and Interpretations* (New Delhi, 2012) is up to date but hard going. David Sinor, ed., *The Cambridge History of Early Inner Asia* (Cambridge, 1990) is now rather dated but is the most comprehensive introduction available. The two beautifully illustrated volumes of Christoph Baumer's *History of Central Asia* (London, 2012) can serve for orientation but are too eccentric to be relied on; briefer and less lavish, but more reliable is Barry Cunliffe, *By Steppe, Desert, and Ocean: The Birth of Eurasia* (New York, 2015). Nicola Di Cosmo, *Ancient China and Its Enemies: The Rise of Nomadic Power in East Asian History* (Cambridge, 2002) is far more relevant to our topic than the Chinese orientation would at first suggest.

On Sasanian Persia, D. T. Potts, ed., *The Oxford Handbook of Ancient Iran* (Oxford, 2013) is the best recent overview – the groundbreaking relevant volumes of the Cambridge History of Iran require updating. On Zoroastrianism, there remains a good annotated anthology of texts in Mary Boyce, *Textual Sources for the Study of Zoroastrianism* (Chicago, 1984). For the relationship between the empires, see the anthology of translations in Michael H. Dodgeon and Samuel N. C. Lieu, *The Roman Eastern Frontier and the Persian Wars* (London, 1991) and the more varied sources and commentary in Beate Dignas and Engelbert Winter, *Rome and Persia in Late Antiquity: Neighbours and Rivals* (Cambridge, 2007). Monographs of importance include Matthew P. Canepa, *The Two Eyes of the Earth: Art and Ritual of Kingship Between Rome and Sasanian Iran* (Berkeley, 2009), M. Rahm Shayegan, *Arsacids and Sasanians: Political Ideology in Post-Hellenistic and Late Antique Persia* (Cambridge, 2011) and Richard E. Payne, *A State of Mixture: Christians, Zoroastrians, and Iranian Political Culture in Late Antiquity* (Berkeley, 2015). David Stronach and Ali Mousavi, *Ancient Iran from the Air: Photographs by Georg Gerster* (Mainz, 2012) is beautifully evocative.

On the lands between the two empires, see: Peter M. Edwell, *Between Rome and Persia: The Middle Euphrates, Mesopotamia and Palmyra under Roman Control* (London, 2008); the magnificently illustrated David Kennedy and Derrick Riley, *Rome's Desert Frontier from the Air* (London, 1990); Andrew M. Smith, *Roman Palmyra: Identity, Community and State Formation* (Oxford, 2013). For Arabia, see: D. T. Potts, *The Arabian Gulf in Antiquity, Volume II: From Alexander the Great to the Coming of Islam* (Oxford, 1990); Greg Fisher, ed., *Arabs and Empires Before Islam* (Oxford, 2015), which aims for comprehensiveness.

For the world of the Black Sea and the European steppe, see: David Braund, *Georgia in Antiquity: A History of Colchis and Transcaucasian Iberia, 550 BC–AD 562* (Oxford, 1994); Roger Batty, *Rome and the Nomads: The Pontic-Danubian Realm in Antiquity* (Oxford, 2007). Ellis H. Minns, *Scythians and Greeks: A Survey of Ancient History and Archaeology on the North Coast of the Euxine from the Danube to the Caucasus* (Cambridge, 1913) is now more than a century old, but no similar survey has ever been attempted.

On the European barbarians, the works of E. A. Thompson, listed in the bibliography, were pathbreaking in their day, but now see John Drinkwater, *The Alamanni and Rome, 213–496* (Oxford, 2007), the finest history of Roman–barbarian relations ever published. My own *Rome's Gothic Wars from the Third Century to Alaric* (Cambridge, 2007) treats the Danubian and Black Sea barbarians and offers non-specialists an introduction to the methodological questions surrounding Roman–barbarian contact. Malcolm Todd, *The Early Germans* (Oxford, 1992) is very old-fashioned in its approach, but it is well illustrated and good on archaeology, while I. M. Ferris, *Enemies of Rome: Barbarians Through Roman Eyes* (Stroud, 2000) is exciting as well as illuminating on the image of the barbarian.

Maximinus I to the Death of Galerius

For the primary sources, see the anthology by Hekster in section 2, above. Our sources are very few, and for the political narrative we rely heavily on the fourth-century breviary histories (see section 1). A major polemical source for the tetrarchy is Lactantius's *De mortibus persecutorum* ('On the deaths of the persecutors'), which is available in the Oxford Early Christian Texts, translated by J. L. Creed (Oxford, 1984). The new fragments of Dexippus, one of the more important historical discoveries of recent decades, are translated and discussed in the works by Martin and Grusková, and by Mallan and Davenport, listed in the bibliography.

Unfortunately, the best single study of the fraught years between 235 and 238 remains a difficult German thesis: Karlheinz Dietz, *Senatus contra Principum: Untersuchungen zur senatorischen Opposition gegen Kaiser Maximinus Thrax* (Munich, 1980). Most biographies or studies of third-century emperors rely excessively and unacceptably upon the *Historia Augusta*. An exception in English is Lukas de Blois, *The Policy of the Emperor Gallienus* (Leiden, 1976), but good recent studies of individual emperors in German appear in the bibliography. Ronald Syme, perhaps the greatest Roman historian of the Anglophone twentieth century, devoted a disproportionate percentage of his huge output to that maddening text:

the third-century studies in his *Emperors and Biography: Studies in the Historia Augusta* (Oxford, 1971) isolate anything even remotely reliable that can be found in its pages.

Ramsay MacMullen, *Roman Government's Response to Crisis* (New Haven, 1976) was and remains controversial but essential reading on the period. Hendrik W. Dey, *The Aurelian Wall and the Refashioning of Imperial Rome, AD 271–855* (Cambridge, 2011) is usefully comprehensive in coverage and moderate in making big claims. On the tetrarchy, Jones's *Later Roman Empire* (introduction, above) got the basics absolutely right. A readable if very traditional biography is Stephen Williams, *Diocletian and the Roman Recovery* (New York, 1985). On the Carausius and Allectus episode, P. J. Casey's *Carausius and Allectus* (New Haven, 1993) remains a good study of the limited evidence. William Leadbetter, *Galerius and the Will of Diocletian* (London, 2009) makes as strong a case for the emperor as can be made. For the tetrarchic palaces, see J. J. Wilkes, *Diocletian's Palace, Split: Residence of a Retired Roman Emperor* (2nd ed., Exeter, 1996).

The coinage, in both its economic and its ideological aspects, looms large as a source for the third century. The most important studies are in French and German and are given in the bibliography, but see Erika Manders, *Coining Images of Power: Patterns in the Representation of Roman Emperors on Imperial Coinage, A.D. 193–284* (Leiden, 2012). The panegyric speeches on which we rely for insight into the tetrarchs' and Constantine's motives are translated with commentary in C. E. V. Nixon and Barbara Saylor Rodgers, *In Praise of Later Roman Emperors: The Panegyrici Latini* (Berkeley, 1994). For imperial rhetoric and its change over time, three difficult but essential books are: Averil Cameron, *Christianity and the Rhetoric of Empire* (Berkeley, 1991); Simon Corcoran, *The Empire of the Tetrarchs: Imperial Pronouncements and Government, AD 284–324* (2nd ed., Oxford, 2000); and John Dillon, *The Justice of Constantine: Law, Communication, and Control* (Ann Arbor, 2012). For frontier relations in late antiquity, A. D. Lee, *Information and Frontiers: Roman Foreign Relations in Late Antiquity* (Cambridge, 1993) remains pathbreaking.

On the spread of Christianity over the centuries there is no clear consensus, but see the essays in William V. Harris, ed., *The Spread of Christianity in the First Four Centuries: Essays in Explanation* (Leiden, 2005). Vastly differing views, all with real value, are expressed in Robin Lane Fox, *Pagans and Christians in the Mediterranean World from the Second Century AD to the Conversion of Constantine* (Harmondsworth, 1986), Keith Hopkins, *A World Full of Gods: The Strange Triumph of Christianity* (Harmondsworth, 1999) and T. D. Barnes, *Early Christian Hagiography and Roman History* (Tübingen, 2010). For a comprehensive if old-fashioned survey of church history, see Henry Chadwick, *The Church in Ancient Society from Galilee to Gregory the Great* (Oxford, 2002). For the role of philosophers in anti-Christian controversy, see Elizabeth DePalma Digeser, *A Threat to Public Piety: Christians, Platonists, and the Great Persecution* (Ithaca, 2012) and for philosophic culture more generally, G. R. Boys-Stones, *Post-Hellenistic Philosophy: A Study of Its Development from the Stoics to Origen* (Oxford, 2001). For monotheism among non-Christians, see Polymnia Athanassiadi and Michael Frede, eds., *Pagan Monotheism in Late Antiquity* (Oxford, 1999). For Manichees, see Samuel N. C. Lieu, *Manichaeism in the Later Roman Empire and Medieval China: A Historical Survey* (Manchester, 1985).

From the Second Tetrarchy to Julian

The primary source evidence gets significantly better at the very end of our period, from 353, when the surviving text of Ammianus Marcellinus becomes available. The Loeb translation is neither readable nor particularly reliable, while a good Penguin translation is abridged in unhelpful ways. My colleague Gavin Kelly and I are currently at work on a new and fully annotated translation of the complete text (to be published by Oxford University Press as *The Landmark Ammianus Marcellinus*). The fourth-century breviary histories (see section 1) are still important for the events of Constantine's reign, as is Lactantius (section 3). The history of the church written by Eusebius of Caesarea (available in Loeb and Penguin translations) provides some – often tendentious – information. Three documents relevant to Constantine's Christianity and generally attributed to him are translated by Mark Edwards as *Constantine and Christendom* (Liverpool, 2003). In the same Liverpool series there are volumes on the Donatist controversy (*Donatist Martyr Stories* and Optatus of Milevis, *Against the Donatists*).

The bibliography on Constantine is enormous and grows continuously, in every language, but biographical treatments should generally be avoided; Paul Stephenson, *Constantine: Roman Emperor, Christian Victor* (London, 2009) is a notable exception. T. D. Barnes, *Constantine and Eusebius* (Cambridge, MA, 1980) is essential if difficult reading, though his *Constantine: Dynasty, Religion and Power in the Later Roman Empire* (Maldon, 2011) is more polemical than necessary. Noel Lenski, ed., *The Cambridge Companion to the Age of Constantine* (Cambridge, 2005) includes a number of significant essays. Dillon's *Justice of Constantine* (section 3, above) is also relevant. The deeply tendentious life of the emperor written by Eusebius of Caesarea is expertly annotated in the fine translation of Averil Cameron and Stuart G. Hall, eds., *Eusebius: Life of Constantine* (Oxford, 1999), while shifting ancient views of Constantine can be traced in Samuel N. C. Lieu and Dominic Montserrat, eds., *From Constantine to Julian: Pagan and Byzantine Views* (London, 1998). See Nixon and Rodgers (section 3, above) for the panegyrics to Constantine.

For Constantius (a deeply unprepossessing character) and his adversary Athanasius (even worse), see T. D. Barnes, *Athanasius and Constantius* (Cambridge, MA, 1993). Julian's intellectual world is well captured by Polymnia Athanassiadi-Fowden, *Julian and Hellenism: An Intellectual Biography* (Oxford, 1981) and his life by G. W. Bowersock, *Julian the Apostate* (Cambridge, MA, 1978). Lendon's *Soldiers and Ghosts* (above, section 1) is excellent on Julian. The classic study of John Matthews, *The Roman Empire of Ammianus* (London, 1989) picks up just at the very end of our period.

For the integration of Christianity into Roman life, the best introduction is Gillian Clark, *Christianity and Roman Society* (Cambridge, 2004). See also Michele Renee Salzman, *The Making of a Christian Aristocracy* (Cambridge, MA, 2002). Brent D. Shaw, *Sacred Violence: African Christians and Sectarian Hatred in the Age of Augustine* (Cambridge, 2011) has revolutionised our understanding of religious thuggery. Economic change is provocatively discussed by Jairus Banaji, *Agrarian Change in Late Antiquity* (revised ed., Oxford, 2007); equally important is Chris Wickham, *Framing the Early Middle Ages* (Oxford, 2005), which sheds light on our period as well. The essays in Claude Brenot and Xavier Loriot, eds., *L'Or monnayé* (Paris, 1992) are essential reading. On the late Roman army, there is a dull but worthy introduction in M. J. Nicasie, *Twilight of Empire* (Amsterdam, 1998), while chapter 17 of Jones's *Later Roman Empire* (introduction, above) on the army is still essentially unsurpassed.

BIBLIOGRAPHY

❦

The works below are the secondary literature I made most use of while working on this book. The relevant primary sources are discussed in the notes on further reading with suggested translations; scholars will already know which critical editions are best consulted, and the *Oxford Classical Dictionary* should point the way on more obscure texts. As I wrote this book, my reading over the years may have come into play without my realising it: I apologise to anyone whose ideas I have absorbed and used without being conscious of it and whose work I have inadvertently omitted.

Absil, Michel. *Les préfets du prétoire d'Auguste à Commode, 2 avant Jésus-Christ-192 après Jésus-Christ*. Paris, 1997.

Alcock, Susan E. *Graecia Capta: The Landscapes of Roman Greece*. Cambridge, 1993.

Alföldi, Andreas. *Studien zur Geschichte der Weltkrise des 3. Jahrh. nach Christus*. Darmstadt, 1967.

Alföldy, Géza. *Konsulat und Senatorenstand unter den Antoninen*. Bonn, 1977.

Alpers, Edward A. *The Indian Ocean in World History*. Oxford, 2014.

Alram, Michael and D. E. Klimburg-Salter, eds. *Coins, Art and Chronology: Essays on the Pre-Islamic History of the Indo-Iranian Borderlands*. Vienna, 1999.

Alram, Michael, D. E. Klimburg-Salter, et al., eds. *Coins, Art and Chronology II: The First Millennium C.E. in the Indo-Iranian Borderlands*. Vienna, 2010.

Anderson, Graham. *The Second Sophistic*. London, 1993.

Ando, Clifford. *Imperial Ideology and Provincial Loyalty in the Roman Empire*. Berkeley, 2000.

Athanassiadi-Fowden, Polymnia. *Julian and Hellenism: An Intellectual Biography*. Oxford, 1981.

Athanassiadi, Polymnia and Michael Frede, eds. *Pagan Monotheism in Late Antiquity*. Oxford, 1999.

Ausbüttel, Frank M. *Die Verwaltung des römischen Kaiserreiches von der Herrschafts des Augustus bis zum Niedergang des weströmischen Reiches*. Darmstadt, 1998.

Austin, N. J. E. and N. B. Rankov. *Exploratio: Military and Political Intelligence in the Roman World from the Second Punic War to the Battle of Adrianople*. London, 1995.

Back, Michael. *Die sassanidischen Staatsinschriften* (Acta Iranica VIII). Leiden, 1978.

Bagnall, Roger S. *Egypt in Late Antiquity*. Princeton, 1993.

Bagnall, Roger S., ed. *Egypt in the Byzantine World, 200–700*. Cambridge, 2007.

Bagnall, Roger S., Alan Cameron, Serh R. Schwartz and K. A. Worp. *Consuls of the Later Roman Empire*. Atlanta, 1987.

Baldini, Antonio. *Storie perdute (III secolo d.C.)*. Bologna, 2000.

Ball, Warwick. *Rome in the East: The Transformation of an Empire*. London, 2000.

Banaji, Jairus. *Agrarian Change in Late Antiquity*. Revised ed., Oxford, 2007.

Bang, Martin. *Die Germanen im römischen Dienst bis zum Regierungsantritt Constantins I*. Berlin, 1906.

Barbieri, G. *L'albo senatoriale da Settimio Severo a Carino (193–285)*. Rome, 1952.

Barceló, Pedro A. *Roms auswärtige Beziehungen unter den Constantinischen Dynastie (306–363)*. Regensburg, 1981.

Barnes, T. D. *Constantine and Eusebius*. Cambridge, MA, 1981.

Barnes, T. D. *The New Empire of Diocletian and Constantine*. Cambridge, MA, 1982.

Barnes, T. D. *Athanasius and Constantius*. Cambridge, MA, 1993.

Barnes, T. D. *Early Christian Hagiography and Roman History*. Tübingen, 2010.

Barnes, T. D. *Constantine: Dynasty, Religion and Power in the Later Roman Empire*. Maldon, 2011.

Batty, Roger. *Rome and the Nomads: The Pontic-Danubian Realm in Antiquity*. Oxford, 2007.

Baumer, Christoph. *The History of Central Asia, Volume One: The Age of the Steppe Warriors*. London, 2012.

Baumer, Christoph. *The History of Central Asia, Volume Two: The Age of the Silk Road*. London, 2012.

Behrwald, Ralf and Christian Witschel, eds. *Rom in der Spätantike: Historische Erinnerung im städtischen Raum*. Stuttgart, 2012.

Bell, H. I., et al., eds.. *The Abinnaeus Archive: Papers of a Roman Officer in the Reign of Constantius II*. Oxford, 1962.

Bemmann, Jan and Michael Schmauder, eds. *Complexity of Interaction Along the Eurasian Steppe Zone in the First Millennium CE*. Bonn, 2015.

Birley, Anthony R. *Marcus Aurelius*. 2nd ed., New Haven, 1987.

Birley, Anthony R. *Septimius Severus: The African Emperor*. 2nd ed., New Haven, 1988.

Birley, Anthony R. *Hadrian: The Restless Emperor*. London, 1997.

Bleckmann, Bruno. *Die Reichskrise des III. Jahrhunderts in der spätantiken und byzantinischen Geschichtsschreibung: Untersuchungen zu den nachdionischen Quellen der Chronik des Johannes Zonaras*. Munich, 1992.

Bowersock, G. W. *Julian the Apostate*. Cambridge, MA, 1978.

Bowersock, G. W. *Hellenism in Late Antiquity*. Ann Arbor, 1990.

Boyce, Mary. *Textual Sources for the Study of Zoroastrianism*. Chicago, 1984.

Boys-Stones, G. R. *Post-Hellenistic Philosophy: A Study of Its Development from the Stoics to Origen*. Oxford, 2001.

Braund, David C. *Rome and the Friendly King: The Character of Client Kingship*. London, 1984.

Braund, David, ed. *The Administration of the Roman Empire, 241 BC–AD 193*. Exeter, 1988.

Braund, David. *Georgia in Antiquity: A History of Colchis and Transcaucasian Iberia, 550 BC–AD 562*. Oxford, 1994.

Brenot, Claude and Xavier Loriot. *L'Or monnayé* (Cahiers Ernest-Babelon). Paris, 1992.

Breyer, Francis. *Das Königreich Aksum: Geschichte und Archäologie Abessiniens in der Spätantike*. Mainz, 2012.

Brown, Peter. *Power and Persuasion in Late Antiquity: Towards a Christian Empire*. Madison, WI, 1992.

Brunt, P. A. *Roman Imperial Themes*. Oxford, 1990.

Bruun, Patrick. *Studies in Constantinian Numismatics: Papers from 1954–1988* (Acta Instituti Romani Finlandiae 12). Rome, 1991.

Burgess, R. W. 'The date of the persecution of Christians in the army', *Journal of Theological Studies* n.s. 47 (1996): 157–8.

Burgess, R. W. *Studies in Eusebian and Post-Eusebian Chronography* (Historia Einzelschriften 135). Stuttgart, 1999.

Burgess, R. W. 'The summer of blood: The "Great Massacre" of 337 and the promotion of the sons of Constantine', *Dumbarton Oaks Papers* 62 (2008): 5–51.

Burnett, Andrew. *Coinage in the Roman World*. London, 1987.

Bursche, Aleksander. 'The battle of Abritus, the imperial treasury and aurei in Barbaricum', *Numismatic Chronicle* 173 (2013): 150–70, with Plates 32–37.

Caldelli, Maria Letizia and Gian Luca Gregori. *Epigrafia e Ordine Senatorio, 30 Anni Dopo* 2 vols. (TITVLI 10). Rome, 2014.

Callu, J.-P. *La politique monétaire des empereurs romains de 238 à 311*. Paris, 1969.

Callu, J.-P. *La monnaie dans l'antiquité tardive: Trente-quatre études de 1972 à 2002*. Bari, 2010.

Cameron, Alan. *The Last Pagans of Rome*. Oxford, 2010.

Cameron, Averil. *Christianity and the Rhetoric of Empire*. Berkeley, 1991.

Cameron, Averil and Stuart G. Hall, eds. *Eusebius: Life of Constantine*. Oxford, 1999.

Canepa, Matthew P. *The Two Eyes of the Earth: Art and Ritual of Kingship Between Rome and Sasanian Iran*. Berkeley, 2009.

Carlà, Filippo. *L'oro nella tarda antichità: aspetti economici e sociali*. Turin, 2009.

Casey. P. J. *Carausius and Allectus: The British Usurpers*. New Haven, 1994.

Chadwick, Henry. *The Church in Ancient Society from Galilee to Gregory the Great*. Oxford, 2002.

Chastagnol, André. *La préfecture urbaine à Rome sous le Bas-Empire*. Paris, 1960.

Chastagnol, André. *Les fastes de la préfecture de Rome au Bas-Empire*. Paris, 1962.

Chaumont, Marie-Louise. *Recherches sur l'histoire d'Arménie de l'avènement des Sassanides à la conversion du royaume*. Paris, 1969.

Cherry, David. *Frontier and Society in Roman North Africa*. Oxford, 1998.

Christensen, Arthur. *L'Iran sous les Sassanides*. 2nd ed., Copenhagen, 1944.

Christol, Michel. *Essai sur l'évolution des carrières sénatoriales dans la 2e moitié du IIIe s. ap. J.-C.* Paris, 1986.

Christol, Michel. *L'empire romain du IIIe siècle*. Paris, 1997.

Clark, Gillian. *Christianity and Roman Society*. Cambridge, 2004.

Clauss, Manfred. *Der magister officiorum in der Spätantike (4–6. Jahrhundert)*. Munich, 1981.

Corbier, Mireille. *L'aerarium saturni et l'aerarium militare*. Paris, 1974.

Corcoran, Simon. *The Empire of the Tetrarchs: Imperial Pronouncements and Government, AD 284–324*. 2nd ed., Oxford, 2000.

Corcoran, Simon and Benet Salway. '*Fragmenta Londiniensia Anteiustiniana*: preliminary observations', *Roman Legal Tradition* 8 (2012): 63–83 http://romanlegaltradition.org/contents/2012/

Creighton, J. D. and R. J. A. Wilson, eds. *Roman Germany: Studies in Cultural Interaction*. Portsmouth, RI, 1999.

Crook, J. A. *Consilium Principis: Imperial Councils and Counsellors from Augustus to Diocletian*. Cambridge, 1955.

Cunliffe, Barry. *By Steppe, Desert, and Ocean: The Birth of Eurasia*. New York, 2015.

Dabrowa, Edward, ed. *Ancient Iran and the Mediterranean World: Studies in Ancient History*. Krakow, 1998.

Dagron, Gilbert. *Naissance d'une capitale: Constantinople et ses institutions de 330 à 451*. Paris, 1974.

Dauge, Yves Albert. *Le Barbare: Recherches sur la conception romaine de la barbarie et de la civilisation*. Brussels, 1981.

Davies, Roy. *Service in the Roman Army*. David Breeze and Valerie Maxfield, eds. New York, 1989.

De Blois, Lukas. *The Policy of the Emperor Gallienus*. Leiden, 1976.

Degrassi, A. *I fasti consolari dell'impero romano*. Rome: Storia e Letteratura, 1952.

De Laet, Siegfried. *Portorium: Étude sur l'organisation douanière chez le romains, surtout à l'époque du Haut-Empire*. Bruges, 1949.

Delbrueck, Richard. *Spätantike Kaiserporträts von Constantinus Magnus bis zum Ende des Westreichs*. 2 vols. Berlin, 1933.

Delmaire, Roland. *Largesses sacrées et Res Privata: L'aerarium impérial et son administration du IVe au VIe siècle*. Rome, 1989.

Delmaire, Roland. *Les responsables des finances impériales au Bas-Empire romain (Ive-VIe s.)*. Brussels, 1989.

Demandt, Alexander. *Die Spätantike: Römische Geschichte von Diocletian bis Justinian 284–565 n. Chr.* (Handbuch der Altertumswissenschaft III.6). Munich, 1989.

Demandt, Alexander, Andreas Goltz and Heinrich Schlange-Schöningen, eds. *Diokletian und die Tetrarchie: Aspekte einer Zeitenwende*. Berlin, 2004.

d'Escurac, Henriette Pavis. *La préfecture de l'annone, service administratif impérial, d'Auguste à Constantin*. Paris, 1976.

Devijner, Hubert. *The Equestrian Officers of the Roman Imperial Army*. Amsterdam, 1989.

Dey, Hendrik W. *The Aurelian Wall and the Refashioning of Imperial Rome, AD 271–855*. Cambridge, 2011.

Dietz, Karlheinz. *Senatus contra Principum: Untersuchungen zur senatorischen Opposition gegen Kaiser Maximinus Thrax*. Munich, 1980.

Digeser, Elizabeth DePalma. *A Threat to Public Piety: Christians, Platonists and the Great Persecution*. Ithaca, 2012.

Dignas, Beate and Engelbert Winter. *Rome and Persia in Late Antiquity: Neighbours and Rivals*. Cambridge, 2007.

Dillon, John. *The Justice of Constantine: Law, Communication, and Control*. Ann Arbor, 2012.

Dittrich, Ursula-Barbara. *Die Beziehungen Roms zu den Sarmaten und Quaden im vierten Jahrhundert n. Chr.* Bonn, 1984.

Dobson, Brian. *Die Primipilares: Entwicklung und Bedeutung, Laufbahnen und Persönlichkeiten eines römischen Offizierranges*. Bonn, 1978.

Dodgeon, Michael H. and Samuel N. C. Lieu. *The Roman Eastern Frontier and the Persian Wars*. London, 1991.

Donciu, Ramiro. *L'empereur Maxence*. Bari, 2012.

Dörries, Hermann. *Das Selbstzeugnis Kaiser Konstantins*. Göttingen, 1954.

Drijvers, Jan Willem. 'Ammianus Marcellinus 30.7.2–3: Observations on the career of Gratianus Maior', *Historia* 64 (2015): 479–86.

Drinkwater, John. *The Gallic Empire: Separatism and Continuity in the North-western Provinces of the Roman Empire, AD 260–274*. Wiesbaden, 1987.

Drinkwater, John. *The Alamanni and Rome, 213–496*. Oxford, 2007.

Duncan-Jones, Richard. *Structure and Scale in the Roman Economy*. Cambridge, 1990.

Edwell, Peter M. *Between Rome and Persia: The Middle Euphrates, Mesopotamia and Palmyra under Roman Control*. London, 2008.

Eich, Peter. *Zur Metamorphose des politischen Systems in der römischen Kaiserzeit. Die Entstehung einer "personalen Bürokratie" im langen dritten Jahrhundert*. Berlin, 2005.

Elsner, Jaś. *Imperial Rome and Christian Triumph*. Oxford, 1998.

Elton, Hugh. *Frontiers of the Roman Empire*. London, 1996.

Ensslin, Wilhelm. *Zur Ostpolitik des Kaisers Diokletian*. Munich, 1942.

Felix, Wolfgang. *Antike literarische Quellen zur Aussenpolitik des Sasanidenstaates, erster Band (224–309)*. Vienna, 1985.

Ferris, I. M. *Enemies of Rome: Barbarians Through Roman Eyes*. Stroud, 2000.

Fischer, Svante. *Roman Imperialism and Runic Literacy: The Westernization of Northern Europe (150–800 AD)*. Uppsala, 2006.

Fisher, Greg. *Between Empires: Arabs, Romans and Sasanians in Late Antiquity*. Oxford, 2011.

Fornasier, Jochen and Burkhard Böttger, eds. *Das Bosporanische Reich*. Mainz, 2002.

Frank, R. I. *Schola Palatinae: The Palace Guards of the Later Roman Empire*. Rome, 1969.

Frézouls, Edmond and Hélène Jouffroy, eds. *Les empereurs illyriens: Actes du colloque de Strasbourg (11–13 Octobre 1990)*. Strasbourg, 1998.

Gagé, J. *Recherches sur les jeux seculaires*. Paris, 1934.

Garnsey, Peter and Richard Saller. *The Roman Empire: Economy, Society, and Culture*. Berkeley, 1987.

Ghirshman, Roman. *Les Chionites-Hephtalites*. Cairo, 1948.

Gibbon, Edward. *The Decline and Fall of the Roman Empire*. D. Womersley, ed. 3 vols. London, 1994.

Göbl, Robert. *Dokumente zur Geschichte der iranischen Hunnen in Baktrien und Indien*. 4 vols. Wiesbaden, 1967.

Goffart, Walter. *Rome's Fall and After*. London, 1989.

Goffart, Walter. *Barbarian Tides*. Philadelphia, 2006.

Goldhill, Simon, ed. *Being Greek under Rome: Cultural Identity, the Second Sophistic and the Development of Empire*. Cambridge, 2001.

Goldsworthy, Adrian and Ian Haynes, eds. *The Roman Army as a Community*. Portsmouth, RI, 1999.

Grey, Cam. *Constructing Communities in the Late Roman Countryside*. Cambridge, 2011.

Grig, Lucy and Gavin Kelly, eds. *Two Romes: Rome and Constantinople in Late Antiquity*. New York, 2012.

Grosse, Robert. *Römische Militärgeschichte von Gallienus bis zum Beginn der byzantinischen Themenverfassung*. Berlin, 1920.

Gurukkal, Rajan and Dick Whittaker. 'In search of Muziris', *Journal of Roman Archaeology* 14 (2001): 335–50.

Haklai-Rotenberg, Merav. 'Aurelian's monetary reform: between debasement and public trust', *Chiron* 43 (2013): 1–39.

Halfmann, Helmut. *Itinera principum: Geschichte und Typologie der Kaiserreisen im römischen Reich*. Stuttgart, 1986.

Hall, Jonathan M. *Hellenicity: Between Ethnicity and Culture*. Chicago, 2002.

Hansen, Ulla Lund. *Römischer Import im Norden: Warenaustausch zwischen dem römischen Reiche und dem freien Germanien*. Copenhagen, 1987.

Harl, Kenneth W. *Coinage in the Roman Economy, 300 BC to AD 700*. Baltimore, 1996.

Harper, Kyle. 'Pandemics and passages to late antiquity: Rethinking the plague of c. 249–70 described by Cyprian', *Journal of Roman Archaeology* 28 (2015): 223–60.

Harris, William V. *Rome's Imperial Economy: Twelve Essays*. New York, 2011.

Haptbroek, Johannes. *Untersuchungen zur Geschichte des Kaisers Septimius Severus*. Heidelberg, 1921.

Haynes, Ian. *Blood of the Provinces: The Roman Auxilia and the Making of Provincial Society from Augustus to the Severans*. Oxford, 2013.

Heather, Peter. *Goths and Romans, 332–489*. Oxford, 1991.

Hedeager, Lotte. *Iron-Age Societies: From Tribe to State in Northern Europe, 500 BC–700 AD*. John Hines, trans. Oxford, 1992.

Hekster, Olivier. *Commodus: An Emperor at the Crossroads*. Amsterdam, 2002.

Hekster, Olivier. *Rome and Its Empire, AD 193–284*. Edinburgh, 2008.

Hirschfeld, Otto. *Die kaiserlichen Verwaltungsbeamten bis auf Diocletian*. Berlin, 1905.

Hodgson, N. 'The abandonment of Antonine Scotland: Its date and causes', in W. S. Hanson, ed., *The Army and Frontiers of Rome: Papers Offered to David J. Breeze*. Portsmouth, RI, 2009, 186–93.

Honoré, Tony. *Emperors and Lawyers*. 2nd ed. Oxford, 1994.

Honoré, Tony. *Ulpian: Pioneer of Human Rights*. 2nd ed. Oxford, 2002.

Hopkins, Keith. *Conquerors and Slaves* (Sociological Studies in Roman History 1). Cambridge, 1978.

Hopkins, Keith. *Death and Renewal* (Sociological Studies in Roman History 2). Cambridge, 1983.

Hopkins, Keith. *A World Full of Gods: The Strange Triumph of Christianity*. Harmondsworth, 1999.

Horbury, William. *Jewish War under Trajan and Hadrian*. Cambridge, 2014.

Howe, L. L. *The Pretorian Prefect from Commodus to Diocletian*. Chicago, 1942.

Isaac, Benjamin. *The Limits of Empire: The Roman Army in the East*. Revised ed. Oxford, 1992.

Jacques, François. *Le privilège de liberté: Politique imperiale et autonomie municipale dans les cités de l'Occident romain (161–244)*. Paris, 1984.

Janiszewski, Pawel. *The Missing Link: Greek Pagan Historiography in the Second Half of the Third Century and in the Fourth Century AD*. Warsaw, 2006.

Jayaswal, Vidula, ed. *Glory of the Kushans: Recent Discoveries and Interpretations*. New Delhi, 2012.

Johne, Klaus-Petcr, ed. *Die Zeit der Soldatenkaiser*. 2 vols. Berlin, 2008.

Johnson, Aaron P. *Religion and Identity in Porphyry of Tyre: The Limits of Hellenism in Late Antiquity*. Cambridge, 2013.

Johnson, Scott Fitzgerald, ed. *The Oxford Handbook of Late Antiquity*. New York, 2012.

Jones, A. H. M. *The Later Roman Empire, 284–602*. 4 vols. Oxford, 1964.

Jones, C. P. *The Roman World of Dio Chrysostom*. Cambridge, 1978.

Jongeward, David and Joe Cribb. *Kushan, Kushano-Sasanian and Kidarite Coins: A Catalogue of the Coins from the American Numismatic Society*. New York, 2015.

Katsari, Constantina. *The Roman Monetary System: The Eastern Provinces from the First to the Third Century AD*. Cambridge, 2011.

Kennedy, David, ed. *The Roman Army in the East*. Ann Arbor, 1996.

Kennedy, David and Derrick Riley. *Rome's Desert Frontier from the Air*. London, 1990.

Keyes, Clinton Walker. *The Rise of the Equites in the Third Century of the Roman Empire*. Princeton, 1915.

Khazanov, A. M. *Nomads and the Outside World*. Cambridge, 1984.

Kienast, Dietmar. *Römische Kaisertabelle: Grundzüge einer römischen Kaiserchronologie*. 2nd ed. Darmstadt, 1996.

Kim, Hyun Jin. *The Huns, Rome and the Birth of Europe*. Cambridge, 2013.

King, Anthony and Martin Henig, eds. *The Roman West in the Third Century*. 2 vols. Oxford, 1981.

Kolb, Frank. *Diocletian und die erste Tetrarchie: Improvisation oder Experiment in der Organisation monarchischer Herrschaft?* Berlin, 1987.

Kolendo, Jerzy. 'Plat avec réprésentation du cirque lors des jeux séculaires de Philippe l'Arabe', *Bayerische Vorgeschichtsblätter* 50 (1985): 463–74.

König, Ingemar. *Die gallischen Usurpatoren von Postumus bis Tetricus*. Munich, 1981.

Körner, Christian. *Philippus Arabs: Ein Soldatenkaiser in der Tradition des antoninisch-severischen Prinzipats*. Berlin, 2002.

Kuhlmann, Peter Alois. *Die Giessener literarischen Papyri und die Caracalla-Erlasse: Edition, Übersetzung und Kommentar*. Giessen, 1994.

Lambrechts, Pierre. *La composition du sénat romain de l'accession au trône d'Hadrien à la mort de Commode (117–192)*. Antwerp, 1936.

Lambrechts, Pierre. *La composition du sénat romain de Septime Sévère a Dioclétien (193–284)*. Budapest, 1937.

Lane Fox, Robin. *Pagans and Christians in the Mediterranean World from the Second Century AD to the Conversion of Constantine*. Harmondsworth, 1986.

Leadbetter, William. *Galerius and the Will of Diocletian*. London, 2009.

Lee, A. D. *Information and Frontiers: Roman Foreign Relations in Late Antiquity*. Cambridge, 1993.

Lendon, J. E. *Empire of Honour*. Oxford, 1998.

Lendon, J. E. *Soldiers and Ghosts: A History of Battle in Classical Antiquity*. New Haven, 2005.

Lenski, Noel, ed. *The Cambridge Companion to the Age of Constantine*. Cambridge, 2005.

Lepper, Frank and Sheppard Frere. *Trajan's Column: A New Edition of the Cichorius Plates, Introduction, Commentary and Notes*. Gloucester, 1988.

Leppin, Hartmut. *Von Constantin dem Grossen zu Theodosius II: Das christliche Kaisertum bei den Kirchenhistorikern Socrates, Sozomenus und Theoderet*. Göttingen, 1995

Leunissen, Paul M. M. *Konsuln und Konsulare in der Zeit von Commodus bis Severus Alexander (180–235 n. Chr.)*. Amsterdam, 1989.

Lieu, Samuel N. C. *Manichaeism in the Later Roman Empire and Medieval China. A Historical Survey*. Manchester, 1985.

Lieu, Samuel N. C. and Dominic Montserrat, eds. *From Constantine to Julian: Pagan and Byzantine Views*. London, 1998.

Lieu, Samuel N. C. and Dominic Montserrat, eds. *Constantine: History, Historiography and Legend*. London, 1998.

Lintott, Andrew. *Imperium Romanum: Politics and Administration*. London, 1993.

Lo Cascio, Elio, ed. *L'impatto della 'peste antonina'*. Bari, 2012.

Löhken, Henrik. *Ordines dignitatum: Untersuchungen zur formalen Konstituierung der spätantiken Führungsschicht*. Cologne, 1982.

L'Orange, H. P. *Studien zur Geschichte des spätantiken Porträts*. Oslo, 1933.

MacDonald, David. *An Introduction to the History and Coinage of the Kingdom of the Bosporus*. Lancaster, PA, 2005.

MacMullen, Ramsay. *Soldier and Civilian in the Later Roman Empire*. Cambridge, 1963.

MacMullen, Ramsay. *Roman Government's Response to Crisis*. New Haven, 1976.

MacMullen, Ramsay. *Paganism in the Roman Empire*. New Haven, 1981.

MacMullen, Ramsay. *Christianizing the Roman Empire, AD 100–400*. New Haven, 1984.

Madsen, Jesper Majbom. *Eager to be Roman: Greek Response to Roman Rule in Pontus and Bithynia*. London, 2009.

Maenchen-Helfen, Otto J. *The World of the Huns: Studies in Their History and Culture*. Berkeley, 1970.

Magie, David. *Roman Rule in Asia Minor*. 2 vols. Princeton, 1950.

Mairs, Rachel. *The Hellenistic Far East: Archaeology, Language, and Identity in Greek Central Asia*. Berkeley, 2014.

Mallan, Christopher and Caillan Davenport, 'Dexippus and the Gothic invasions: interpreting the new Vienna Fragment (*Codex Vindobonensis Hist. gr.* 73, ff. 192v–193r)', *Journal of Roman Studies* 105 (2015): 203–26.

Manders, Erika. *Coining Images of Power: Patterns in the Representation of Roman Emperors on Imperial Coinage, AD 193–284*. Leiden, 2012.

Markwart, Josef. *Wehrot und Arang: Untersuchungen zur mythischen und geschichtlichen Landeskunde von Ostiran*. Leiden, 1938.

Martin, Gunther and Jana Grusková. "'Dexippus Vindobonensis". Ein neues Handschriftenfragment zum sog. Herulereinfall der Jahre 267/268', *Wiener Studien* 127 (2014): 101–20.

Martin, Gunther and Jana Grusková. "'Scythica Vindobonensia" by Dexippus(?): New fragments on Decius' Gothic wars', *Greek, Roman, and Byzantine Studies* 54 (2014): 728–54.

Matthews, John. *The Roman Empire of Ammianus*. Baltimore, 1989.

Mattingly, David J. *Tripolitania*. Ann Arbor, 1994.

Maurice, Jules. *Numismatique Constantinienne*. 3 vols. Paris, 1908.

Mazza, Mario. *Lotte sociali e restaurazione autoritaria nel terza secolo d. C.* Catania, 1970.

Mazzarino, Santo. *Il basso impero: Antico, tardoantico ed èra costantiniana*. 2 vols. Bari, 1974.

McCormick, Michael. *Origins of the European Economy: Communications and Commerce, AD 300–900*. Cambridge, 2001.

McGill, Scott, Cristiana Sogno and Edward Watts, eds. *From the Tetrarchs to the Theodosians: Later Roman History and Culture, 284–450 CE* (Yale Classical Studies 34). Cambridge, 2010.

McGovern, William Montgomery. *The Early Empires of Central Asia: A Study of the Scythians and the Huns and the Part They Played in World History with Special Reference to the Chinese Sources*. Chapel Hill, 1939.

Mecela, Laura. *Dexippo di Atene: Testimonianze e frammenti*. Rome, 2013.

Mennen, Inge. *Power and Status in the Roman Empire, AD 193–284* (Impact of Empire Volume 12). Leiden, 2011.

Meslin, Michel. *Les Ariens d'Occident, 335–430*. Paris, 1967.

Mickwitz, Gunnar. *Geld und Wirtschaft im römischen Reich des vierten Jahrhunderts n. Chr.* Helsingfors, 1932.

Migl, Joachim. *Die Ordnung der Ämter: Prätorianerpräfektur und Vikariat in der Regionalverwaltung des römischen Reiches von Konstantin bis zur Valentinianischen Dynastie*. Frankfurt, 1994.

Miles, Richard, ed. *Constructing Identities in Late Antiquity*. London, 1999.

Millar, Fergus. *A Study of Cassius Dio*. Oxford, 1964.

Millar, Fergus. *The Emperor in the Roman World*. Ithaca, 1977.

Millar, Fergus. *The Roman Empire and Its Neighbours*. 2nd ed., London, 1981.

Millar, Fergus. *The Roman Near East, 31 BC–AD 337*. Cambridge, MA, 1993.

Minns, Ellis H. *Scythians and Greeks: A Survey of Ancient History and Archaeology on the North Coast of the Euxine from the Danube to the Caucasus*. Cambridge, 1913.

Mitchell, Stephen. *Anatolia: Land, Men, and Gods in Asia Minor. Volume I: The Celts and the Impact of Roman Rule*. Oxford, 1993.

Mitchell, Stephen. *Anatolia: Land, Men, and Gods in Asia Minor. Volume II: The Rise of the Church*. Oxford, 1993.

Modéran, Yves. *Les Maures et l'Afrique romaine (iv-e–vii-e siècle)*. Paris, 2003.

Nelson, Bradley R. *Numismatic Art of Persia. The Sunrise Collection Part I: Ancient – 650 BC–AD 650*. Lancaster, PA, 2011.

Neri, Valerio. *Medius princeps: Storia e immagine di Costantino nella storiografia latina pagana*. Bologna, 1992.

Nicasie, M. J. *Twilight of Empire*. Amsterdam, 1998.

Nixon, C. E. V. and Barbara Saylor Rodgers. *In Praise of Later Roman Emperors: The Panegyrici Latini*. Berkeley, 1994.

Okon, Danuta. *Septimius Severus et Senatores: Septimius Severus' Personal Policy Towards Senators in the Light of Prosopographic Research*. Szczecin, 2012.

Opper, Thorsten. *Hadrian: Empire and Conflict*. Cambridge, MA, 2008.

Palanque, J. R. *Essai sur la préfecture du prétoire du Bas-Empire*. Paris, 1933.

Parker, Grant. *The Making of Roman India*. Cambridge, 2008.

Parker, H. M. D. *The Roman Legions*. 2nd ed., London, 1957.

Paschoud, François and Joachim Szidat, eds. *Usurpationen in der Spätantike* (Historia Einzelschriften 111). Stuttgart, 1997.

Passerini, Alfredo. *Le coorti pretorie*. Rome, 1939.

Payne, Richard E. *A State of Mixture: Christians, Zoroastrians, and Iranian Political Culture in Late Antiquity*. Berkeley, 2015.

Peachin, Michael. *Iudex vice Caesaris: Deputy Emperors and the Administration of Justice During the Principate*. Stuttgart, 1996.

Perea Yébenes, Sabino. *La Legión XII y el prodigio de la lluvia en época del emperador Marco Aurelio/ Epigrafía de la Legión XII Fulminata*. Madrid, 2002.

Peter, Hermann. *Wahrheit und Kunst*. Leipzig, 1911.

Pfisterer, Matthias. *Hunnen in Indien: Die Münzen der Kidariten und Alchan aus dem Bernischen Historischen Museum und der Sammlung Jean-Pierre Righetti*. Vienna, 2012.

Pflaum, H.-G. *Les procurateurs équestres sous le Haut-Empire romain*. Paris, 1950.

Pflaum, H.-G. *Les carrières procuratoriennes équestres sous le Haut-Empire romain*. 4 vols. Paris, 1960–61.

Pietri, Charles. *Roma Christiana*. 2 vols. Paris, 1976.

Plass, Paul. *Wit and the Writing of History: The Rhetoric of Historiography in Imperial Rome*. Madison, 1988.

Pohl, Walter, ed. *Kingdoms of the Empire: The Integration of Barbarians in Late Antiquity*. Leiden, 1998.

Pohl, Walter and Gerda Heydemann, eds. *Strategies of Identification: Ethnicity and Religion in Early Medieval Europe*. Turnhout, 2013.

Pohl, Walter and Helmut Reimitz, eds. *Strategies of Distinction: The Construction of Ethnic Communities, 300–800*. Leiden, 1998.

Potter, Davis S. *Prophecy and History in the Crisis of the Roman Empire: A Historical Commentary on the Thirteenth Sibylline Oracle*. Oxford, 1990.

Potter, David S. *The Roman Empire at Bay AD 180–395*. London, 2004.

Potter, David S., ed. *A Companion to the Roman Empire*. Oxford, 2006.

Potts, D. T. *The Arabian Gulf in Antiquity, Volume II: From Alexander the Great to the Coming of Islam*. Oxford, 1990.

Potts, D. T. *Nomadism in Iran from Antiquity to the Modern Era*. Oxford, 2014.

Potts, D. T., ed. *The Oxford Handbook of Ancient Iran*. Oxford, 2013.

Reddé, Michel. *Mare Nostrum: Les infrastructures, le dispositif et l'histoire de la marine militaire sous l'empire romain*. Paris, 1986.

Richardson, John. *The Language of Empire: Rome and the Idea of Empire from the Third Century BC to the Second Century AD*. Cambridge, 2008.

Riggs, Christina, ed. *The Oxford Handbook of Roman Egypt*. Oxford, 2012.

Rives, J. B. 'Christian expansion and Christian ideology' in W. V. Harris, ed., *The Spread of Christianity in the First Four Centuries: Essays in Explanation*. Leiden, 2005, 15–41.

Rosenfeld, John M. *The Dynastic Arts of the Kushans*. Berkeley, 1967.

Rowan, Clare. *Under Divine Auspices: Divine Ideology and the Visualisation of Imperial Power in the Severan Period*. Cambridge, 2012.

Russell, D. A., ed. *Antonine Literature*. Oxford, 1990.

Salzman, Michele Renee. *The Making of a Christian Aristocracy*. Cambridge, 2002.

Samuel, Alan. *Greek and Roman Chronology*. Munich, 1972.

Šašel, Jaroslav. *Opera Selecta*. Ljubljana, 1992.

Schallmayer, Egon, ed. *Niederbieber, Postumus und der Limesfall: Stationen eines politischen Prozesses: Bericht des ersten Saalburgkolloquiums*. Saalburg, 1996.

Scheidel, Walter, Ian Morris and Richard Saller, eds. *The Cambridge Economic History of the Greco-Roman World*. Cambridge, 2007.

Schmidt, Erich F. *Persepolis III. The Royal Tombs and Other Monuments*. Chicago, 1970.

Schmidt, Ludwig. *Geschichte der deutschen Stämme: Die Ostgermanen*. 2nd ed., Munich, 1938.

Schulte, Bernhard. *Die Goldprägung der gallischen Kaiser von Postumus bis Tetricus*. Aarau, 1983.

Schwartz, Eduard. *Kaiser Constantin und die christliche Kirche: Funf Vorträge*. Darmstadt, 1969.

Seeck, Otto. *Regesten der Kaiser und Päpste für die Jahre 311 bis 476 n. Chr*. Stuttgart, 1919.

Sellinger, Reinhard. *The Mid-Third Century Persecutions of Decius and Valentinian*. Frankfurt, 2002.

Seston, William. *Dioclétien et la Tétrachie I: Guerres et réformes (284–300)*. Paris, 1946.

Shaw, Brent D. *Sacred Violence: African Christians and Sectarian Hatred in the Age of Augustine*. Cambridge, 2011.

Shayegan, M. Rahm. *Arsacids and Sasanians: Political Ideology in Post-Hellenistic and Late Antique Persia*. Cambridge, 2011.

Sherwin-White, A. N. *Roman Society and Roman Law in the New Testament*. Oxford, 1963.

Sherwin-White, A. N. *The Roman Citizenship*. 2nd ed., Oxford, 1973.

Sherwin-White, Susan and Amélie Kuhrt. *From Samarkand to Sardis: A New Approach to the Seleucid Empire*. Berkeley, 1993.

Sidebotham, Steven E. *Berenike and the Ancient Maritime Spice Route*. Berkeley, 2011.

Sinnigen, William Gurnee. *The Officium of the Urban Prefecture During the Later Roman Empire*. Rome, 1957.

Sinor, David, ed. *The Cambridge History of Early Inner Asia*. Cambridge, 1990.

Skjaervo, Prods O. *The Sassanian Inscriptions of Paikuli, Part 3.1: Restored Text and Translation. Part 3.2: Commentary*. 2 vols. Wiesbaden, 1983.

Smith, Andrew M., II. *Roman Palymyra: Identity, Community and State Formation*. Oxford, 2013.

Smith, Andrew, ed. *The Philosopher and Society in Late Antique Society*. Swansea, 2005.

Sondermann, Sebastian. *Neue Aurei, Quinare und Abschläge der gallischen Kaiser von Postumus bis Tetricus*. Bonn, 2010.

Speidel, Michael Alexander. *Heer und Herrschaft im römischen Reich der hohen Kaiserzeit*. (MAVORS 16.) Stuttgart, 2009.

Speidel, Michael P. *Roman Army Studies I*. (MAVORS 1.) Amsterdam, 1984.

Speidel, Michael P. *Roman Army Studies II*. (MAVORS 8.) Stuttgart, 1992.

Stallknecht, Bernt. *Untersuchungen zur römischen Aussenpolitik in der Spätantike (306–395 n. Chr.)*. Bonn, 1967.

Staviskij, B. Ja. *La Bactriane sous les Kushans: Problèmes d'histoire et de culture*. Paris, 1987.

Ste Croix, G. E. M. de. *The Class Struggle in the Ancient Greek World from the Archaic Age to the Arab Conquests*. Ithaca, 1983.

Stein, Arthur. *Der römische Ritterstand*. Munich, 1927.

Stein, Ernst. *Histoire du Bas-Empire 1: De l'état romain à l'état byzantin*. Paris, 1959.

Stephenson, Paul. *Constantine: Roman Emperor, Christian Victor*. London, 2009.

Straub, Johannes. *Vom Herrscherideal in der Spätantike*. Stuttgart, 1939.

Straub, Johannes. *Regeneratio Imperii: Aufsätze über Roms Kaisertum und Reich im Spiegel der heidnischen und christlichen Publiztik*. Darmstadt, 1972.

Straub, Johannes. *Regeneratio Imperii. Aufsätze über Roms Kaisertum und Reich im Spiegel der heidnischen und christlichen Publiztik II*. Darmstadt, 1986.

Strobel, Karl. *Das Imperium Romanum im 3. Jahrhundert: Modell einer Krise?* (Historia Einzelschriften 75). Stuttgart, 1993.

Stronach, David and Ali Mousavi. *Ancient Iran from the Air: Photographs by Georg Gerster*. Mainz, 2012.

Swain, Simon. *Hellenism and Empire: Language, Classicism, and Power in the Greek World, AD 50–250*. Oxford, 1996.

Swain, Simon and Mark Edwards, eds. *Approaching Late Antiquity: The Transformation from Early to Late Empire*. Oxford, 2004.

Swain, Simon, Stephen Harrison and Jas Elsner, eds. *Severan Culture*. Cambridge, 2007.

Syme, Ronald. *Tacitus*. 2 vols. Oxford, 1958.

Syme, Ronald. *Danubian Papers*. Bucharest, 1971.

Syme, Ronald. *Emperors and Biography: Studies in the Historia Augusta*. Oxford, 1971.

Syme, Ronald. *Roman Papers*. A. R. Birley, ed. 7 vols. Oxford, 1979–91.

Szidat, Joachim. *Usurpator tanti nominis. Kaiser und Usurpator in der Spätantike (337–476 n.Chr.)*. (Historia Einzelschriften 210.) Stuttgart, 2010.

Talbert, Richard J. A. *The Senate of Imperial Rome*. Princeton, 1984.

Talbert, Richard J. A., ed. *The Barrington Atlas of the Greek and Roman World*. Princeton, 2000.

Tarpin, Michel. *Vici et pagi dans l'Occident romain*. Rome, 2002.

Thompson, E. A. *The Early Germans*. Oxford, 1965.

Thompson, E. A. *The Visigoths in the Time of Ulfila*. 2nd ed. with a foreword by Michael Kulikowski, London, 2008.

Todd, Malcolm. *The Early Germans*. Oxford, 1992.

Toynbee, J. M. C. *Roman Medallions*. New York, 1944.

Vallet, Françoise and Michel Kazanski, eds. *L'Armée romaine et les barbares du IIIe au VIIe siècle*. Paris, 1993.

Vallet, Françoise and Michel Kazanski, eds. *La noblesse romaine et les barbares du IIIe au VIIe siècle*. Paris, 1995.

Van Berchem, Denis. *L'armée de Dioclétien et la réforme constantinienne*. Paris, 1952.

Vannesse, Michaël. *La défense de l'Occident romain pendant l'Antiquité tardive*. Brussels, 2010.

Vogler, Chantal. *Constance II et l'administration impériale*. Strasbourg, 1979.

Vondrovec, Klaus. *Coinage of the Iranian Huns and Their Successors from Bactria to Gandhara (4th to 8th century CE)*. 2 vols. Vienna, 2014.

von Haehling, Raban. *Die Religionszugehörigkeit der hohen Amsträger des römischen Reiches seit Constantins I: Alleinherrschaft bis zum Ende der theodosianischen Dynastie*. Bonn, 1978.

von Reden, Sitta. *Money in Classical Antiquity*. Cambridge, 2011.

von Rummel, Philipp. *Habitus barbarus: Kleidung und Repräsentation spätantiker Eliten im 4. und 5. Jahrhundert*. Berlin, 2007.

Waas, Manfred. *Germanen im römischen Dienst im 4. Jahrhundert nach Christus*. Bonn, 1965.

Watts, Edward J. *City and School in Late Antique Athens and Alexandria*. Berkeley, 2006.

Weaver, P. R. C. *Familia Caesaris*. Cambridge, 1970.

Weber, Wilhelm. *Untersuchungen zur Geschichte des Kaisers Hadrianus*. Leipzig: Teubner, 1907.

Webster, Graham. *The Roman Imperial Army*. 3rd ed., New York, 1985.

Wells, Peter, ed. *Rome Beyond Its Frontiers: Imports, Attitudes and Practices*. Portsmouth, RI, 2013.

Wenskus, Reinhard. *Stammesbildung und Verfassung: Das Werden der frühmittelalterlichen gentes*. Köln-Vienna, 1961.

Whitby, Mary, ed. *The Propaganda of Power: The Role of Panegyric in Late Antiquity*. Leiden, 1998.

Whittaker, C. R. *Frontiers of the Roman Empire: A Social and Economic Study*. Baltimore, 1994.

Whittaker, C. R. *Rome and Its Frontiers: The Dynamics of Empire*. London, 2004.

Wickham, Chris. *Framing the Early Middle Ages*. Oxford, 2005.

Wilkes, J. J. *Diocletian's Palace, Split: Residence of a Retired Roman Emperor*. 2nd ed., Exeter, 1996.

Willger, Hermann-Joseph. *Studien zur Chronologie des Gallienus und Postumus*. Saarbrücken, 1966.

Williams, Hugh. *Carausius*. Oxford, 2004.

Williams, Stephen. *Diocletian and the Roman Recovery*. New York, 1985.

Winkelmann, Friedhelm. *Ausgewählte Aufsätze: Studien zu Konstantin dem Grossen und zur byzantinischen Kirchengeschichte*. Wolfram Brandes and John Haldon, eds. Birmingham, 1993.

Witschel, Christian. *Krise-Rezession-Stagnation? Der Westen des römischen Reiches im 3. Jahrhundert n. Chr.* Frankfurt, 1999.

Wolff, Hartmut. *Die Constitutio Antoniniana und Papyrus Gissensis 40 I.* 2 vols. Cologne, 1976.

Wolski, Jozef. *Seleucid and Arsacid Studies: A Progress Report on Developments in Source Research.* Krakow, 2003.

Wood, Philip, ed. *History and Identity in the Late Antique Near East.* Oxford, 2013.

Woolf, Greg. *Becoming Roman: The Origins of Provincial Civilization in Gaul.* Cambridge, 1998.

Yavetz, Zvi. *Plebs and Princeps.* Oxford, 1969.

Zöllner, Erich. *Geschichte der Franken bis zur Mitte des 6. Jahrhunderts.* Munich, 1970.

INDEX

Note

Roman nomenclature is a nightmare for indexers and alphabetisers. Not only are Roman naming patterns sometimes maddeningly complex, they also undergo a major change in the period covered by this book. When the story opens, anyone with Roman citizenship conforms to a fairly standardised three-name system (the so-called *tria nomina*) of *praenomen*, *nomen* and *cognomen*; this is fairly straightforward, but also means that identical names can appear in every generation of a particular family with all the potential for misidentification that brings. By the time we end, and really by the late third century, there is no system and much confusion. Names are either bafflingly multiple, with as many as ten elements and often no way of telling which one was primary, or so generic as to be uninterpretable – the *nomen* Aurelius is close to universal among the low-born emperors of the third century; in the fourth century, the *nomen* Flavius originally borne by the family of Constantine becomes the equivalent of our 'Mr' Scholarly conventions complicate matters, because it is traditional to alphabetise names under the *nomen*, or family name, up to Severan period or slightly later, when we can still generally tell what the *nomen* is. Thus Gaius Julius Caesar, the Republican dictator and adoptive father of the emperor Augustus, is alphabetised under Julius. For the later period, however, we can only occasionally discern the main *nomen* (what we call the diacritic *nomen*), which makes alphabetisation tricky. In the following index, individuals are alphabetised under the name most commonly used in the book's text (thus C. Vibius Trebonianus Gallus, a short-lived emperor of the third century, appears under Trebonianus). Where there is a heightened potential for confusion, cross-references are given.